THE CHRISTMAS COMPANION

Edited by John Hadfield
with contributions by
the Dean of Saint Paul's
Father Martindale, J. B. Morton
Rose Macaulay, Mrs. Arthur Webb
the Rev. Leslie D. Weatherhead
Hubert Phillips and Caliban
James Bridie, Harry Price
D. B. Wyndham Lewis
James Hilton, Frank Sullivan
Instructor-Captain R. Weatherhead
Edmond Segrave, H. H. Blanchard
Constance Spry, Miles Hadfield
and many others

No Longer
the Property of
Bluffton University

LONDON
J. M. DENT & SONS LTD
NEW YORK: E. P. DUTTON & CO. INC.

Bluffton College Library

Copyright 1941
E. P. Dutton & Co., Inc.
All rights reserved
Printed in U. S. A.

First Printing

THE EDITOR'S PREFACE

Miss Rose Macaulay defines Christmas books as 'a disease which is contracted by publishers, literary editors, and reviewers.' You will find Miss Macaulay's description of this 'disagreeable malady' printed in full and shocking particularity within these covers. Having thus recognized the principle of free expression, however, I intend to dispose of her alarmism with healthy brusquerie.

Undoubtedly some febrile constitutions are disturbed by Christmas books. Like many another malady, however, this ailment supplies an essential human need. What would there be for Uncle Percy to talk about if he did not suffer from rheumatism? How miserable Matilda would be without her catarrh! Where would young Augustus be without his complexes? And where would publishers and booksellers be without 'Christmas books'?

To those who cannot take their ailments gladly, and persistently remain allergic to Christmas books, I would offer three simple remedies. First, a teaspoonful of *sod. bicarb.* three times a day, in water, after meals. Second, a rest-cure in some foreign spa where the spirit of Christmas has been purged, and 'goodwill' has been decontaminated by totalitarian hygiene. Third, a copy of *The Christmas Companion.*

The last cure, being new to the pharmacopoeia, needs to have its formula stated. The underlying constituents are some two thousand years old, and it would be presumptuous for me to refer to them in lay terms when I have so fortunately obtained illuminating comments on them from the Dean of St Paul's, from Father Martindale, and from the Reverend Leslie Weatherhead. They will speak of the meaning and message of Christmas, two elements which are all too seldom embodied in 'Christmas books.'

As a further expression of the legend and meaning of the birth of Christ I have assembled about a hundred poems. In these days every anthologist is on the defensive; but although I claim no originality for this collection of Christmas poems I make no apologies for it. The lyrical genius of the English has surpassed itself in celebrating the birth of Christ. I have not been able to include in this anthology all the verses I could have wished; I have tried, however, to make the selection a fair image of Christmas in its several aspects—the Christmas of the Nativity, of adoration, of goodwill, the prime festival of winter, of tradition, of song, and of indulgent companionship.

The Christmas chronicles I have gathered together are fragmentary. But perhaps they indicate something of the feeling and continuity that lie behind Christmas—the count-less brave and odd and gay and tragic happenings that are the unseen fabric of the Twelve Days.

It is easy to take the view that Christmas is an outmoded convention (this view has been advanced persistently for several hundred years). It is less easy, but flattering to one's sense of superiority, to disapprove of the way in which Christ-mas is celebrated to-day—to inveigh against fake-Gothic carols, pagan mistletoe, over-indulgence in food and drink, and the muddled, unhistorical attitude which the 'little man' brings to his jolly little beano.

I would make a plea for a more catholic and comprehensive outlook. Christmas is what it is. In its very nature it accepts human inconsistency and frailty, and postulates human goodwill. 'Good King Wenceslas' may be—is, of course—a nineteenth-century fake. What does that matter? Every one is familiar with it, and every one can join in singing it. By the beards of the three kings let us welcome and encourage any song, ceremony, or jovial custom that will bring people together in fellowship and peace. Is not this the current news-value in the tidings that the shepherds heard?

This book, therefore, is deliberately intended to be 'everybody's book.' I have attempted to pack all the conventional elements of Christmas into it, from St Luke on the Nativity to Washington Irving on Bracebridge Hall. Here, once again, the page treads in his master's steps, and Mr Winkle treads nervously upon the ice at Dingley Dell.

On the other hand, the spirit of Christmas demands novelty of expression. Ronald Knox has aptly commented on the *unexpectedness* of the season. 'Just when you are expecting burglars to prowl about other people's houses in disguise, and take things away, you instead, the householder, are expected to disguise yourself and prowl about your own house, putting things there. Instead of waking up to find ladders in her stockings, your small daughter wakes up to find that the stocking itself has become a ladder, for Santa Claus to come down the chimney. Just when the boughs should be at their barest, one tree manages to reverse the whole process, *miraturque novas frondes et non sua poma* (burgeons into leaves of flame and fruits of glittering glass).' I hope that this book may modestly continue the topsy-turvy tradition. Here you will find J. B. Morton's brilliant foolery about Christmas folk-lore in timely juxtaposition with more sober history. Miss Rose Macaulay's irony will clean the palate of any who may be sated with sentiment. Frank Sullivan, that jovial cynic of American humour, will gaily poke a pin into any balloons that come his way.

In the collection of twelve Christmas tales, only one, Le Fanu's 'Madam Crowl's Ghost,' is not strictly about Christmas. But it is one of Le Fanu's best, and Christmas demands nothing but the best in ghost stories. I make no excuse for including it here. The company it keeps is select, and many old friends could not be invited. I hope, however, that some of the guests are at least agreeably surprising.

Christmas would not be Christmas without . . . one need not continue. This book is intended to be useful, no less than amusing. My idea is that the purchaser should get at least half of his or her money's worth out of it before sending it to the ultimate recipient. Buy your copies early, therefore, and, before you pack them for the post, plan your own decorations under Mrs Spry's guidance, see to your garden under the tutelage of my brother Miles, arrange your Christmas dinner with Mrs Webb, and ask Edmond Segrave to choose your wines. When you have done this, and posted your copies to fond friends, perhaps it would be just as well if you bought another copy to be kept in the home. Let it be a gift for husband or father; you can leave it about where he is likely to find it, before the Day. He will then be able to keep the dinner table in a roar with Blanchard's chestnuts, and after dinner he can tell the assembled guests about the ghostly phenomena which Harry Price 'heard with his own ears and saw with his own eyes.' Later he will be able to raise the corporal spirits of the guests with Hubert Phillips's games.

On Boxing Day, and, indeed, all twelve days of Christmas, he can amuse and instruct himself with the 888 quiz questions which I have been privileged to borrow from the collection of that learned and witty member of the Senior Service, the late 'Scun' Weatherhead. Of Caliban's puzzles and problems, and Hubert Phillips's Xmas X-words, I am not qualified to speak, as I will never be able to solve any of them myself. I am assured, however, that nobody, except perhaps Hubert Phillips, could have set such ingenious problems as those of Caliban; and only Caliban could have equalled the finesse of Hubert Phillips's crosswords.

None of the carols is unfamiliar, but I have tried to make a pleasant blend of the universally loved religious carols with some curious songs of legend. If any one takes me to task for including that luscious nineteenth-century sentimentality,

'The Mistletoe Bough,' I ask him to try out Mr Rubbra's in‑
genious setting on his piano (if he is still paying the instalments
on it), and I am sure he will soon have the party in full song.

Writing, as I do, in the second month of what would appear
to be a second Great War, I cannot end even this brief preface
without a sidelong reference to that Herodian ideology under
which many millions are to‑day deprived of the essential
spirit of Christmas. This has given a pathetic irony to the
section of the book called 'Christmas round the World.'
When the power of radio became so strikingly manifest in
that series of international Christmas broadcasts which began
in 1932, there seemed to be a hope that Christmas would
spread invisible wings of peace over a wider world. Since
then, alas, radio has been turned to other uses. I am happy
that I have been able to print for the first time some extracts
from those broadcasts of goodwill; but I have had to make
some obvious omissions from this part of the book lest I
appear to be sarcastic about an erratic but for the most part
kindly people.

Enough of uneasiness, however. Friends, present and
absent, have good day! I give you the toast of the good,
grey old head and beard of Christmas. I invite you to read
of goodwill and gaiety among men, with a seasoning of
seasonable shudders. And I beg to conclude with the
following words, which introduced a little book called *The
Vindication of Christmas* in the year 1653: 'This very good time
of Christ's birth some men do not greatly desire to have this
day sanctified with thanksgiving, nor yet their poor kinred
and poor neighbours feasted with Christian mirth and love,
but I hope these men will change their judgement, when it
shall please God to increase faith and knowledge, and it may
please God this book may show a little light to their knowledge.'

J. H.

October 1939.

It is the fashion, I believe, to regard Christmas as a bore of rather a gross description, and as a time when you are invited to overeat yourself, and pretend to be merry without just cause. As a matter of fact, it is one of the prettiest and most poetic institutions possible, if observed in the proper manner, and after having been more or less unpleasant to everybody for a whole year, it is a blessing to be forced on that one day to be amiable.

Elizabeth and her German Garden.

Now winter nights enlarge
The number of their hours,
And clouds their storms discharge
Upon the airy towers.
Let now the chimneys blaze,
And cups o'erflow with wine;
Let well-tuned words amaze
With harmony divine.
Now yellow waxen lights
Shall wait on honey love,
While youthful revels, masques,
    and courtly sights
Sleep's leaden spells remove.
All do not all things well;
Some measures comely tread,
Some knotted riddles tell,
Some poems smoothly read.

THOMAS CAMPION.

This book of Christmas is a sound and good persuasion for gentlemen . . . to keep a good Christmas. Here is proved the cause of Free-will offerings, here is sound and good Arguments.

A Ha! Christmas, 1647.

THE CONTENTS

PAGE

THE EDITOR'S PREFACE v

THE MESSAGE OF CHRISTMAS. The Dean of St Paul's . 1

THIS CHRISTMAS BUSINESS. Rose Macaulay . . 6

POEMS OF CHRISTMAS. Chosen by John Hadfield . 12

    Awake and Sing 14

    Nativity 22

    Adoration 38

    Wintry Pleasures 55

    Merry my Sprights! 66

    Christmas Voices 82

    The New Year 92

    Now fare ye well 99

DOES CHRISTMAS MEAN ANYTHING? Father Martindale . 103

FACTS ABOUT CHRISTMAS. J. B. Morton . . 109

CHRONICLES OF CHRISTMAS 113

    The Wise Men 114

    The Three Poor Shepherds 115

    The Three Kings of Cologne . . . 115

    As the Romans did 117

    Christmas in the Catacombs 118

    A Christmas Massacre 119

    The Evolution of Christmas 120

    The Sword in the Stone 121

    Paganism at York, 521 124

    The Word 'Christmas' 125

    The Coronation of the Conqueror . . . 126

    Murder in the Cathedral 126

    Feast of Fools 128

    No Greetings for King John 129

    The First Crib, 1223 130

CHRONICLES OF CHRISTMAS—*continued*   PAGE

Aggression in 1403 130
Christmas Box Menace, 1419 131
None Loud Disports 132
Columbus in Cuba 132
Henry VIII makes Merry, 1512 133
Revels of the Inner Temple, *c.* 1560 . . . 134
My Lorde of Misserule 134
Hampton Court, 1604 135
Great Golden Play, etc. 136
With the Pilgrim Fathers, Plymouth Rock, 1620 . 137
St Noël 138
Abominable Disorders 140
Insurrection at Canterbury, 1648 . . . 141
Abolition of Christmas 142
Mournfullest Day, 1655 142
Musketts at the Altar, 1657 143
Thornes and Walnutts 144
Mr Pepys's Christmas Reading . . . 145
Half a Crown for Patrick 145
Sir Roger de Coverley 146
The Pantomime comes to England . . . 147
Pantomime Transformation Scene, 1728 . . 147
The Thorns and the Calendar . . . 148
Traffic in Turkeys, 1793 149
Christmas with the Wordsworths . . . 149
At Bracebridge Hall 150
A Warning to Waits 159
A Little Fête at Panshanger, 1829 . . . 160
Tyrone Power on Broadway 160
Origin of the Christmas Card . . . 161
Besieged Paris 162
Captain Scott's Last Journey 162
Christmas, 1914 163
The First Air Raid 163

THE CONTENTS xiii

CHRONICLES OF CHRISTMAS—*continued*   PAGE

The King's First Christmas Broadcast   .   .   . 164
Coldest Christmas of the Century   165

SWINGING TO A STAR. The Rev. Leslie D. Weatherhead . 166

THE CHRISTMAS OF THE FUTURE. Frank Sullivan . 171

CHRISTMAS DECORATIONS. Constance Spry   .   . 176

COOK'S CHRISTMAS. Mrs Arthur Webb   .   .   . 184

WINE IN THE CELLAR. Edmond Segrave   .   .   . 196

GARDENER'S CHRISTMAS. Miles Hadfield   .   .   . 218

CHRISTMAS GHOSTS. Harry Price   231

CHESTNUTS. Roasted by H. H. Blanchard   .   . 248

GAMES FOR THE PARTY. Hubert Phillips   .   .   . 258

TWELVE TALES FOR CHRISTMAS 274

Twilight of the Wise. James Hilton   .   .   . 275
Crisp New Bills for Mr Teagle. Frank Sullivan . 285
A Wise Man from the East. Charles Heywood .   . 292
The White Road. E. F. Bozman   299
Christmas with Our Bill. Frederick H. Grisewood . 311
How Santa Claus came to Simpson's Bar. Francis
Bret Harte   315
Oh, what a Horrid Tale! P. S.   332
Madam Crowl's Ghost. J. Sheridan Le Fanu .   . 337
The Christmas Card. James Bridie   .   .   . 353
A Curious Mistake. After 'Beachcomber'   .   . 369
The Pickwick Club on the Ice. Charles Dickens . 370
Ring out, Wild Bells. D. B. Wyndham Lewis .   . 378

PUZZLES AND PROBLEMS. Caliban   383

Answers to the Puzzles and Problems   .   .   . 396

CHRISTMAS QUIZ. Instructor-Captain R. Weatherhead . 404

Answers to the Christmas Quiz   440

TWELVE X-WORDS FOR XMAS. Hubert Phillips .   . 460

Solutions to the X-words   483

CHRISTMAS ROUND THE WORLD 485

  PAGE

CAROLS AND CHRISTMAS SONGS   506
    A Babe is born   506
    God rest you Merry, Gentlemen   508
    The First Nowell 511
    In Dulci Jubilo   514
    O come, All ye Faithful   516
    The Carnal and the Crane   518
    Hark! the Herald Angels sing   520
    While Shepherds watch'd   522
    Winter's Snow   524
    Christians, awake 526
    I saw Three Ships   529
    Good King Wenceslas 531
    The Seven Joys of Mary   533
    Three Kings of Orient 536
    The Cherry Tree Carol 538
    The Holly and the Ivy 540
    The Moon shines Bright   542
    The Wassail Song   544
    The Boar's Head 546
    The Mistletoe Bough   548

OUT OF THE STOCKING   551

INDEX OF AUTHORS 557

FIRST LINES OF ANONYMOUS POEMS AND CAROLS   . 560

ACKNOWLEDGMENTS

In traversing so well-trodden a country as the literature of Christmas one cannot pose as a pioneer, and one's debt to those who have gone before is manifest. I would make particular acknowledgment to *A Christmas Book* (1928), that anthology by D. B. Wyndham Lewis and G. C. Heseltine, which is, I hope, possessed by those who will read this book. I would also express my indebtedness for material and information derived from *An Anthology of Christmas Prose and Verse* (1928) collected by D. L. Kelleher, *Christmas and its Associations* (1902) by W. F. Dawson, *Yule and Christmas* by Alexander Tille, *The Book of Christmas* (New York, 1909) with an Introduction by Hamilton W. Mabie, *The Book of Christmas* (1888) by Thomas K. Hervey, *A Righte Merrie Christmasse* by John Ashton, *Christmas with the Poets* (1855), and *A Christmas Holiday Book* (1934) edited by Alice Daglish and Ernest Rhys.

I acknowledge, too, the use I have made of *A Winter Miscellany* edited by Humbert Wolfe, *The Aldine Bible* edited by the late M. R. James, *The English Galaxy of Shorter Poems* (1933) edited by Gerald Bullett, *Scottish Poetry* (1935) edited by M. M. Gray, J. W. Tibble's edition of *The Poems of John Clare* (1935), Geoffrey Keynes's edition of *The Works of Sir Thomas Browne* (1928–31), Bramley & Stainer's *Christmas Carols, Old and New* (1871), the *Oxford Hymn Book* (1925), and the *Oxford Book of Carols* (1928). My grateful thanks are due to those who have contributed specially to this book, and to the following authors and publishers who have kindly consented to my use of copyright material: Mr E. F. Bozman for 'The White Road'; Mr James Bridie for 'The Christmas Card'; Fr Brodrick for his essay on St Noël; the British

Broadcasting Corporation, Mr Laurence Gilliam, and Mr Igor Vinogradoff for extracts from Christmas broadcasts of 1932, 1934, 1935, 1937; Mr Walter de la Mare, Messrs Constable & Company, Ltd, and Messrs Henry Holt & Company for 'Before Dawn' from *The Veil*; Messrs J. M. Dent & Sons Ltd for 'The Christ-Child' and 'A Portrait' from *The Wild Knight* by G. K. Chesterton; Messrs J. M. Dent & Sons Ltd and Mr Frank Sullivan for 'The Christmas of the Future' and 'Crisp New Bills for Mr Teagle' from *Sullivan at Bay*; Messrs Faber & Faber and Mr T. S. Eliot for 'The Journey of the Magi'; Miss Viola Gerard Garvin for 'Holy Thorn'; Count Alfred A. Hessenstein for 'A Child in Hungary'; Mr Charles Heywood for 'A Wise Man from the East'; Mr James Hilton for 'Twilight of the Wise'; Mr D. B. Wyndham Lewis for 'Ring out, Wild Bells'; Miss Rose Macaulay for 'This Christmas Business'; Miss Anna McMullen for 'Christmas 1938'; Mr J. B. Morton for 'Facts about Christmas'; P. S. for 'Oh, what a Horrid Tale!'; the Editor of the *Radio Times* for 'Christmas with Our Bill' by Mr Frederick H. Grisewood, which is reprinted by permission of the British Broadcasting Corporation; Mr Ernest Rhys for 'A New-Old Song'; Messrs Simon & Schuster and Mr Ogden Nash for 'A Carol for the Children' from *The Bad Parents' Garden of Verse*; Messrs Stainer & Bell for Dr R. Vaughan Williams's setting of 'The Carnal and the Crane'; Dr Walter Starkie for 'Christmas with the Gipsies'; the proprietors of *The Times* for several extracts from its columns; and the executors of the late Instructor-Captain R. Weatherhead for the questions in the 'Christmas Quiz' which were first printed in his *Dozens of Whos and Whats*.

THE MESSAGE OF CHRISTMAS

BY THE DEAN OF SAINT PAUL'S

Let us now go even unto Bethlehem and see this thing which is come to pass.—LUKE ii. 15.

Herein was the love of God manifested in us, that God hath sent his only begotten son into the world that we might live through him.—1 JOHN iv. 9.

A WRITER on the meaning of Christmas is given a hard task, for the message and meaning of the festival are so profound and so far-reaching that he can do no more than skim over the surface. The two texts with which I have headed this essay indicate the double aspect of the Christmas story. On Christmas Day we celebrate an event which happened long ago, and also a truth which remains for ever. The shepherds with the thirst for fact of simple folk go to Bethlehem to see this thing which has come to pass, this event. The mystical writer of the second text interprets the event. 'The love of God is manifested,' an eternal truth about the Divine nature is disclosed and made clear. But we should be very far from the truth, and certainly in utter contradiction with the New Testament, if we supposed that one side of the Christmas message could be separated from the other, or that we might accept the one and reject the other. The thing that happened and the eternal truth about God are indissolubly connected, they stand or fall together. The one is meaningless without the other: together they are the centre of the gospel.

Suppose for a moment that we tried to think of the Christmas story as just an account of an event and nothing more—only a thing which came to pass. Well, what is there in it which could justify our celebration or even claim our attention? One baby more has appeared in the world among the millions which have been born. No doubt there is a sense in which every birth is of profound importance, and we do wrong to consider any one as ordinary or uninteresting. But the miracle of birth has become commonplace by repetition. This fact would not be altered though choirs of angels sang, and all the portents which history or legend records were concentrated in the natal hour. The birth of Jesus has no significance for us unless it is the bearer of a meaning which is eternal. 'The tender mercy from on high has visited us': 'in this was manifested the love of God.'

Just as there are some who think they can be satisfied with the experience of the shepherds without going on to the experience of St John, so there are others who think they can hold fast to the insight of St John without sharing the simple, direct attitude of the shepherds. I mean that they would say: 'We hold the essence of the Christian faith, God is love. We do not need to buttress that belief by the doctrine of the Incarnation, we are not interested in what came to pass, in an event which happened long ago. We are interested only in eternal truths. Sufficient for us to believe that God is love.'

God forbid that I should seek to disturb the faith of any one who finds it easy to believe in the love of God, but we are bound to notice that the faith in the love of God has, in fact, been bound up with the event at Bethlehem. Doubtless, the love of God has been conjectured, it has been conceived as a hypothesis, adumbrated as a faint but glorious hope, but it has never been accepted as the central truth, the clue to life and the victory over death, except by those who drew their assurance from what came to pass at Bethlehem and Calvary.

Would you say that it is easy to believe that God is love? Simple perhaps to understand, but not surely easy to accept. Take the world and human life as they present themselves to us. We may find order in them; and, as I believe, very good evidence that they are the creations of a great superhuman mind. But how difficult it is to pass from the perception of the Divine power and the Divine intelligence to a firm conviction of Divine loving-kindness! Just when we think we have found a way, some grim and sombre facet of existence rises against us. We encounter pain which seems purposeless and cruelty triumphant, and our faith in the love of God quivers and declines into a mere conjecture or a faint hope. Is there love behind the world? We want more than possibility, more than hints: we want the love of God manifested.

In the infant whose birth came to pass on the first Christmas Day, St John tells us the love of God *was* manifested. But how? How, you may ask, does Jesus help us to be sure? Not, I would reply, by giving us a reason which cannot be gainsaid, but by presenting us with a challenge which cannot be escaped. The baby who was born in Bethlehem was a person who claimed to set up God's kingdom, to be its centre, to represent the Creator of the world, to speak with the authority of the Divine lawgiver, to demand the utmost devotion and obedience from men. And, at the same time, He was one who manifested throughout His life love without reserve, a devotion which knew no limits, and a compassion which embraced all men, so that those who had lived with Him and known Him best could find no words to describe Him short of divine. When they looked at Him they said: 'Here is the Divine life. Here, and not in the blind forces of nature or the strange turns of history, here in this personal life we find God manifested.'

That faith is the unchanging Christian gospel. It is a faith which cannot be proved, but also a faith which cannot be quenched. It comes to us, not with the persuasive words of man's wisdom, but with the summons to face the implications of one personal life. We are confronted with a dilemma. Either that life, which began at Bethlehem, was the most futile of all lives, based on illusion, utterly at odds with the realities: or else it was, as Jesus Himself believed, the most significant of all lives, the nearest to Reality, the most in harmony with the true nature of things—in short, the manifestation of the life and love of God.

Thus one faith embraces the two aspects: event and truth, fact and idea. 'Let us now go and see this thing which has come to pass: in this was the love of God manifested.'

We cannot deny that this faith of ours has to be kept alive in evil times. We live under a darkening sky, and it would be mere folly to pretend that we have much ground for imme‐diate optimism. It is only too obvious that the nations and their leaders have learned very little from the dreadful experiences of world war. The path of Progress is so shadowed that no one can confidently say he knows where it lies.

In times such as these, when hopes are dying, there is a great temptation to withdraw from the conflict and wash our hands of responsibility. If we have no faith in God we may take Voltaire's advice and cultivate our private gardens. We may allow the world to go on its foolish way without our assistance, and gain such quiet and satisfaction as life can give. But even if we have faith in God we may fall victims to the same kind of temptation. We may try to lay hold on eternal life for ourselves, and be content with a peace within while the world outside tears itself to tatters. But the Christian faith would not allow either of these retreats from conflict. The love of God was manifested, not in some quiet and retired mystic, but in Jesus Christ, who was born to suffer and struggle to the end, who did not renounce the world but took all its evil and pain into His soul that He might redeem it. So now and always the love of God is manifested through persons who do not turn away from the turmoil, who are not daunted by the dark, who increasingly strive to overcome evil with good.

We who have the Christian faith and believe that something came to pass at Bethlehem of eternal meaning and moment can never take short views or be overborne by the difficulties of our time. For the Eternal is with us, and God establishes His own Kingdom in His own time. The Dayspring from on high has visited us, and soon or late the morning star will lead us to the perfect day.

W. R. MATTHEWS.

We will sing a new song
That sounds like the old:
    Noël.

We will tell an old tale
That has often been told:
    Noël.

We will build a tall town;
We will watch for the Star:
    Noël.

We will build a new world,
    Without War.

ERNEST RHYS.

THIS CHRISTMAS BUSINESS

BY ROSE MACAULAY

THERE are whispers of another Christmas revolt. There have been such whispers and such revolts on and off for the last twenty or thirty centuries, for neither the keeping of 25th December nor of any other day is a novelty to the human race, and, where a day is observed, you may be sure that there will be some who will desire that it should not be observed. Our pagan ancestors, in the chilly regions of the Danube and the Baltic, waged intertribal wars on this point, some maintaining that too much fuss was made of Woden, Freya, and Thor on the days appointed for them; others that fuss, like mead, was one of those things of which one cannot make too much, be the occasion what it will. The same difference of opinion concerning their festal occasions occurred among the Greeks, the Romans, the Chinese, the Jews, the Mithraic Persians (whose great day was the same as ours, 25th December), the ancient Britons, and the Christians from the third century down to the twentieth. There will always be those who feel, with Jehovah, that your new moons and sabbaths, your calling of assemblies and appointed feasts, they cannot away with, they are a trouble unto them, they are weary to bear them. Origen pronounced the festal keeping of Christmas to be positively irreverent, and so, since his day, have thought many others, such as Quakers, Presbyterians, and Plymouth Brethren (though these have all come partially round to it now). The curious thing about some of these objectors is that, even at

6

their most anti-Christmas periods, they have not, apparently, felt the same distaste for the observance of other days, such as Sunday. Even when the Long Parliament passed its ordinance for the suppression of blasphemies and heresies, including among these the keeping of Christmas, it did not, it appears, include Sunday. Illogical human beings, they suspected Christmas for its pagan ancestry and rites, yet suffered *dies solis,* far more nakedly pagan in association though it was, despite the Christian dress and Christian name which had been given it by the discreet converters of the heathen. (Can the reason that the weekly Lord's Day was so beloved of Christendom, from apostolic times on, while other Lord's days were often looked at somewhat reluctantly and askance, be that the one gave no trouble, was, in fact, a day of rest, whereas Christmas was suspect from the first as a season of immeasurable toil?) Anyhow, it seems that human creatures must needs observe some appointed feast-days, and if they get rid of one they fall with all the more zeal for another. We have our fancies among days as among pets; we pick and we choose; some will keep Christmas and some Easter, some the New Year, some the new moon, some Sunday, some Saturday, some birthdays, some dogs, some canaries, and some cats. So long as we keep something or other we are content. Unless, like the hermits and ascetics, we decide to keep nothing except our dignity.

The Teutonic and Scandinavian races have always had a peculiar addiction to the keeping of Christmas. There seems to be no record of an age before our rude forefathers observed this festival with feasting, shouting, gaming, mumming, and, in general, with what the English used to call good cheer. These races have ever been the world's best Christmas-keepers; so intent have they been on Yule revelry that nothing has been able to keep them from it for long together. The Christian missionaries had to permit them their revelry, their feasting, their dancing, their decking of houses and temples with green, in spite of the prohibitions of these pagan vanities by the austere Councils of the Church. Not all the decrees of Church Councils, the wrath of parish priests, the ordinances of Puritan parliaments, could suppress the Saxon Christmas, which always reappeared, noisier, jollier, more Bacchanalian than ever, through every change of land, religion, dynasty, and constitution.

The Scots, on the other hand, not being Saxons, took the opportunity of the establishment of the Presbyterian Church in their land practically to abolish Christmas, which had for some centuries been troubling their thrifty souls. In this matter, as in so many others, they were obviously influenced by their allies the French, an even thriftier race, who have never troubled about Christmas much. Both these nations prefer to observe New Year's Day, which gives them all the outlet they require for their high spirits and goodwill.

In this country the Christmas business has become, for many centuries, a steady progress upward. True, we eat and drink less to-day than of yore; our consumption of boars' heads, turkeys, geese, puddings and pies, tankards of ale and brandy-punch is, by comparison, contemptible. On the other hand, we have, during the last century, acquired Christmas trees and Christmas cards, and multiplied Christmas books, Christmas numbers, and Christmas shopping. It is said that we English were originally responsible for Christmas trees, those pretty monuments of German industry, since St Boniface, our good Devonshire missionary to the German heathen, made his converts cut down the trees of their sacred groves, but consoled them by encouraging them to use them as Christmas trees to brighten their strange new faith, which the poor Germans have done laboriously ever since, and in the nineteenth century rewarded us for our missionary's happy idea by sending it back to us through our Germanic court. Against Christmas trees, none but those who have to deck them need murmur;

indeed, they make a pretty sight, flourishing in churches, houses, shops, and streets, for all the world as if we were still Druids, and wished, like them, to provide the comforts of their forest homes for the sylvan deities who must come and dwell under roofs until the bitter weather be past. No; the revolt of which I speak has little to do with Christmas trees, or even with Christmas decorations, which are mainly resented only by the wives of the clergy and their parochial assistants, who have to wreathe the holly and twine the bay round pulpit and font.

Let us pass to Christmas cards, that strange, bright, fascinat/ ing shower which began to rain on us early in the Victorian era, and is raining yet. Every one likes to receive these agree/ able and bizarre picturettes, these tokens of goodwill that fly like birds from home to home, winging over land and sea, reminding us, alas! too often of those whom it were wiser to forget, and whom we have, in point of fact, forgotten; we all, I say, or nearly all, like to receive these charming little objects — but how few of us like sending them! On the vast expenditure of time, envelopes, ink, stamps, and, above all, thought, involved in this industry to those who tackle it seriously I will not here dwell. Some people settle down to it in August, in the so/called leisure of their summer holidays in this country or another; these will purchase some hundreds of picture postcards, write 'Happy Christmas' on them, and dispatch them, and then, think they, they are done with Christ/ mas for the year. But they have underestimated the hypnotic power of Christmas, for by December they have quite forgotten having dispatched these cards, and begin the good work all over again.

In the same category as Christmas cards are Christmas presents, only worse, as involving more time, more thought, more money, more trouble, and (if fewer envelopes) brown paper and string in addition. They also make the shops very crowded and peculiar. What a wonderful place Selfridge's will be at Christmas time, we are told; and so, indeed, it proves. The stir of revolt is reported to be very active among shop assistants and shoppers. A certain amount of buying things in shops, a tedious and painful business at best, is necessary in most lives, but how much wearier a task does this become when some thousands of others are buying in the same shop at the same time! The revolt against buying and sending presents is joined, naturally, by the postmen, who develop at this season a very painful ailment which they call 'Christmas back.'

A disease not very dissimilar in name is that called Christmas books, which is contracted by publishers, literary editors, and reviewers. The symptoms of this disagreeable malady closely resemble those experienced by the drowning: a feeling of over-whelming suffocation, partial or total loss of memory and power to think, pallor, nausea, and faintness, alternating with spasms of insane rage, and, when the patient is coming round (for happily this complaint is not as a rule fatal), sensations of apathy, lassitude, and morbid disgust at the sight or thought of that element which occasioned the disease. So painful and pre-valent a disease is this that it has driven a large section of our publishers and editors into the van of the revolt.

Allied to this ailment, and similar in symptoms, is the one caused by Christmas numbers, which mainly affects editors, authors, reviewers, and printers. This is a disease of some age, and editors have sickened with it annually from the mid-eighteenth century onwards. I understand that they are at last getting tired of doing so, and mean to make a stand.

Of Christmas bills, Christmas boxes, Christmas carols, and Christmas cocks (for the bird of dawning croweth all night long, which is very disturbing) I need scarcely here speak. We all know of these oppressions, and we have supported them for some two thousand years with that impatience which is the mark of the British race. But it is now rumoured that Christmas reached its zenith about three years back, and has begun to decline. There are certainly signs of this. It is, as I write, as late as the feast of St Andrew, yet I have not yet heard a single street carol singer, though these little songsters are wont to warble from St Luke's little summer on. Neither has shopping set in, so far, with its customary rigour, and it is rumoured in commercial circles that it will be what they call a poor Christmas in the shops.

Can it be that our increasingly frequent visits abroad have infected us with something of the continental—at least of the French, Italian, Spanish, and Portuguese—spirit with regard to Christmas, and that our old English Yule is beginning to decay, to go the way of our old English Twelfth Night, May Day, St John's Eve, Lammas, Michaelmas, All Hallowe'en, Sunday, and the rest of our ceremonial feasts? For this is the fate of feasts when they have been carried too far—farther, that is, than the spirit of a people will endure. The breaking-point comes.

But, for my part, I think it will be a pity. I like these exuberant seasonal feasts, and see no reason why we English should become like those Roman Catholic, Presbyterian, and atheistical countries which pass Christmas Day by, only giving it the tribute of a service or two in church in the morning, a carol or two in chapel at night. So I hope that the rumour is baseless, or that the revolt will come to no more than the other revolts of the last two thousand years.

POEMS OF CHRISTMAS

CHOSEN BY JOHN HADFIELD

THIS is the month, and this the happy morn,
Wherein the Son of Heaven's Eternal King,
Of wedded maid and virgin mother born,
Our great redemption from above did bring;
For so the holy sages once did sing,
 That He our deadly forfeit should release,
And with His Father work us a perpetual peace.

That glorious form, that light unsufferable,
And that far-beaming blaze of majesty,
Wherewith He wont at Heaven's high council-table
To sit the midst of Trinal Unity,
He laid aside, and, here with us to be,
 Forsook the courts of everlasting day,
And chose with us a darksome house of mortal clay.

Say, Heavenly Muse, shall not thy sacred vein
Afford a present to the Infant God?
Hast thou no verse, no hymn, or solemn strain,
To welcome Him to this His new abode,
Now while the heaven, by the Sun's team untrod,
 Hath took no print of the approaching light,
And all the spangled host keep watch in squadrons bright?

See how from far upon the eastern road
The star-led wizards haste with odours sweet!

Oh! run; prevent them with thy humble ode,
And lay it lowly at His blessèd feet;
Have thou the honour first thy Lord to greet,
   And join thy voice unto the Angel Quire,
From out His secret altar touched with hallowed fire.

JOHN MILTON (1608–74).

From Virgin's womb this day did spring
The precious Seed that only savèd man:
This day let man rejoice and sweetly sing,
Since on this day salvation first began.
This day did Christ man's soul from death remove,
With glorious saints to dwell in heaven above.

This day to man came pledge of perfect peace,
This day to man came love and unity,
This day man's grief began for to surcease,
This day did man receive a remedy
For each offence and every deadly sin
With guilty heart that erst he wandered in.

In Christes flock let love be surely placed,
From Christes flock let concord hate expel:
Of Christes flock let love be so embraced,
As we in Christ, and Christ in us may dwell.
Christ is the author of all unity,
From whence proceedeth all felicity.

O sing unto this glittering glorious king,
O praise His name let every living thing:
Let heart and voice like bells of silver ring,
For comfort that this day to man did bring,
Let lute, let shalm, with sound of sweet delight,
The joy of Christes birth this day recite.

FRANCIS KINWELMERSHE (c. 1540–80).

AWAKE AND SING

Immortal Babe, who this dear day
Didst change Thine heaven for our clay,
And didst with flesh Thy godhead veil,
Eternal Son of God, all hail!

Shine, happy star, ye angels, sing
Glory on high to heaven's King.
Run, shepherds, leave your nightly watch,
See heaven come down to Bethlehem's cratch.

Worship, ye sages of the east,
The King of gods in meanness dressed.
O blessed maid, smile and adore
The God thy womb and arms have bore.

Star, angels, shepherds, and wise sages,
Thou virgin glory of all ages,
Restorèd frame of heaven and earth,
Joy in your dear Redeemer's birth!

JOSEPH HALL (1574–1656).

Voices in the Mist

The time draws near the birth of Christ:
  The moon is hid; the night is still;
  The Christmas bells from hill to hill
Answer each other in the mist.

Four voices of four hamlets round,
  From far and near, on mead and moor,
  Swell out and fail, as if a door
Were shut between me and the sound:

Each voice four changes on the wind,
  That now dilate, and now decrease,
  Peace and goodwill, goodwill and peace,
Peace and goodwill, to all mankind.

           ALFRED, LORD TENNYSON (1809–92).

Heaven cannot hold Him

In the bleak midwinter
  Frosty wind made moan,
Earth stood hard as iron,
  Water like a stone;
Snow had fallen, snow on snow,
  Snow on snow,
In the bleak midwinter
  Long ago.

Our God, heaven cannot hold Him,
  Nor earth sustain;
Heaven and earth shall flee away
  When He comes to reign:
In the bleak midwinter
  A stable place sufficed
The Lord God Almighty
  Jesus Christ.

Enough for Him, whom cherubim
  Worship night and day,

A breastful of milk
  And a mangerful of hay;
Enough for Him, whom angels
  Fall down before,
The ox and ass and camel
  Which adore.

Angels and archangels
  May have gathered there,
Cherubim and seraphim
  Thronged the air;
But only His mother
  In her maiden bliss
Worshipped the Belovèd
  With a kiss.

What can I give Him,
  Poor as I am?
If I were a shepherd
  I would bring a lamb,
If I were a Wise Man
  I would do my part,—
Yet what I can I give Him,
  Give my heart.

CHRISTINA ROSSETTI (1830–94).

O Sweetest Night!

O sweetest night! my mind I ne'er can wean
From thoughts of thee, in which the heavens do rain
Huge showers of grace: the hillocks flow with sweets,
And from the mountains milk and honey sweats.

O sweetest night! my starvèd soul doth die
To have a full draught of thy ambrosy.
Tertullian gravely said: 'Some goods there are
As well as evils, which e'en oppress and bear
Us to the ground.' The wonders of this night
Are such, to find our God in such a plight:
That hardly such a bastard soul is found
Who sends not knees and heart to kiss the ground.

MYLES PINKNEY (1599–1674).

Before Dawn

Dim-berried is the mistletoe
With globes of sheenless grey,
The holly mid ten thousand thorns
Smoulders its fires away;
And in the manger Jesu sleeps
    This Christmas Day.

Bull unto bull with hollow throat
Makes echo every hill,
Cold sheep in pastures thick with snow
The air with bleatings fill;
While of his mother's heart this Babe
    Takes His sweet will.

All flowers and butterflies lie hid,
The blackbird and the thrush
Pipe but a little as they flit
Restless from bush to bush;
Even to the robin Gabriel hath
    Cried softly, 'Hush!'

Now night is astir with burning stars
In darkness of the snow;
Burdened with frankincense and myrrh
And gold the strangers go
Into a dusk where one dim lamp
    Burns faintly, Lo!

No snowdrop yet its small head nods,
In winds of winter drear;
No lark at casement in the sky
Sings matins shrill and clear;
Yet in this frozen mirk the Dawn
    Breathes, Spring is here!

WALTER DE LA MARE.

I sing the Birth

I sing the birth was born to-night,
The Author both of life and light;
    The angels so did sound it.
And like the ravish'd shepherds said,
Who saw the light, and were afraid,
    Yet search'd, and true they found it.

The Son of God, th' Eternal King,
That did us all salvation bring,
    And freed the soul from danger;
He whom the whole world could not take,
The Word, which heaven and earth did make,
    Was now laid in a manger.

The Father's wisdom will'd it so,
The Son's obedience knew no No,
    Both wills were in one stature;

And as that wisdom had decreed,
The Word was now made flesh indeed,
    And took on Him our nature.

What comfort by Him do we win,
Who made Himself the price of sin,
    To make us heirs of glory.
To see this Babe, all innocence;
A martyr born in our defence:
    Can man forget this story?

                    BEN JONSON (1573–1637).

Let us kneel with Mary Maid

Before the paling of the stars,
    Before the winter morn,
Before the earliest cockcrow,
    Jesus Christ was born:
Born in a stable,
    Cradled in a manger,
In the world His hands had made,
    Born a stranger.

Priest and king lay fast asleep
    In Jerusalem,
Young and old lay fast asleep
    In crowded Bethlehem:
Saint and angel, ox and ass,
    Kept a watch together,
Before the Christmas daybreak
    In the winter weather.

Jesus on His Mother's breast
  In the stable cold,
Spotless Lamb of God was He,
  Shepherd of the fold.
Let us kneel with Mary Maid,
  With Joseph bent and hoary,
With saint and angel, ox and ass,
  To hail the King of Glory.

CHRISTINA ROSSETTI (1830–94).

It is the Birthday of thy King

Awake, glad heart! get up, and sing!
It is the birthday of thy King.
    Awake! awake!
    The sun doth shake
Light from his locks, and all the way
Breathing perfumes, doth spice the day.

Awake! awake! hark how th' wood rings,
Winds whisper, and the busy springs
    A concert make;
    Awake! awake!
Man is their high priest, and should rise
To offer up the sacrifice.

I would I were some bird, or star,
Fluttering in woods, or lifted far
    Above this inn
    And road of sin;
Then either star or bird should be
Shining or singing still to Thee.

I would I had in my best part
Fit rooms for Thee! or that my heart
   Were so clean as
   Thy manger was!
But I am all filth, and obscene;
Yet, if Thou wilt, Thou canst make me clean.

Sweet Jesu! will then. Let no more
This leper haunt and soil Thy door!
   Cure him, ease him,
   O release him!
And let once more, by mystic birth,
The Lord of life be born in earth.

            HENRY VAUGHAN (1622–95).

Where is the Babe?

Tell us, thou clear and heavenly tongue,
Where is the Babe but lately sprung?
Lies He the lily-banks among?

Or say if this new Birth of ours
Sleeps, laid within some ark of flowers,
Spangled with dew-light; thou canst clear
All doubts, and manifest the where.

Declare to us, bright star, if we shall seek
Him in the morning's blushing cheek,
Or search the beds of spices through,
To find Him out?

            ROBERT HERRICK (1591–1674).

NATIVITY

The shepherd upon a hill he sat;
He had on him his tabard and his hat,
His tarbox, his pipe, and his flagat;
His name was called Joly Joly Wat,
For he was a good herdes boy
　　　　Ut hoy!
　　For in his pipe he made so much joy.

The shepherd upon a hill was laid;
His dog unto his girdle was tied;
He had not slept but a little braid,
But '*Gloria in excelsis!*' was to him said.
　　　　Ut hoy!
　　For in his pipe he made so much joy.

The shepherd on a hill he stood;
Round about him his sheep they yode;
He put his hand under his hood,
He saw a star as red as blood.
　　　　Ut hoy!
　　For in his pipe he made so much joy.

The shepherd said anon right,
'I will go see yon farly sight,
Whereas the angel singeth on height,
And the star that shineth so bright.'
　　　　Ut hoy!
　　For in his pipe he made so much joy.

'Now farewell, Moll, and also Will!
For my love go ye all still
Unto I come again you till,
And evermore, Will, ring well thy bell.'
     Ut hoy!
  For in his pipe he made so much joy.

'Now must I go where Christ was born;
Farewell! I come again to-morn.
Dog, keep well my sheep from the corn,
And warn well "Warroke" when I blow my horn!'
     Ut hoy!
  For in his pipe he made so much joy.

When Wat to Bethlehem comen was,
He sweat, he had gone faster than a pace;
He found Jesu in a simple place,
Between an ox but and an ass.
     Ut hoy!
  For in his pipe he made so much joy.

'Jesu, I offer to thee here my pipe,
My skirt, my tarbox, and my scrip;
Home to my fellows now will I skip,
And also look unto my sheep.'
     Ut hoy!
  For in his pipe he made so much joy.

'Now farewell, mine own herdsman Wat!'
'Yea, for God, lady, even so I hat;
Lull well Jesus in thy lap,
And farewell, Joseph, with thy round cap!'
     Ut hoy!
  For in his pipe he made so much joy.

'Now may I well both hop and sing,
For I have been at Christ's bearing;
Home to my fellows now will I fling,
Christ of heaven to his bliss us bring!'
            Ut hoy!
    For in his pipe he made so much joy.

                    ANONYMOUS (*fifteenth century*).

Shepherds, sit we here?

    Sweet music, sweeter far
    Than any song is sweet;
    Sweet music, heavenly rare,
    Mine ears (O peers!) doth greet.
You gentle flocks, whose fleeces, pearl'd with dew,
Resemble heaven, whom golden drops make bright,
Listen, O listen! now, O not to you
Our pipes make sport to shorten weary night.
    But voices most divine,
    Make blissful harmony;
    Voices that seem to shine,
    For what else clears the sky?
Tunes can we hear, but not the singers see;
The tunes divine, and so the singers be.

    Lo! how the firmament
    Within an azure fold
    The flock of stars hath pent,
    That we might them behold.
Yet from their beams proceedeth not this light,
Nor can their crystals such reflection give.
What, then, doth make the element so bright?
The heavens are come down upon earth to live.

But hearken to the song:
'Glory to glory's King!
And peace all men among!'
These choristers do sing.
Angels they are, as also, shepherds, he
Whom in our fear we do admire to see.

'Let not amazement blind
Your souls,' said he, 'annoy;
To you and all mankind,
My message bringeth joy.
For, lo! the world's great Shepherd now is born,
A blessèd babe, an infant full of power;
After long night uprisen is the morn,
Renowning Bethlem in the Saviour.

Sprung is the perfect day,
By prophets seen afar;
Sprung is the mirthful May,
Which Winter cannot mar.'
In David's city doth this sun appear,
Clouded in flesh, yet, shepherds, sit we here?

EDMUND BOLTON (*c*. 1575–1633).

Chantons Noé

Une pastourelle gentille
Et ung bergier en ung verger
L'autr'hyer en jouant à la bille
S'entredisoient, pour abréger:
Roger
Bergier
Legière
Bergière,
C'est trop à la bille joué;
Chantons Noé, Noé, Noé.

Te souvient-il plus du prophète
Qui nous dit cas de si hault faict,
Que d'une Pucelle parfaicte
Naistroit ung Enfant tout parfaict?
L'effect
Est faict;
La belle
Pucelle
A eu ung filz du ciel voué:
Chantons Noé, Noé, Noé.

CLÉMENT MAROT (c. 1496–1544).

Faire Maiden, Swete Lording

I saw a faire maiden
Sitten and sing.
She lulled a litel child,
A swete lording.

That eché lord is that
That made allé thing;
Of allé lordès he is lord,
Of allé kingès king.

There was mekel melody
At that childès birth;
Alle tho wern in hevené bliss
They made mekel mirth.

Aungels bright they song that night,
And seiden to that child:
Blessèd be thou and so be she
That is both meke and mild.

Pray we now to that child
And to his moder deare,
Graunt them his blessing
That now maken cheere.

ANONYMOUS.

This Stable is a Prince's Court

Behold, a silly tender Babe,
In freezing winter night,
In homely manger trembling lies—
Alas, a piteous sight!

The inns are full; no man will yield
This little Pilgrim bed.
But forced He is with silly beasts
In crib to shroud His head.

This stable is a Prince's court,
This crib His chair of state;
The beasts are parcel of His pomp,
The wooden dish His plate.

The persons in that poor attire
His royal liveries wear;
The Prince Himself is come from heaven;
This pomp is prizèd there.

With joy approach, O Christian wight,
Do homage to thy King;
And highly praise this humble pomp,
Which He from heaven doth bring.

ROBERT SOUTHWELL (c. 1561–95)

The Christ-child

The Christ-child lay on Mary's lap,
  His hair was like a light.
(O weary, weary were the world,
  But here is all aright.)

The Christ-child lay on Mary's breast,
  His hair was like a star.
(O stern and cunning are the kings,
  But here the true hearts are.)

The Christ-child lay on Mary's heart,
  His hair was like a fire.
(O weary, weary is the world,
  But here the world's desire.)

The Christ-child stood at Mary's knee,
  His hair was like a crown,
And all the flowers looked up at Him,
And all the stars looked down.

G. K. CHESTERTON (1874–1936).

The Shepherds' Hymn

Come, we shepherds whose blest sight
Hath met Love's noon in Nature's night:
Come, lift we up our loftier song,
And wake the sun that lies too long.

To all our world of well-stol'n joy,
  He slept, and dreamt of no such thing;

While we found out heaven's fairer eye,
    And kissed the cradle of our King;
Tell him he rises now too late
To show us aught worth looking at.

Tell him we now can show him more
    Than he e'er showed to mortal sight,
Than he himself e'er saw before,—
    Which to be seen needs not his light;
Tell him, Tityrus, where th' hast been;
Tell him, Thyrsis, what th' hast seen.

Tityrus.   Gloomy night embraced the place
    Where the noble Infant lay;
The Babe looked up and showed His face—
    In spite of darkness it was day;
It was Thy day, Sweet, and did rise,
Not from the East, but from Thine eyes.

Thyrsis.   Winter chid aloud, and sent
    The angry North to wage his wars;
The North forgot his fierce intent,
    And left perfumes instead of scars:
By those sweet eyes' persuasive powers,
Where he meant frost he scattered flowers.

Both.   We saw Thee in Thy balmy nest,
    Young dawn of our eternal day!
We saw Thine eyes break from their East,
    And chase the trembling shades away:
We saw Thee, and we blessed the sight,
We saw Thee by Thine own sweet light.

Tityrus. Poor world, said I, what wilt thou do
    To entertain this starry Stranger?
Is this the best thou canst bestow,
    A cold and not too cleanly manger?
Contend, ye powers of heaven and earth,
To fit a bed for this huge birth.

Thyrsis. Proud world, said I, cease your contest,
    And let the mighty Babe alone;
The phoenix build the phoenix' nest,
    Love's architecture is His own:
The Babe whose birth embraves this morn,
Made His own bed ere He was born.

Tityrus. I saw the curl'd drops, soft and slow,
    Come hovering o'er the place's head,
Offering their whitest sheets of snow,
    To furnish the fair Infant's bed:
Forbear, said I, be not too bold,
Your fleece is white, but 't is too cold.

Thyrsis. I saw the obsequious seraphims
    Their rosy fleece of fire bestow,
For well they now can spare their wings,
    Since heaven itself lies here below:
Well done, said I; but are you sure
Your down, so warm, will pass for pure?

Tityrus. No, no, your King's not yet to seek
    Where to repose His royal head;
See, see how soon His new-bloom'd check
    'Twixt mother's breasts is gone to bed.
Sweet choice, said I, no way but so
Not to lie cold, yet sleep in snow.

Chorus. Welcome all wonders in one sight!
   Eternity shut in a span!
Summer in winter! day in night!
   Heaven in earth! and God in man!
Great little one, whose all-embracing birth
Lifts earth to heaven, stoops heaven to earth!

Welcome, tho' nor to gold, nor silk,
   To more than Caesar's birthright is:
Two sister seas of virgin's milk,
   With many a rarely-temper'd kiss,
That breathes at once both maid and mother,
Warms in the one, cools in the other.

She sings Thy tears asleep, and dips
   Her kisses in Thy weeping eye:
She spreads the red leaves of Thy lips
   That in their buds yet blushing lie.
She 'gainst those mother diamonds tries
The points of her young eagle's eyes.

Welcome—tho' not to those gay flies,
   Gilded i' th' beams of earthly kings,
Slippery souls in smiling eyes—
   But to poor shepherds, homespun things,
Whose wealth 's their flocks, whose wit 's to be
Well read in their simplicity.

Yet, when young April's husband show'rs
   Shall bless the fruitful Maia's bed,
We 'll bring the first-born of her flowers,
   To kiss Thy feet and crown Thy head.
To Thee, dread Lamb! whose love must keep
The shepherds while they feed their sheep.

To Thee, meek Majesty, soft King
    Of simple graces and sweet loves!
Each of us his lamb will bring,
    Each his pair of silver doves;
At last, in fire of Thy fair eyes,
Ourselves become our own best sacrifice.

RICHARD CRASHAW (1613–49).

And Springs ran Nectar

O than the fairest day, thrice fairer night!
    Night to best days in which a sun doth rise,
    Of which that golden eye, which clears the skies,
Is but a sparkling ray, a shadow light:
And blessed ye, in silly pastor's sight,
    Mild creatures, in whose warm crib now lies
That heaven-sent Youngling, holy maid-born Wight,
    Midst, end, beginning of our prophecies;
Blest cottage that hath flowers in winter spread,
    Though withered; blessed grass, that hath the grace
    To deck, and be a carpet to that place.
Thus sang, unto the sounds of oaten reèd,
Before the Babe, the shepherds bowed on knees,
And springs ran nectar, honey dropt from trees.

WILLIAM DRUMMOND (1585–1649).

Le Cher Petit Enfant

Le ciel est noir, la terre est blanche.
Cloches, carillonnez gaîment!
Jésus est né; la Vierge penche
Sur lui son visage charmant.

Pas de courtines festonnées
Pour préserver l'Enfant du froid;
Rien que les toiles d'araignées
Qui pendent des poutres du toit.

Il tremble sur la paille fraîche,
Ce cher petit enfant Jésus,
Et pour l'échauffer dans sa crèche
L'âne et le bœuf soufflent dessus.

La neige au chaume pend ses franges,
Mais sur le toit s'ouvre le Ciel,
Et, tout en blanc, le chœur des anges
Chante aux bergers: 'Noël! Noël!'

THÉOPHILE GAUTIER (1811–72).

How he shakes for Cold!

Look, how He shakes for cold!
How pale His lips are grown!
Wherein His limbs to fold
Yet mantle has He none.
His pretty feet and hands
(Of late more pure and white
Than is the snow
That pains them so),
Have lost their colour quite.
His lips are blue
Where roses grew,
He's frozen everywhere:
All the heat He has
Joseph, alas!
Gives in a groan; or Mary in a tear.

HON. PATRICK CAREY (1623–57).

A Maiden that is Makeless

I sing of a maiden
  That is makeless.
King of all kinges
  To her son she chose.

He came all so stille
  There his mother was
As dew in Aprille
  That falleth on the grass.

He came all so stille
  To his mother's bower,
As dew in Aprille
  That falleth on the flower.

He came all so stille
  There his mother lay,
As dew in Aprille
  That falleth on the spray.

Mother and maiden
  Was never none but she;
Well may such a lady
  Godes mother be.

ANONYMOUS.

Our Lady's Lullaby

Upon my lap my Sovereign sits,
And sucks upon my breast;
Meanwhile, His love sustains my life,
And gives my body rest.
  Sing lullaby, my little Boy,
  Sing lullaby, my life's Joy.

When thou hast taken thy repast
Repose, my Babe, on me;
So may Thy mother and Thy nurse
Thy cradle also be.
 Sing lullaby.

My Babe, my Bliss, my Child, my Choice,
My Fruit, my Flower, and Bud,
My Jesus, and my only Joy,
The Sum of all my good.
 Sing lullaby.

The shepherds left their keeping sheep
For joy to see my Lamb;
How may I more rejoice to see
Myself to be the Dam.
 Sing lullaby.

Three kings their treasure hither brought
Of incense, myrrh, and gold,
The heaven's Treasure and the King
That here they might behold.
 Sing lullaby.

One sort an angel did direct,
A star did guide the other;
And all the fairest Son to see
That ever had a Mother.
 Sing lullaby, my little Boy,
 Sing lullaby, my life's Joy.

RICHARD ROWLANDS (1565–1620).

On the Blessed Virgin's Bashfulness

That on her lap she casts her humble eye,
'Tis the sweet pride of her humility.
The fair star is well fix'd, for where, O where
Could she have fix'd it on a fairer sphere?
'Tis heaven, 'tis heaven she sees; heaven's God there lies,
She can see heaven, and ne'er lift up her eyes;
This new guest to her eyes new laws hath given,
'Twas once look up, 'tis now look down to heaven.

RICHARD CRASHAW (1613–49).

Cradle Hymn

Sleep, sweet babe! my cares beguiling:
Mother sits beside thee smiling:
  Sleep, my darling, tenderly!
If thou sleep not, mother mourneth,
Singing as her wheel she turneth:
  Come, soft slumber, balmily!

SAMUEL TAYLOR COLERIDGE (1772–1834).

The Journey of the Magi

'A cold coming we had of it,
Just the worst time of the year
For a journey, and such a long journey:
The ways deep and the weather sharp,
The very dead of winter.'
And the camels galled, sore-footed, refractory,
Lying down in the melting snow.
There were times we regretted
The summer palaces on slopes, the terraces,
And the silken girls bringing sherbet.
Then the camel men cursing and grumbling
And running away, and wanting their liquor and women,

And the night-fires going out, and the lack of shelters,
And the cities hostile and the towns unfriendly
And the villages dirty and charging high prices:
A hard time we had of it.

At the end we preferred to travel all night,
Sleeping in snatches,
With the voices singing in our eyes, saying
That this was all folly.
Then at dawn we came down to a temperate valley,
Wet, below the snow line, smelling of vegetation;
With a running stream and a water-mill beating the darkness,
And three trees on the low sky,
And an old white horse galloped away in the meadow.
Then we came to a tavern with vine-leaves over the lintel,
Six hands at an open door dicing for pieces of silver,
And feet kicking the empty wine-skins.
But there was no information, and so we continued
And arrived at evening, not a moment too soon
Finding the place; it was (you may say) satisfactory.

All this was a long time ago, I remember,
And I would do it again, but set down
This set down
This: were we led all that way for
Birth or Death? There was a Birth, certainly,
We had evidence and no doubt. I had seen birth and death,
But had thought they were different; this Birth was
Hard and bitter agony for us, like Death, our death.
We returned to our places, these kingdoms,
But no longer at ease here, in the old dispensation,
With an alien people clutching their gods.
I should be glad of another death.

                                        T. S. ELIOT.

ADORATION

He who did wear
God's radiant boundless Form
Shrinks Himself here
Into a simple worm.
Heaven's moulded up in earth, Eternity
Grasped in a span of Time doth bounded lie.

All Paradise
Collected in one bud
Doth sweetly rise
From its fair virgin bed,
Omnipotence an infant's shape puts on:
Immensity becomes a Little One.

JOSEPH BEAUMONT (1616–99).

This Heavenly Boy

Come to your heaven, you heavenly choirs!
Earth hath the heaven of your desires.
Remove your dwelling to your God;
A stall is now His best abode.
Sith men their homage do deny,
Come, angels, all their fault supply.

His chilling cold doth heat require,
Come, seraphins, in lieu of fire;
This little ark no cover hath,
Let cherubs' wings His body swathe.
Come, Raphael, this Babe must eat—
Provide our little Toby meat.

Let Gabriel be now His groom
That first took up His earthly room;
Let Michael stand in His defence
Whom love hath linkt to feeble sense;
Let Graces rock when He doth cry,
And angels sing His lullaby.

The same you saw in heavenly seat
Is He that now sucks Mary's teat;
Agnize your King a mortal wight,
His borrow'd weed lets not your sight.
Come, kiss the manger where He lies
That is your bliss above the skies.

This little Babe, so few days old,
Is come to rifle Satan's fold;
All hell doth at His presence quake,
Though He Himself for cold do shake;
For in this weak unarmèd wise
The gates of hell He will surprise.

With tears He fights and wins the field,
His naked breast stands for a shield;
His battering shot are babish cries,
His arrows looks of weeping eyes,
His martial ensigns Cold and Need,
And feeble Flesh His warrior's steed.

His camp is pitchèd in a stall,
His bulwark but a broken wall;
The crib His trench, hay-stalks His stakes;
Of shepherds He His muster makes;
And thus, as sure His foe to wound,
The angels' trumps alarum sound.

My soul, with Christ join thou in fight;
Stick to the tents that He hath pight.
Within His crib is surest ward;
This little Babe will be thy guard.
If thou wilt foil thy foes with joy.
Then flit not from this heavenly Boy.

ROBERT SOUTHWELL (*c.* 1561–95).

No Rose of such Vertu

There is no rose of such vertu
As is the rose that bare Jesu.
Alleluia.

For in this rose conteinèd was
Heaven and erth in litel space,
Res miranda.

By that rose we may well see
There be one God in persons three,
Pares forma.

The aungels sungen the shepherds to:
Gloria in excelsis Deo.
Gaudeamus.

Leave we all this werldly mirth,
And folwè we this joyful birth.
Transeamus.

ANONYMOUS.

O grant this Boon

Hail, blessèd virgin, full of heavenly grace,
Blest above all that sprang from human race;
Whose heav'n-saluted womb brought forth in one,
A blessèd Saviour and a blessèd Son;
O! what a ravishment 't had been to see
Thy little Saviour perking on thy knee!
To see Him nuzzle in thy virgin breast
His milk-white body all unclad, all undressed!
To see thy busy fingers clothe and wrap
His spraddling limbs in thy indulgent lap!
To see His desperate eyes, with childish grace
Smiling upon His smiling mother's face!
And when His forward strength began to bloom,
To see Him diddle up and down the room!
O, who would think so sweet a Babe as this,
Should e'er be slain by a false-hearted kiss!
Had I a rag, if sure Thy Body wore it,
Pardon, sweet Babe, I think I should adore it.
Till then, O grant this boon (a boon far dearer),
The weed not being, I may adore the wearer.

FRANCIS QUARLES (1592–1644).

Jerusalem rejoice

Jerusalem rejoice for joy,
Jesus the sterne of most beauty
In thee is risen as richteous roy,
Fro darkness to illumine thee;
With glorious sound of angel glee,
Thy Prince is born in Bethlehem,
Whilk sall thee mak of thraldom free;
Illuminare Jerusalem!

With angellis licht, in legionis,
Thou art illumynit all about;
Three kingis of strange regionis
To thee are come with lusty rout,
All drest with diamantis but doubt,
Reverst with gold in every hem;
Sounding attonis with a shout,
    Illuminare Jerusalem.

His coming knew all element;
The air be sterne did Him persave;
The water, when dry He on it went;
The erd that trymlit all and rave;
The sun, when he no lichtis gave;
The cross, when it was done contem;
The stanis when they in piecis clave:
    Illuminare Jerusalem!

The deid Him knew that raiss upricht,
Whilk lang time had the erd lain under;
Crookit and blind declarit His micht,
That healit of them so many hunder;
Nature Him knew and had great wonder,
When He of virgin was born but wem;
Hell when their yettis were broken asunder:
    Illuminare Jerusalem!

ANONYMOUS (*from the Bannatyne MS.*, 1568).

Ode

In numbers, and but these few,
I sing Thy birth, O Jesu!
Thou pretty Baby, born here
With sup'rabundant scorn here.

Who for Thy princely port here,
    Hadst for Thy place
    Of birth a base
Out-stable for Thy court here.

Instead of neat enclosures
Of interwoven osiers,
Instead of fragrant posies
Of daffodils and roses,
Thy cradle, Kingly Stranger,
    As Gospel tells,
    Was nothing else
But here a homely manger.

But we with silks, not crewels,
With sundry precious jewels,
And lily-work, will dress Thee;
And as we dispossess Thee
Of clouts, we'll make a chamber,
    Sweet Babe, for Thee
    Of ivory,
And plastered round with amber.

The Jews they did disdain Thee,
But we will entertain Thee
With glories to await here
Upon Thy princely state here,
And more for love than pity,
    From year to year
    We'll make Thee, here,
A freeborn of our city.

ROBERT HERRICK (1591–1674).

Hymn

It was the winter wild,
While the heaven-born Child
All meanly wrapt in the rude manger lies;
Nature, in awe to Him,
Hath doffed her gaudy trim.
With her great Master so to sympathize:
It was no season then for her
To wanton with the Sun, her lusty paramour.

Only with speeches fair
She woos the gentle air
To hide her guilty front with innocent snow,
And on her naked shame,
Pollute with sinful blame,
The saintly veil of maiden white to throw;
Confounded, that her Maker's eyes
Should look so near upon her foul deformities.

But He, her fears to cease,
Sent down the meek-eyed Peace:
She, crowned with olive green, came softly sliding
Down through the turning sphere,
His ready harbinger,
With turtle wing the amorous clouds dividing;
And, waving wide her myrtle wand,
She strikes a universal peace through sea and land.

No war, or battle's sound,
Was heard the world around;
The idle spear and shield were high uphung;
The hookèd chariot stood,
Unstained with hostile blood;

The trumpet spake not to the armèd throng;
And kings sat still with awful eye,
As if they surely knew their sovran Lord was by.

But peaceful was the night
Wherein the Prince of Light
His reign of peace upon the earth began.
The winds, with wonder whist,
Smoothly the waters kissed,
Whispering new joys to the mild Ocean,
Who now hath quite forgot to rave,
While birds of calm sit brooding on the charmèd wave.

The stars, with deep amaze,
Stand fixed in steadfast gaze,
Bending one way their precious influence,
And will not take their flight,
For all the morning light,
Or Lucifer that often warned them thence;
But in their glimmering orbs did glow,
Until their Lord Himself bespake, and bid them go.

And, though the shady gloom
Had given day her room,
The Sun himself withheld his wonted speed,
And hid his head for shame,
As his inferior flame
The new-enlightened world no more should need:
He saw a greater Sun appear
Than his bright throne or burning axletree could bear.

The shepherds on the lawn,
Or ere the point of dawn,
Sat simply chatting in a rustic row;

Full little thought they than
That the mighty Pan
Was kindly come to live with them below:
Perhaps their loves, or else their sheep,
Was all that did their silly thoughts so busy keep.

When such music sweet
Their hearts and ears did greet
As never was by mortal finger strook,
Divinely-warbled voice
Answering the stringèd noise,
As all their souls in blissful rapture took:
The air, such pleasure loth to lose,
With thousand echoes still prolongs each heavenly close.

Nature, that heard such sound
Beneath the hollow round
Of Cynthia's seat the Airy region thrilling,
Now was almost won
To think her part was done,
And that her reign had here its last fulfilling:
She knew such harmony alone
Could hold all Heaven and Earth in happier union.

At last surrounds their sight
A globe of circular light,
That with long beams the shamefaced Night arrayed;
The helmèd cherubim
And sworded seraphim
Are seen in glittering ranks with wings displayed,
Harping in loud and solemn quire,
With unexpressive notes, to Heaven's new-born Heir.

Such music (as 'tis said)
Before was never made,

But when of old the Sons of Morning sung,
  While the Creator great
  His constellations set,
And the well balanced World on hinges hung,
And cast the dark foundations deep,
And bid the weltering waves their oozy channel keep.

  Ring out, ye crystal spheres!
  Once bless our human ears,
If ye have power to touch our senses so;
  And let your silver chime
  Move in melodious time;
And let the bass of Heaven's deep organ blow;
And with your ninefold harmony
Make up full consort to the angelic symphony.

  For, if such holy song
  Enwrap our fancy long,
Time will run back and fetch the Age of Gold;
  And speckled Vanity
  Will sicken soon and die;
And leprous Sin will melt from earthly mould;
And Hell itself will pass away,
And leave her dolorous mansions to the peering day.

  Yea, Truth and Justice then
  Will down return to men,
Orbed in a rainbow; and, like glories wearing,
  Mercy will sit between,
  Throned in celestial sheen,
With radiant feet the tissued clouds down steering;
And Heaven, as at some festival,
Will open wide the gates of her high palace-hall.

But wisest Fate says No,
This must not yet be so;
The Babe yet lies in smiling infancy
That on the bitter cross
Must redeem our loss,
So both Himself and us to glorify:
Yet first, to those ychained in sleep,
The wakeful trump of doom must thunder through the deep,

With such a horrid clang
As on Mount Sinai rang,
While the red fire and smouldering clouds outbrake:
The aged Earth, agast,
With terror of that blast,
Shall from the surface to the centre shake,
When, at the world's last session,
The dreadful Judge in middle air shall spread His throne.

And then at last our bliss
Full and perfect is,
But now begins; for from this happy day
The Old Dragon under ground,
In straiter limits bound,
Not half so far casts his usurpèd sway,
And, wroth to see his kingdom fail,
Swinges the scaly horror of his folded tail.

The Oracles are dumb;
No voice or hideous hum
Runs through the archèd roofs in words deceiving.
Apollo from his shrine
Can no more divine,
With hollow shriek the steep of Delphos leaving.
No nightly trance, or breathèd spell,
Inspires the pale-eyed priest from the prophetic cell.

The lonely mountains o'er,
And the resounding shore,
A voice of weeping heard and loud lament;
From haunted spring, and dale
Edged with poplar pale,
The parting Genius is with sighing sent;
With flower-inwoven tresses torn
The Nymphs in twilight shade of tangled thickets mourn.

In consecrated earth,
And on the holy hearth,
The Lars and Lemures moan with midnight plaint;
In urns, and altars round,
A drear and dying sound
Affrights the flamens at their service quaint;
And the chill marble seems to sweat,
While each peculiar Power forgoes his wonted seat.

Peor and Baälim
Forsake their temples dim,
With that twice-battered God of Palestine;
And moonèd Ashtaroth,
Heaven's queen and mother both,
Now sits not girt with tapers' holy shine:
The Libyc Hammon shrinks his horn;
In vain the Tyrian maids their wounded Thammuz mourn.

And sullen Moloch, fled,
Hath left in shadows dread
His burning idol all of blackest hue;
In vain with cymbal's ring
They call the grisly king,
In dismal dance about the furnace blue;
The brutish gods of Nile as fast,
Isis, and Orus, and the dog Anubis, haste.

Nor is Osiris seen
In Memphian grove or green,
Tramping the unshowered grass with lowings loud;
Nor can he be at rest
Within his sacred chest;
Nought but profoundest Hell can be his shroud;
In vain, with timbrelled anthems dark,
The sable-stolèd sorcerers bear his worshipped ark.

He feels from Juda's land
The dreaded Infant's hand;
The rays of Bethlehem blind his dusky eyn;
Nor all the gods beside
Longer dare abide,
Not Typhon huge ending in snaky twine:
Our Babe, to show His Godhead true,
Can in His swaddling bands control the damnèd crew.

So, when the sun in bed,
Curtained with cloudy red,
Pillows his chin upon an orient wave,
The flocking shadows pale
Troop to the infernal jail,
Each fettered ghost slips to his several grave,
And the yellow-skirted fays
Fly after the night-steeds, leaving their moon-loved maze.

But see! the Virgin blest
Hath laid her Babe to rest.
Time is our tedious song should here have ending:
Heaven's youngest-teemèd star
Hath fixed her polished car,
Her sleeping Lord with handmaid lamp attending;
And all about the courtly stable
Bright-harnessed Angels sit in order serviceable.

JOHN MILTON (1608–74).

Rorate Coeli desuper

Rorate coeli desuper!
Heavens distil your balmy shouris,
For now is risen the bricht day ster,
Fro the rose Mary, flour of flouris;
The clear Son, whom no cloud devouris,
Surmounting Phoebus in the east,
Is comen of his heavenly touris;
Et nobis Puer natus est.

Archangellis, angellis, and dompnationis,
Tronis, potestatis, and martyris seir,
And all ye heavenly operationis,
Star, planet, firmament, and sphere,
Fire, erd, air, and water clear,
To him give loving, most and least,
That come in/to so meek mannér;
Et nobis Puer natus est.

Sinneris be glaid, and penance do,
And thank your Maker hairtfully;
For he that ye micht nocht come to,
To you is comen full humyly,
Your saulis sith his blude to buy,
And loose you of the Fiendis arrest,
And only of his awn mercy;
Pro nobis Puer natus est.

All clergy do to him incline,
And bow unto that bairn bening,
And do your observance divine
To him that is of kingis King;

Ensence his altar, read, and sing
In haly kirk, with mind degest,
Him honouring attour all thing,
Qui nobis Puer natus est.

Celestial fowlis in the air,
Sing with your notis upon hicht;
In firthis and in forestis fair
Be mirthful now, at all your micht,
For passit is your dully nicht;
Aurora has the cloudis pierc'd,
The sun is risen with glaidsome licht,
Et nobis Puer natus est.

Now spring up flouris fra the root,
Revert you upward naturally,
In honour of the blissit fruit
That raise up fro the rose Mary;
Lay out your leavës lustily,
Fro deid tak life now at the lest
In worship of that Prince worthy,
Qui nobis Puer natus est.

Sing heaven imperial, most of hicht,
Regions of air mak harmony;
All fish in flood and fowl of flicht,
Be mirthful and mak melody;
All GLORIA IN EXCELSIS cry,
Heaven, erd, sez, man, bird, and beast,
He that is crownit abune the sky
Pro nobis Puer natus est.

WILLIAM DUNBAR (c. 1460–1530).

And shall I Silent be ?

All after pleasures as I rid one day,
  My horse and I, both tir'd, body and mind,
  With full cry of affections, quite astray;
I took up in the next inn I could find.

There when I came, whom found I but my dear,
  My dearest Lord, expecting till the grief
  Of pleasures brought me to Him, ready there
To be all passengers' most sweet relief?

O Thou, whose glorious, yet contracted light,
  Wrapt in night's mantle, stole into a manger;
  Since my dark soul and brutish is Thy right,
To man of all beasts be not Thou a stranger:
  Furnish and deck my soul, that Thou mayst have
  A better lodging, then a rack, or grave.

The shepherds sing; and shall I silent be?
        My God, no hymn for Thee?
My soul's a shepherd too; a flock it feeds
        Of thoughts, and words, and deeds.
The pasture is Thy word: the streams, Thy grace
        Enriching all the place.
Shepherd and flock shall sing, and all my powers
        Out-sing the day-light hours.
Then we will chide the sun for letting night
        Take up his place and right:
We sing one common Lord; wherefore He should
        Himself the candle hold.
I will go searching, till I find a sun
        Shall stay, till we have done;

A willing shiner, that shall shine as gladly,
    As frost-nipt suns look sadly,
Then we will sing, and shine all our own day,
    And one another pay:
His beams shall cheer my breast, and both so twine,
Till ev'n His beams sing, and my music shine.

                GEORGE HERBERT (1593–1633).

To a Child

Go, pretty child, and bear this flower
Unto thy little Saviour,
And tell Him, by that bud now blown,
He is the Rose of Sharon known.
When thou hast said so, stick it there
Upon His bib or stomacher;
And tell Him, for good handsel too,
That thou hast brought a whistle new,
Made of a clean straight oaten reed,
To charm His cries at time of need.
Tell Him, for coral thou hast none,
But, if thou hadst, He should have one;
But poor thou art, and known to be
Even as moneyless as He.
Lastly, if thou canst win a kiss
From those mellifluous lips of His,
Then never take a second on,
To spoil the first impression.

                ROBERT HERRICK (1591–1674).

WINTRY PLEASURES

With footstep slow, in furry pall yclad,
His brows enwreathed with holly never sere,
Old Christmas comes, to close the wanèd year,
And aye the shepherd's heart to make right glad;
Who, when his teeming flocks are homeward had,
To blazing hearth repairs, and nut-brown beer;
And views, well pleased, the ruddy prattlers dear
Hug the grey mongrel; meanwhile, maid and lad
Squabble for roasted crabs. Thee, sire, we hail,
Whether thine aged limbs thou dost enshroud
In vest of snowy white and hoary veil,
Or wrapp'st thy visage in a sable cloud;
Thee we proclaim with mirth and cheer, nor fail
To greet thee well with many a carol loud.

JOHN BAMPFYLDE (1754–96).

In Praise of Winter

O Winter, ruler of the inverted year,
Thy scattered hair with sleet like ashes filled,
Thy breath congealed upon thy lips, thy cheeks
Fringed with a beard made white with other snows
Than those of age, thy forehead wrapped in clouds,
A leafless branch thy sceptre, and thy throne
A sliding car, indebted to no wheels,
But urged by storms along its slippery way;
I love thee, all unlovely as thou seem'st,
And dreaded as thou art! Thou hold'st the sun
A prisoner in the yet undawning east,
Shortening his journey between morn and noon

And hurrying him, impatient of his stay,
Down to the rosy west; but kindly still
Compensating his loss with added hours
Of social converse and instructive ease,
And gathering, at short notice, in one group
The family dispersed, and fixing thought,
Not less dispersed by daylight and its cares.
I crown thee king of intimate delights,
Fireside enjoyments, homeborn happiness,
And all the comforts that the lowly roof
Of undisturbed retirement, and the hours
Of long uninterrupted evening know.

WILLIAM COWPER (1731-1800).

Morning

The morning wakens with the lumping flails,
Chilly and cold; the early-rising clown
Hurkles along and blows his finger nails;
Icicles from the cottage eaves hang down,
Which peeping children wish for in their play.
The field, once clad in autumn's russet brown,
Spreads from the eye its circle far away
In one huge sheet of snow; from the white wood
The crows all silent seek the dreary fens,
And starnels blacken through the air in crowds;
The sheep stand bleating in their turnip pen
And loathe their frozen food; while labouring men
Button their coats more close from angry clouds
And wish for night and its snug fire agen.

JOHN CLARE (1793-1864).

Noon

But now, at noon,
Upon the southern side of the slant hills,
And where the woods fence off the northern blast,
The season smiles, resigning all its rage,
And has the warmth of May. The vault is blue
Without a cloud, and white without a speck
The dazzling splendour of the scene below.
Again the harmony comes o'er the vale;
And through the trees I view the embattled tower,
Whence all the music. I again perceive
The soothing influence of the wafted strains,
And settle in soft musings as I tread
The walk, still verdant, under oaks and elms
Whose outspread branches overarch the glade.

WILLIAM COWPER (1731–1800).

Night

The shutter closed, the lamp alight,
The faggot chopt and blazing bright—
The shepherd now, from labour free,
Dances his children on his knee;
While, underneath his master's seat,
The tired dog lies in slumbers sweet,
Starting and whimpering in his sleep,
Chasing still the straying sheep.
The cat's rolled round in vacant chair,
Or leaping children's knees to lair
—Or purring on the warmer hearth
Sweet chorus to the crickets' mirth.

The redcap, hanging over head
In cage of wire, is perch'd abed;
Slumbering in his painted feathers
Unconscious of the out-door weathers;
Ev'n things without the cottage walls
Meet comfort as the evening falls,—
As happy in the winter's dearth
As those around the blazing hearth.
The ass (frost-driven from the moor
Where storms through naked bushes roar)
Litter'd with straw, now dozes warm,
Beneath his shed, from snow and storm;
The swine are fed and in the sty;
And fowls snug perch'd in hovel nigh,
With head in feathers safe asleep,
Where foxes cannot hope to creep;
And geese are gabbling in their dreams
Of littered corn and thawing streams—
The sparrow, too, a daily guest,
Is in the cottage eaves at rest;
And robin small, and smaller wren,
Are in their warm holes safe again
From falling snows, that winnow by
The hovels where they nightly lie.

JOHN CLARE (1793–1864).

Images in the Fire

Me oft has fancy ludicrous and wild
Soothed with a waking dream of houses, towers,
Trees, churches, and strange visages, express'd
In the red cinders, while with poring eye
I gazed, myself creating what I saw.

WILLIAM COWPER (1731–1800).

Heigh ho, the Holly!

Blow, blow, thou winter wind,
Thou art not so unkind
    As man's ingratitude;
Thy tooth is not so keen,
Because thou art not seen,
    Although thy breath be rude.
Heigh ho, sing heigh ho, unto the green holly:
Most friendship is feigning, most loving mere folly:
    Then, heigh ho, the holly!
    This life is most jolly.

Freeze, freeze, thou bitter sky,
That dost not bite so nigh
    As benefits forgot:
Though thou the waters warp,
Thy sting is not so sharp
    As friend remember'd not.
Heigh ho, sing heigh ho, unto the green holly:
Most friendship is feigning, most loving mere folly:
    Then, heigh ho, the holly!
    This life is most jolly.

WILLIAM SHAKESPEARE (1564–1616).

To dream Alone

I used to love on winter nights
    To lie and dream alone
Of all the rare and real delights
    My lovely years had known;

EMILY BRONTË (1818–48).

Chimney Corner Days

How am I to sing your praise,
Happy chimney corner days,
Sitting safe in nursery nooks,
Reading picture story-books?

ROBERT LOUIS STEVENSON (1850–94).

Fog by the Shore

The ocean too has winter views serene,
When all you see through densest fog is seen;
When you can hear the fishers near at hand
Distinctly speak, yet see not where they stand;
Or sometimes them and not their boat discern,
Or half-conceal'd some figure at the stern;
The view's all bounded, and from side to side
Your utmost prospect but a few ells wide . . .
'Tis pleasant then to view the nets float past,
Net after net till you have seen the last;
And as you wait till all beyond you slip,
A boat comes gliding from an anchor'd ship,
Breaking the silence with the dipping oar,
And their own tones, as labouring for the shore;
Those measured tones which with the scene agree,
And give a sadness to serenity.

GEORGE CRABBE (1754–1832).

Imitation of Horace: Vides ut Alta . . .

Bless me, 'tis cold! how chill the air!
How naked does the world appear!
But see (big with the offspring of the north)
The teeming clouds bring forth:

A shower of soft and fleecy rain
Falls, to new-clothe the earth again.
Behold the mountain-tops around,
As if with fur or ermine crown'd:
　　And lo! how by degrees
The universal mantle hides the trees,
　In hoary flakes which downward fly,
As if it were the autumn of the sky,
　Whose fall of leaf would theirs supply:
Trembling, the groves sustain the weight, and bow
　Like aged limbs, which feebly go
Beneath a venerable head of snow.

Diffusive cold does the whole earth invade,
Like a disease, through all its veins 'tis spread,
And each late living stream is numbed and dead.
Let's melt the frozen hours, make warm the air;
Let cheerful fire Sol's feeble beams repair;
　Fill the large bowl with sparkling wine,
　Let's drink till our own faces shine,
　　Till we like suns appear,
　To light and warm the hemisphere.
Wine can dispense to all both light and heat,
　They are with wine incorporate:
That pow'rful juice, with which no cold dares mix,
Which still is fluid, and no frost can fix;
　Let that but in abundance flow,
And let it storm and thunder, hail and snow,
　'Tis heav'n's concern, and let it be
　The care of heaven still for me:
These winds which rend the oaks and plough the seas,
　　Great Jove can, if he please,
With one commanding nod appease.

Seek not to know to-morrow's doom;
That is not ours which is to come.
The present moment's all our store:
    The next, shou'd Heav'n allow,
Than this will be no more:
So all our life is but one instant now.
    Look on each day you've past
    To be a mighty treasure won:
And lay each moment out in haste;
    We're sure to live too fast,
    And cannot live too soon.
Youth does a thousand pleasures bring,
    Which from decrepit age will fly;
Sweets that wanton i' th' bosom of the spring,
    In winter's cold embraces die.

WILLIAM CONGREVE (1670–1729).

Pleasures of Melancholy

Let others love soft summer's evening smiles,
As, listening to the distant waterfall,
They mark the blushes of the streaky west;
I choose the pale December's foggy glooms.
Then, when the sullen shades of evening close,
Where thro' the room a blindly-glimmering gleam
The dying embers scatter, far remote
From Mirth's mad shouts that thro' the illumin'd roof
Resound with festive echo, let me sit,
Blest with the lowly cricket's drowsy dirge.
Then let my thought contemplative explore
This fleeting state of things, the vain delights,
The fruitless toils that still our search elude,
As thro' the wilderness of life we rove.

THOMAS WARTON (1728–90).

Trophonian Pallor

I, singularly moved
To love the lovely that are not beloved,
Of all the seasons, most
Love Winter, and to trace
The sense of the Trophonian pallor on her face.
It is not death, but plenitude of peace;
And the dim cloud that does the world enfold
Hath less the characters of dark and cold
Than warmth and light asleep,
And correspondent breathing seems to keep
With the infant harvest, breathing soft below
Its eider coverlet of snow.

COVENTRY PATMORE (1823–96).

Skating

All shod with steel
We hissed along the polished ice in games
Confederate, imitative of the chase
And woodland pleasures,—the resounding horn,
The pack loud chiming, and the hunted hare.
So through the darkness and the cold we flew,
And not a voice was idle: with the din
Smitten, the precipices rang aloud;
The leafless trees and every icy crag
Tinkled like iron; while far distant hills
Into the tumult sent an alien sound
Of melancholy not unnoticed, while the stars
Eastward were sparkling clear, and in the west
The orange sky of evening died away.

Not seldom from the uproar I retired
Into a silent bay, or sportively
Glanced sideway, leaving the tumultuous throng,
To cut across the reflex of a star
That fled, and, flying still before me, gleamed
Upon the glassy plain: and oftentimes,
When we had given our bodies to the wind,
And all the shadowy banks on either side
Came sweeping through the darkness, spinning still
The rapid line of motion, then at once
Have I, reclining back upon my heels,
Stopped short; yet still the solitary cliffs
Wheeled by me—even as if the earth had rolled
With visible motion her diurnal round!
Behind me did they stretch in solemn train,
Feebler and feebler, and I stood and watched
Till all was tranquil as a dreamless sleep.

WILLIAM WORDSWORTH (1770–1850).

Reading

'Tis winter, and I love to read indoors,
    When the moon hangs her crescent up on high;
While on the window shutters the wind roars,
    And storms like furies pass remorseless by.
How pleasant on a feather bed to lie,
    Or, sitting by the fire, in fancy soar
With Dante or with Milton to regions high,
    Or read fresh volumes we've not seen before,
    Or o'er old Burton's Melancholy pore.

JOHN CLARE (1793–1864).

Kings in Conceit

Now thrice welcome Christmas,
    Which brings us good cheer,
Minced pies and plum porridge,
    Good ale and strong beer;
With pig, goose, and capon,
    The best that can be.
So well doth the weather
    And our stomachs agree.

Observe how the chimneys
    Do smoke all about,
The cooks are providing
    For dinner, no doubt;
But those on whose tables
    No victuals appear,
O may they keep Lent
    All the rest of the year!

With holly and ivy
    So green and so gay;
We deck up our houses
    As fresh as the day,
With bays and rosemary,
    And laurel complete,
And every one now
    Is a king in conceit.

Poor Robin's Almanack, 1695.

Frontispiece to THE VINDICATION OF
CHRISTMAS, *1653*

MERRY MY SPRIGHTS!

Give me leave to ask, for I bring you a masque
    From little, little, little London,
Which say the king likes, I have passed the pikes,
    If not, old Christmas is undone.

                BEN JONSON (1573–1637).

Aye, chairman, set us down. We're for a ball
    Where neither sword nor stekes is allowed,
But only the simple heart that, stripped of all
    But love, can dance lavoltas on a cloud.

                HUMBERT WOLFE.

When rosemary, and bays, the poet's crown,
Are bawled, in frequent cries, through all the town;
Then judge the festival of Christmas near,—
Christmas, the joyous period of the year.
Now with bright holly all your temples strow,
With laurel green, and sacred mistletoe,
Now, heaven-born Charity! thy blessings shed;
Bid meagre Want uprear her sickly head;
Bid shivering limbs be warm; let Plenty's bowl
In humble roofs make glad the needy soul!
See, see! the heaven-born maid her blessings shed;
Lo! meagre Want uprears her sickly head;
Clothed are the naked, and the needy glad,
While selfish Avarice alone is sad.

JOHN GAY (1685–1732), *Trivia.*

Advice to Housewives

Get ivy and hull, woman, deck up thine house,
And take this same brawn for to seethe and to souse;
Provide us good cheer, for thou knowest the old guise,
Old customs that good be, let no man despise.
At Christmas be merry and thank God of all,
And feast thy poor neighbours, the great and the small.
Yea, all the year long have an eye to the poor,
And God shall send luck to keep open thy door.
Good fruit and good plenty do well in thy loft,
Then lay for an orchard and cherish it oft.
The profit is mickle, the pleasure is much;
At pleasure with profit few wise men will grutch.
For plants and for stocks lay aforehand to cast,
But set or remove them, while Twelve-tide do last.

THOMAS TUSSER (c. 1524–80).

Fun and Games, 1734

O you merry, merry souls,
  Christmas is a coming;
We shall have flowing bowls,
  Dancing, piping, drumming.

Delicate minced pies,
  To feast every virgin,
Capon and goose likewise,
  Brawn, and dish of sturgeon.

Then for your Christmas-box
  Sweet plum-cakes and money,
Delicate Holland smocks,
  Kisses sweet as honey.

Hey for the Christmas ball,
  Where we shall be jolly;
Coupling short and tall,
  Kate, Dick, Ralph, and Molly.

Then to the hop we'll go,
  Where we'll jig and caper;
Dancers all a-row,
  Will shall pay the scraper.

Hodge shall dance with Prue,
  Keeping time with kisses;
We'll have a jovial crew
  Of sweet smirking misses.

Round about our Coal Fire, 1734.

Stop Thief!

Come, guard this night the Christmas-pie,
That the thief, though ne'er so sly,
With his flesh-hooks, don't come nigh
        To catch it

From him who all alone sits there,
Having his eyes still in his ear,
And a deal of nightly fear,
        To watch it.

ROBERT HERRICK (1591–1674).

The Yule Log

Come bring with a noise,
   My merry, merry boys,
The Christmas log to the firing;
   While my good dame, she
   Bids ye all be free,
And drink to your heart's desiring.

   With the last year's brand
   Light the new block, and
For good success in his spending,
   On your psalteries play,
   That sweet luck may
Come while the log is a teending.

ROBERT HERRICK.

But a Single Thought

Bring us in good ale, and bring us in good ale:
For our blessèd Lady's sake, bring us in good ale!

Bring us in no beef, for there is many bones,
Bring us in good ale, for *that* goth down at ones.

Bring us in no bacon, for that is passing fat,
But bring us in good ale, and give us enough of that.

Bring us in no mutton, for that is often lene,
Nor bring us in no trypes, for they be seldom clene.

Bring us in no egges, for there are many shelles,
But bring us in good ale, and give us nothing elles.

Bring us in no butter, for therein are many heres,
Nor bring us in no pigges flesh, for that will make us
     boars.

Bring us in good ale, and bring us in good ale:
For our blessèd Lady's sake, bring us in good ale!

                    ANONYMOUS (*fifteenth century*).

In Honour of the Boar's Head

SUNG AT QUEENS' COLLEGE, CAMBRIDGE

I sing not of Rome or Grecian mad games,
The Pythian, Olympic, and such like hard names;
Your patience awhile, with submission I beg,
I strive but to honour the feast of Coll. Reg.
          Derry down, down, derry down.

No Thracian brawls at our rites shall prevail,
We temper our mirth with plain, sober mild ale;
The tricks of old Circe deter us from wine,
Though we honour a boar we won't make ourselves swine.
    Derry down, down, derry down.

Great Milo was famous for slaying his ox,
Yet he prov'd but an ass in the cleaving of blocks;
But we had a hero for all things was fit,
Our motto displays both his valour and wit.
    Derry down, down, derry down.

Stout Hercules labour'd and looked mighty big
When he slew the half starv'd Erymanthian pig;
But we can relate such a stratagem taken,
That the stoutest of boars may not save his own bacon.
    Derry down, down, derry down.

So dreadful this bristle-back'd foe did appear,
You 'd have sworn he had got the wrong pig by the ear,
But instead of avoiding the mouth of the beast,
He rammed in a volume and cried—Graecum est.
    Derry down, down, derry down.

In this gallant action such fortitude shown is
As proves him no coward nor tender Adonis;
No armour but logic, by which we may find
That logic's the bulwark of body and mind.
    Derry down, down, derry down.

Ye 'squires that fear neither hills nor rough rocks,
And think you 're full wise when you outwit a fox,
Enrich your poor brains and expose them no more,
Learn Greek and seek glory from hunting the boar.
    Derry down, down, derry down.

          ANONYMOUS.

Wat Nane how Lang he livis here

In honour of this Christinmas
Now every man suld him address
. To sing and dance and mak gud cheer;
Wat nane how lang he livis here.

Tak ye no thocht, nor yet despair
Of this false warld, however it fare,
That changeis fashion every year:
Wat nane how lang he livis here.

When we believe it is most stable,
To change on us it is most able,
Fortune so quaintly does it steir:
Wat nane how lang he livis here.

For when we of this countree flit,
Have we nocht all alike of it,
Though we it buy nocht alike dear?
Wat nane how lang he livis here.

Wharefore me think their part is best,
That can with truth be merriest,
For angel life he goes maist near;
Wat nane how lang he livis here.

ANONYMOUS (*from the Maitland MSS.*).

Dorset Song

Come down to marra night, an' mind
Don't leave thy fiddle-bag behind.
We'll shiake a lag an' drink a cup
O' yal to kip wold Chris'mas up.

An' let thy sister tiake thy yarm,
The wa'k woont do 'er any harm:
Ther 's noo dirt now to spwile her frock
Var 'tis a⁄vroze so hard 's a rock.

Ther bent noo stranngers that 'ull come,
But only a vew naighbours: zome
Vrom Stowe, an' Combe, an' two ar dree
Vrom uncle's up at Rookery.

An' thee woot vine a ruozy fiace,
An' pair ov eyes so black as sloos,
The pirtiest oones in al the pliace.
I 'm sure I needen tell thee whose.

We got a back bran', dree girt logs
So much as dree ov us can car:
We 'll put 'em up athirt the dogs,
An' miake a vier to the bar,

An' ev'ry oone wull tell his tiale,
An' ev'ry oone wull zing his zong,
An' ev'ry oone wull drunk his yal,
To love an' frien'ship al night long.

We 'll snap the tongs, we 'll have a bal,
We 'll shiake the house, we 'll rise the ruf,
We 'll romp an' miake the maidens squal,
A catchen o'm at bline⁄man's bluff.

Zoo come to marra night, an' mind
Don't leave thy fiddle⁄bag behind.
We 'll shiake a lag an' drink a cup
O' yal to kip wold Chris'mas up.

WILLIAM BARNES (1801–86).

Have you brought your Music?

Lett no man cum into this hall,
Grome, page, nor yet marshall,
But that sum sport he bryng withall;
 For now ys the tyme of Crystymas!

Yff that he say he can not sing
Some oder sport then let him bring,
That yt may please at thys festyng;
 For now ys the tyme of Crystymas!

Yff he say he can nowght do,
Then for my love aske hym no mo,
But to the stokkis then lett hym go;
 For now ys the tyme of Crystymas!

Commonplace Book of Richard Hill, 1500–35.

Seventeenth-century Gaieties

So, now is come our joyfull'st feast;
 Let every man be jolly;
Each room with ivy leaves is drest,
 And every post with holly.
Though some churls at our mirth repine,
Round your foreheads garlands twine;
Drown sorrow in a cup of wine,
 And let us all be merry.

Now all our neighbours' chimneys smoke,
 And Christmas blocks are burning;
Their ovens they with baked meats choke,
 And all their spits are turning.

Without the door let sorrow lie;
And if for cold it hap to die,
We'll bury't in a Christmas pie,
    And ever more be merry.

Now every lad is wondrous trim,
    And no man minds his labour;
Our lasses have provided them
    A bag-pipe and a tabour;
Young men and maids, and girls and boys
Give life to one another's joys;
And you anon shall by their noise
    Perceive that they are merry.

Ned Squash hath fetched his bands from pawn,
    And all his best apparel;
Brisk Nell hath brought a ruff of lawn
    With droppings of the barrel;
And those that hardly all the year
Had bread to eat, or rags to wear,
Will have both clothes and dainty fare,
    And all the day be merry.

Now poor men to the justices
    With capons make their errants;
And if they hap to fail of these,
    They plague them with their warrants:
But now they feed them with good cheer,
And what they want they take in beer;
For Christmas comes but once a year,
    And then they shall be merry.

Good farmers in the country nurse
    The poor that else were undone;
Some landlords spend their money worse,
    On lust and pride at London.

There the roysters they do play,
Drab and dice their lands away,
Which may be ours another day;
    And therefore let's be merry.

The client now his suit forbears,
    The prisoner's heart is easèd:
The debter drinks away his cares,
    And for the time is pleasèd.
Though other purses be more fat,
Why should we pine or grieve at that?
Hang sorrow! care will kill a cat,
    And therefore let's be merry.

Hark! how the wags abroad do call
    Each other forth to rambling:
Anon you'll see them in the hall
    For nuts and apples scrambling.
Hark! how the roofs with laughter sound!
Anon they'll think the house goes round;
For they the cellar's depth have found,
    And there they will be merry.

The wenches with the wassail bowls
    About the streets are singing;
The boys are come to catch the owls,
    The wild mare in is bringing.
Our kitchen-boy hath broke his box,
And to the dealing of the ox
Our honest neighbours come by flocks,
    And here they will be merry.

Now kings and queens poor sheep cotes have,
    And mate with every body;
The honest now may play the knave,
    And wise men play the noddy.

Some youths will now a mumming go,
Some others play at Rowland-ho,
And twenty other gambles mo,
    Because they will be merry.

Then wherefore in these merry days
    Should we, I pray, be duller?
No, let us sing some roundelays,
    To make our mirth the fuller.
And, whilst thus inspired we sing,
Let all the streets with echoes ring,
Woods and hills, and every thing,
    Bear witness we are merry.

GEORGE WITHER (1588–1667).

Merry my hey down derry

I gave her Cakes and I gave her Ale,
    I gave her Sack and Sherry;
I kist her once and I kist her twice,
    And we were wondrous merry.

I gave her Beads and Bracelets fine,
    I gave her Gold down derry.
I thought she was afeard till she stroked my Beard,
    And we were wondrous merry.

Merry my Hearts, merry my Cocks, merry my Sprights,
    Merry merry merry my hey down derry.
I kist her once and I kist her twice,
    And we were wondrous merry.

ANONYMOUS.

The Mahogany Tree

Christmas is here;
Winds whistle shrill,
Icy and chill,
Little care we:
Little we fear
Weather without,
Sheltered about
The Mahogany Tree.

Commoner greens,
Ivy and oaks,
Poets, in jokes,
Sing, do you see?
Good fellows' shins
Here, boys, are found,
Twisting around
The Mahogany Tree.

Once on the boughs
Birds of rare plume
Sang, in its bloom;
Night birds are we:
Here we carouse,
Singing like them,
Perched round the stem
Of the jolly old tree.

Here let us sport,
Boys, as we sit;
Laughter and wit
Flashing so free.

Life is but short—
When we are gone,
Let them sing on,
Round the old tree.

Evenings we knew,
Happy as this;
Faces we miss,
Pleasant to see.
Kind hearts and true,
Gentle and just,
Peace to your dust!
We sing round the tree.

Care, like a dun,
Lurks at the gate:
Let the dog wait;
Happy we'll be!
Drink every one;
Pile up the coals,
Fill the red bowls,
Round the old tree.

Drain we the cup.—
Friend, art afraid?
Spirits are laid
In the Red Sea.
Mantle it up;
Empty it yet;
Let us forget,
Round the old tree.

Sorrows, begone!
Life and its ills,
Duns and their bills,
Bid we to flee.

Come with the dawn,
Blue-devil sprite;
Leave us to-night,
Round the old tree.

WILLIAM MAKEPEACE THACKERAY (1811–63).

A Portrait

Fair faces crowd on Christmas night
  Like seven suns a-row,
But all beyond is the wolfish wind
  And the crafty feet of the snow.

But through the rout one figure goes
  With quick and quiet tread;
Her robe is plain, her form is frail—
  Wait if she turn her head.

I say no word of line or hue,
  But if that face you see,
Your soul shall know the smile of faith's
  Awful frivolity.

Know that in this grotesque old masque
  Too loud we cannot sing,
Or dance too wild, or speak too wide
  To praise a hidden thing.

That though the jest be old as night,
  Still shaketh sun and sphere
An everlasting laughter
  Too loud for us to hear.

G. K. CHESTERTON (1874–1936).

Those were the Days!

How happy were those days so old,
When feasting did all twelve days hold;
When tables groaned with boiled and roast,
And key of buttery door was lost;
When cooks had hardly time to eat,
For serving up of others' meat;
When the old hall with gambols rung,
And merry carols they were sung;
While many tales and jests were saying,
Some were Whisk and Cross Ruff playing,
Primero, Gleek, Picquet, All Fours,
In harmless mirth they spent the hours;
Knaves out of Town who may not hurt ye.
And tom-fool's game called One and Thirty,
Winning and Losing, Loudum, Put,
Then Post and Pair, and next New Cut.
Some were a shoeing the wild mare,
With other ticks that usèd were.
But those things now are laid aside,
The better to maintain our pride,
And Christmas scarcely should we know,
Did not the almanacks it show.

Poor Robin's Almanack, 1709.

The Stay-at-home's Complaint

Now Christmas draweth near, and most men make good cheer,
    With heigh-ho, care away!
I, like a sickly mome, in drowsy dumps at home,
    Will naught but fast and pray.

Some sing and dance for life, some card and dice as rife,
    Some use old Christmas games;
But I, oh wretched wight! in dole both day and night,
    Must dwell; the world so frames.

In Court, what pretty toys, what fine and pleasant joys
    To pass the time away!
In country naught but care; four cheese-curds, chiefest fare;
    For wine, a bowl of whey.

For every dainty dish, of flesh or else of fish,
    And for your drink in Court,
A dish of young fried frogs, sod houghs of measled hogs,
    A cup of small tap-wort.

And for each courtly sight, each show that may delight
    The eye or else the mind;
In country thorns and brakes, and many miry lakes,
    Is all the good you find.

And for fine enteries, halls, chambers, galleries,
    And lodgings many moe;
Here desert woods and plains, where no delight remains,
    To walk in to and fro.

In Court, for to be short, for every pretty sport
    That may the heart delight;
In country many a grief, and small or no relief,
    To aid the wounded wight.

And in this desert place, I, wretch! in woful case,
    This merry Christmas time,
Content myself perforce to rest my careful corse,
    And so I end my rime.

NICHOLAS BRETON (1545-1626).

CHRISTMAS VOICES

Some say, that ever 'gainst that season comes
Wherein our Saviour's birth is celebrated,
This bird of dawning singeth all night long:
And then, they say, no spirit dare stir abroad;
The nights are wholesome; then no planets strike,
No fairy takes, nor witch hath power to charm,
So hallowed and so gracious is the time.

WILLIAM SHAKESPEARE (1564–1616).

As I in hoary winter's night stood shivering in the snow,
Surpris'd I was with sudden heat which made my heart to
  glow;
And lifting up a fearful eye to view what fire was near,
A pretty Babe all burning bright did in the air appear;
Who, scorchèd with excessive heat, such floods of tears
  did shed,
As tho' his floods should quench his flames which with his
  tears were fed.
'Alas!' quoth he, 'but newly born in fiery heats I fry,
Yet none approach to warm their hearts or feel my fire but I.
My faultless breast the furnace is, the fuel wounding thorns;
Love is the fire, and sighs the smoke, the ashes shame and
  scorns;
The fuel justice layeth on, and mercy blows the coals;
The metal in this furnace wrought are men's defilèd souls:
For which, as now on fire I am to work them to their good,
So will I melt into a bath to wash them in my blood.'
With this he vanish'd out of sight and swiftly shrunk away,
And straight I callèd unto mind that it was Christmas day.

ROBERT SOUTHWELL (c. 1561–95).

Minstrels

The minstrels played their Christmas tune
  To-night beneath my cottage-eaves;
While, smitten by a lofty moon,
  The encircling laurels, thick with leaves,
Gave back a rich and dazzling sheen,
That overpowered their natural green.

Through hill and valley every breeze
  Had sunk to rest with folded wings:
Keen was the air, but could not freeze,
  Nor check, the music of the strings;
So stout and hardy were the band
That scraped the chords with strenuous hand.

And who but listened?—till was paid
  Respect to every inmate's claim,
The greeting given, the music played
  In honour of each household name,
Duly pronounced with lusty call,
And 'merry Christmas' wished to all.

WILLIAM WORDSWORTH (1770–1850).

The Lamb

  Little lamb, who made thee?
  Dost thou know who made thee,
Gave thee life, and bid thee feed
By the stream and o'er the mead;
Gave thee clothing of delight,
Softest clothing, woolly, bright,
Gave thee such a tender voice,
Making all the vales rejoice?
  Little lamb, who made thee?
  Dost thou know who made thee?

Little lamb, I'll tell thee;
Little lamb, I'll tell thee:
He is callèd by thy name,
For He calls Himself a Lamb.
He is meek, and He is mild,
He became a little child.
I a child, and thou a lamb,
We are callèd by His name.
   Little lamb, God bless thee?
   Little lamb, God bless thee!

WILLIAM BLAKE (1757–1827).

Holy Thorn

At the dead turning of the year
This hawthorn tree stands winter-bare,
And dazed with storm, and numb with rime,
Forgets the processes of time.

What is it to this rocky grief,
That the tides broke in bud and leaf
On the old shores of vanished May?

What is it to this chill dismay
That the unsighted May shall be
Warm and translucent as the sea,
With naiad flowers drifting upon
Its green, sun-calmèd ocean?

These things, like fairy-stories, are
Legendary, faint and far;
They have no meaning for a tree
So islanded in misery.

But there are set, even for this,
To-night, the rescuing sails of peace. . . .

For now snow softly falls, and weaves
A silver dream of summer eves,
And the tree stretches twig and bough,
Thinking the glimmering weight of snow
Honey-hearted as blossom was
That once leaned over the tall, May grass.
The sap remembers how, between
Night and morning, a wind serene
Brushed the ghost petals, and set moving
Love, and the fragrances of loving:
And the tree muses how night's blue
Trembled to green, and how strange dew,
Repeating heaven star for star,
Made the field unfamiliar.

And now, like that lost nightingale
Who sang till the moon burned cold and pale
On the grave pyre of dawn, the air
Is tuned to an invisible, rare
Music; and luminous-feathered song
Dives and wheels and flits among
The listening branches, till the tree,
Lit with antiphonal ecstasy,
Jets from the sealed and silent ground
In crystal fountains, whose clear sound
Sings upward to the singing sky
A rapt and fiery symphony.
And while the tree resolves all pain
In the pure silver of that strain,

Behold, in darkness suddenly
Another and a holier tree
Invests with candid, radiant light
The long, dus' haunted groves of night;
Those blossoms gleam more milky fair
Than Eve's blanched flowers in Eden were;
Those boughs spread out like arms to take
A world to shelter, for love's sake,
And at its heart those green leaves fold
A child, whose head is ringed with gold.
Is he a king? his courtiers then
Are falcons and throstle, dove and wren;
A general? his armies are
Butterflies winging the wide air;
A god? his only priestess is
Maid Mary kneeling in the grass. . . .
Now through her tears the petals fall
Red and white and beautiful,
Until she prays in snow, and stark
A thorn crowned tree upbraids the dark
A moment, and the vision
Melts in the morning, and is gone.
The bells ring out for Christmas day
With 'Gloria' and 'Gloria,'
And on the eastern horizon
Flowers a rose enfolding sun,
Fulfilling life.

            The hawthorn tree,
Waking from what epiphany,
Ponders what winters, what high spring
Met in that heavenly blossoming.

                    VIOLA GERARD GARVIN.

The Ghost's Song

'Tis late and cold, stir up the fire;
Sit close and draw the table nigher;
Be merry and drink wine that's old,
A hearty medicine 'gainst a cold.
Your beds of wanton down the best,
Where you shall tumble to your rest.
Call for the best the house may ring,
Sack, white, and claret let them bring,
And drink apace, whilst breath you have,
You'll find but cold drink in the grave;
Plover, partridge for your dinner,
And a capon for the sinner,
You shall find ready when you're up,
And your horse shall have his sup.
Welcome, welcome shall fly round,
And I shall smile, though underground.

ANONYMOUS (*seventeenth century*).

Quho is at my Windou

Quho is at my windou, quho?
Go fro my windou, go.
Quho callis thair, sa lyk a strangeir?
Go fro my windou, go.

(Lord, I am here, a wretchit mortal
That for thy mercy does cry and call
Unto thee my lord celestial.)
See quho is at my windou, quho?

Remember thy sin and als thy smart,
And als for thee what was my part:
Remember the speir that thirlit my hart,
And in at my dure thou sall go.

I ask na thing of thee thairfor
But love for love to lay in store.
Gif me thy hart, I ask na more,
And in at my dure thou sall go.

Quho is at my windou, quho?
Go fro my windou, go.
Cry na mair thair, lyk a strangeir,
But in at my dure thou go.

ANONYMOUS.

Then sings the Owl

When icicles hang by the wall,
    And Dick the shepherd blows his nail,
And Tom bears logs into the hall,
    And milk comes frozen home in pail,
When blood is nipp'd, and ways be foul,
Then nightly sings the staring owl,
        To⌣whit!
To⌣who!—a merry note,
While greasy Joan doth keel the pot.

When all aloud the wind doth blow,
    And coughing drowns the parson's saw,
And birds sit brooding in the snow,
    And Marian's nose looks red and raw,

When roasted crabs hiss in the bowl,
Then nightly sings the staring owl,
    To-whit!
To-who!—a merry note,
While greasy Joan doth keel the pot.

        WILLIAM SHAKESPEARE (1564–1616).

A Carol for the Children

God rest you merry, Innocents,
  Let nothing you dismay,
Let nothing wound an eager heart
  Upon this Christmas day.

Yours be the genial holly wreaths,
  The stockings and the tree;
An aged world to you bequeaths
  Its own forgotten glee.

Soon, soon enough come crueller gifts,
  The anger and the tears;
Between you now there sparsely drifts
  A handful yet of years.

Oh, dimly, dimly glows the star
  Through the electric throng;
The bidding in temple and bazaar
  Drowns out the silver song.

The ancient altars smoke afresh,
  The ancient idols stir;
Faint in the reek of burning flesh
  Sink frankincense and myrrh.

Gaspar, Balthazar, Melchior!
  Where are your offerings now?
What greetings to the Prince of War,
  His darkly branded brow?

Two ultimate laws alone we know,
  The ledger and the sword—
So far away, so long ago,
  We lost the infant Lord.

Only the children clasp His hand;
  His voice speaks low to them,
And still for them the shining band
  Wings over Bethlehem.

God rest you merry, Innocents,
  While innocence endures.
A sweeter Christmas than we to ours
  May you bequeath to yours.

                          OGDEN NASH.

Christmas 1938

  Peace on earth?
  The tinsell'd Tree
  Shines again on infancy.
  Now, unshutter'd windows glow
  Through the softly falling snow.
  But goodwill?
  No.

  Remember,
  The celebration of this Birth
  Might have mocked a ravaged earth.
  No merry bells, no reindeer sledge,

But a screaming, tearing wedge
Of pain and death.
No sleeping child—a choking breath
And blood upon the snow.

God rest ye merry, gentlemen,
Let nothing you dismay.
But watch, and pray.

ANNA MCMULLEN.

THE NEW YEAR

While the bald trees stretch forth their long lank arms,
And starving birds peck nigh the reeky farms:
While houseless cattle paw the yellow field,
Or coughing shiver in the pervious bield,
And nought more gladsome in the hedge is seen,
Than the dark holly's grimly glistening green—
At such a time, the ancient year goes by
To join its parents in eternity—
At such a time the merry year is born,
Like the bright berry from the naked thorn.

HARTLEY COLERIDGE (1796–1849).

The Death of the Old Year

Full knee-deep lies the winter snow,
    And the winter winds are wearily sighing:
Toll ye the church-bell sad and slow,
    And tread softly, and speak low,
    For the old year lies a-dying.
        Old year, you must not die;
        You came to us so readily,
        You lived with us so steadily,
        Old year, you shall not die.

He lieth still: he doth not move:
    He will not see the dawn of day.
He hath no other life above.
He gave me a friend, and a true, true love,
    And the new year will take 'em away.

Old year, you must not go;
So long as you have been with us,
Such joy as you have seen with us,
Old year, you shall not go.

He frothed his bumpers to the brim;
  A jollier year we shall not see.
But though his eyes are waxing dim,
And though his foes speak ill of him,
  He was a friend to me,
    Old year, you shall not die;
    We did so laugh and cry with you,
    I 've half a mind to die with you,
    Old year, if you must die.

He was full of joke and jest,
  But all his merry quips are o'er.
To see him die, across the waste
His son and heir doth ride post-haste,
  But he 'll be dead before.
    Every one for his own.
    The night is starry and cold, my friend,
    And the new year blithe and bold, my friend,
    Comes up to take his own.

How hard he breathes! over the snow
  I heard just now the crowing cock.
The shadows flicker to and fro:
The cricket chirps: the light burns low:
  'Tis nearly twelve o'clock.
    Shake hands, before you die.
    Old year, we 'll dearly rue for you:
    What is it we can do for you?
    Speak out before you die.

His face is growing sharp and thin.
  Alack! our friend is gone.
Close up his eyes: tie up his chin:
Step from the corpse, and let him in
  That standeth there alone,
    And waiteth at the door.
      There's a new foot on the floor, my friend,
      And a new face at the door, my friend,
      A new face at the door.

ALFRED, LORD TENNYSON (1809-92).

Tract for the Times

Ring out, wild bells, to the wild sky,
  The flying cloud, the frosty light:
  The year is dying in the night;
Ring out, wild bells, and let him die.

Ring out the old, ring in the new,
  Ring, happy bells, across the snow:
  The year is going, let him go;
Ring out the false, ring in the true.

Ring out the grief that saps the mind,
  For those that here we see no more;
  Ring out the feud of rich and poor,
Ring in redress to all mankind.

Ring out a slowly dying cause,
  And ancient forms of party strife;
  Ring in the nobler modes of life,
With sweeter manners, purer laws.

Ring out the want, the care, the sin,
  The faithless coldness of the times;
  Ring out, ring out my mournful rhymes,
But ring the fuller minstrel in.

Ring out false pride in place and blood,
  The civic slander and the spite;
  Ring in the love of truth and right,
Ring in the common love of good.

Ring out old shapes of foul disease,
  Ring out the narrowing lust of gold;
  Ring out the thousand wars of old,
Ring in the thousand years of peace.

Ring in the valiant man and free,
  The larger heart, the kindlier hand;
  Ring out the darkness of the land,
Ring in the Christ that is to be.

                    ALFRED, LORD TENNYSON.

The Cock crows

Hark! the cock crows, and yon bright star
Tells us the day himself 's not far;
And see where, breaking from the night,
He gilds the western hills with light.
With him old Janus doth appear,
Peeping into the future year,
With such a look as seems to say,
The prospect is not good that way.
Thus do we rise ill sights to see,
And 'gainst ourselves to prophesy;
When the prophetic fear of things

A more tormenting mischief brings,
More dull of soul-tormenting gall,
Than direct mischiefs can befall.
But stay! but stay! methinks my sight,
Better inform'd by clearer light,
Discerns sereneness in that brow,
That all contracted seem'd but now.
His revers'd face may show distaste,
And frown upon the ills are past;
But that which this way looks is clear,
And smiles upon the new-born year.
He looks too from a place so high,
The year lies open to his eye;
And all the moments open are
To the exact discoverer.
Yet more and more he smiles upon
The happy revolution.
Why should we then suspect or fear
The influences of a year,
So smiles upon us the first morn,
And speaks us good so soon as born?
Plague on 't! the last was ill enough,
This cannot but make better proof;
Or, at the worst, as we brush'd through
The last, why so we may this too:
And then the next in reason should
Be superexcellently good:
For the worst ills (we daily see)
Have no more perpetuity,
Than the best fortunes that do fall;
Which also bring us wherewithal
Longer their being to support,
Than those do of the other sort:
And who has one good year in three,

And yet repines at destiny,
Appears ungrateful in the case,
And merits not the good he has.
Then let us welcome the new guest
With lusty brimmers of the best;
Mirth always should good fortune meet,
And render e'en disaster sweet:
And though the princess turn her back,
Let us but line ourselves with sack,
We better shall by far hold out,
Till the next year she face about.

CHARLES COTTON (1630–87).

A New Year's Gift

SENT TO SIR SIMEON STEWARD

No news of navies burnt at seas;
No news of late-spawned Tittyries;
No closet-plot, or open vent,
That frights men with a Parliament;
No new device or late-found trick,
To read by th' stars the kingdom's sick;
No gin to catch the state, or wring
The free-born nostrils of the king,
We send to you;—but here a jolly
Verse, crowned with ivy and with holly,
That tells of winter's tales and mirth,
That milk-maids make about the hearth;
Of Christmas sports, the wassail bowl,
That's tossed up after Fox-i'-th'-Hole;
Of Blind-man's-buff, and of the care
That young men have to shoe the mare;
Of twelfth-tide cakes, of peas and beans,
Wherewith ye make those merry scenes,

Whenas ye choose your king and queen,
And cry out, 'Hey for our town green';
Of ash-heaps, in the which ye use
Husbands and wives by streaks to choose;
Of crackling laurel, which fore-sounds
A plenteous harvest to your grounds;—
Of these, and such like things, for shift,
We send, instead of new year's gift.
Read, then, and when your faces shine
With bucksome meat and cap'ring wine,
Remember us in cups full crowned,
And let our city health go round,
Quite through the young maids and the men,
To the ninth number, if not ten,
Until the firèd chestnuts leap
For joy to see the fruits ye reap,
From the plump chalice and the cup
That tempts till it be tossèd up.
Then as ye sit about your embers,
Call not to mind those fled Decembers;
But think on these, that are t' appear,
As daughters to the instant year;
Sit crowned with rose-buds, and carouse,
Till *Liber Pater* twirls the house
About your ears, and lay upon
The year, your cares, that's fled and gone.
And let the russet swains the plough
And harrow hang up, resting now;
And to the bagpipe all address,
Till sleep takes place of weariness.
And thus, throughout, with Christmas plays,
Frolic the full twelve holydays.

ROBERT HERRICK (1591–1674).

NOW FARE YE WELL

Orphan hours, the year is dead;
  Come and sigh, come and weep;
Merry hours, smile instead,
  For the year is but asleep:
See, it smiles as it is sleeping,
Mocking your untimely weeping.

As an earthquake rocks a corse
  In its coffin in the clay,
So white winter, that rough nurse,
  Rocks the dead-cold year to-day.
Solemn hours! wail aloud
For your mother in her shroud.

As the wild air stirs and sways
  The tree-swung cradle of a child,
So the breath of these rude days
  Rocks the year:—be calm and mild,
Trembling hours; she will arise
With new love within her eyes.

January grey is here,
  Like a sexton by her grave;
February bears the bier,
  March with grief doth howl and rave;
And April weeps—but, O ye hours!
Follow with May's fairest flowers.

PERCY BYSSHE SHELLEY (1792–1822).

Twelfth Night, or King and Queen

Now, now the mirth comes,
With the cake full of plums,
Where bean's the king of the sport here;
Beside we must know,
The pea also
Must revel as queen in the court here.

Begin then to choose,
This night as you use,
Who shall for the present delight here;
Be a king by the lot,
And who shall not
Be twelfth-day queen for the night here.

Which known, let us make
Joy-sops with the cake;
And let not a man then be seen here,
Who unurged will not drink,
To the base from the brink,
A health to the king and the queen here.

Next crown the bowl full
With gentle lamb's-wool;
Add sugar, nutmeg, and ginger,
With store of ale too;
And thus ye must do
To make the wassail a swinger.

Give then to the king
And queen wassailing;
And though with ale ye be whet here,

Yet part ye from hence,
As free from offence,
As when ye innocent met here.

ROBERT HERRICK (1591–1674).

Spring Cleaning

Down with the rosemary and bays,
  Down with the mistletoe;
Instead of holly, now up⁄raise
  The greener box, for show.

The holly hitherto did sway;
  Let box now dominere,
Until the dancing Easter⁄day,
  On Easter's Eve appear.

ROBERT HERRICK.

St Distaff's Day

Partly work and partly play
Ye must on St Distaff's Day;
From the plough soon free your team,
Then come home and fother them.
If the maids a spinning go,
Burn the flax, and fire the tow;
Bring in pails of water then,
Let the maids bewash the men;
Give St Distaff all the right,
Then bid Christmas sport good night;
And next morrow, every one
To his own vocation.

ROBERT HERRICK.

Now have Good Day

Now have good day, now have good day.
I am Christmas, and now I go my way.

Here have I dwelt with more or less,
From Hallow/tide till Candlemas,
And now must I from you hence pass,
   Now have good day.

I take my leave of King and Knight,
And Earl, Baron, and lady bright,
To wilderness I must me dight,
   Now have good day.

And at the good lord of this hall,
I take my leave, and of guestes all,
Methinks I hear Lent doth call,
   Now have good day.

And at every worthy officer,
Marshal, panter, and butler,
I take my leave as for this year,
   Now have good day.

Another year I trust I shall
Make merry in this hall,
If rest and peace in England may fall,
   Now have good day.

But oftentimes I have heard say,
That he is loth to part away,
That often biddeth 'have good day,'
   Now have good day.

ANONYMOUS (c. 1540).

DOES CHRISTMAS MEAN ANYTHING?

BY C. C. MARTINDALE, S.J.

WE are asked to write a page or two on the 'essential' 'meaning' of 'Christmas' to 'our age.' By 'Christmas Day' we mean December the twenty-fifth. Do we mean more than that? Does Christmas Day mean more than Boxing Day? We cannot pretend that Candlemas, Lammas, or Michaelmas 'mean' anything special to most of our contemporaries; nor does Lady Day; nor, to many, does Good Friday. We re-member a young bank-clerk, a friend of ours, whom his mate asked what he meant to do next Friday, which was 'Good' Friday. He said: 'Church a.m.; golf, p.m.' 'Church?' said the other, flustered. 'Well,' said his friend, 'Catholics do go to church on Good Friday.' 'Do they?' he asked. 'Why?' He was a pleasant and honest lad; but Good Friday 'meant' to him no more than an extra holiday which happened on a Friday.

Had our friend used the word 'Christian' instead of 'Catho-lic' he might have got further out of the realm of the 'queer' into that of the vaguely familiar: but anyhow, he attached no 'meaning' to Good Friday, certainly not any 'essential' meaning; it *meant* to him a day on which he had a holiday—he didn't inquire 'why' (very characteristic, I'm afraid: 'Rates are so and so. Who settles them? Don't know. Why "so much"? Why on this or that? God knows . . .!' Mr Hasluck wrote a whole book on that). . . .

Well, we are asked what 'Christmas Day' 'essentially' 'means' to 'our age.' Evidently not, therefore, what it meant to our grandparents, or to Dickens. Whatever it then meant, it implied snow, ice, holly, frosted Christmas cards (which in their turn implied frightful illness, if not mortality, among those who made them—because they swallowed the powdered glass and died of it, rather as workers in the Johannesburg gold-mines swallow white dust and get silicosis; and as match-makers—we don't mean matrimonialists—swallowed phos-phorus with horrible results: all this was an 'essential' though disregarded element in that period, and we only hope it is less so now). Now, when we long for summer to be over so that we may have the chance at least of some fine weather, we are ready to discard the sparkling *mise-en-scène* of the traditional Christmas.

But a *mise-en-scène* is certainly not essential; it is 'acci-dental'—and it is even that because *we* think that midwinter ought to be cold and so on, and not because we have any reason to suppose that the first Christmas was cold or even that it occurred in the winter. In any case, Palestinian winters are wet rather than cold; and in the exquisite idyll of the shepherds who 'kept their watch by night' we have, on the whole, the right to observe this first: it is known that the night-watchmen of flocks were usually extremely rough men, hired from over-Jordan; so the first worshippers of Christ *were* very rough men, and not even moderately highbrow men, which (to the present writer) provides a certain satisfaction.

However, in our grandparents' days, Christmas was cer-tainly felt as 'essentially' a family and indeed a children's feast. Stockings: Father Christmas: presents: surprises. This latter aspect of Christmas, essential or not, has not vanished. We are very glad that certain non-ecclesiastical organizations (like this or that newspaper, let alone the hospitals) make a point of collecting toys for children. We wish this enterprise all possible success. We would like children, especially very poor ones, to be made happy at

Christmas—though we would also like them to know why Christmas is chosen for this effort rather than, say, August Bank Holiday or Derby Day.

But Christmas used not to be treated as a day for children separately. The entire family was involved, and so were the servants (if you had any), and so were friends who mightn't be going to have too good a Christmas because they would otherwise have been lonely—such as young men, studying in London away from their homes. In a word, Christmas was a 'home-feast.' And this was certainly due to sympathy with Mary and Joseph, who, so long ago, found 'no room' in the Bethlehem inn. The notion of dining in a restaurant on that day would have been regarded as not only absurd, but irreverent, and also as spoiling the whole 'flavour' of the day. This did not mean that the servants were overworked. The 'family' not only arranged that servants should have plenty of time for their own festivities, but went to share in them so far as the servants might be supposed to like them to. Ser-vants have, as they used to say, their 'feelings' and their privacy and their social preferences; and these were respected. It remained that the feast was a 'household' feast, in which every one concerned took a common part, and also a personal part. We do not feel convinced that Christmas is so regarded nowadays: we shall say why we regret it, if it is not.

Finally, Christmas was certainly treated as, to some extent, a religious celebration, and as the only one which combined in the same way what was religious with what was 'merry' and—frankly—gastronomic. Easter eggs were not an equiva-lent for plum-pudding; and again, no hymns took the same place as *Hark, the Herald Angels* and *While Shepherds watch'd*.

Abroad, all religious feasts were, and are, regarded more as 'all round' festivals. This may seem to deprive Christmas of its unique quality; but then the Crib, with the Holy Child, the ox and the ass, Mary and Joseph, and the straw, restore to it an unshared fascination. The Crib remains in the church till, as a rule, February the second; but meanwhile, on January the sixth, the Wise Men and their Star have replaced the Shepherds, so that just enough variety is introduced. In certain districts, like Provence, children and whole families bring presents, like cheeses, to the Child Jesus. These are distributed to the neediest, and, as it were, from His hands. Christmas-tide, almost more than Christmas Day, is cele brated, and the impression is not only charming but enduring and unselfish in its effects.

Here, then, is one element of lasting value. Christmas Day is associated with a *person*; not merely with a ceremony, like Ash Wednesday; nor with an obligation, financial or other, like quarter-days. Moreover, the story of this Birth has an incomparable charm, unlike the story of, for example, the victory at Trafalgar which, while impressive, is none the less grim.[1] In consequence Christmas can inspire children them selves with generous inclusive kindness, in terms of affection and not of a bleak theory. Not only was Christ born in extreme poverty, but His first friends were the very poor. It is true that He did not forthwith provide His parents nor the shepherds with a suitable capital or even with a dole; but the radiant atmosphere of St Luke's narrative certainly suggests happiness, which does not seem to be the result of contemporary theories or methods.

Again, the angelic hymn contained the words: 'Peace to men of good will.' That Aramaic turn of phrase means, practically, 'goodwill-men,' and its bearing is universal, whether you consider it to mean 'men whose will is good'

[1] Perhaps we ought to add that we regard the Childhood stories in the gospels as by no mean mythical but quite good history. We do this on critical grounds, and not *a priori*, or because we are bound to. The date, 25th December, is a quite separate topic, and in no way connected with the scriptural narrative.

or 'men who are the object of God's good will.' The ancient story is still so powerful as to generate at least the affectation of 'good will all round.' Indeed, the sending (and even the receiving!) of Christmas cards has become almost an exasperation: 'I suppose I ought—I've got—to send a card to X!' And indeed, for my part, such cards are meaningless unless they suggest *why* men, at Christmas, ought all of them to be friends. The reason is nothing less than that God is the good Father of all of them—has 'good will' towards all of them. In the last war, most men were somehow 'shocked' if they had to fight on Christmas Day. Vague dreams mounted from long ago into their confused and tortured minds; they never wanted to cause pain to one another; and on Christmas Day to do so seemed especially anomalous. 'Fraternization' had to be stopped by order.

Of course, everything of Christian origin ultimately comes back to the question: 'What think ye of Christ?' If the answer be in terms of divine authority, then the object-lessons of Christmas have their unique sanction: 'Riches are *not* to be your main objective; the least-befriended ought to be your primary friends; yet *no* one should be excluded from your friendship; and this should not be only a beautiful ideal, but should incarnate and reveal itself in your personal life and action— tending towards complete self-sacrifice. And this, because anything else is out of keeping with the will and love of God.'

Even if a man cannot regard Jesus Christ as the Son of God made Man for our sakes, yet if he allows 'Christmas' to exercise its intrinsic spell upon him, he will find that it at least can generate a Christian 'mood' in him. If he touches but the fringe of Christ's garment he will find that 'virtue—influence— goes out from Him,' that he is being healed, and in his turn becomes a healer, and a health-giving influence not only within his personal life (many parts of which are as a rule somewhat suffering—often, so habitually that he has ceased to notice it), but within his home, within his environment and country, and between the peoples of the world.

We pray then that many may continue to 'go over unto Bethlehem'; to bring gifts to the Divine Child and receive yet greater ones from Himself: to join with Mary, who 'kept all these things, pondering them—seeing deeper into them— 'putting them together,' and interconnecting them and observing their implications—in her heart; and not fear to share in the enormous responsibility of St Joseph, who had to safeguard, and to transmit, the greatest treasure in the world.

Presumably what I hold to be the 'essential meaning' of Christmas—that God united to His Divine Nature this our human nature, and was born of Mary at Bethlehem for our sakes—has its value for every age. But it certainly has not less for to-day, when, on the one hand, too many men are as egoistic as ever, and on the other, the individual and his worth are being, so often, quite suppressed; when horrible social injustices are still perpetrated at the expense of the poor and weak, and, again, the 'poor' are so often urged towards hate and violence; when race is pitted against race. 'But you are all one thing—one person—in Christ Jesus!'

———

They all were looking for a king
    To slay their foes and lift them high:
Thou cam'st, a little baby thing
    That made a woman cry.

GEORGE MACDONALD (1824–1905).

FACTS ABOUT CHRISTMAS

BY J. B. MORTON ('BEACHCOMBER')

I THINK it was Professor Gibus who proved to his own satisfaction, if to nobody else's, that Christmas, like every other good
thing, has an English origin. The professor's argument, if
I remember rightly, was that the feast which we keep on Christmas Day got its name from Christmas Island, which is one of
the Straits Settlements, in the Eastern Indian Ocean, south of
Java. For its Saxon origin he adduced the presence of the
letters HRIS, which, of course, is the Anglo-Saxon word for
feasting. The word appears as Hros in the old Chronicle of
Stigulf of Northumbria, as Hras in the Song of Beofrith, as
Hrus in the Charter of the City of Verulam, and as Hres in
the Book of the Forty-Two Werewolves of Mercia. But, as
Gibus pointed out, the interchanging of vowel-sounds was
common up to the middle of the reign of Æthelfrith the Bald.[1]

It was left to the Ancient Society of Twentieth Century
Astrologers [2] to build on the foundations laid by Gibus.
The astrologers showed that the distance from the central
point of Christmas Island to the 'Old Cheshire Cheese' in
Little Essex Street was rather less than seventeen times more
than the distance from Rome to Avignon. They took this
as being a conclusive proof that Christmas was originally an
English custom, handed down from the ancient Druids. The
very name Stonehenge, they said, showed this, coming as it
did from the root-word Stonehenge.

In 1896 (I think) Namskill [3] of St John's College, Cambridge, discovered in a book called *Bewifmannes Beweddunge*

---

[1] q.v. [2] Founded by Plodder. [3] Toby Namskill, of course.

Bewolf, by the Abbess Hthicea, a tacit reference to something called Hnoel. This was obviously a corruption of the later French *Noël*, and referred to the feast which had begun so long ago on Christmas Island.

Here the reader is referred, for a fuller discussion, to the work of Smeldt, Stench, and Sir Alexander Filthie; as also to the famous *Untersuchungen Angelsachsischen Germanischen Gesetzgebung*, which is the earliest attempt to collate the various texts of the Liebermann glossaries. The whole thing is a monument of beastliness.

It was Poole (of Poole Harbour) who first drew the attention of scholars and others to the word HTRE in many of the oldest Saxon dialects. This, he said, could only refer to the Htre or Tree of Christmas.[1] King (of King's Cross) held a different view. He said that the word Htre meant the small swivel-pipe on the end of a revolving paget-valve, and not, as had been suggested, a tree. Then Ponder (of Ponder's End) rushed in with his sensational thesis. Ponder contended that the paget-valve does not make its appearance until well on in the nineteenth century, and that, therefore, King must be wrong. The battle raged for many years, until Dr Anthony van Gystich of Antwerp [2] settled the matter by pointing out that Htre was a corruption of Hootre, meaning a sidelong glance at a crowded Witanagemot.

The crackers which we pull at Christmas are, of course, the KRAKAS of the natives of Christmas Island. It was customary when the sun appeared above the horizon on 25th December to salute the dawn in this way. One of these old krakas can be seen to-day in the South Croydon Museum of Extraordinary Antiquities. Our word crack, of course, comes from the same root, the ER being merely what philologists call a terminal ending, or final conclusion. We see the same principle at work in such words as water, character, daughter,

[1] Now, now!   [2] Such a nice man.

helicopter, and so on. In later words, like sugar, the penulti-
mate vowel undergoes a change and emerges different (*see*
Mabel Chadwick's *The Origin of Word-Roots*).[1]

The earliest crackers were evidently larger than ours. They
were made of the leaves of trees, and contained small figures
in unfossiliferous basalt or cretaceous sandstone—not always
triassic, however. We know all this from the admirable
reconstruction made by Mrs Denton,[2] while she was at Wool-
wich, the darling.

Pudding, obviously, is a word of pure Saxon root. The old
verb was Pud, which meant to roll anything about so as to get
it into shape. The noun, a Puding, meant a thing rolled into
shape. The old Portuguese explorer, da Voda, tells how, in
the fifteenth century, he found the Christmas Islanders making
puddings in this primitive fashion, and he discovered in some
caves very ancient (possibly pre-Plasticene) drawings of puddings. Some of them had what was evidently meant to be
a sprig of holly stuck into them. Holly, is, of course the old
word holly. The natives used to put rings and armlets into
their puddings to appease evil spirits, just as we, to-day, put
in money to appease our guests. This money the Anglo-
Saxons called Pudingeld or pudding-gold. They regarded
it as a tribute paid to the malignant deities, as Dr Fluffer has
shown. Hotair, a monk of Thuringia, wrote a long treatise
on the subject in the seventh century.

When we come to the word mistletoe, we are confronted
with a problem which has remained unsolved even to this day.
Jungsturm says that it is the old Saxon word Gasprachtulf;
a far-fetched explanation. Singermann traces the word to
viscivorus, the adjective applied by Tertullian to the missel-
thrush. He says that the V became M after the Wars of the
Roses, and the rest of the word changed when Alva invaded

---

[1] A sickening book.
[2] The 'Babs' referred to in Adam Smith's *Wealth of Nations*.

the Netherlands. Grant (of Grant, Dewsbury & Co.) holds
that it should be spelt misseltoe, because the leaves, according
to Linnaeus, are obovate and, when young, the size of the toe
of a missel-thrush. Holbourne (of Holbourne Viaduct) and
Cannon (of Cannon Street) both distinguish between the
Californian and the Chinese mistletoe.[1] But no authority
is rash enough [2] to deny that the plant has grown on Christmas
Island since the beginning of recorded history. Incidentally,
the word thrush is simply the old Anglo-Saxon word Throsh,
meaning to maltreat by thrusting into the slush. The man so
used would naturally cry out like a startled bird. And so
the term came to be applied to the bird which we know as the
thrush. The earlier root survives in our word throstle, which
originally meant to thrust and hostle someone. The reader is
referred to Tottie Smithson's *Romance of Words; with a foreword
by Colonel Sir Edgar Walham-Green, T.U.C.*

Professor Mornington (of Mornington Crescent) has, I think,
expressed what most of us feel about things, in words that have
been too often quoted for me not to quote them again: 'Though
so little is known about anything, that should not deter the
scholar and the scientist from writing and talking until everybody is blue in the face. Where should we be without guesswork? If we did not pretend to omniscience, who on earth
would ever pay the slightest attention to us? To teach hypothesis as accepted fact, that is our task; to suggest that what
we have invented is a commonplace of scholarship; to disguise,
beneath a layer of jargon, our lack of evidence; to cloak,
beneath a blanket of words, our ignorance of the principles of
thought; to substitute for logic, rhetoric; for argument, statistics;
for lucidity, dogmatic reiteration; to blind the reader with foot-
notes and humbugging allusions; to stun him with bogus
"authorities."'

A blessing upon you, one and all.

[1] Why not?   [2] Why?

CHRONICLES OF CHRISTMAS

AND it came to pass in those days, that there went out a decree from Caesar Augustus, that all the world should be taxed. . . . And all went to be taxed, every one into his own city.

And Joseph also went up from Galilee, out of the city of Nazareth, into Judaea, unto the city of David which is called Bethlehem, (because he was of the house and lineage of David,) to be taxed with Mary his espoused wife, being great with child. And so it was that, while they were there, the days were accomplished that she should be delivered. And she brought forth her firstborn son; and wrapped him in swaddling clothes, and laid him in a manger; because there was no room for them in the inn.

And there were in the same country shepherds abiding in the field, keeping watch over their flock by night. And, lo, the angel of the Lord came upon them, and the glory of the Lord shone round about them: and they were sore afraid.

And the angel said unto them, Fear not; for, behold, I bring you good tidings of great joy, which shall be to all people. For unto you is born this day in the city of David a Saviour, which is Christ the Lord. And this shall be a sign unto you; ye shall find the babe wrapped in swaddling clothes, lying in a manger.

And suddenly there was with the angel a multitude of the heavenly host praising God, and saying, Glory to God in the highest, and on earth peace, goodwill toward men.

And it came to pass, as the angels were gone away from them into heaven, the shepherds said one to another, Let us now go even unto Bethlehem, and see this thing which is come to pass, which the Lord hath made known unto us.

And they came with haste, and found Mary, and Joseph, and the babe lying in a manger. And when they had seen it, they made known abroad the saying which was told them concerning this child. And all they that heard it wondered at those things which were told them by the shepherds. But Mary kept all these things, and pondered them in her heart. And the shepherds returned, glorifying and praising God for all the things that they had heard and seen, as it was told unto them.

The Gospel according to ST LUKE.

The Wise Men

Now when Jesus was born in Bethlehem of Judaea in the days of Herod the king, behold, there came wise men from the east to Jerusalem, saying, Where is he that is born King of the Jews? for we have seen his star in the east, and are come to worship him.

When Herod the king had heard these things, he was troubled, and all Jerusalem with him. And when he had gathered all the chief priests and scribes of the people together, he demanded of them where Christ should be born.

And they said unto him, In Bethlehem of Judaea: for thus it is written by the prophet:

'And thou Bethlehem, in the land of Juda,
Art not the least among the princes of Juda:
For out of thee shall come a Governor,
That shall rule my people Israel.'

Then Herod, when he had privily called the wise men, inquired of them diligently what time the star appeared. And he sent them to Bethlehem, and said, Go and search diligently for the young child; and when ye have found him, bring me word again, that I may come and worship him also.

When they had heard the king, they departed; and, lo, the star, which they saw in the east, went before them, till it came and stood over where the young child was. When they saw the star, they rejoiced with exceeding great joy. And when they were come into the house, they saw the young child with Mary his mother, and fell down, and worshipped him: and when they had opened their treasures, they presented unto him gifts; gold, and frankincense, and myrrh. And being warned of God in a dream that they should not return to Herod, they departed into their own country another way.

The Gospel according to ST MATTHEW.

The Three Poor Shepherds

According to the carol, *The First Nowell*, and many legends, the Angel spake to 'three poor shepherds.' Other sources, however, give the number as four. Their names, Misael, Achael, Cyriacus, and Stephanus, were, together with the names of the three Kings, used as a charm in the Middle Ages to cure the bites of snakes and other venomous reptiles. In the seventh of the Chester Mysteries the shepherds, three in number, have the more homely names of Harvey, Tudd, and Trowle. By birth and habits they are yokels of Cheshire or Lancashire. Trowle's gift to Jesus is 'a pair of his wife's old hose.'

The Three Kings of Cologne

A common conceit there is of the three Kings of Collein, conceived to be the wise men that travelled unto our Saviour by the direction of the Star, Wherein (omitting the large Discourses of Baronius, Pineda, and Montacutius,) that they might be Kings, beside the Ancient Tradition and Authority of many Fathers, the Scripture also implieth: The Gentiles shall come to thy light, and Kings to the brightness of thy rising. The Kings of Tharsis and the Isles, the Kings of Arabia and Saba shall offer gifts; which places most Christians and many Rabbins interpret of the Messiah. Not that they are to be conceived potent Monarchs, or mighty Kings; but Toparks, Kings of Cities or narrow Territories; such as were the Kings of Sodom and Gomorrah, the Kings of Jericho and Ai, the one and thirty which Joshuah subdued, and such as some conceive the Friends of Job to have been.

But although we grant they were Kings, yet can we not be assured they were three. For the Scripture maketh no mention of any number; and the number of their presents, Gold, Myrrhe, and Frankincense, concludeth not the number of their persons; for these were the commodities of their Country, and such as probably the Queen of Sheba in one person had brought before unto Solomon. So did not the sons of Jacob divide the present unto Joseph, but are conceived to carry one for them all, according to the expression of their Father: Take of the best fruits of the land in your vessels, and carry down the man a present. And therefore their number being uncertain, what credit is to be given unto their names, Gasper, Melchior, Balthazar, what to the charm thereof against the falling sickness, or what unto their habits, complexions, and corporal accidents, we must rely on their uncertain story, and received pourtraits of Collein.

Lastly, Although we grant them Kings, and three in number, yet could we not conceive that they were Kings of Collein. For though Collein were the chief City of the Ubii, then called Ubiopolis, and afterwards Agrippina, yet will no History inform us there were three Kings thereof. Beside, these being rulers in their Countries, and returning home, would have probably converted their subjects; but according unto Munster, their conversion was not wrought until seventy years after by Maternus a disciple of Peter. And lastly, it is said that the wise men came from the East; but Collein is seated Westward from Jerusalem; for Collein hath of longitude thirty four degrees, but Jerusalem seventy two.

The ground of all was this. These wise men or Kings, were probably of Arabia, and descended from Abraham by Keturah, who apprehending the mystery of this Star, either by the Spirit of God, the prophesie of Balaam, the prophesie which Suetonius mentions, received and constantly believed through all the East, that out of Jury one should come that should rule the whole world: or the divulged expectation of the Jews from the expiring prediction of Daniel: were by the same conducted unto Judea, returned into their Country, and were after baptized by Thomas. From whence about three hundred years after, by Helena the Empress their bodies were translated to Constantinople. From thence by Eustathius unto Millane, and at last by Renatus the Bishop unto Collein: where they are believed at present to remain, their monuments shewn unto strangers, and having lost their Arabian titles, are crowned Kings of Collein.

SIR THOMAS BROWNE, *Pseudodoxia Epidemica.*

As the Romans did

It is now the month of December, when the greatest part of the city is in a bustle. Loose reins are given to public dissipation; everywhere you may hear the sound of great preparations, as if there were some real difference between the days devoted to Saturn and those for transacting business. . . . Were you here, I would willingly confer with you as to the plan of our conduct; whether we should live in our usual way, or, to avoid singularity, both take a better supper and throw off the toga.

SENECA, *Epistolae,* xviii.

Christmas in the Catacombs

It is known that the Feast of the Nativity was observed as early as the first century, and that it was kept by the primitive Christians even in dark days of persecution. 'They wandered in deserts, and in mountains, and in dens and caves of the earth' (Heb. xi. 38). Yet they were faithful to Christ, and the Catacombs of Rome contain evidence that they celebrated the Nativity.

The opening up of these Catacombs has brought to light many most interesting relics of primitive Christianity. In these Christian cemeteries and places of worship there are signs not only of the deep emotion and hope with which they buried their dead, but also of their simple forms of worship and the festive joy with which they commemorated the Nativity of Christ. On the rock-hewn tombs these primitive Christians wrote the thoughts that were most consoling to themselves, or painted on the walls the figures which gave them the most pleasure. The subjects of these paintings are for the most part taken from the Bible, and the one which illustrates the earliest and most universal of these pictures, and exhibits their Christmas joy, is 'The Adoration of the Magi.' Another of these emblems of joyous festivity which is frequently seen, is a vine, with its branches and purple clusters spreading in every direction, reminding us that in Eastern countries the vintage is the great holiday of the year. In the Jewish Church there was no festival so joyous as the Feast of Tabernacles, when they gathered the fruit of the vineyard, and in some of the earlier celebrations of the Nativity these festivities were closely copied. And as all down the ages pagan elements have mingled in the festivities of Christmas, so in the Catacombs they are not absent. There is Orpheus playing on his harp to the beasts; Bacchus as the god of the vintage; Psyche, the butterfly of the soul; the Jordan as the god of the rivers. The classical and the Christian, the Hebrew and the Hellenic elements had not yet parted; and the unearthing of these pictures after the lapse of centuries affords another interesting clue to the origin of some of the customs of Christmastide. It is astonishing how many of the Catacomb decorations are taken from heathen sources and copied from heathen paintings; yet we need not wonder when we reflect that the vine was used by the early Christians as an emblem of gladness, and it was scarcely possible for them to celebrate the Feast of the Nativity—a festival of glad tidings—without some sort of *Bacchanalia*. Thus it appears that even beneath the palaces and temples of pagan Rome the birth of Christ was celebrated, this early undermining of paganism by Christianity being, as it were, the germ of the final victory, and the secret praise, which came like muffled music from the Catacombs in honour of the Nativity, the prelude to the triumphsong in which they shall unite who receive from Christ the unwithering crown.

W. F. DAWSON, *Christmas, its Origins and Associations.*

A Christmas Massacre

The early years of Diocletian's reign were characterized by some sort of religious toleration, but when his persecutions began many endured martyrdom, and the storm of his fury burst on the Christians in the year 303. A multitude of Christians of all ages had assembled to commemorate the Nativity in the temple of Nicomedia, in Bithynia, when the Emperor had the town surrounded by soldiers and set on fire. About twenty thousand people were believed to have perished.

The Evolution of Christmas

The early Church did not regard Christ as a God from birth, but merely as having become one when He was thirty years, and when the Holy Ghost descended upon Him at the baptism in Jordan. . . . The festival in commemoration of the deification of Christ was Epiphany. About the beginning of the third century there arose in the western countries a new opinion on the person of the Saviour. . . . It was the Roman Bishop Liberius (A.D. 352–366) who had the courage to draw the consequences from the new belief. On 6th January 354 he celebrated, as before, the appearance of Christ in God-like glory, but in the same year he celebrated a second birthday of the God in Christ on 25th December, and used henceforth all his authority to lead this new festival to victory throughout the whole Church.

The new day of Christ's deification could only be successful in outshining the old one if it was celebrated earlier than the old one and at the same time with higher splendour. Although everything was done in that direction, attempts were not lacking to build a bridge from the new days to the old one, by proclaiming holy the twelve days between them. This was done as early as the fourth century by Ephraim the Syrian, and became by and by an ecclesiastical institution; so that the Synod of Tours of 567 declared it to be a festive tide of the Church under the name Δωδεκαήμερον or Twelve-days tide —called on Germanic soil, several centuries later, the *Twelve nights*—and in the course of time becoming so popular that a thousand years later so great a mythologist as Professor Weinhold could mistake them for a relic of ancient Germanic worship.

In Constantinople the first festival of Christ's birth on 25th December was celebrated in 379, in Nyssa of Cappadocia in 382, in Antioch in 388. It took about a century and a half to win for it legal authority among the Eastern Germanics. By the commentary to the Law Book of Alarich, which originated with it in 506, Christ's birthday became a day on which no law courts were allowed to be held. In Eastern Rome it gained the same position not much later, the *Codex Justinianus* of 543 ordaining it to be a *dies nefastus*. On the other hand, the Church tried to make it a real day of worldly joy, excluding from it all fasting as early as A.D. 561.

ALEXANDER TILLE, *Yule and Christmas.*

The Sword in the Stone

Then Merlin went to the Archbishop of Canterbury, and counselled him for to send for all the lords of the realm, and all the gentlemen of arms, that they should to London come by Christmas, upon pain of cursing; and for this cause, that Jesus, that was born on that night, that he would of his great mercy show some miracle, as he was come to be King of mankind, for to show some miracle who should be rightways king of this realm. So the Archbishop, by the advice of Merlin, sent for all the lords and gentlemen of arms that they should come by Christmas even unto London. And many of them made them clean of their life, that their prayer might be the more acceptable unto God. So in the greatest church of London, whether it were Paul's nor not the French book maketh no mention, all the estates were long or day in the church for to pray. And when Matins and the first Mass was done, there was seen in the church-yard, against the high altar, a great stone four square, like unto a marble stone, and in the midst thereof was like an anvil of steel a foot on high, and therein stuck a fair sword naked by the point, and letters there were written in gold about the sword that said thus:

Whoso pulleth out this sword of this stone and anvil, is rightwise king-born of all England.

Then the people marvelled, and told it to the Archbishop. I command, said the Archbishop, that ye keep you within your church, and pray unto God still; that no man touch the sword till the high Mass be all done. So when the Masses were done all the lords went to behold the stone and the sword. And when they saw the scripture, some assayed; such as would have been king. But none might stir the sword nor move it. He is not here, said the Archbishop, that shall achieve the sword, but doubt not God will make him known. But this is my counsel, said the Archbishop, that we let purvey ten knights, men of good fame, and they to keep this sword. So it was ordained, and then there was made a cry, that every man should essay that would, for to win the sword. And upon New Year's day the barons let make a jousts and a tournament, that all the knights that would joust or tourney there might play, and all this was ordained for to keep the lords and the commons together, for the Archbishop trusted that God would make him known that should win the sword. So upon New Year's day, when the service was done, the barons rode unto the field, some to joust and some to tourney, and so it happened that Sir Ector, that had great livelihood about London, rode unto the jousts, and with him rode Sir Kay his son, and young Arthur that was his nourished brother; and Sir Kay was made knight at All Hallowmass afore. So as they rode to the jousts-ward, Sir Kay had lost his sword, for he had left it at his father's lodging, and so he prayed young Arthur for to ride for his sword. I will well, said Arthur, and rode fast after the sword, and when he came home, the lady and all were out to see the jousting. Then was Arthur wroth, and said to himself, I will ride to the churchyard, and take the sword with me that sticketh in the stone, for my brother Sir Kay shall not be without a sword this day. So when he came to the churchyard, Arthur alit and tied his horse to the stile, and so he went to the tent, and found no knights there, for they were at jousting; and so he handled the sword by the handles, and lightly and fiercely pulled it out of the stone, and took his horse and rode his way until he came to his brother Sir Kay, and delivered him the sword. And as soon as Sir Kay saw the sword, he wist well it was the sword of the stone, and so he rode to his father Sir Ector, and said: Sir, lo here is the sword of the stone, wherefore I must be king of this land. When Sir Ector beheld the sword, he returned again and came to the church, and there they alit all three, and went into the church. And anon he made Sir Kay to swear upon a book how he came by that sword. Sir, said Sir Kay, by my brother Arthur, for he brought it to me. How gat ye this sword? said Sir Ector to Arthur. Sir, I will tell you. When I came home for my brother's sword, I found nobody at home to deliver me his sword, and so I thought my brother Sir Kay should not be swordless, and so I came hither eagerly and pulled it out of the stone without any pain. Found ye any knights about this sword? said Sir Ector. Nay, said Arthur. Now, said Sir Ector to Arthur, I understand ye must be king of this land. Wherefore I, said Arthur, and for what cause? Sir, said Ector, for God will have it so, for there should never man have drawn out this sword, but that he shall be rightways king of this land. Now let me see whether ye can put the sword there as it was, and pull it out again. That is no mastery, said Arthur, and so he put it in the stone, therewithal Sir Ector essayed to pull out the sword and failed.

Now assay, said Sir Ector unto Sir Kay. And anon he pulled at the sword with all his might, but it would not be. Now shall ye essay, said Sir Ector unto Arthur. I will well, said Arthur, and pulled it out easily. And therewithal Sir

Ector knelt down to the earth, and Sir Kay. Alas, said Arthur, my own dear father and brother, why kneel ye to me? Nay, nay, my lord Arthur, it is not so, I was never your father nor of your blood, but I wot well ye are of an higher blood than I weened ye were. . . .

Therewithal they went unto the Archbishop, and told him how the sword was achieved, and by whom; and on Twelfth Day all the barons came thither, and to essay to take the sword, who that would essay. But there afore them all, there might none take it out but Arthur.

SIR THOMAS MALORY, *Morte d'Arthur.*

Paganism at York, 521

At this time that great Monarch Arthur, with his Clergy, all his Nobility, and Soldiers, kept *Christmas* in *York*, whither resorted to him the prime Persons of the Neighbourhood, and spent the latter End of *December* in Mirth, Jollity, Drinking and the Vices that are too often the Consequence of them; so that the Representations of the old Heathenish Feasts dedicated to Saturn were here again revived; but the Number of Days they lasted were doubled and amongst the wealthier Sort trebled; during which Time they counted it almost a Sin to treat of any serious Matter. . . . Our Countrymen call this Jule-tide, substituting the name of *Julius Caesar* for that of *Saturn.* The Vulgar are yet persuaded that the Nativity of Christ is then celebrated, but mistakenly; for 'tis plain they imitate the Lasciviousness of *Bacchanalians,* rather than the memory of *Christ.*

History of York, 1785.

The Word 'Christmas'

The Parker MS. of the *Saxon Chronicle* under A.D. 763 has the entry: 'on thone feowertegan dæg ofer midne winter,' showing midwinter to be a pure calendar term; whilst half a century after, in 827, that term has evolved into an official mass of the Church: 'on middes wintres mæsse niht.' Another half century, and a new element again joins the two which are united in that term, the twelfth night after December 25: 'here on midne wiñt. ofer tuelftan niht.' In 885 there occurs the term used as a means of determining a day previous to it: 'thy ilcan geare ær middum wintra,' to which in 898 a similar dating by midsummer is added: 'nigum nihtum ær middum sumere.' In the Laud MS. of the *Chronicle* (E), which represents the larger group of versions, *midewinter* appears first in 762. But after the year 810 (when a new mode of annal-writing was adopted) the same date is mentioned as 'on middes wintres messa niht,' in 827; and in 878 as 'on midne winter ofer twelftan niht,' all three entries being contained in the Parker MS. (A), though the first of them under A.D. 763. Then *middan wintra* (A.D. 885) is for a long time the only denomination for December 25 (to which 918 *middan sumera* is added, which is at the same time clearly marked to mean June 24), now and then 'in thære midde wintres tide' (A.D. 1006 and 1016) appearing instead. Subsequently, with the year 1017, an altogether new method of dating commenced—in 1038 the same date is named for the first time *Cristes mæssan*, 1043 having 'to Cristes mæssan on Stephanes mæsse dæg,' whilst *mide winter* again appears from 1075 to 1086. In 1091 several changes set in. Midwinter is replaced by *Cristes mæssa*; regular mention is made of the king staying at a certain place at Christmas—this statement thenceforward being always the first in the year, making it appear that from that date the year was no longer begun with January 1, but with December 25. In 1002 December 25 is called for the first time *to Natiuitedh*, whilst in 1103 *to mide-wintra* turns up again, and 1115, 1116, 1122, and 1123 add new terms: 1122, 'on thære nihte uigilia Natalis Domini'; and 1123, 'on Cristes tyde.' In 1131 *Cristemesse* is for the first time written in one word, so that then it can be said to have become a regular compound, with only one main emphasis. Other sources are in perfect agreement with this system of nomenclature.

ALEXANDER TILLE, *Yule and Christmas.*

The Coronation of the Conqueror

A.D. 1066. Willielmus . . . ipsa Nativitatis die, quae illo anno evenit, ab Aldredo Eboracensium archiepiscopo in Westmonasterio consecratus est honorifice.

FLORENCE OF WORCESTER.

[From this date onwards Christmas Day was often chosen for ceremonies, coronations, and courts.]

Murder in the Cathedral

[On 29th December 1170, Thomas à Becket, Archbishop of Canterbury, was slain by four of King Henry the Second's knights. The following narrative is from the Sloane MS. of the fifteenth century.]

Lestenytz lordyngs both grete and smale
I xal you telyn a wonder tale
How holy cherche was browt in bale
    Cum magna injuria

The greteste clerk of al this lond
Of Cauntyrbery ye understond
Slawyn he was by wykkyd hond
    Demonis potentia
Knytes kemyn fro Hendry kyng
Wykkyd men, with-oute lesyng
Ther they dedyn a wonder thing
    Ferventes insania
They sowtyn hym al abowtyn
Withine the paleys and withoutyn
Of Jhesu Cryst hadde they non dowte
    In sua malicia
They openyd here mowthis wonder wyde
To Thomeys they spokyn mekyl pryde
Here, tretour, thu xalt abyde
    Ferens mortis tedia
Thomas answerid with mylde chere
If ye wil me slon in this manere
Let hem pasyn alle tho arn here
    Sine contumelia
Beforn his aunter he knelyd adoun
Ther they gunne to paryn his crown
He sterdyn the braynys up and doun
    Optans celi gaudia
The turmentowrs abowtyn sterte
With dedly wondys thei gunne him hurte
Thomas deyid in moder cherche
    Pergens ad celestia
Moder, clerke, wedue, and wyf
Worchepe ye Thomeys in al your lyf
For lii poyntes he les his lyf
    Contra regis consilia.

Feast of Fools

Beletus, who lived in 1182, mentions the Feast of Fools, as celebrated in some places on New Year's Day, in others on Twelfth Night and in still others the week following. It seems at any rate to have been one of the recognized revels of the Christmas season. In France, at different cathedral churches there was a Bishop or an Archbishop of Fools elected, and in the churches immediately dependent upon the papal see a Pope of Fools.

These mock pontiffs had usually a proper suite of ecclesiastics, and one of their ridiculous ceremonies was to shave the Precentor of Fools upon a stage erected before the church in the presence of the jeering 'vulgar populace.'

They were mostly attired in the ridiculous dresses of pantomime players and buffoons, and so habited entered the church, and performed the ceremony accompanied by crowds of followers representing monsters or so disguised as to excite fear or laughter. During this mockery of a divine service they sang indecent songs in the choir, ate rich puddings on the corner of the altar, played at dice upon it during the celebration of a mass, incensed it with smoke from old burnt shoes, and ran leaping all over the church. The Bishop or Pope of Fools performed the service and gave benediction, dressed in pontifical robes. When it was concluded he was seated in an open carriage and drawn about the town followed by his train, who in place of carnival confetti threw filth from a cart upon the people who crowded to see the procession.

These 'December liberties,' as they were called, were always held at Christmas time or near it, but were not confined to one particular day, and seem to have lasted through the chief part of January. When the ceremony took place upon St Stephen's Day they said as part of the Mass a burlesque composition called the Fool's Prose.

WILLIAM HONE, *Ancient Mysteries.*

No Greetings for King John

The Christmas of 1214 is memorable in English history as the festival at which the barons demanded from King John that document which as the foundation of our English liberties is known to us by the name of *Magna Charta.* John's tyranny and lawlessness had become intolerable, and the people's hope hung on the fortunes of the French campaign in which he was then engaged. His defeat at the battle of Bouvines, fought on 27th July 1214, gave strength to his opponents; and after his return to England the barons secretly met at St Edmondsbury and swore to demand from him, if needful by force of arms, the restoration of their liberties by charter under the king's seal. Having agreed to assemble at the Court for this purpose during the approaching festival of Christmas they separated. When Christmas Day arrived John was at Worcester, attended only by a few of his immediate retainers and some foreign mer⁄ cenaries. None of his great vassals came, as was customary at Christmas, to offer their congratulations. His attendants tried in vain to assume an appearance of cheerfulness and festivity; but John, alarmed at the absence of the barons, hastily rode to London and there shut himself up in the house of the Knights Templars. On the Feast of the Epiphany the barons assembled in great force at London and presenting themselves in arms before the King formally demanded his confirmation of the laws of Edward the Confessor and Henry I.

W. F. DAWSON, *Christmas, its Origin and Associations.*

The First Crib, 1223

Now three years before his death it befell that he was minded, at the town of Greccio, to celebrate the memory of the Birth of the Child Jesus, with all the added solemnity that he might, for the kindling of devotion. That this might not seem an innovation, he sought and obtained licence from the Supreme Pontiff, and then made ready a manger, and bade hay, together with an ox and an ass, be brought unto the place. The Brethren were called together, the folk assembled, the wood echoed with their voices, and that August night was made radiant and solemn with many bright lights, and with tuneful and sonorous praises. The man of God, filled with tender love, stood before the manger, bathed in tears, and overflowing with joy. Solemn Masses were celebrated over the manger, Francis, the Levite of Christ, chanting the Holy Gospel. Then he preached unto the folk standing round the Birth of the King in poverty, calling Him, when he wished to name Him, the Child of Bethlehem, by reason of his tender love for Him. A certain knight, valorous and true, Messer John of Greccio, who for the love of Christ had left the secular army, and was bound by closest friendship unto the man of God, declared that he beheld a little Child right fair to see sleeping in that manger, who seemed to be awakened from sleep when the blessed Father Francis embraced Him in both arms.

ST BONAVENTURE, *Life of St Francis of Assisi.*

Aggression in 1403

A little before Christmass the Frenchmen came into the Ile of Wight, boasting that they would keep their Christmass there and when a thousand of the Frenchmen were entred into the Ilande, and driving flockes of Catell towarde the Sea, sodainely there came upon them a companie of the Ilande menne, that forced them to leave their praye behinde them, and to gette them gone (with shame ynough) to their shippes with no small losse of their men.

JOHN STOW, *Annales*.

Christmas Box Menace, 1419

Regulation made that the Serjeants and other officers of the Mayor, Sheriffs, or City, shall not beg for Christmas gifts. Forasmuch as it is not becoming or agreeable to propriety that those who are in the service of reverend men, and from them, or through them, have the advantage of befitting food and raiment, as also of reward, or remuneration, in a competent degree, should, after a perverse custom, be begging aught of people, like paupers; and seeing that in times past, every year at the feast of our Lord's Nativity (25th December), according to a certain custom, which has grown to be an abuse, the vadlets of the Mayor, the Sheriffs and the Chamber of the said city—persons who have food, raiment, and appropriate advantages, resulting from their office—under colour of asking for an oblation, have begged many sums of money of brewers, bakers, cooks, and other victuallers; and, in some instances, have, more than once, threatened wrongfully to do them an injury if they should refuse to give them something; and have frequently made promises to others that, in return for a present, they would pass over their unlawful doings in mute silence; to the great dishonour of their masters, and to the common loss of all the city: therefore, on Wednesday, the last day of April, in the 7th year of King Henry the Fifth, by William Sevenok, the Mayor, and the Aldermen of London, it was ordered and established that no vadlet, or other sergeant of the Mayor,

Sheriffs, or City, should in future beg or require of any person, of any rank, degree, or condition whatsoever, any moneys, under colour of an oblation, or in any other way, on pain of losing his office.

Corporation Letter-book.

None Loud Disports

[Margery Paston to her husband, John Paston, 24th Dec. 1483.]

Right worshipful husband, I recommend me unto you: please it you to weet [know] that I sent your eldest son John to my Lady Morley, to have knowledge what sports were used in her house in Christmas next following after the decease of my lord her husband; and she said that there were none disguisings, nor harpings, nor lutings, nor singing, nor none loud disports; but playing at the tables, and chess, and cards; such disports she gave her folks leave to play, and none other. I am sorry that ye shall not at home be for Christmas. I pray you that ye will come as soon as ye may; I shall think myself half a widow, because ye shall not be at home, &c. God have you in his keeping. Written on Christmas even.

By your servant and beadwoman,

MARGERY PASTON.

Columbus in Cuba

On Christmas Day, 1492, Christopher Columbus landed at the newly-discovered port in Cuba which he named Navidad, in honour of the Nativity.

Henry VIII makes Merry, 1512

In this yeare the king kept his Christmasse at Greenewich, where was such abundance of viands served to all comers of anie honest behaviour, as hath beene few times seene. And against New Yeeres night was made in the hall a castell, gates, towers, and dungeon, garnished with artillerie and weapon, after the most warlike fashion: and on the front of the castell was written *Le fortresse dangereux*, and, within the castell were six ladies cloathed in russet satin, laid all over with leaves of gold, and everie one knit with laces of blew silke and gold. On their heads, coifs and caps all of gold. After this castell had beene caried about the hall, and the queene had beheld it, in came the king with five other, apparelled in coats, the one halfe of russet sattin, the other halfe of rich cloth of gold; on their heads caps of russet sattin embrodered with works of fine gold bullion.

These six assaulted the castell. The ladies seeing them so lustie and couragious, were content to solace with them, and upon further communication to yeeld the castell, and so they came downe and dansed a long space. And after, the ladies led the knights into the castell, and then the castell suddenlie vanished out of their sights. On the daie of the Epiphanie at night, the king, with eleven other, were disguised, after the manner of Italie; called a maske, a thing not seene before, in England; they were apparelled in garments long and broad, wrought all with gold, with visors and caps of gold. And, after the banket done, these maskers came in, with six gentlemen disguised in silke, bearing staffe torches, and desired the ladies to danse: some were content, and some refused. And, after they had dansed, and communed togither, as the fashion of the maske is, they tooke their leave and departed, and so did the queene and all the ladies.

EDWARD HALL'S *Chronicle*.

Revels of the Inner Temple, c. 1560

First, the solemn Revells (after dinner, and the play ended,) are begun by the whole House, Judges, Serjeants at Law, Benchers; the Utter and Inner Barr; and they led by the Master of the Revells: and one of the Gentlemen of the Utter Barr is chosen to sing a song to the Judges, Serjeants, or Masters of the Bench; which is usually performed; and in default thereof, there may be an amerciament. Then the Judges and Benchers take their places, and sit down at the upper end of the Hall. Which done, the Utter-Barristers and Inner-Barristers, perform a second solemn Revell before them. Which ended, the Utter-Barristers take their places and sit down. Some of the Gentlemen of the Inner-Barr, do present the House with dancing, which is called the Post Revells, and continue their Dances, till the Judges or Bench think meet to rise and depart.

SIR WILLIAM DUGDALE, *Origines Juridiciales*

My Lorde of Misserule

Firste all the wilde heades of the parishe conventynge together, chuse them a grand Capitaine (of mischeef) whom they innoble with the title of my *Lorde of Misserule*, and hym they crown with great solemnitie, and adopt for their kyng. This kyng anoynted, chuseth for the twentie, fourtie, three score, or a hundred lustie guttes like to hymself, to waite uppon his lordely majestie, and to guard his noble persone. Then every one of these his menne he investeth with his liveries of greene, yellowe or some other light wanton colour. And as though that were not baudie enough I should saie, they be-decke themselves with scarffes, ribons, and laces, hanged all

over with golde rynges, precious stones, and other jewelles:
this doen, they tye about either legge twentie or fourtie belles
with rich handkercheefes in their handes, and sometymes
laied acrosse over their shoulders and neckes, borrowed for
the moste parte of their pretie Mopsies and loovying Bessies,
for bussyng them in the darcke. Thus thinges sette in order,
they have their hobbie horses, dragons, and other antiques,
together with their baudie pipers, and thunderyng drommers,
to strike up the Deville's Daunce withall, then marche these
heathen companie towardes the church and churche yarde,
their pipers pipyng, drommers thonderyng, their stumppes
dauncyng, their belles iynglyng, their handkerchiefes swyngyng
about their heades like madmen, their hobbie horses and other
monsters skyrmishyng amongst the throng: and in this sorte
they goe to the churche (though the minister bee at praier or
preachyng) dauncyng and swingyng their handkercheefes
over their heades, in the churche, like devilles incarnate, with
suche a confused noise that no man can heare his owene voice.
Then the foolishe people, they looke, they stare, they laugh,
they fleere, and mount upon formes and pewes, to see these
goodly pageauntes, solemnized in this sort.

PHILIP STUBBS, *The Anatomie of Abuses,* 1585.

Hampton Court, 1604

The Twelfth Day the French ambassador was feasted
publicly, and at night there was a play in the Queen's presence,
with a masquerade of certain Scotchmen; who came in with
a sword dance, not unlike a matachin; and performed it
cleanly; from whence the King went to dice, into his own
presence, and lost 500 crowns which marred a gamester; for
since he appeared not there but once before was it at in the same

place and parted a winner. The Sunday following was the great day of the Queen's masque, at which was present the Spanish and Polack ambassadors with their whole trains, and the most part of the Florentines and Savoyards, but not the ambassadors themselves, who were in so strong competition for place and precedence, that to displease neither it was thought best to let both alone.

SIR DUDLEY CARLETON.

Great Golden Play, etc.

[January 8th, 1607]. On the Twelfth-eve there was great golden play at Court. No Gamester admitted that brought not £300 at least. Montgomery played the King's money, and won him £750, which he had for his labour. The Lord Montegle lost the Queen £400. Sir Robert Cary, for the Prince, £300; and the Earl Salisbury, £300; the Lord Buckhurst, £500; *et sic de coeteris*. So that I heard of no winner but the King and Sir Francis Wolley, who got above £800. The King went a hawking-journey yesterday to Theobalds and returns tomorrow.

Above Westminster the Thames is quite frozen over; and the Archbishop came from Lambeth, on Twelfth-day, over the ice to Court. Many fanciful experiments are daily put in practice; as certain youths burnt a gallon of wine upon the ice, and made all the passengers partakers. But the best is, of an honest woman (they say) that had a great longing to encrease her family on the Thames.

JOHN CHAMBERLAINE, in a letter to
Sir Dudley Carleton.

With the Pilgrim Fathers, Plymouth Rock, 1620

Munday, the 25 Day, we went on shore, some to fell tymber, some to saw, some to riue, and some to carry, so that no man rested all that day, but towards night, some, as they were at worke, heard a noyse of some Indians, which caused vs all to goe to our Muskets, but we heard no further, so we came aboord againe, and left some twentie to keepe the court of gard; that night we had a sore storme of winde and raine. Munday the 25 being Christmas day, we began to drinke water aboord, but at night, the Master caused vs to have some Beere, and so on board we had diverse times now and then some Beere, but on shore none at all.

One ye day called Christmas-day, ye Gov'r caled them out to worke (as was used), but ye most of this new company excused themselves, and said it went against their consciences to worke on ye day. So ye Gov'r tould them that if they made it a mater of conscience, he would spare them till they were better informed. So he led away ye rest, and left them: but when they came home at noone from their worke, he found them in ye streete at play, openly; some pitching ye barr, and some at stoole ball, and such like sports. So he went to them and tooke away their implements, and told them it was against his conscience that they should play, and others worke. If they made ye keeping of it matter of devotion, let them kepe their houses, but there should be no gameing or revelling in ye streets. Since which time nothing hath been attempted that way, at least, openly.

WILLIAM BRADFORD'S Journal.

St Noël

Noël's family name was Chabanel, and he came into this world at some unidentified place in the department of Lozère, France, on 2nd February, 1613. Seventeen years later he joined the Society of Jesus at Toulouse, and then for the following thirteen years lay *perdu* in colleges, and other such levelling institutions. Not a word remains to tell us what he was like during all that period, except the remark that 'God had given him a strong vocation' for work among the Red Indians of New France. To that work he sailed at the age of thirty, in a small, insanitary ship that heaved and tossed on the Atlantic for three solid months before making Quebec. Conditions on board would have turned the stomach of the toughest Grimsby fisherman, for, as one who made the voyage feelingly recorded, the passengers were 'packed into the dismal and noisome hold like sardines in a barrel.' It was a good initiation for the shy and sensitive humanist whose company hitherto had been aristocratic French boys and the gentle ghosts of Vergil and Cicero.

St Noël's first trial in his land of heart's desire was the Indian language. For five years he slaved away, endeavouring to master whatever grammar it possessed and to commit its dreadful vocabulary, which sounded like the chattering of monkeys, to a memory saturated with the cadences of Greece and Rome. At the end of that long effort he was almost in despair, for, as his superior, Père Ragueneau, reported, 'he found his progress so slight that hardly could he make himself understood, even in the most ordinary matters, which was no little mortification to a man who burned with desire for the conversion of the savages.' And what savages they were, among the vilest and most degraded known to anthropology. Their habits nauseated St Noël from the very first, despite his utmost efforts to overcome the loathing. He had to live in closest contact with those dirty, malodorous, vermin-ridden, cruel, foul-tongued travesties of human nature; to share their disgusting food, and to work all day in a hovel described by Père Ragueneau as 'un petit enfer de fumée.' The place was crawling with vermin, as well as with scrubby children who fought and squalled and yelled from morning to night. One's bed was the bare ground, and often in the morning Noël woke to find that Nature, for a frolic, had provided him with a counterpane of snow. His food when times were good consisted of a paste made with Indian meal boiled in water; when times were bad, of acorns.

These physical discomforts were, however, only the fringe of St Noël's bloodless martyrdom. Even the constant dread in which, being a timid soul, afraid of pain, he passed his days that he would be captured and tortured by the sadistic Iroquois, did not mark the limits of his unhappiness. There was a far worse trial even than that. Other saints, his companions on the terrible mission—the lion-hearted de Brébuf, the gentle Jogues, the sturdy, indomitable Garnier, had visits from the angels to cheer them, or tokens no less plain of God's benevo- lence; but for St Noël, Heaven kept silent up to the very end.

When parting for his last mission, where he was to be the companion of St Charles Garnier, Noël said to the Father who used to hear his confession: 'My dear Father, may it be for good and all this time that I give myself to God, and may I belong to Him.'

And so Noël went into the wilds to starve with Garnier. At last food of any kind became so scarce on their mission that there was not enough to keep the two of them alive, and Ragueneau therefore sent Noël instructions to repair to another station. He had been gone only two days when the Iroquois arrived and gave Garnier his crown.

Meantime, St Noël, having tramped about thirty miles

accompanied by seven or eight Christian Hurons, found himself overtaken by night in the thick of a vast forest. Bidding his men lie down and sleep as best they could in the perishing December cold, he knelt by them to keep guard and pray. Towards midnight he heard shouting in the forest, and roused his companions, who at once melted into the darkness. For a time he kept up with some of them, but at last fell to his knees, exhausted. It didn't matter about him, he said; let them go on and save themselves. What happened after that is a mystery which has never been solved. At dawn, apparently Noël struggled on alone to his destination, but he never reached it. 'Mine will be a martyrdom in the gloom,' he had once said, and sure enough he died, like John the Baptist, without any glory or human comfort, under the tomahawk of a prowling Indian who hated him for his faith. His last words to two of his brethren whom he had met on the journey were these: 'I am going where obedience summons me. I may never arrive there, but if I do I shall ask my superior to send me back again to the mission which was my share of work, for I must serve God until I die.'

J. BRODRICK, S.J.

Abominable Disorders

Our Christmas lords of Misrule, together with dancing, masques, mummeries, stage-players, and such other Christmas disorders, now in use with Christians, were derived from these Roman Saturnalia and Bacchanalian festivals; which should cause all pious Christians eternally to abominate them.

WILLIAM PRYNNE, *Histrio-Mastix*, 1633.

Insurrection at Canterbury, 1648

Upon Wednesday, Decem. 22, the Cryer of Canterbury by the appointment of Master Major [Mayor], openly proclaimed that Christmas day, and all other Superstitious Festivals should be put downe, and that a Market should be kept upon Christmas day. Which not being observed (but very ill taken by the Country) the towne was thereby unserved with provision, and trading very much hindered; which occasioned great discontent among the people, caused them to rise in a Rebellious way.

The Major being slighted, and his Commands observed only of a few who opened their Shops, to the number of 12 at the most: They were commanded by the multitude to shut up again, but refusing to obey, their ware was thrown up and down, and they, at last, forced to shut in.

The Major and his assistants used their best endeavours to qualifie this tumult, but the fire being once kindled, was not easily quenched. The Sheriffe laying hold of a fellow, was stoutly resisted; which the Major perceiving, took a Cudgell and strook the man: who, being no puny, pulled up his courage, and knockt down the Major, whereby his Cloak was much torne and durty, beside the hurt he received. The Major hereupon made strict Proclamation for keeping the Peace and that every man depart to his own house. The multitude hollowing thereat, in disorderly manner; the Aldermen and Constables caught two or three of the rout, and sent them to the Jayle, but they soon broke loose, and jeered Master Alderman.

Soone after, issued forth the Commanders of this Rabble, with an addition of Souldiers, into the high street, and brought with them two Foot-balls, whereby their company increased. Which the Major and Aldermen perceiving, took what prisoners they had got, and would have carried them to the

Jayle. But the multitude following after to the King's Bench, were opposed by Captain Bridg, who was straight knoct down, and had his head broke in two places, not being able to withstand the multitude, who, getting betwixt him and the Jayle, rescued their fellowes, and beat the Major and Aldermen into their houses, and then cried Conquest.

> *Canterbury Christmas; or, a True Relation of the Insurrection in Canterbury.*

Abolition of Christmas

The House spent much Time this Day about the businesse of the Navie, for settling the Affairs at Sea, and before they rose, were presented with a terrible Remonstrance against Christ-mas-day, grounded upon divine Scriptures: 2 Cor. v. 16; 1 Cor. xv. 14, 17; and in honour of the Lord's-day, grounded on these Scriptures: John xx. 1; Rev. i. 10; Psalms cxviii. 24; Lev. xxiii. 7, 11; Mark xv. 8; Psalms lxxxiv. 10; in which Christmas is called Anti-Christ's-masse, and those Masse-mongers and Papists who observe it, &c.

In consequence of which, Parliament spent some Time in Consultation about the Abolition of Christmas-day, pass'd Orders to that Effect, and resolv'd to sit on the following Day, which was commonly called Christmas-day.

> *The Flying Eagle,* London; 24th December 1652.

Mournfullest Day, 1655

25 Dec. There was no more notice taken of Christmas day in Churches. I went to London, where Dr Wild preached the funeral sermon of Preaching, this being the last day; after which,

Cromwell's proclamation was to take place, that none of the Church of England should dare either to preach, or administer Sacraments, teach school, etc., on pain of imprisonment or exile. So this was the mournfullest day that in my life I had seen, or the Church of England herself, since the Reformation; to the great rejoicing of both Papist and Presbyter. So pathetic was his discourse. that it drew many tears from the auditory. Myself, wife, and some of our family received the Communion: God make me thankful, who hath hitherto provided for us the food of our souls as well as bodies! The Lord Jesus pity our distressed Church, and bring back the captivity of Zion!

JOHN EVELYN, *Diary*.

Musketts at the Altar, 1657

25 Dec. I went to London with my wife, to celebrate Christmas-day, Mr Gunning preaching in Exeter-Chapell, on 7 Micah 2. Sermon ended, as he was giving us the holy sacrament, the chapell was surrounded with souldiers, and all the communicants and assembly surpriz'd and kept prisoner by them, some in the house, others carried away. It fell to my share to be confin'd to a room in the house, where yet I was permitted to dine with the master of it, the Countess of Dorset, Lady Hatton, and some others of quality who invited me. In the afternoone came Col. Whaly, Goffe, and others, from White-hall, to examine us one by one; some they committed to the Marshall, some to prison. When I came before them they took my name and abode, examin'd me why, contrarie to an ordinance made that none should any longer observe the superstitious time of the Nativity (so esteem'd by them) I durst offend, and particularly be at Common Prayers, which they told me was but the Masse in English, and particularly pray for Charles Steuart, for which we had no Scripture.

I told them we did not pray for Cha. Steuart, but for all Christian Kings, Princes, and Governours. They replied, in so doing we praid for the K. of Spaine too, who was their enemie and a papist, with other frivolous and insnaring questions and much threatning: and finding no colour to detaine me, they dismiss'd me with much pitty of my ignor-ance. These were men of high flight and above ordinances, and spake spiteful things of our Lord's Nativity. As we went up to receive the sacrament the miscreants held their musketts against us as if they would have shot us at the altar, but yet suffering us to finish the office of Communion, as perhaps not having instructions what to do in case they found us in that action. So I got home late the next day, blessed be God.

JOHN EVELYN, Diary.

Thornes and Walnutts

Mr Anthony Hinton, one of the officers of the Earle of Pem-broke, did inoculate, not long before the late civill warres (ten yeares or more), a bud of Glastonbury Thorne, on a thorne, at his farmhouse, at Wilton, which blossoms at Christmas, as the other did. My mother has had branches of them for a flowerpott, several Christmasses, which I have seen. Elias Ashmole, Esq., in his notes upon *Theatrum Chymicum*, saies that in the churchyard of Glastonbury grew a walnutt tree that did putt out young leaves at Christmas, as doth the King's Oak in the New Forest. In Parham Park, in Suffolk (Mr Boutele's), is a pretty ancient thorne, that blossomes like that at Glastonbury, the people flock hither to see it on Christmas Day. But in the rode that leades from Worcester to Droit-wiche is a black thorne hedge at Clayes, half a mile long or more, that blossoms about Christmas-day, for a week or more together. Dr Ezerel Tong sayd that about Rumly-Marsh, in Kent, are thornes naturally like that near Glastonbury.

The Soldiers did cutt downe that near Glastonbury; the stump remaines.

JOHN AUBREY, *Memoires of Remarques in Wilts.*

Mr Pepys's Christmas Reading

Dec. 25th, 1667. Being a fine, light, moonshine morning, home round the city, and stopped and dropped money at five or six places, which I was the willinger to do, it being Christmas-day, and so home, and there find my wife in bed, and Jane and the maid making pyes. So I to bed. Rose about nine, and to church, and there heard a dull sermon of Mr Mills, but a great many fine people at church; and so home. Wife and girl and I alone at dinner—a good Christmas dinner. My wife reading to me 'The History of the Drummer of Mr Mompesson,' which is a strange story of spies, and worth reading indeed.

SAMUEL PEPYS, *Diary.*

Half a Crown for Patrick

London, 24th Dec. 1711. I went into the City to-day in a coach, and dined there. My cold is going. It is now bitter hard frost, and has been so these three or four days. . . . I gave Patrick half a crown for his Christmas-box, on con- dition he would be good, and he came home drunk at mid- night. I have taken a memorandum of it; because I never design to give him a groat more. 'Tis cruel-cold.

JONATHAN SWIFT, *Journal to Stella.*

Sir Roger de Coverley

Sir Roger, after the laudable Custom of his Ancestors, always keeps open House at Christmas. I learned from him that he had killed eight Fat Hogs for this Season, that he had dealt about his Chines very liberally amongst his Neighbours, and that in particular he had sent a String of Hogs'-puddings with a Pack of Cards to every poor Family in the Parish. I have often thought, says Sir Roger, it happens very well that Christmas should fall out in the Middle of Winter. It is the most dead uncomfortable Time of the Year, when the poor People would suffer very much from their Poverty and Cold, if they had not good Chear, warm Fires, and Christmas Gambols to support them. I love to rejoice their poor Hearts at this season, and to see the whole Village merry in my great Hall. I allow a double Quantity of Malt to my Small Beer, and set it a-running for twelve Days to every one that calls for it. I have always a Piece of Cold Beef and Mince-pye upon the Table, and am wonderfully pleased to see my Tenants pass away a whole Evening in playing their innocent Tricks, and smutting one another. Our Friend Will Wimble is as merry as any of them, and shows a thousand Roguish Tricks upon these Occasions.

I was very much delighted with the Reflexion of my old Friend, which carried so much Goodness with it. He then launched out into the Praise of the late Act of Parliament for securing the Church of England, and told me with great Satisfaction, that he believed it already began to take Effect, for that a rigid Dissenter who chanced to dine at his House on Christmas-day, had been observed to eat away very plentifully of his Plumb-porridge.

JOSEPH ADDISON.

The Pantomime comes to England

The theatre in Lincoln's Inn Fields, which Christopher Rich had been restoring, his son, John Rich, was allowed to open on the 18th of December, 1714. John Rich was a clever mimic, and after a year or two he found it to his advantage to compete with the actors in a fashion of his own. He was the inventor of the modern English form of pantomime, with a serious part that he took from Ovid's *Metamorphoses* or any fabulous history, and a comic addition of the courtship of harlequin and columbine, with surprising tricks and transformations. He introduced the old Italian characters of pantomime under changed conditions, and beginning with *Harlequin Sorcerer* in 1717, continued to produce these entertainments until a year before his death in 1761.

HENRY MORLEY, *English Plays.*

Pantomime Transformation Scene, 1728

All the extravagancies in the lines following were introduced on the stage, and frequented by persons of the first quality in England, to the twentieth and thirtieth time.

> See now, what Dulness and her sons admire!
> See what the charms, that smite the simple heart
> Not touch'd by Nature, and not reach'd by Art.
> He look'd, and saw a sable Sorcerer rise,
> Swift to whose hand a winged volume flies:
> All sudden, gorgons hiss, and dragons glare,
> And ten-horn'd fiends and giants rush to war:
> Hell rises, heav'n descends, and dance on earth;
> Gods, imps, and monsters; music, rage, and mirth;

A fire, a jig, a battle, and a ball,
Till one wide conflagration swallows all.
Thence a new world, to nature's laws unknown,
Breaks out refulgent, with a heav'n its own:
Another Cynthia her new journey runs,
And other planets circle other suns.
The forests dance, the rivers upward rise,
Whales sport in woods, and dolphins in the skies;
And last, to give the whole creation grace,
Lo! one vast egg produces human race.
Joy fills his soul, joy innocent of thought:
'What power,' he cries, 'what power these wonders
    wrought?'

ALEXANDER POPE, *The Dunciad.*

The Thorns and the Calendar

[The following occurrences were the result of the change in the calendar in 1752, when 2nd September was by law changed into 14th September, and Christmas was accordingly celebrated twelve days earlier.]

Quainton in Buckinghamshire, December 24. Above 2,000 people came here this night, with lanthorns and candles, to view a black thorn which grows in the neighbourhood, and which was remembered (this year only) to be a slip from the famous Glastonbury Thorne, that it always budded on the 24th, was full blown the next day, and went all off at night; but the people, finding no appearance of a bud, 'twas agreed by all, that 25 December, N.S., could not be the right Christmas Day, and accordingly, refused going to Church and treating their friends on that day, as usual: at length the affair became so serious that the ministers of the neighbouring villages, in order to appease the people, thought it prudent to give notice that the old Christmas Day should be kept holy as before.

Glastonbury. A vast concourse of people attended the noted thorns on Christmas Eve, New Stile; but, to their great disappointment, there was no appearance of its blowing, which made them watch it narrowly the 5th of Jan., the Christmas day, Old Style, when it blow'd as usual.

The Gentleman's Magazine, 1753.

Traffic in Turkeys, 1793

Hone, in his *Every-Day Book*, quotes from an historical account of Norwich a statement of the amount of turkeys which were sent from that city to London between a Saturday morning and the night of Sunday, in December 1793, It gives the number as one thousand seven hundred, the weight as nine tons, two hundredweight, and two pounds, and the value as £680. It is added that in the two following days these were followed by half as many more.

Christmas with the Wordsworths

24th December 1802.—Christmas Eve. William is now sitting by me, at half-past ten o'clock. I have been . . . repeating some of his sonnets to him, listening to his own repeating, reading some of Milton's and the *Allegro* and *Penseroso*. It is a quick, keen frost. . . . Coleridge came this morning with Wedgwood. . . . He looked well. We had to tell him of the birth of his little girl, born yesterday morning at six o'clock. William went with them to Wytheburn in the

chaise, and M. and I met W. on the Raise. . . . The sun
shone now and then, and there was no wind, but all things
looked cheerless and distinct; no meltings of sky into mountains, the mountains like stone work wrought up with huge
hammers. . . . It is Christmas Day, Saturday, 25th December,
1802. I am thirty-one years of age. It is a dull, frosty day.

DOROTHY WORDSWORTH.

At Bracebridge Hall

The dinner was served up in the great hall, where the Squire
always held his Christmas banquet. A blazing crackling
fire of logs had been heaped on to warm the spacious apartment, and the flame went sparkling and wreathing up the
wide-mouthed chimney. The great picture of the crusader and
his white horse had been profusely decorated with greens for
the occasion; and holly and ivy had likewise been wreathed
round the helmet and weapons on the opposite wall, which I
understood were the arms of the same warrior. I must own,
by the bye, I had strong doubts about the authenticity of the
painting and armour as having belonged to the crusader, they
certainly having the stamp of more recent days; but I was told
that the painting had been so considered time out of mind;
and that as to the armour, it had been found in a lumber
room, and elevated to its present situation by the Squire, who
at once determined it to be the armour of the family hero; and
as he was absolute authority on all such subjects in his own
household, the matter had passed into current acceptation.
A sideboard was set out just under this chivalric trophy, on
which was a display of plate that might have vied (at least in
variety) with Belshazzar's parade of the vessels of the temple;
'flagons, cans, cups, beakers, goblets, basins, and ewers'; the

gorgeous utensils of good companionship, that had gradually accumulated through many generations of jovial housekeepers. Before these stood the two Yule candles beaming like two stars of the first magnitude; other lights were distributed in branches, and the whole array glittered like a firmament of silver.

We were ushered into this banqueting scene with the sound of minstrelsy, the old harper being seated on a stool beside the fireplace, and twanging his instrument with a vast deal more power than melody. Never did Christmas board display a more goodly and gracious assemblage of countenances: those who were not handsome were, at least, happy; and happiness is a rare improver of your hard-favoured visage. I always consider an old English family as well worth studying as a collection of Holbein's portraits or Albert Durer's prints. There is much antiquarian lore to be acquired; much knowledge of the physiognomies of former times. Perhaps it may be from having continually before their eyes those rows of old family portraits, with which the mansions of this country are stocked; certain it is, that the quaint features of antiquity are often most faithfully perpetuated in these ancient lines; and I have traced an old family nose through a whole picture gallery, legitimately handed down from generation to generation, almost from the time of the Conquest. Something of the kind was to be observed in the worthy company around me. Many of their faces had evidently originated in a Gothic age, and been merely copied by succeeding generations; and there was one little girl, in particular, of staid demeanour, with a high Roman nose, and an antique vinegar aspect, who was a great favourite of the Squire's, being, as he said, a Bracebridge all over, and the very counterpart of one of his ancestors who figured in the court of Henry VIII.

The parson said grace, which was not a short familiar one, such as is commonly addressed to the Deity, in these unceremonious days; but a long, courtly, well-worded one of the ancient school. There was now a pause, as if something was expected; when suddenly the butler entered the hall with some degree of bustle; he was attended by a servant on each side with a large wax-light, and bore a silver dish, on which was an enormous pig's head decorated with rosemary, with a lemon in its mouth, which was placed with great formality at the head of the table. The moment this pageant made its appearance, the harper struck up a flourish; at the conclusion of which the young Oxonian, on receiving a hint from the Squire, gave, with an air of the most comic gravity, an old carol, the first verse of which was as follows:

> Caput apri defero
> Reddens laudes Domino.
> The boar's head in hand bring I,
> With garlands gay and rosemary.
> I pray you all sing merrily
> Qui estis in convivio.

Though prepared to witness many of these little eccentricities, from being apprised of the peculiar hobby of mine host; yet, I confess, the parade with which so odd a dish was introduced somewhat perplexed me, until I gathered from the conversation of the Squire and the parson that it was meant to represent the bringing in of the boar's head: a dish formerly served up with much ceremony, and the sound of minstrelsy and song, at great tables on Christmas day. 'I like the old custom,' said the Squire, 'not merely because it is stately and pleasing in itself, but because it was observed at the College of Oxford, at which I was educated. When I hear the old song chanted, it brings to mind the time when I was young and gamesome —and the noble old college-hall—and my fellow students loitering about in their black gowns; many of whom, poor lads, are now in their graves!'

The parson, however, whose mind was not haunted by such associations, and who was always more taken up with the text than the sentiment, objected to the Oxonian's version of the carol: which he affirmed was different from that sung at college. He went on, with the dry perseverance of a commentator, to give the college reading, accompanied by sundry annotations: addressing himself at first to the company at large; but finding their attention gradually diverted to other talk, and other objects, he lowered his tone as his number of auditors diminished, until he concluded his remarks, in an under voice, to a fat-headed old gentleman next him, who was silently engaged in the discussion of a huge plateful of turkey.

The table was literally loaded with good cheer, and presented an epitome of country abundance, in this season of overflowing larders. A distinguished post was allotted to 'ancient sirloin,' as mine host termed it; being, as he added, 'the standard of old English hospitality, and a joint of goodly presence, and full of expectation.' There were several dishes quaintly decorated, and which had evidently something traditionary in their embellishments; but about which, as I did not like to appear over-curious, I asked no questions.

I could not, however, but notice a pie, magnificently decorated with peacocks' feathers, in imitation of the tail of that bird, which overshadowed a considerable tract of the table. This the Squire confessed, with some little hesitation, was a pheasant-pie, though a peacock-pie was certainly the most authentical; but there had been such a mortality among the peacocks this season, that he could not prevail upon himself to have one killed.

When the cloth was removed, the butler brought in a huge silver vessel of rare and curious workmanship, which he placed before the Squire. Its appearance was hailed with acclamation; being the Wassail Bowl, so renowned in Christmas festivity. The contents had been prepared by the Squire himself; for it was a beverage in the skilful mixture of which he particularly prided himself; alleging that it was too abstruse and complex for the comprehension of an ordinary servant. It was a potation, indeed, that might well make the heart of a toper leap within him; being composed of the richest and raciest wines, highly spiced and sweetened, with roasted apples bobbing about the surface.

The old gentleman's whole countenance beamed with a serene look of indwelling delight, as he stirred this mighty bowl. Having raised it to his lips, with a hearty wish of a merry Christmas to all present, he sent it brimming round the board, for every one to follow his example, according to the primitive style; pronouncing it 'the ancient fountain of good feeling, where all hearts met together.'

There was much laughing and rallying as the honest emblem of Christmas joviality circulated, and was kissed rather coyly by the ladies. When it reached Master Simon he raised it in both hands, and with the air of a boon companion struck up an old Wassail chanson. . . .

Much of the conversation during dinner turned upon family topics, to which I was a stranger. There was, however, a great deal of rallying of Master Simon about some gay widow, with whom he was accused of having a flirtation. This attack was commenced by the ladies; but it was continued throughout the dinner by the fat-headed old gentleman next the parson, with the persevering assiduity of a slow-hound; being one of those long-winded jokers, who, though rather dull at starting game, are unrivalled for their talents in hunting it down. At every pause in the general conversation, he renewed his bantering in pretty much the same terms; winking hard at me with both eyes whenever he gave Master Simon what he considered a home thrust. The latter, indeed, seemed fond of being teased on the subject, as old bachelors are apt to be; and he took occasion to inform me, in an under-tone, that the lady in question was a prodigiously fine woman, and drove her own curricle.

The dinner-time passed away in this flow of innocent hilarity; and, though the old hall may have resounded in its time with many a scene of broader rout and revel, yet I doubt whether it ever witnessed more honest and genuine enjoyment. How easy it is for one benevolent being to diffuse pleasure around him; and how truly is a kind heart a fountain of gladness, making everything in its vicinity to freshen into smiles! The joyous disposition of the worthy Squire was perfectly contagious; he was happy himself, and disposed to make all the world happy; and the little eccentricities of his humour did but season, in a manner, the sweetness of his philanthropy.

When the ladies had retired, the conversation, as usual, became still more animated; many good things were broached which had been thought of during dinner, but which would not exactly do for a lady's ear; and though I cannot positively affirm that there was much wit uttered, yet I have certainly heard many contests of rare wit produce much less laughter.

I found the tide of wine and wassail fast gaining on the dry land of sober judgment. The company grew merrier and louder as their jokes grew duller. Master Simon was in as chirping a humour as a grasshopper filled with dew; his old songs grew of a warmer complexion, and he began to talk maudlin about the widow. He even gave a long song about the wooing of a widow, which he informed me he had gathered from an excellent black-letter work, entitled ' *Cupid's Solicitor for Love,* containing store of good advice for bachelors, and which he promised to lend me. The first verse was to this effect:

> He that will woo a widow must not dally,
> He must make hay while the sun doth shine;
> He must not stand with her, Shall I, Shall I?
> But boldly say, Widow, thou must be mine.

This song inspired the fat-headed old gentleman, who made several attempts to tell a rather broad story out of Joe Miller, that was pat to the purpose; but he always stuck in the middle, everybody recollecting the latter part excepting himself. The parson, too, began to show the effects of good cheer, having gradually settled down into a doze, and his wig sitting most suspiciously on one side. Just at this juncture we were summoned to the drawing-room, and, I suspect, at the private instigation of mine host, whose joviality seemed always tempered with a proper love of decorum.

After the dinner-table was removed, the hall was given up to the younger members of the family, who, prompted to all kind of noisy mirth by the Oxonian and Master Simon, made its old walls ring with their merriment, as they played at romping games. I delight in witnessing the gambols of children, and particularly at this happy holiday-season, and could not help stealing out of the drawing-room on hearing one of their peals of laughter. I found them at the game of blind-man's buff. Master Simon, who was the leader of their revels, and seemed on all occasions to fulfil the office that of ancient potentate, the Lord of Misrule, was blinded in the midst of the hall. The little beings were as busy about him as the mock fairies about Falstaff, pinching him, plucking at the skirts of his coat, and tickling him with straws. One fine blue-eyed girl of about thirteen, with her flaxen hair all in beautiful confusion, her frolic face in a glow, her frock half torn off her shoulders, a complete picture of a romp, was the chief tormentor; and from the slyness with which Master Simon avoided the smaller game, and hemmed this wild little nymph in corners, and obliged her to jump shrieking over chairs, I suspected the rogue of being not a whit more blinded than was convenient. . . .

Whilst we were all attention to the parson's stories, our ears were suddenly assailed by a burst of heterogeneous sounds from the hall, in which was mingled something like the clang of rude minstrelsy, with the uproar of many small voices and girlish laughter. The door suddenly flew open, and a train came trooping into the room, that might almost have been mistaken for the breaking up of the court of Fairy. That indefatigable spirit, Master Simon, in the faithful discharge of his duties as Lord of Misrule, had conceived the idea of a Christmas mummery, or masking; and having called in to his assist-ance the Oxonian and the young officer, who were equally ripe for anything that should occasion romping and merri-ment, they had carried it into instant effect. The old house-keeper had been consulted; the antique clothes-presses and wardrobes rummaged and made to yield up the relics of finery that had not seen the light for several generations; the younger part of the company had been privately convened from the parlour and hall, and the whole had been bedizened out, into a burlesque imitation of an antique masque.

Master Simon led the van, as 'Ancient Christmas,' quaintly apparelled in a ruff, a short cloak, which had very much the aspect of one of the old housekeeper's petticoats, and a hat that might have served for a village steeple, and must indubit-ably have figured in the days of the Covenanters. From under this his nose curved boldly forth, flushed with a frost-bitten bloom, that seemed the very trophy of a December blast. He was accompanied by the blue-eyed romp, dished up as 'Dame Mince-Pie,' in the venerable magnificence of faded brocade, long stomacher, peaked hat, and high-heeled shoes. The young officer appeared as Robin Hood, in a sporting dress of Kendal green, and a foraging cap with a gold tassel. The costume, to be sure, did not bear testimony to deep research, and there was an evident eye to the picturesque, natural to a young gallant in the presence of his mistress. The fair Julia hung on his arm in a pretty rustic dress, as 'Maid Marian.' The rest of the train had been metamorphosed in various ways; the girls trussed up in the finery of the ancient belles of the Bracebridge line, and the striplings bewhiskered with burnt cork, and gravely clad in broad skirts, hanging sleeves, and full-bottomed wigs, to represent the characters of Roast Beef, Plum Pudding, and other worthies celebrated in ancient maskings. The whole was under the control of the Oxonian, in the appropriate character of Misrule; and I observed that he exercised rather a mischievous sway with his wand over the smaller personages of the pageant.

The irruption of this motley crew, with beat of drum, according to ancient custom, was the consummation of up-roar and merriment. Master Simon covered himself with glory by the stateliness with which, as Ancient Christmas, he walked a minuet with the peerless, though giggling, Dame Mince-Pie. It was followed by a dance of all the characters, which, from its medley of costumes, seemed as though the old family por-traits had skipped down from their frames to join in the sport. Different centuries were figuring at cross hands and right and left; the dark ages were cutting pirouettes and rigadoons; and the days of Queen Bess jigging merrily down the middle, through a line of succeeding generations.

The worthy Squire contemplated these fantastic sports, and this resurrection of his old wardrobe, with the simple relish of childish delight. He stood chuckling and rubbing his hands, and scarcely hearing a word the parson said, notwithstanding that the latter was discoursing most authentically on the ancient and stately dance of the Paon, or Peacock, from which he conceived the minuet to be derived. For my part, I was in a continual excitement, from the varied scenes of whim and innocent gaiety passing before me. It was inspiring to see wild-eyed frolic and warm-hearted hospitality breaking out from among the chills and glooms of winter, and old age throw-ing off his apathy, and catching once more the freshness of youthful enjoyment. I felt also an interest in the scene, from the consideration that these fleeting customs were posting fast into oblivion, and that this was, perhaps, the only family in England in which the whole of them were still punctiliously observed. There was a quaintness, too, mingled with all this revelry that gave it a peculiar zest; it was suited to the time and place; and as the old Manor House almost reeled with mirth and wassail, it seemed echoing back the joviality of long/departed years.

WASHINGTON IRVING, *The Sketch Book of Geoffrey Crayon, Gent.* (1820).

A Warning to Waits

Charles Clapp, Benjamin Jackson, Denis Jelks, and Robert Prinset, were brought to Bow Street Office by O. Bond, the constable, charged with performing on several musical instruments in St Martin's Lane, at half/past twelve o'clock on Christmas morning, by Mr Munroe, the authorized principal Wait, appointed by the Court of Burgesses for the City and Liberty of Westminster, who alone considers him/self entitled, by his appointment, to apply for Christmas Boxes. He also urged that the prisoners, acting as minstrels, came under the meaning of the Vagrant Act, alluded to in 17th Geo. II.; however, on reference to the last Vagrant Act of the present King, the word 'minstrels' is omitted; consequently they are no longer cognizable under that Act of Parliament; and in addition to that, Mr Charles Clapp, one of the prisoners, pro/duced his indenture of having served seven years as an appren/tice to the profession of a musician to Mr Clay, who held the same appointment as Mr Munroe does under the Court of Burgesses. The prisoners were discharged, after receiving an admonition from Mr Hall, the sitting magistrate, not to collect Christmas Boxes.

The Gentleman's Magazine, 1822.

A Little Fête at Panshanger, 1829

The Princess Lieven got up a little fête such as is customary all over Germany. Three trees in great pots were put upon a long table covered with pink linen; each tree was illuminated with three circular tiers of coloured wax candles—blue, green, red, and white. Before each tree was displayed a quantity of toys, gloves, pocket handkerchiefs, work boxes, books, and various articles—presents made to the owner of the tree. It was very pretty. Here it was only for the children; in Germany the custom extends to persons of all ages.

CHARLES GREVILLE, *Memoirs*.

Tyrone Power on Broadway

January 1, 1834. On this day from an early hour every door in New York is open and all the good things possessed by the inmates paraded in lavish profusion. Every sort of vehicle is put in requisition. At an early hour a gentleman of whom I had a slight knowledge entered my room, accompanied by an elderly person I had never before seen, and who, on being named, excused himself for adopting such a frank mode of making my acquaintance, which he was pleased to add he much desired, and at once requested me to fall in with the custom of the day, whose privilege he had thus availed himself of, and accompany him on a visit to his family.

I was the last man on earth likely to decline an offer made in such a spirit; so entering his carriage, which was waiting, we drove to his house on Broadway, where, after being presented to a very amiable lady, his wife, and a pretty gentle-looking girl, his daughter, I partook of a sumptuous luncheon, drank a glass of champagne, and on the arrival of other visitors, made my bow, well pleased with my visit.

My host now begged me to make a few calls with him, explaining, as we drove along, the strict observances paid to this day throughout the State, and tracing the excellent custom to the early Dutch colonists. I paid several calls in company with my new friend, and at each place met a hearty welcome, when my companion suggested that I might have some compliments to make on my own account, and so leaving me, begged me to consider his carriage perfectly at my disposal. I left a card or two and made a couple of hurried visits, then returned to my hotel to think over the many beneficial effects likely to grow out of such a charitable custom which makes even the stranger sensible of the benevolent influence of this kindly day, and to wish for its continued observance.

TYRONE POWER, *Impressions of America.*

Origin of the Christmas Card

The Christmas Card proper had its tentative origin in 1846. Mr Joseph Cundall, a London artist, claims to have issued the first in that year. It was printed in lithography, coloured by hand, and was of the usual size of a lady's card.

Not until 1862, however, did the custom obtain any foot-hold. Then experiments were made with cards of the size of an ordinary *carte de visite*, inscribed simply 'A Merry Christmas' and 'A Happy New Year.' After that came to be added robins and holly branches, embossed figures and landscapes. 'I have the original designs before me now,' wrote 'Luke Limner' (John Leighton) to the London *Publishers' Circular*, 31st Dec. 1883: 'they were produced by Goodall & Son. Seeing a growing want and the great sale obtained abroad, this house produced (1868) a Little Red Riding Hood, a Hermit and his Cell, and many other subjects in which snow and the robin played a part.'

W. S. WALSH, *Curiosities of Popular Customs.*

Besieged Paris

Dec. 25th, 1870, *98th day of the Siege.* Never has a sadder Christmas dawned on any city. Cold, hunger, agony, grief, and despair sit enthroned at every habitation in Paris. It is the coldest day of the season and the fuel is very short; and the government has had to take hold of the fuel question, and the magnificent shade-trees that have for ages adorned the avenues of this city are all likely to go in the vain struggle to save France. So says the Official Journal of this morning. The sufferings of the past week exceed by far anything we have seen. There is scarcely any meat but horsemeat, and the government is now rationing. It carries out its work with impartiality. The omnibus-horse, the cab-horse, the work-horse, and the fancy-horse, all go alike in the mournful procession to the butchery shops—the magnificent blooded steed of the Roths-childs by the side of the old plug of the cabman. Fresh beef, mutton, pork are now out of the question. A little poultry yet remains at fabulous prices. In walking through the Rue St Lazare I saw a middling-sized goose and chicken for sale in a shop-window, and I had the curiosity to step in and inquire the price (rash man that I was). The price of the goose was twenty-five dollars, and the chicken seven dollars.

E. B. WASHBURNE, *Reminiscences of the*
Siege and Commune of Paris.

Captain Scott's Last Journey

Jan. 1st, 1911. At Christmas I got your letter, put into my hands by the radiant Teddy. . . . I wonder what you are doing. More especially of course I try to picture you on special dates. Where were you when we were making discord for the penguins at Christmas? You were to be nearing Colombo, weren't you? I sent glad thoughts to you, I wonder if you felt them. I looked out-of-doors in the evening on a truly Christmassy scene. On all sides an expanse of snow covered floes, a dull grey sky shedding fleecy snow flakes, every rope and spar had its little white deposit like the sugaring on a cake. A group of penguins were having highly amusing antics close by, and the sounds of revelry followed behind, but on the white curtain of feathery crystals I tried to picture your face, and I said God bless her for having been an unselfish wife, and the best of friends to an undeserving man.

CAPTAIN SCOTT, *in a letter to his wife.*

Christmas, 1914

We have all read what happened between the opposing armies, and how it came unexpected, undesigned, and yet willed with all the unconscious force of their natures. Not once or twice but again and again we hear of this sudden change upon the night of Christmas Eve, how there was singing upon one side answered by the other, and how the men rose and advanced to meet each other as if they had been released from a spell. Every one who tells of it speaks also of his own wonder as if he had seen a miracle; and some say that the darkness became strange and beautiful with lights as well as music, as if the armies had been gathered together there not for war but for the Christmas feast.

A. CLUTTON-BROCK, in *The Times.*

The First Air Raid

Christmas Day has come and gone and has left no memories even of the shortest truce behind it. We in England received, moreover, on Christmas Eve a new kind of warning of the activity of the enemy.　A hostile aeroplane, which had crossed the Channel, dropped a bomb into a garden not far from Dover Castle.　Except for the breaking of some windows by the concussion, no damage was done, and the aeroplane, which was only seen for a few seconds, disappeared over sea.

> Leading Article in *The Times*,
> 26th December 1914.

The King's First Christmas Broadcast

Broadcast by King George V on 25th December 1932: 'Through one of the marvels of modern science I am enabled this Christmas Day to speak to all my peoples throughout the Empire.　I take it as a good omen that wireless should have reached its present perfection at a time when the Empire has been linked in closer union, for it offers us immense possibilities to make that union closer still.

'It may be that our future will lay upon us more than one stern test.　Our past will have taught us how to meet it unshaken.　For the present the work to which we are all equally bound is to arrive at a reasoned tranquillity within our borders, to regain prosperity without self-seeking, and to carry with us those whom the burden of past years has disheartened or overborne.

'My life's aim has been to serve as I might towards those ends.　Your loyalty, your confidence in me has been my abundant reward.　I speak now from my home and from my heart to you all; to men and women so cut off by the snows, the desert, or the sea that only voices out of the air can reach them; to those cut off from fuller life by blindness, sickness, or infirmity, and to those who are celebrating this day with their children and their grandchildren—to all, to each, I wish a happy Christmas.　God bless you.'

Coldest Christmas of the Century

Severe cold at Christmas has been so rare since the nineties of last century that the very moderate degree of cold left over in the south-east of England from the bitter weather of December 18th and 19th sufficed to establish this Christmas a record for the present century for London. Compared with the previous coldest, which was in 1906, Kew mean temperature was 2½ degrees colder on Christmas Eve, 1 degree colder on Christmas Day, and ½ degree warmer yesterday. In 1906 the mean for the 3 days was 33·3 degrees and this Christmas 32·3 degrees.

The Times, 27th December 1938.

SWINGING TO A STAR

BY LESLIE D. WEATHERHEAD

SOME years ago a benefit night was arranged in a famous theatre in honour of a former music-hall star. In earlier days she had been a leading lady. Now she was old and frail and strangely timid. She arrived at the stage door in good time when the great night came. She was greeted almost perfunctorily. Some did not even seem to know her, nor did they care to do so. She flitted about noiselessly in the wings, sometimes pushed and elbowed by those who were to perform. They were more eager to know their place in the bill than even to nod a greeting to her. Many asked who she was. The whole evening of revelry was in her honour. Yet she was all but forgotten.

On Christmas night, this night of nights, when thousands of us are reunited with our families, giving ourselves up to mirth and song, let us pause to pay honour to Him from whom all this happiness comes. Let us remember that this is Christmass, the festival of Christ. Let us, on the wings of those lovely carols, go back in imagination to that mystic, starlight night, when God spoke to the world a new word, the word that became flesh and dwelt among us, until, in a human life—full of love, full of tenderness, full of utter self-giving—the nature of God was fully revealed.

It is the habit of some fathers, having given their child a present, to amuse themselves with it all Christmas afternoon. I have seen a father, having given his boy a Meccano set or a Hornby train, sneak off into a corner and play by himself, under the pretence of showing the child how the thing worked. But one wise father gave his little girl materials with which to make a model village and he played with her. They made a pretty little village with a church spire peeping up among the trees.

Then the father said: 'Betty, this is a Christian village. Let's turn it into a heathen one. What shall we have to take out?' 'The church,' said Betty; so that was lifted up and put back into the box. But before long Betty was nearly in tears, for her father said that it was the influence of Jesus that had been responsible for starting most of the healing work in the world. He explained that the first hospital, dating back to the end of the third century, was a place where hospitality was offered to Christian pilgrims on the way to Jerusalem. Many fell sick and were healed there or in an annexe of the building, called an infirmary. So the hospital was put back into the box. The orphanage followed and the old people's home, and even the jolly little school, for the first schools were church schools. When all these buildings had been removed, Betty said to her father: 'Daddy, I wouldn't like to live in that village, would you?' I am sure not one of my readers would.

I know how the churches have fallen into disfavour with some folk; but have we ever realized that, if we could remove from the fabric we call civilization all the influences which come from Christ, we should reduce it to a tattered and dirty rag? Perhaps only those of us who have lived in obscure places of the earth, such as an eastern village entirely untouched by the spirit of Christ, can realize just how awful life can be without His influence or how dark is that night which is unreached by the faintest glimmer of His grace. Do not let us forget on Christmas Day what we owe to Him!

It is His spirit which makes this day so wonderful. It is not merely the holiday spirit, for August does not produce anything like the spirit of goodwill which permeates Christmas Day. On that day, throughout the whole of Christendom there is a new spirit in the air. And it comes from Him. If only the spirit that is abroad in our land on Christmas Day could be maintained and deepened and secured, the era for which we all long would begin at once. For one day the great miracle happens. Man loves his brother man. The thing we've been preaching about for two thousand years is here. To-night a beggar will scarcely be turned away from any door. There is scarcely a heart that is not kind and loving and responsive to human need.

Isn't it a thrilling thought? I like to think that dignified directors of important companies at this moment are wearing pink tissue-paper hats taken out of crackers. They would rather die than let their smart and well-dressed typists see them like that. But there they are. It's Christmas. In a day or two they will be sitting back in leather-covered arm-chairs, the tips of their fingers together, dictating in sonorous tones letters to difficult customers or clients. Maiden aunts of severe demeanour, who usually affect a lorgnette—not that it helps them to see better, but it looks impressive!—are found declaring at the tops of their voices that 'John Brown's baby's got a cold upon his chest.' Solemn doctors put aside their bedside manner and are to-night found on all fours on the carpet making farmyard noises which make the kiddies squeal with delight. Theological professors eat nuts at Christmas instead of proving in other ways the theory of evolution!

And, in spite of much unhappiness and want, war and its many hardships, and the loneliness of some to whom our hearts go out in greeting, wherever they are, it is true to say that life is happier, hearts are lighter, minds are quickened to deeds of love and thoughts of others. It is Christmas!

The thought makes one almost sick with longing. Why can't it go on? Why can't this spirit be kept up? I don't mean the hilarity. I don't mean the mince pies and crackers. There must be an end to them. But why must we let go the spirit of unconquerable goodwill which holds our hearts at this hour? We need not. Listen to this bit of the good news: 'As many as received Him, to them gave He the right to become children of God.'

There are those who say that all Christ stood for is impracticable in this modern world; that His teaching is a beautiful ideal which could never possibly come true. It's a lie! Christmas Day is the proof that it's a lie. Why must we for ever call grim, ugly, beastly things 'facts' and lovely things 'ideals'? Can't an ideal ever become a fact? Of course it can, given only persisting will. Here is a sentence which came to me as I sat and pondered over these things: 'An ideal is a baby fact cradled in the minds of those who believe in God.'

During Christmas Day the world gets its sense of values right. Love, tenderness, sympathy, understanding, kindness, thought for others, unselfishness, humility—these qualities get full marks. For most of the year they are assessed at little value. They lie like gems in a drawer covered with dust. Sometimes we open the drawer and look at them—on Sundays for instance. We see them gleam dully, but we put them away and shut the drawer. At Christmas we take them out and wear them as a crown. They shine with all their glorious divine light and make glad the hearts of men.

Are you going to put them back to-morrow and take out greed, aggression, pride, self-assertion? The world thinks *they* are jewels worth having. By means of them one 'gets on in the world.' They are not jewels. They are fakes. The world has got its sense of values wrong and men are deceived by them. For this reason, in a world where all want peace, men make war. In a world where there is plenty for all, men starve. In a world which might be as happy as a spring morning, our hates and fears and suspicions and distrusts make bitter winter, heartless and cold as death. In a few weeks, ah, for some, in a few hours, we shall be back in the old, selfish habit tracks. Scrooge will be himself once more.

Will you join with me in a new resolution made in this witching hour? It is Christmas. His feast. For a few hours the world breathes a rarer, lovelier air. The nursery in every man's heart is unlocked. The Christ-child draws our stubborn necks as low as His manger. Let Him but rule our hearts all the year and a millennium will dawn.

A few years ago one of our most brilliant essayists wrote an article in which he said that the world was in such a state that, unless something happened to ameliorate it, pious men would do well to pray that God would swing this great planet so near to a star that the whole earth would be burnt up, and human quarrelling and strife and folly be brought to an end. I mused on the words until they took on a different meaning —'Swing the earth so near to a star—and bring human quarrel-ling, strife, and folly, to an end.' Yes, I agree, so long as the star is the Star of Bethlehem.

O my deir hert, young Jesus sweit,
Prepare thy creddil in my spreit,
And I sall rock thee in my hert
And never mair from thee depart.

But I sall praise thee evermoir
With sangis sweit unto thy gloir;
The knees of my hert sall I bow,
And sing that richt *Balulalow*.

ANONYMOUS.

THE CHRISTMAS OF THE FUTURE

BY FRANK SULLIVAN

THERE is every reason to believe that the old haphazard and unscientific methods of celebrating Christmas are slowly dying out and that the Christmas of the future will be observed with a maximum of efficiency and a minimum loss of energy.

In the past, Christmas as a holiday has often been fraught with danger to life and limb, but science is making rapid strides in the direction of making the Yuletide safe for democracy. An example of this: I heard only the other day of the admirable work a prominent inventor is doing to combat the holly menace. There are few of us who at one time or another have not received flesh wounds—not serious, to be sure, but none the less painful—as a result of sitting unawares on barbed holly left in chairs by frenzied Christmas-tree trimmers. Such lesions will soon be a thing of the past. I am not authorized to give details but I understand that within the year this inventor I speak of will have a serviceable and cheap rubber holly on the market, guaranteed not to puncture.

Other time-honoured Christmas features seem to have out-lived their day. You no longer find Christmas trees festooned with ropes of popcorn. Those of us who are in our forties can remember when days were spent popping corn and string-ing it into yards of trimming for the Christmas tree. By the time the tree was taken down at Twelfth Night the popcorn had hung long enough to acquire an attractively gamey tang, with a flavour of tinsel dust, lint, and dried evergreen needles. It was considered quite a delicacy by the small fry of those times. For years hot buttered popcorn seemed quite tame to me by comparison. This eating of mummified popcorn and the wholesale consumption by tots of Christmas-tree candles were probably, with the recent depression, the main factors in producing the dyspepsia which is so marked a characteristic of the generation of the present writer. (Popcorn and wax candles have joined the dodo and the Yule log.) The children of to-day must find some other means of acquiring acute indigestion. They are resourceful and ingenious, and will no doubt have little trouble doing so.

Another Christmas reform impends. I am told that within a year or two science will have stripped the kiss under the mistletoe of its terrors. For some time past experiments have been proceeding with a new automatic antiseptic mistletoe. The leaves are of sterilized green satin and the berries are made of indurated milk. It will function on the principle of the automatic sprinkler, in this manner: Two kissers approach the mistletoe in a spirit of holiday lust. As they square off under the mistletoe the heat generated by their fondness for each other releases hundreds of tiny sprinklers concealed in the mistletoe 'berries' and a spray of healing formaldehyde sifts gently down upon them like a benison, destroying all coryza, grippe, influenza, pneumonia, or tetanus germs that may be lurking about the kissers' kissers.

Of course, the antiseptic mistletoe is only a temporary measure. Eventually the kiss under the mistletoe must go, bag and baggage. It is unhygienic, sloppy, and sentimental; and it breeds unscientific thinking. It has no place in our modern life.

The Christmas of the future will be a triumph of science over waste. Energy now frittered away in futile holiday pursuits will be conserved for more constructive purposes. For one thing, Christmas will be made to end immediately after dinner on Christmas Day, thus eliminating the demoralizing Christmas afternoon, the most depressing few hours in the Christian calendar. I refer to the period from about three o'clock on, when reaction from the hysteria of trimming the tree and opening the presents has set in and all the world seems dark and dreary; when the fruit cake is irrevocably inside the celebrant and has made unmistakably clear its determination not to merge with the port wine, walnuts, oyster stuffing, cranberry sauce, and the rest of the Christmas viands. It is the time when the kiddies begin to do battle for the possession of the few toys that remain unbroken; and it is the time when daddy, called upon to fix the electric train, trips over the track—or the baby—and plunges headlong into the Christmas tree, ripping off the electrical trimmings and causing a short circuit. Christmas afternoon must go.

In the Christmas of the future the gift problem, with its associated problems of shopping, mailing, wrapping, ex-changing, etc., will cease to be the *bête noire* it is to-day. Every one will co-operate. Christmas cards will be mailed earlier and earlier until the bulk of them will have been delivered about the time the second income-tax instalments begin to clog the mails. Parcels will be wrapped more and more securely as the years go by until he will be a fast worker indeed who gets his presents all unwrapped by the second Sunday after Epiphany.

Shopping will not be the bedlam it is to-day. It will be controlled. The energies of women will be harnessed. There will be national leagues of shoppers. Teams from stores will compete with each other in shopping bouts under the rules now governing wrestling. It will be no time at all before controlled Christmas shopping has developed a hardy, buxom race of woman shoppers which might well serve as a first line of national defence in case of emergency. Perhaps it may eventually be said of the democratic countries that our victories were won on the counters of Wanamaker's or Selfridge's

One of the worst psychological effects of Christmas on people is the rage that follows when a person gives a friend a gift and the friend fails to reciprocate. This will be eliminated in the Christmas of the future by the Declaration of Gift. This will simply be a public notice of every citizen's Christmas intentions. Early in the fall every one will be required by law to file a list with the Collector of Internal Revenue of the persons to whom he proposes to give Christmas presents, with the nature and the planned cost of each gift.

These lists will be tacked up at the post office and department stores of each city for public scrutiny. Each person can examine the lists, find out what his friends are doing, and act accordingly. If I have you on my list for a necktie or a compact and I find from the public list that you have not put me down for anything, I can just cross you off my list. Or, if a citizen thinks he has a right to expect a present from a friend who has failed to declare to that effect, the injured party shall have the legal right to apply to the courts for a writ of mandamus compelling the defendant, or recalcitrant donor, to show cause why the aforesaid present should not be given to the plaintiff, or piqued donee.

Two people who find that they are giving each other presents of equal value can pair off like senators voting at Washington and cancel both gifts, taking the will for the deed. This practice will be called phantom giving.

As Christmas becomes more and more scientific and less encumbered with sentimental flubdub children will play less and less part in its celebration. The heaviest burden of the Christmas celebration has always fallen on the tots, for it is the season of the year when parents have to be coddled and humoured more than at any other time. The child has to simulate an unfelt curiosity in mysterious packages that arrive during December and are whisked furtively to the attic. Children have to compose letters to Santa Claus to placate

Christmas-crazed parents, and they are hauled off to depart-ment stores, where they are expected to display glee at the sight of a Santa Claus in palpably fake whiskers.

All this is too much of a strain on their little libidos. It fills their subconsciousnesses with impressions that pop out twenty or thirty years later in the most blood-curdling mani-festations. In the future it is probable that Santa Claus will be required to be clean-shaven and that only disciples of Dr Freud will be allowed to continue wearing a beard.

So it will go. As we progress scientifically we shall slough off the antiquated customs and leave off saying 'Merry Christ-mas' or drinking wassail (of slight nutritive value and totally lacking in the essential vitamins). The celebration of Christ-mas will become more and more efficient until it will at last be so efficient that it will become unnecessary to keep Christmas at all.

The Greeks Have No Words for It

Christmas time to a Greek is by no means considered as festive; in fact they look upon the twelve days which intervene between Christmas and Epiphany rather with abhorrence than otherwise; it is to them the season when ghosts and hob-goblins are supposed to be most rampant; it is generally cold, ungenial weather, and the Greeks of to-day, like their an-cestors, live contented only when the warm rays of the life-giving sun scorch them. They can get up no enthusiasm as we can about yule logs and blazing fires, for they have nothing to warm themselves with save small charcoal braziers capable of communicating heat to not more than one limb at a time.

                                        J. THEODORE BENT.

CHRISTMAS DECORATIONS

BY CONSTANCE SPRY

HAVE you ever, at a party, joined in a sort of game where you are asked to show how you strike a match, light a cigarette, or contemplate the perfections or imperfections of your manicure —the questioner undertaking to tell from the way you perform these simple and generally unconsidered actions whether you have a preponderance of masculine or feminine characteristics? It smacks of fortune-telling or character-reading, and has its charm.

I sometimes feel I should like to ask people: 'What is your vision of an ideal Christmas? Do you fall for evergreens tied up with shiny red ribbons? Would the boughs of your Christmas tree be bowed to the ground with brightly coloured ornaments, electric lights, and parcels tied with gay bows? Do you like the groaning board to be decorated with heaped fruits, scarlet bon-bons, and red candles, and do you listen for the sound of lusty carol singers? Or, on the other hand, do you fancy something more fairy-like, crystalline and delicate? Is your dream tree nothing but a glistening white form floodlit, or, at most, illuminated by slender white candles, the boughs bending slightly under the weight of swinging icicles and iridescent bubbles of glass? Do you see your table in terms of silver and white and glitter, and your Christmas music nothing louder than the tinkle of glass bells? I have an idea that if I knew these things I might hazard a guess about the sort of books you liked as a child and even, perhaps, have some idea about your taste in beauty and ornament.

In any case, I am sure one's feeling about Christmas derives from memories of one's childhood. These may be dim recollections of stories of snow maidens, or sleighs drawn by reindeer: the vision of pictures on a nursery screen, perhaps of little girls in bonnets and furry white pelisses, skating on gleaming lakes in improbable scenery. It may be just the line of a poem, 'sheds new-roofed with Carrara' dropping into one's memory from nowhere—or just a recollection of beholding in a toy-shop window the glorious, glamorous Christmas fairy, shimmering in silver gauze, flaxen-haired and star-crowned.

Whatever your taste may be, one thing is certain: Christmas is the time, in the matter of decoration, to let the fancy roam: to be inventive, creative, gay, light-hearted, and unafraid. I have often noticed that uninspired people, released by the Christmas spirit from fear of being criticized or laughed at, will show a taste and inventiveness—will produce decorative effects surprisingly more beautiful—than they will at other times of the year.

Since one idea begets another, and the description of one decoration will start a dozen ideas, I will tell you of some pretty and successful Christmas arrangements that I have made and which I hope and believe will start you off on a series of Christmas notions.

A Kissing Bunch

The simplest and oldest I remember from my nursery days, and its origin is buried in the mists of antiquity. We called it a kissing bunch: that was, I imagine, on account of the bunch of mistletoe which formed an important part of it; and it may be that it was popular at a time when mistletoe was a far more expensive item than it is now, so that a small spray often had to serve in place of the fine bunches one sees to-day. The kissing bunch is made with three (or, for large ones, four) hoops fixed one inside another to form a globe. Each hoop is bound separately with any material and colour you like— I use sometimes silver ribbons, or cellophane cut like a ham frill, or frosted holly leaves, or little sprigs of box or fir, or gold or red ribbons—whatever suits the case. When the binding is finished they are fitted together and tied firmly at top and bottom. Within this globe you may hang witch balls, Christmas bells, whatever you please, and at its base you should tie, with ribbons to match the binding, as big a spray of mistletoe as possible, touched with white paint, frost, or gilded and glittered with gold. The outside of the hoops may be hung with ornaments or you may leave them plain. When we were little, the making of the kissing bunch was one of the greatest pleasures of Christmas. The nursery curtains were drawn, the fire glowed, and oil lamps made an illuminated island of the table which was littered with tissue paper of gaudy colours and saucers of home-made paste, encircled by intent, pre-occupied and probably paste-smeared faces. Our business was to cut neat 'ham-frills' of the paper, and we were allowed to choose in turn from the range of colours—arsenic green, magenta pink, and wash-bag blue. When we had turned the frills inside out and pasted the edges together our nurse bound them in what we thought a delicious contrasting of colours round the hoops. Then came the thrill of tying on bags of coloured tarlatan filled with unwholesome-looking candies, sugar bird-cages, pink and white sugar mice, red and green Christmas ornaments—everything gaudy and gay, and to modern eyes impossibly tawdry. But to-day's version of the kissing bunch may be far from tawdry. The shape, a most important factor in all decoration, is good, and it is possible to make of it something quite beautiful; and I am grateful to those days when a Christmas tree was an expensive luxury, for the remembrance of that old nurse who delved among her childhood's memories to find a way to let us 'make something for Christmas.'

The Tree

The tree, of course, is the *clou* of Christmas decorations. My vision of this is something more stylized, more regular, than one usually succeeds in achieving with the ordinary fir-trees. This is due, I expect, to an early book I had, illustrated with old-fashioned wood-cuts, in which the Christmas trees looked like Noah's Ark trees—straight stems, straight branches holding a quite symmetrical arrangement of candles. Where a tree is to bear a heavy crop of presents this is of little use, and a child might be disappointed if aesthetic beauty were allowed to replace tradition. So you can really only use stylized versions of the Christmas tree as a decoration either in addition to an ordinary tree or for grown-up people with sophisticated taste. But when you find a chance to use them they can be lovely.

These are some of the ways I have made them. Three rings in graduated sizes are fastened to a central post which is fixed firmly in a pot. The post is first suitably bound. To the top four long ribbons are attached firmly. The first and smallest hoop is secured, at four equidistant points, to the ribbons, a few inches from the top. The second and third follow at whatever intervals appeal to your eye. In other words, your three hoops are suspended by four ribbons, crinoline fashion, from a central post which is fixed in a flower pot. This is the skeleton or framework on which you build up your formal trees. The prettiest ones I ever made had a silver post, silver ribbons, and the hoops were covered with fragile white wax camellias. Next, perhaps even tying with

it, was one in which the hoops were bound with whitened and
frosted holly leaves pointed at intervals with bunches of
scarlet berries. I have made others with evergreen leaves
and scarlet ribbons. The point of beauty is the symmetry
of the whole, and the precision with which the hoops are
bound. If, in the making, one loses form and neatness, there
is a chance that the whole may deteriorate into something
meaningless, even tawdry.

Frosted Boughs

At the extreme opposite of this stylized tree is something
that I like perhaps best of all. Sometimes I have cut a huge
and lovely bough from a tree, choosing one which has a good
shape and plenty of delicate bare branches and twigs. Very
often with me it is a branch of wild plum or damson, because
these trees have lots of small branchlets and twigs. I fix this
in a large pot or tub (it is generally so heavy that I have to get
a wedge of wood made to take it, and then use cement to secure
it); then I whiten it all over with distemper or flat paint, and
while this is still tacky I sprinkle it all over with 'frost' (the
white kind, not the silver glitter). At this stage, without any
ornaments at all, it has real beauty, and I am sparing and careful
in decorating it. A few iridescent glass bubbles, icicles, here
and there a delicate white frosted leaf, are all that it needs—
nothing tawdry or heavy.

It is an ethereally beautiful thing if one spot-lights it. Once
such a 'tree' as this was put in the recess formed by a window
in a large room and a good lighting effect arranged. When
the guests entered the room they caught their breath at its
beauty, and it was many a long week before any one could bear
to part with it: it had an essential quality of beauty which did
not depend on the Christmas season. It is difficult to convey

in words its quality of delicacy and grace: the nearest I can get
to it is to say that it looked like a delicate frosty tree in moonlight, but with a little fantasy added.

Two other pretty trees I remember. They were quite
simple: one was a well-pruned and shaped tree, whitened and
frosted, set in a frosted flower pot and decorated entirely with
delicate silver ornaments. Each white candle rose from the
heart of a white rosette. The second tree was left green and
pruned to a very regular shape. The branches had here and
there a few strands of silver fringe hung over them and the
white candles were tied on with small neat white bows.
This tree had dignity—almost a sort of austerity—and I remember thinking it a relief after having seen far too much
Christmas gaudiness.

How to avoid Tawdriness

I have a great dislike of tawdriness: no amount of gaiety
will excuse it to my mind, and yet one can use almost any
material and any colour if one uses it with feeling.

Decorations with evergreens can be beautiful: they can also
be rather dreary and untidy. To be really decorative I think
evergreens need to be harnessed to a shape and not spattered
about a room without any particular rhyme or reason. I use
two simple forms. For large rooms where I want to have
garlands on the walls I cut out of chicken wire the shape of a
formal swag—a crescent, really. This is covered with a layer of
moss which is bound in place with twine, and on to this
foundation I can fix leaves or sprays of fir and keep a regular
and formal outline. At the point of meeting of each crescent
one can make a drop-piece, or hang ribbons weighted with a
knot of evergreens and berries. For small rooms I prefer
what we call wall-drops; for these you cut out a shape—a star,

or circle, whatever you please—in chicken wire, and cover first with moss and then with leaves. Sometimes we whiten and frost them. These are then hung on long ribbons from the top of the wall or from the picture rail, and come to within about four feet of the floor. The ribbons hang like old-fashioned bell pulls and the 'drop' lies flat against the wall. One or two of these hung in suitable positions will give a room a decorated and gay air but without the untidiness, and in some cases destructiveness, of some types of Christmas decoration.

Mistletoe

Of course, Christmas isn't Christmas without mistletoe, but I do not think this always looks as pretty as it might. I have tried various ways of hanging it, and I think the most effective was as follows. I took a wide, straw garden hat, silvered and frosted it, and hung it with silver gauze ribbons. In this I arranged the mistletoe so that it cascaded out of the two ends of the hat, showed a little over the sides and was caught also in the bow that finished off the ends of ribbon. The mistletoe also was just touched here and there with white and frosted lightly.

Frosting and Glittering

For those who are not accustomed to 'frosting and glittering' I ought to say that the easiest way to make these powders adhere to the surface is either to sprinkle them on while the paint (white, silver or gold) is still sticky or, where no paint is used, to brush on a thin coating of artists' gum or ordinary gum made very thin with the addition of water. When this is nearly dry but still tacky the frost may be applied. I use a cheap sugar sifter for the purpose, and work always over sheets

of newspaper—otherwise I should waste far more than I used
of the glitter. Silver glitter is pretty and brilliant, but tarnishes
soon. The white powder sold as 'frost' is less brilliant—
prettier in some ways—and does not tarnish. Gold glitter
lasts well. White paint with silver glitter or frost is prettier
than silver paint, which looks to my taste too like aluminium,
so I rarely use it.

———————

La Galette du Roi

In France, where it probably originated, the Twelfth Night
cake, known as La Galette du Roi ('the king's cake'), still
survives.

The cake is generally made of pastry, and baked in a round
sheet like a pie. The size of the cake depends on the number
of persons in the company. In former times a broad bean
was baked in the cake, but now a small china doll is substituted

The cake is the last course in the dinner. One of the
youngest people at the table is asked to say to whom each
piece shall be given. This creates a little excitement and all
watch breathlessly to see who gets the doll. The person who
gets it is king or queen, and immediately chooses a king or
queen for a partner. So soon as the king and queen are
announced they are under the constant observation of the rest
of the party and whatever they do is immediately commented
upon. In a short time there is a perfect uproar: 'The king
drinks,' 'the queen speaks,' 'the queen laughs.' This is kept
up for a long time; then there are games, music, and dancing.

WILLIAM HONE, *The Everyday Book.*

COOK'S CHRISTMAS

BY MRS ARTHUR WEBB

THE British constitution is based and built upon tradition, and our Christmas meals are based upon tradition, and in spite of the prophesying to the contrary, British constitutions still survive the annual feast, and welcome each Christmas with appetites renewed.

From those great breakfast pasties, made with goose and capons, partridge and duck, chicken and hare, arranged one within the other like a Chinese puzzle box, and cooked under a canopy of thick pastry in enormous dishes, has survived the present breakfast of goose giblet pie, but for this the crust is no longer thick, but thin and light and short; the giblets, prepared with the utmost care, are stewed until tender in well-flavoured stock, then placed in a pie dish and left to cool and set in jelly, ready to receive the pastry top, and be baked for an hour in a hot oven, then left to serve cold.

To the unthinking, our Christmas feast is a collection of heavy-weights; but it is really a cleverly conceived and balanced collection of appetizing foods. Let's take the Christmas pudding, which has been evolved from that old, old mess of 'plum porridge,' which was too sloppy to be called pudding, and too thick to be eaten as soup. Our pudding is light in weight and dark in colour, pleasantly flavoured, with all the items so well blended and thoroughly cooked that no charge for indigestion can be brought against it. It has a great advantage inasmuch as it can be prepared and cooked months before Christmas, and, if well and truly made, any of its companions that are left over will keep for months after, so:—

The Christmas Pudding

1 lb. flour, 1 lb. breadcrumbs, 1 lb. each raisins, sultanas, and currants, ¼ lb. citron, ½ lb. mixed peel, 1 lb. shredded or chopped beef suet, 1 lb. Demerara sugar, 3 oz. sweet almonds, grated rinds and strained juice of 2 lemons, 1 teaspoonful each of salt, and mixed pudding spice, 3 teaspoonfuls of baking powder, 6 eggs, 1 pint of milk, 1 teaspoonful of essence of almonds.

Have everything ready before starting to make the pudding, the raisins stoned, almonds split very small, sultanas and currants picked over and rubbed in a coarse clean cloth to get rid of stalks, etc. Be sure that the sugar coating has been removed from the orange and lemon peel, and each piece slightly warmed to allow of quick and easy slicing, the fresh lemon rinds grated, juice strained, the bread rubbed into fine crumbs, and the suet shredded or chopped.

Take a large bowl, see that it is quite dry, put in all the other dry ingredients and mix them well together before adding suet and lemon rind which should be distributed evenly. Make a well in the centre, pour in the lemon juice, essence, beaten eggs, and more gradually the milk, beating all the time and blending everything so that all the ingredients are thoroughly moistened. Cover with a cloth, then leave for one hour (taking care that each member of the household has had a stir, and a wish).

Grease as many basins as you need, smearing lard over the insides so that there won't be any fear of sticking. After filling, cover with scalded cloths dusted with flour. Make a fold in centre of each cloth to allow for the pudding swelling, and tie with strong tape. Place in steamer or in a boiler and cook eight to ten hours.

You may object to so much bread, but take my word for it, if you cut a slice of this pudding cold, you'll find it tastes like cake, and eats like cake. Breadcrumbs make the puddings much more digestible than if flour only is used.

The pudding mixture can, of course, be varied to suit the tastes of the family, for instance, a few spoonfuls of brandy, half a dozen bitter almonds, a pinch of powdered ginger, or an ounce of crystallized ginger finely minced, or even the merest sprinkling of cayenne pepper, or the addition of strained orange juice, or maybe a more generous allowance of citron sliced and chopped, or perhaps more liberal proportions of sugar and shredded suet.

Many people have an idea that brandy or rum is essential to the safe keeping of the pudding, but this isn't correct; the skilfully made pudding, thoroughly boiled and kept in a dry, cool place, should be safe for many weeks, or even months.

With a pudding mixture in which breadcrumbs play so large a part, when it is so good cold, it may be worth while to make a

Pudding Cake Lady

that is, turn out one of the puddings after a long boiling of eight or nine hours and allow it to get cold; then brush it all over with white of egg lightly beaten. Into the centre top, tuck the base of the bust and head of a tiny china lady of the crinoline period. The cake—because that's what it is—is ready for a coating of white icing, and when the icing is set, the whole is decorated with delicate frills and flounces produced by means of the finest end of the icing tube loaded with smooth cream-like icing, perhaps tinted with a spot or two of carmine.

Alas! however elegant the Pudding Cake Lady may appear, she is better fitted for any other day than that on which the pudding is part of the feast, so another and much more conventional cake must be made ready, and here are the ingredients for

The Christmas Cake

1 lb. flour, ½ lb. butter, ½ lb. castor sugar, 12 oz. currants, 8 oz. sultanas, 4 oz. mixed peel and citron, 3 oz. glacé cherries, 3 oz almonds, 3 oz. ground almonds, 1½ teaspoonfuls baking powder, 1 teaspoonful mixed spice, 4 eggs, 1 eggcupful milk.

Clean the fruit, chop the peel and citron, halve and quarter the cherries, blanch and split the almonds, then mix the fruits together. Beat the butter and sugar to a creamy mixture, beat the eggs until frothy, then add them gradually to the butter and sugar. Sift the baking powder and flour into a bowl, add the mixed spice, and the ground almonds. Mix the fruit with the flour, then add it all lightly to the egg mixture, and finally stir in the milk very carefully. Have ready a suitable sized cake tin, greased and lined with double lining of greaseproof paper, cut to fit, and extend two inches above the tin. Turn the cake mixture into the tin and bake in a moderate oven 3½ hours.

This cake also calls for icing and decorations, but they can be added the day before Christmas, while the cake itself is better for keeping a week or two; the delay appears to give it substance, and enrich the flavour. And, speaking of flavour, perhaps a little essence of vanilla, or almond, or a spoonful of orange and lemon juice, or a dessertspoonful of brandy may be added in the making; again, it is a matter of taste, the cake is sufficiently good in itself.

It is pleasant to know that mincemeat will also improve with keeping, and as many of the ingredients in it are similar to those in the pudding, it's common sense to prepare extra raisins, currants, sultanas, etc. It's a very simple business, this matter of

Making the Mincemeat

1½ lb. apples, 1 lb. currants, 1 lb. raisins, ½ lb. sultanas, ¼ lb. mixed candied peel, 3 oz. citron, 1 lb. suet chopped fine or shredded, 1 lb. Demerara sugar, 3 oz. shredded almonds, (or Brazil nuts chopped very small), the grated rinds and juice of two lemons, 2 teaspoonfuls of mixed spice, 1 saltspoonful ground ginger, 1 saltspoonful salt, 1 teaspoonful vanilla essence.

Stone the raisins, and prepare the other fruit. Put raisins, sultanas and peel, citron, nuts and half the currants and apples through the mincer, using the coarse knife. After mincing, place in a bowl, add the sugar, currants, suet, shredded or chopped, and the remaining apples chopped small. Mix all well together, stir in the essence, spice, ginger, grated lemon rind, juice and essence. Put into jars and cover securely.

When choosing apples for mincemeat, select good firm fruit and let there be lots of nice chunky bits of apple in the mincemeat mixture. When the pies are cooked, they will be much tastier for the solid scraps of nicely flavoured apples.

Sometimes in winter the lemons arrive looking very green and unattractive. Don't use them like that, but hang them in a paper bag near the stove for a few days, and you'll find that the skins will have turned just the clear ripe-looking yellow that you need for grating, and besides, the warmth will have made the juice run more freely.

There is another matter of some importance, the pastry for the mince pies. This can be either 'short,' 'puff,' or 'flaky.' Whichever is chosen, the mince pies are more conveniently made the day before, because on Christmas Day the cook's time, and the oven, are taxed to their utmost capacity.

Mince Pies

1 lb. of flour, 10 oz. of butter or margarine, 1 level teaspoonful cream of tartar, 1 saltspoonful salt, very cold water to mix.

Sift together the flour, salt, and cream of tartar, and put through a sieve into a bowl. Divide the butter or margarine into small rounds like marbles, drop one by one into the flour. Don't rub them in, but see that they are well distributed, add the cold water very sparingly, stirring all the time. See that you only allow just sufficient to make a fairly firm paste. Dredge a board with flour, roll out pastry lightly, then fold in three, and leave for quarter of an hour before repeating the light rolling and folding; leave again for fifteen minutes before giving the third rolling and allowing it to remain flat, it's then ready to cut out into rounds to line small well-greased patty pans. Into each lined patty pan place a generous spoonful of mincemeat, wet the edge of pastry, cover with pastry round, press edges together, brush over with milk, sprinkle over a little castor sugar, and put at once into a hot oven and bake to a nice golden brown.

Mince pies were once wayfarers' pies, dispensed to every man, woman, and child who might call at the house, with or without a reason, on Christmas Day or New Year's Day.

The short crust pastry is not so delectable as 'flaky'; but it has merits, it is easily and quickly made, takes less fat, and needs only one rolling, and is held to be more digestible. For a small quantity, allow ½ lb. flour, ¼ teaspoonful baking powder, 1 teaspoonful castor sugar, 5 oz. butter or margarine, pinch of salt, 1 yolk of egg, ½ teaspoonful lemon juice, a spoonful or so of cold water.

Sift flour, baking powder, and salt and castor sugar into bowl. Cut the butter or margarine very small and rub lightly into the flour until fine as breadcrumbs. Mix the egg yolk and lemon juice with a tablespoonful of water, use it to mix the paste to a light dough. Knead it lightly, place on floured board, roll out to required thickness, cut into rounds, line the greased patty pans, fill, and cover with pastry tops. Bake in a good oven, and when cooked, dust over with castor sugar.

Roast Goose and Stuffing

For those Christmas dinners in the long ago, poultry and game, meat and fish, loaded the tables, and it is doubtful whether all of it was cooked properly, for however hot the huge fire, and however hard the wretched kitchen boys worked, turning and basting the birds and joints, sufficient heat could not reach them all. Think of the herons and peacocks, bustards and swans with which the guests were regaled. It seems that they loved very fishy fowls.

To-day, a goose or a duck is looked upon as strong meat, and so it is with all the succulent forcemeat lining, that generous stuffing of onions, sage, and breadcrumbs, spiced with pepper and salt. It has always been a matter for conjecture whether the stuffing flavours the goose, or the goose flavours the stuffing, but whoever invented the mixture was a genius, because it is exactly right for the purpose.

As you will want to make giblet pie, when you purchase the goose give directions for all the giblets to be prepared and sent home with the goose. These should include the head, all scalded and clean, attached to the long neck, freed of feathers and ready to cut into sections, the webbed feet, the big meaty gizzard, the large liver, and the heart, and the pair of secondary wing bones. They are a considerable weight, but they were paid for and weighed with the goose. Two hours' gentle stewing, in water just to cover, with a teaspoonful of salt, two onions, a carrot and a turnip, and those giblets will be welcome pie meat, as suggested in the beginning.

Don't accept anybody's word that the goose itself is clean inside, but wipe it out with a cloth wrung out of hot water. To stuff the goose economically, prepare plenty of onions and breadcrumbs the day before. For a 10-lb. goose have 12 oz. fine crumbs, 3 teaspoonfuls sage finely chopped, 6 medium-sized onions, boiled until tender, then chopped small. Mix these together with a seasoning of pepper and salt. The stuffing can be left. When ready to start the cooking, melt a tablespoonful of butter and stir into the stuffing. Push the mixture into the body of the goose, make a slit in the loose skin or apron at the end of breast, and slip the rump through the slit. Tie the skin at neck and bring the string back to and under the rump, thus securing both ends. Place wings and legs close to the sides and fasten with two strong clean skewers thrust through the bird from side to side. Put the goose in a deep baking tin, arrange the 'leaf,' as the piece of loose fat from the body is called, on the breast, place in a hot oven for the first half hour; the heat should be reduced a little for the next two hours. Baste with the fat which will flow from the 'leaf' and dredge with flour, thus forming a crisp appetizing crust which will save the bird from hardening. (For a smaller goose 1½ to 2 hours will be sufficient time for cooking.) See that the dish to receive the goose is very hot, then take out the skewers and cut away the string. Have ready a nice brown gravy and plenty of apple sauce.

Apple Sauce

No one can afford to be called mean for the sake of saving three or four apples, so be generous with the fruit when making the sauce, and don't grudge a little extra trouble to keep the sauce an appetizingly light colour—it is easy enough. Choose good cooking apples, peel them quickly, cut and core them, and slip each piece as prepared into a basin containing a quart of cold water with a teaspoonful of salt in it. Keep the apples down with a saucer or small plate, and when sufficient are prepared, drain quickly, put into a saucepan, add 2 table-spoonfuls water, put on the lid, place pan over gentle heat until apples are simmering; shake occasionally to prevent them sticking to the bottom of the pan, add sugar to taste, a knob of butter, a pinch of salt, and, if liked, a sprinkling of nutmeg, beat with wooden spoon, serve, hot in a hot tureen, and a *tablespoonful or more* will be appreciated better than the teaspoonful that is occasionally thought to be a 'helping.'

If the family is very small, it may be policy to order a good chicken, plump and white and tender. It can be stuffed and roasted like turkey, and have all the trimmings served with it, not forgetting very small sausages to drape it at the moment of dishing. Bread sauce may be served, but just add a little cranberry sauce as well. It will look and taste more Christ-massy.

Choosing the Turkey

While for many years Goose was Lord of the Christmas feast, and the little black turkey, that didn't weigh much more than half of the present type of turkey, was a third or fourth choice, to-day the order is reversed, and turkey is crowned; so if you are buying one of these noble birds choose a turkey that is short and plump rather than long and thin. See that the skin is white, and the legs are very glossy. And when you have bought it, wait while a label bearing your name and address is attached to the neck. That care may save a lot of disappointment. Are you good at trussing a turkey, or will you get it done for you? Be sure you have the giblets, the long neck, the gizzard, liver, and heart, returned with the turkey. They are all valuable food, and with them you can make gravy, and perhaps a light nourishing soup, and still have them to serve as part of a secondary dish of curry or stew another day.

Preparing the Turkey

You must be particular to see that the loose skin at the neck-end, left by the removal of the crop, is clean and ready to receive the stuffing, which should be prepared on a generous scale. Extra expense, you think? Not a bit of it. Every item of which forcemeat is made is cheaper than turkey, and if it makes the bird go further—well, there you have it—an economy. Before we deal with the stuffing, let me remind you to draw the sinews from the legs, otherwise they'll be tough. If the sinews have not been removed when you receive your bird, follow these simple directions. Break each leg just above the foot, fasten each foot down on the table with a small nail or a bradawl, catch hold of the strong white sinews, and then pull. They should come out. There's the forcemeat to make, and you should be *sure* to get this ready the day before. Here is a useful forcemeat:

½ lb. fine breadcrumbs, 3 oz. shredded suet, 2 teaspoonfuls parsley, 1 teaspoonful mixed herbs, 1 egg, ½ teacupful milk, pepper, salt, nutmeg, and a pinch of grated lemon rind.

Mix all these ingredients thoroughly, stuff into the neck, follow with 1½ lb. of sausage meat, then fasten the skin over securely with the help of a short skewer. Don't forget the chestnuts, they should be ready beforehand, because you may like to blanch and steam ½ lb. and add them at the last moment to the forcemeat, and put them in with the sausage-meat. And anyway, about 2 dozen cooked chestnuts should be ready to slip into the body of the bird to serve with it.

See that the legs are skewered through and tied, and that the wings also are skewered firmly in place. Make sure you have both sides alike, or the bird will be lopsided when ready to serve.

How to cook the Turkey

Have the oven hot at first, then reduce the heat a little. If you have any bacon dripping, or a little fat bacon, put it on the turkey. Keep the bird basted, and allow fifteen minutes to each pound. It should be browned all over. Twenty minutes before it is served put a string of small sausages in a pan and cook them ready to hang round the turkey. Make plenty of rich brown gravy. It is easy enough if you pour nearly all the fat out of the meat pan, put in a spoonful of flour, and cook it over the fire, stirring until smooth, then add a large cupful of the stock from boiling the giblets. For vegetables you have a choice of stewed celery, browned potatoes, Brussels sprouts, and, of course, the delicious chestnuts. And for sauce, what? Cranberry or bread sauce? If cranberry, allow one pound of berries, half a teacupful of sugar, rind of half a lemon. Wash the cranberries, put into saucepan, cover with water, add sugar and rind, simmer until soft. Press through sieve, warm up, serve!

Beef and Pork

Perhaps, after all, beef may be chosen, in which case, sirloin, large or small, seems more in keeping; and, while less lordly in appearance, if boned and rolled into a neat round it is much easier to carve. But whichever piece of beef is chosen for roasting, the Christmas joint demands, as a garnish, small heaps of shavings from the very freshest of horse radish. If the top of the meat is rubbed with a level tablespoonful of flour in which a saltspoon each of sugar and salt and a pinch of pepper have been mixed, the flavour of the gravy will be doubled in value, and the meat itself will be all the tastier.

If the beef is English or Scotch, place it in a hot oven for the first half hour and reduce the heat afterwards, but if it is imported meat, a cool oven first and after half an hour let the heat be gradually increased to a hot oven temperature. Why? Because the juices in the home-killed meat are required to be sealed in at once, and so the hot oven is expected to cause a crust to form for this purpose, but the imported joint has been chilled, and all the juices in it must flow freely before the real cooking starts.

If a leg or loin of pork finds favour for the Christmas dinner, see that it has plenty of time to cook right through to the bone. Underdone pork can never be digestible, so 25 minutes for each pound, and an extra 20 minutes at the end to make sure, is a safe roasting time for pork, and don't allow less. Again, apple sauce is the rightful companion to serve with it.

Hard Sauce

Finally, one last word about a sauce for the Christmas pudding. Possibly the cream jug, filled with real or synthetic cream, or the tureen with custard flavoured with a little wine have reduced the demand for hard sauce, once so popular. This sauce is made with 6 oz. castor sugar, 3 oz. butter, 4 tablespoonfuls brandy or rum.

See that the butter chosen is unsalted, place in basin with the sugar, beat until light and frothy, then add the spirit a little at a time and beat into the mixture. Press into a small glass dish, and put away in a cool place until required.

WINE IN THE CELLAR

BY EDMOND SEGRAVE

'By the belly of Sanct Buf,' cried Pantagruel, unpolished as ever, but to the point, 'let us talk of our drink.' At Christ-mas time it is a wise and pleasant counsel; for Christmas and wine go hand in hand as companionably as the Gemini and their divorce presents as unnatural and pitiful a spectacle as ever made good men sigh. Surely we may refuse to argue about this lawful and beautiful union. If some cantankerous Pussy-foot rises to forbid the banns, let his foolish protests die without an echo. Indeed, let us be a model to him in temperateness as in lovingkindness, wish him the compliments of the season, and hope that he will have no trouble with his water-pipes if the weather turns frosty. Let him go hence. This book is called *The Christmas Companion*; Christmas means peace and goodwill, and Companion, so the dictionaries say, means 'table-fellow.' The matter is settled; let us see to our cellar.

First, a reassurance about cellars. Much of the literature on wine and not a few wine-merchants' lists give explicit and careful instructions about the care of the wine cellar. These hints, excellent in themselves, and kindly intended for our guidance, do little more than bring home to most of us a sense of our limitations. The cellar must be constructed in this way and not that, it must be on that soil and not this, we must beware of cobwebs or the smell of cats, and avoid draughts and a window that does not face north. To the man living in a top-floor flat these counsels of perfection are vaguely distressing. He would like to keep a small store of

196

wine under his roof, but feels there is little point in doing so
if it is doomed to ruin. Let him not despair. A good cellar
simplifies the storing of wine, but it is by no means essential.
If it were, the wine trade, at any rate in London (where new
blocks of flats grow like asparagus in May and the few houses
that remain are proudly advertised as 'non-basement'), is
surely sunk. Actually, a cupboard will serve the purpose
admirably. It should be fairly free from draughts yet not
absolutely airtight. It should also be cool. *It should also be cool.*
When first I inspected my own London flat the landlord's
agent showed off to me, with justifiable pride, the admirably
capacious wine cupboard. In due course the lease was signed
and the keys handed over, the wine cupboard key arriving with
suitable decorum on its own key-ring. With enthusiasm I
had bins made to measure and fitted. In high summer their
occupants moved in. Came the autumn, the turning on of
the central heating, and the discovery that the wine cupboard
was flanked on two of its sides by a ruthlessly efficient hot-
water system. Perhaps the architect was fond of mulled claret.

Having selected and appropriated your cupboard, store
your bottles of wine therein in a horizontal position, so that
the corks may be kept moist; otherwise they may shrink and
allow air to get to the wine, which will then be spoilt. The
best and most convenient manner of storing wine is to procure
a bin of the sort made of strips of wood and metal with a
separate compartment for each bottle. These can be made in
units of any size or shape and their cost works out at from
threepence to fourpence a compartment. A small cupboard
four feet high and three feet wide will hold a bin that
will take nine dozen bottles of wine. Such a bin will
cost about thirty shillings, which does not seem to be
an extravagant sum to expend on a piece of furniture that
will keep your wines in perfect condition, and which, when
inhabited, will unfailingly gladden your eye and heart. It

lasts for ever and, with its precious complement, may be left in your will to some worthy and much-loved friend.   At this point somebody may possibly ask: 'But why store wine at all? What are wine merchants' delivery-men for?'   The answer is twofold.   Firstly, good wine is disturbed by violent move-ment and needs time to collect itself after travel, a point to be remembered if you are ordering in the Christmas rush: secondly, all wine is much cheaper when young than in its maturity.   It is possible this year, for instance, to buy a Château Cos d'Estournel of 1934 vintage, a classed growth of St Estèphe, at four shillings a bottle.   If it runs true to the form it is showing now it will be worth at least half as much again a few years hence.   In matters of this sort you will depend on the wise judgment and kindly advice of your wine merchant. Go to a good man: he will not only sell you better wine, but in all probability will sell it you more cheaply.   I would not wantonly say a word to hurt the feelings of grocers: they are hard-working and honest men; but they have too many things to worry about and cannot give their minds and hearts to any one of them.   The good wine-seller is necessarily a specialist.

Let us go to him.

Claret

Claret is the generic name given in England to the red wines of Bordeaux.   It comes first by natural right; for to a degree that no other wine in the world can equal it offers a range of style, quality, and price to suit all tastes and all pockets.   Un-excelled in its delicacy and purity it is yet sufficiently robust of itself to require no fortification by sugar or alcohol.   There is scarcely any limit to its variety.   The palate that is tired of claret is probably worn out.

Claret is made in the department of the Gironde in the south-western corner of France. There are four main districts in the region: Médoc, Saint-Émilion, Pomerol, Graves. (A word here about the last-named: Graves produces some of the noblest red wine in France, but because the name in this country has become a synonym for inexpensive sweet white wine, the makers of red Graves generally prefer to omit the name. Château Haut-Brion, always a wine to say grace for, is a red Graves.) These districts are divided into parishes or communes, of which the best known are Margaux, Saint-Julien, Saint-Estèphe, and Pauillac. Each parish contains innumerable vineyards, each of which has its château. You will thus find some bottles labelled with the name of the château where the wine was made, others bearing only the name of the parish or the district whence it came, and still others bearing simply the name of the province. An obvious and reasonable assumption to be made is that the more accurately detailed the name and address on the label, the better will be the wine. Therefore, a bottle of wine labelled 'Bordeaux,' *tout court*, may contain anything at all, probably comes from Africa's sunny shores, and should not cost more than one and ninepence. You ought not, in fairness, to bring it to any higher hopes or demands than you would to a bottle of unsponsored whisky labelled with the one word 'Scotch.' Nearly all the châteaux make a practice of bottling their own wines; accordingly you will look for, and accept with confidence, the legend 'Mis en bouteilles au château,' printed on the label, as a guarantee that all such wine is genuine. It is also a guarantee of quality, for wine growers possess a fine *amour-propre* and their signed pieces have to be very good indeed. There are thousands of châteaux: of these some sixty are listed in an official classification of clarets according to their merits. This is given in the following pages. The names of the parishes in which the châteaux are situated are printed in italics.

THE OFFICIAL CLASSIFICATION OF CLARETS

First Growths

Château Lafite (*Pauillac*).
Château Margaux (*Margaux*).
Château Latour (*Pauillac*).
Château Haut-Brion (*Pessac*).

Second Growths

Mouton-Rothschild (*Pauillac*).
Rausan-Segla (*Margaux*).
Rausan-Gassies (*Margaux*).
Léoville-Lascases (*Saint-Julien*)
Léoville-Poyferre (*Saint-Julien*).
Léoville-Barton (*Saint-Julien*).
Durfort-Vivens (*Margaux*).
Gruaud-Larose-Sarget (*Saint-Julien*).
Gruaud-Larose-Faure (*Saint-Julien*).
Lascombes (*Margaux*).
Brane-Cantenac (*Cantenac*).
Pichon-Longueville (*Pauillac*).
Pichon-Longueville-Lalande (*Pauillac*).
Ducru-Beaucaillou (*Saint-Julien*).
Cos d'Estournel (*Saint-Estèphe*).
Montrose (*Saint-Estèphe*).

Third Growths

Kirwan (*Cantenac*).
D'Issan (*Cantenac*).
Lagrange (*Saint-Julien*).
Langoa (*Saint-Julien*).

Giscours (*Labarde*).
Malescot-Saint-Exupéry (*Margaux*).
Cantenac-Brown (*Cantenac*).
Palmer (*Cantenac*).
La Lagune (*Ludon*).
Desmirail (*Margaux*).
Calon-Ségur (*Sainte-Estèphe*).
Ferrière (*Margaux*).
Marquis d'Alesme-Becker (*Margaux*).

Fourth Growths

Saint-Pierre-Sevaistre (*Saint-Julien*).
Saint-Pierre-Bontemps-Dubarry (*Saint-Julien*).
Branaire-Ducru (*Saint-Julien*).
Talbot d'Aux (*Saint-Julien*).
Duhart-Milon (*Pauillac*).
Poujet (*Cantenac*).
La Tour-Carnet (*Saint-Laurent*).
Rochet (*Saint-Estèphe*).
Beychevelle (*Saint-Julien*).
Le Prieuré (*Cantenac*).
Marquis de Terme (*Margaux*).

Fifth Growths

Pontet-Canet (*Pauillac*).
Betailley (*Pauillac*).
Grand-Puy-Lacoste (*Pauillac*).
Grand-Puy-Ducasse (*Pauillac*).
Lynch-Bages (*Pauillac*).
Lynch-Moussas (*Pauillac*).
Dauzac (*Labarde*).
Mouton-d'Armailhacq (*Pauillac*).
Du Tertre (*Arsac*).

Haut-Bages (*Pauillac*).

Pédesclaux (*Pauillac*).

Belgrave (*Saint-Laurent*).

Camensac (*Saint-Laurent*).

Cos-Labory (*Saint-Estèphe*).

Clerc-Milon (*Pauillac*).

Croizet-Bages (*Pauillac*).

Cantemerle (*Macau*).

Graves

Among the best red Graves are La Mission-Haut-Brion, Pape-Clément, Haut-Bailly, Olivier, and Bellegrave.

Saint-Émilion

The wine of Saint-Émilion, say the Bordelais, is the claret nearest in style to Burgundy. The outstanding growths in this district are Château Ausone, Château Cheval Blanc, and Château Figeac.

The foregoing lists form the Debrett of Claret. Some of its members are great princes and command reverence; all of them are noble. The classification of the Médoc châteaux was made in the middle of the last century, and nowadays the experts agree that it requires some readjustment, for while the excellences of the higher growths remain undimmed, some of the lower growths have improved greatly and merit a higher rank. It must not be forgotten, however, that outside these honours lists are very many wines of more bourgeois breeding which are altogether excellent, and are generally cheaper, particularly if they have been bottled in this country.

A bottle of good ordinary red Bordeaux can be bought sometimes for half a crown, frequently for three shillings. For four shillings a bottle, you can drink excellent district wine of a good year; for five, you can get château wine, bottled in

England, good enough to satisfy all but the most pampered palates; for six, you can buy château-bottled wine. The figure seven, in terms of shillings per bottle, is the mystic number which makes you free of the great names and the vintage years of claret. At that price and over you can set wine upon your table that will allow you to look your most important guest boldly in the eye. For claret worth half a guinea a bottle you can safely have Lucullus to dine.

THE SERVING OF CLARET. The classic rule that claret should be drunk at the temperature of the room requires some little qualification in this country, for dining-rooms in the stately homes of England can be chilly places, while in the new, centrally-heated flats they can be constantly hot. It may be clearer to say that a glass of claret should not strike cold to the encircling fingers nor to the lips. It should be gently and gradually warmed. Some hours before it is to be drunk remove the bottle of wine from its horizontal position in its place of storage and stand it upright in a room of average warmth. Be careful not to overdo this warming business; do not put the wine in front of a cheerful Christmassy fire; the nearest it should come to the fire is the end of a wide mantelshelf. An hour or so before the meal remove the cork, in order to let the wine 'breathe.' An efficacious method of bringing the wine into contact with the air is to transfer it to a decanter which is perfectly dry and has had the chill taken off it. Pour the wine carefully down the side of the decanter neck, with your eye watchful for the appearance of any sediment towards the end. If and when it does appear, cease pouring; better to sacrifice the last half-glassful than spoil the whole.

Claret is best drunk from large glasses which should be only half filled: in that way its fragrance can best be perceived and appreciated. Claret goes well with all red meat and game, and can be served throughout the meal from the end of the fish course onwards.

Burgundy

Burgundy is a wine of such splendour and glory that men have sacked the tongues of Europe to find words to convey its solemn grandeur. This chapter will not rush limping in where the lords of language have already trodden so fearfully, but will merely state that genuine burgundy is hard to find in this country and is pretty expensive when you do find it. The piled pyramids of bottles labelled Beaune and Pommard which confront you in the windows of every off-licence that calls itself a wine shop do not contradict this fact; they merely illustrate what Lord Baldwin once called the many-sidedness of truth. The matter is largely one of simple geometry. Côte d'Or, the burgundy district, is smaller than the Bordeaux district, and some of the most famous burgundy estates are tiny. The estate of Chambertin consists of an area of 67 acres divided among twenty-five owners, each owner having, on an average, about 2½ acres. Romanée-Conti has an area of only 4½ acres and is divided between two owners. Clos-Vougeot, the largest of the growths of burgundy, has 125 acres and thirty-eight owners. Compare the size of these estates with that of Château Margaux, which holds equivalent rank in the hierarchy of claret, and which has 225 acres of vines producing annually well over 1,000 hogsheads of first-quality wine. Add to this comparison the further considerations that the yield per acre in the Côte d'Or is smaller than it is in the Gironde, and that such burgundy as is exported goes chiefly to Belgium, and you will perceive that its scarcity and comparatively high cost are reasonable. But, you ask, does this mean that nearly all the burgundy in this country is inferior? It does not. It merely emphasizes the need of dealing with a good wine merchant. Since the Burgundian owner is a small holder and cannot support the general costs of a business house on the same scale as do his confrères of Bordeaux, who bottle and dispatch their wines themselves, he reaches his public through mer-chants. If you buy a château-bottled claret, say a Château Margaux 1928, you will find the name printed boldly on the label and branded on the cork. It is a guarantee as unim-peachable as the government hall-mark stamped on your silver. Moreover it does not matter whether you buy this wine from Jones in London, or Smith in Edinburgh, or Brown in Liver-pool: they will all sell you the same wine, and any variations in it will be due only to variation in cellar treatment. With burgundy it is different. The Chambertin 1928 of Messrs A, stocked by Jones of London, may be entirely different from the Chambertin 1928 of Messrs B, retailed by Brown of Liverpool. M. de Cassagnac puts the matter succinctly when he says: 'The only guarantee of authenticity is the honesty of the merchant. The owner doesn't come into it at all and provides no security. The value of the wine is the value of the seller.'

The following are some of the famous vineyards:

> Chambertin (*Gevrey-Chambertin*).
> Richebourg (*Vosne-Romanée*).
> Romanée-Conti (*Vosne-Romanée*).
> Clos de Bèze (*Gevrey-Chambertin*).
> Clos de Vougeot (*Vougeot*).
> Corton (*Aloxe-Corton*).
> Saint-Georges (*Nuits Saint-Georges*).
> Les Grandes Échezeaux (*Flagey-Échezeaux*).
> Romanée-Saint-Vivant (*Vosne-Romanée*).
> Musigny (*Chambolle-Musigny*).

For burgundy of goodish quality you must be prepared to pay seven shillings (you see the mystic number in the Gironde becomes the lowest entrance fee in the Côte d'Or); a first-rate wine will cost you ten shillings and more. Many burgundy drinkers in this country urge that it should be bottled here. With only a few precious hogsheads to do credit to their name, runs the argument, English merchants would bring to the bottling a degree of care and zeal which the wine does not now always receive. There is sense in the argument and I confess that, for my own part, I like the labels on my burgundy to bear some prosaic superscription such as: '*Specially imported, bottled and guaranteed by* . . . ' followed by a name of a tried and trusty friend. Some burgundy labels bear the letters 'P. T. G.,' which stand for *Passe tous grains*, and mean that no process of selection or rejection has impeded the grapes' journey to the vat.

THE SERVING OF BURGUNDY. Opinion seems to be divided upon the question of whether burgundy should be drunk warmed, like claret, or brought to the table with the cellar chill still upon it. The latter school maintain that the gradual expansion of the wine's bouquet in the glass offers a pleasure equal to that of drinking it. Obviously it is a matter to be decided by individual taste. Burgundy, like claret, is served with red meat and game. Even more than claret it demands large glasses, and the 'only-half-full' instruction, a precept as regards claret, becomes a command for burgundy.

White Burgundy

The white wines of Burgundy are equal in quality to the red wines of their own or any other district. For similar reasons the genuine ones are relatively scarce and are expensive.

Chablis (not, geographically, a burgundy, but so closely associated with it in character, and so well known by name that some wine merchants use it in their catalogues as a generic title for all white burgundies) is a dry and very pale wine.

Montrachet, Pouilly, Meursault are other great names deserving of all honour. Every now and again I hear—always at second or third hand—of wonderful bottles of Montrachet or Meursault that have been procured at three or four shillings apiece, but whenever I have myself embarked on such speculative bargain-hunting my subsequent repent-ance has been of both body and soul. There is nothing nastier than bad white wine.

White burgundies must be served cold; but they must not be frozen to death.

White Bordeaux

There are two main groups of white Bordeaux: Sauternes and Graves. Let it be emphasized at once that Sauternes are dessert wines. (Repeat three times after me—it is important: 'Sauternes with dessert, Sauternes with dessert, Sauternes with dessert.') Matchmaking hints in cookery books, and even in wine merchants' catalogues, invite one to serve Sauternes with the fish course. It is an incompatible marriage, and is largely responsible, I should say, for the low esteem in which sweet white wines are held in this country. Similarly, the absurd convention that 'white wines for the ladies' must be ordered in restaurants is probably the cause of many women thinking that they do not like wine, poor things. A Château Pey-raguey drunk at its right place—i.e. the end of a meal—is sheer ambrosia; but to consume it with the *entrée* would be like eating a beefsteak garnished with treacle.

The greatest of Sauternes is the incomparable Château Yquem. There is no other wine in the world quite like it, and, though it is expensive, every man owes it to his palate to have tasted it once. Fifteen shillings, for which you can procure a choice vintage, is not an excessive price to pay to sup on Olympus.

The classification of the white wines of Sauternes was drawn up thus in 1855:

Great First Growth

Château Yquem (*Sauternes*).

First Growths

Château Climens (*Barsac*).
Château Coutet (*Barsac*).
Château la Tour Blanche (*Bommes*).
Château Peyraguey: Clos Haut Peyraguey (*Bommes*).
Château Peyraguey: Château Lafaurie Peyraguey (*Bommes*).
Château Rabaud: Rabaud Promis (*Bommes*).
Château Rabaud: Rabaud Sigalas (*Bommes*).
Château Vigneau (*Bommes*).
Château Rieussec (*Fargues*).
Château de Suduiraut (*Preignac*).
Château Guiraud (*Sauternes*).

Second Growths

Château Broustet Nérac (*Barsac*).
Château Caillou (*Barsac*).
Château Doisy: Doisy Baene (*Barsac*).
Château Doisy: Doisy Dubroca (*Barsac*).
Château Myrat (*Barsac*).
Château Suau (*Barsac*).
Château de Malle (*Preignac*).
Château Romer (*Preignac*).
Château d'Arche (*Sauternes*).
Château Filhot (*Sauternes*).
Château Lamothe (*Sauternes*).

SERVING OF SAUTERNES. Sauternes must be served very cold. The sweeter a wine is the longer it takes to make cold, and some Sauternes are very sweet. They will require to be on ice for three hours. Last summer a Lafaurie-Peyraguey of mine, inadvertently left in the refrigerator for twenty-seven hours, was voted to be 'just the right temperature.'

Graves

White Graves, although much lighter in body and less sweet than Sauternes is not naturally a dry wine. Château Carbonnieux, Château Olivier, and Château Duc d'Epernon are among the best-known growths, and cost about five to six shillings a bottle. A vast amount of cheap white wine sold in this country bears only the name 'Graves' on the label. It should be bought with circumspection.

Hock and Moselle

Nobody, it seems, can explain why we in England call the good Rheinwein by the name of hock, since Hochheim, of which the word is an abbreviation, is neither the largest Rhenish vineyard nor the greatest. It suggests an over-simplified attitude to the subtlest of all wines.

The hock district is divided into the Rheingau, Rheinessen, and the Palatinate. From these three districts, none of them extensive, come wines so varied in character—some robust, others slight; some austerely dry, others lusciously sweet; some lusty as four-year-olds, others noble as centenarians; some palest topaz in colour, others almost golden—that the Rhinelanders say a man could spend his whole life seeking to know them all and would die without coming to the end of them. It would be a noble life's work.

Among the outstanding names are Hochheimer, Johannis-berger, Rudesheimer, Geisenheimer, Rauenthaler (from the Rheingau); Niersteiner, Bodenheimer, Laubenheimer (from Rheinessen), Förster, Deidesheimer, Dürkheimer, Rupperts-berger (Palatinate wines). The most famous and most abused name of all is Liebfraumilch, which has become almost a sort of generic name for all Rhenish wine that no other vine-yard seems anxious to own. A good name to remember, if you are lunching at a restaurant with an indulgent and wealthy relative, is Förster Jesuitgarten. The date to remember is 1934.

Do not be oppressed or intimidated by the polysyllabic unpronounceability of the names on hock labels. Wine mer-chants, even the travelled ones, tolerate and often themselves use an anglicized pronunciation of names which their German owners might not quickly recognize. In addition to the names themselves, hock labels have a special vocabulary which is worth learning: *Wachstum* means 'grown by'; *Naturwein* is natural wine, not *Verbessert* ('improved') with the sugar permitted by German law in poor years. *Original Keller-abfüllung* means pretty much the same as the French 'mis en bouteilles au château.' *Auslese* means selected bunches from the vineyards; *Beeren Auslese* means specially selected berries from those selected bunches; *Spätlese* means late-gathered bunches of grapes that have been left in the vineyard to get all the sun they can: these yield rich wines. *Edelbeeren Auslese* means specially selected grapes from the *Spätlese*. A hock lover finding 'Edelbeeren Auslese' on a bottle of wine and an Alpine climber finding an edelweiss on a rock know the same rapture.

Hock is altogether a joyous wine; the only saddening thing about it is its price. I am afraid that there is nothing to be done about it, since Nature herself is the culprit; the German vineyards are not large and seldom give enormous yields. The costs of production are comparatively higher than in other wine-growing districts and, as one wine merchant explains to me sadly, some years are so disappointing that the vine-dresser does not recoup his expenses, and must, therefore, make his good years pay for the bad. Pleasant wines can be got for five and six shillings a bottle, but you will find that the great wines are the costliest on your wine merchant's list.

Moselle is a near kinsman of hock and comes from a neigh-bouring district. (Those who find difficulty in telling t'other from which should remember that hock comes in brown bottles, Moselle in green.) Moselle is lighter in body than hock, is drunk younger and—good news—is cheaper. Bern-casteler, Zeltinger, and Piesporter are the greatest names.

(*Passing Note.* Since 1933, although the vintages have been good, there has been a progressive decrease in the quan-tities of good German wine sent abroad. As these notes are being written Hitler seems to be steadily employing himself in arranging the doom of Europe: by the time they are printed, further supplies of German wine may have ceased altogether. This is part of the price that has to be paid when a great nation delivers itself into the hands of a rabid teetotaller.)

Sherry

Sherry is the Admirable Crichton of wines: it gives im-peccable service and is always on duty. It improves pro-gressively in bottle; when opened or decanted it keeps longer than any other wine; it permits the drinker to smoke; it is the ideal aperitif before a meal, sharpening the appetite, and at the same time making the palate willingly receptive of other wines; it is delicious with clear soup; it is one of the pleasantest dessert wines. Taken with a slice of cake or a biscuit as elevenses it is a faithful strengthener of flagging energies (and pre-Christmas readers of this book who are observing the Advent fast may be glad to know that drinking does not break the fast: furthermore, Canon Law permits a biscuit with the drink, *ne potus noceat*—'lest the drink should harm'—and gives no ruling on the size of the biscuit).

Sherry comes from the wine-growing district round Jerez, in Spain, and is a wine blended from many vineyards and various vintages. The blending is done in a series of casks, the young wine progressing slowly from cask to cask imparting strength to, and deriving mellowness from, its elders and betters. This process is continued over the years, and the same standard can be maintained to suit the requirements of individual shippers for a long time. Once you have found the brand that best suits your taste, therefore, you can continue with it from year to year reasonably confident that every bottle will be like the last.

The following are the main blends of sherry: Manzanilla (very dry); Amontillado (dry); Vino de Pasto (dry); Oloroso, Amoroso (both are 'golden' blends). Solera is the name of the mother cask in the sherry-making system: in this country the word is often used to indicate any dark brown dessert sherry.

Dry sherry, served as an aperitif, should be served cold. 'Better drop a lump of ice into your sherry than try to appreciate it lukewarm,' says Mr H. Warner Allen in his book on the wine; he admits that this is a drastic remedy for a desperate need.

The best sherry seems to be available in clubs; the worst, certainly, is in pubs. An excellent everyday sherry can be bought for five shillings a bottle, but for a quality sherry you must be prepared to pay seven shillings.

Champagne

Genuine champagne is made at Épernay or Rheims. The manifestations of Dom Pérignon's epoch-making discovery that wine could be made to sparkle are known to every man, woman, and newly baptized child. It is drunk at christenings, weddings, and on other private and public occasions of rejoicing. Wine lists in restaurants appear to be specially constructed so that they mysteriously open themselves at the champagne page: every man who has ever entertained guests at a restaurant knows the sonorous litany of illustrious and familiar names:

> Bollinger, Heidsieck, Lanson, Mumm,
> Pommery, Rœderer, Veuve Cliquot,
> Moët & Chandon, Perrier Jouet, Deutz & Gelderman.
>> Pol Roger.

Et al.

I am embarrassed by the suspicion that I do not greatly enjoy champagne with my dinner, although I like to see stout opulent bottles of good vintage standing by, an earnest of the quality of the other wines to come. Drunk in the forenoon, preferably on a sunny day, champagne is the most joyous tonic in the world.

The price of champagne bearing the aforementioned names ranges from 12s. 6d. a bottle upwards. An outstanding wine will cost considerably more. Most good wine merchants usually keep a 'Private Cuvée' or a 'Special Reserve' on their lists which sells at about ten shillings a bottle and which will be found a good serviceable drink.

Port

Port is part of the British constitution. Although grown in Portugal it is controlled by British capital and British tastes. In 1934 over four million imperial gallons of wine were imported into this country from Portugal (as against rather less than one and three-quarter million gallons imported from France). Of that amount such wine as was grown on the banks of the river Douro past the bar of Oporto can legally be described as port wine.

Port is divided into two categories. There is vintage port (which includes, as a sub-division, crusted port) and wood port. Wood port is of two kinds, ruby and tawny.

Vintage port bears the shipper's name, vintage year, and date of bottling. Wood wines are matured in cask and are bottled as required: these bear the hearty kind of names you see in every wine catalogue: 'Choice Old Ruby,' 'Fine Old Tawny,' 'Jolly Old Huntsman,' and so on. Vintage port and wood port are entirely different from each other, not with a qualitative difference but with a difference of kind. Crusted port is vintage port which has been left to mature in specially prepared bottles which induce the sediment of the wine to form into a crust (you will see a whitewash mark on such bottles: this must be kept uppermost to prevent the crust from being disturbed). The decanting of vintage port and, in particular, of crusted port can be a ticklish job for unskilled hands. Your wine merchant will decant it for you at the bin, either into a clean bottle or into your decanter. It is advisable, if you are not an expert, to leave it to him.

Brandy

Brandy is a spirit and therefore on technical grounds should perhaps be excluded from a chapter professing to deal only with wine. But if it is not actually situated within the kingdom of wine, it is to brandy that all the good roads of that kingdom go. Therefore it shall receive brief mention here. All spirit distilled from grape juice can be described as brandy and brandy is made in every wine-growing district in the world. Immeasurably superior to all others is the brandy of Cognac.

There is nothing much to say about brandy except that there is good brandy and brandy that is not good. Mr Edward Bunyard gives the one and only efficacious recipe for providing yourself with the good sort: he says, 'Pay a good price to a good man.' A fair price to pay for a good honest liqueur brandy is twenty / five shillings a bottle. For outstanding quality you will have to pay considerably more. Do not pre/occupy yourself with so/called Napoleon brandy: it *may* have come from a cask which *did* contain brandy during Napoleon's lifetime and nevertheless be like the farmer's axe that has had three heads and two handles and is still as good as new.

Other Wines

Space runs out and the cellar remains unexplored: whole countries and continents have not even been visited. Spain, for one, produces much excellent table wine which is available in this country in large quantities at an inexpensive price.

Italy also produces much wine, both red and white. Chianti is a district name which seems to cover every conceivable quality of wine; much of it is fearsomely acid, some of it is as mellow as good claret. Try before you buy in quantity. All Chianti seems to be improved by the addition of a little water, a characteristic which will recommend it to the econo/mically/minded. In its container of gaily coloured straw a flask of Chianti has a pleasantly festive air: it is perhaps unfortunate that *fiasco*, the name of the straw container, has been borrowed by the English language for another meaning. Barolo is a Burgundyish sort of wine. Asti Spumante is a white sparkling wine: I have always found it, as Mrs Browning found the pipings of Pan, 'sweet, sweet, blinding sweet.'

I would like to have found room for Madeira, which can be drunk at the end of dinner instead of port, or which can be used as an all/hour occasional drink like sherry. It seems to be temporarily out of favour in this country: that is doubtless the reason why excellent Madeira can be bought for five shillings a bottle.

Empire wines have never revealed themselves to me at their reputed best. I am told that Australian burgundy, if fostered to maturity, can be a magnificent wine. It is my misfortune that I have only encountered it in its unruly and unlovable youth. I must confess that I might like Empire wines better if they surrendered their claim to names which do not belong to them. Whenever I drink Australian wine boldly calling itself 'Burgundy,' I am reminded of the story of Oscar Browning, that legendary Fellow of King's College, meeting Tennyson in a Cambridge street. 'I am Browning,' said O. B. 'No, you are not,' replied Tennyson, and walked on.

Of British wines I know nothing save this entry in a list of Excise Duties and Licences:

WINE, BRITISH, manufacturers for sale, *see* SWEETS.

Reading maketh a full man

A considerable literature has flowered round the making and appreciation of wine. It charts, very thoroughly and in exact detail, the fascinating country round which this chapter has provided some slap-dash signposting. Many of the works composing this literature are for the connoisseur or the trade specialist: there are, however, a number of good books written by experts in non-technical language, which will usefully serve the inquiring amateur of wine and which, in addition, will offer him much pleasant vicarious drinking. *The Epicure's Companion* by Edward and Lorna Bunyard (a sister volume to the present one) contains an admirable compendium of wine knowledge written in a style as mellow and as fastidiously delicate as its subject-matter. *French Wines* by Paul de Cassagnac (Chatto & Windus) is the best *little* book on its subject that I know. That I have read these two books many times may, indeed, be apparent in what is printed in the foregoing pages. *The Book of Wine*, by Morton Shand, is de-

servedly a classic. Constable's *Wine Miscellany* has volumes
on Sherry, Port, Madeira, Claret, Champagne, written by
experts and edited by André L. Simon, certainly the greatest
oenologist of our time. The wine itself is the thing; but
there is much pleasure, as well as profit, to be derived from reading about it. Sometimes it can be discovered in unlooked-for
places. The last volume of the *Encyclopaedia Britannica*, that
objective and unemotional work, contains an article on wine
beginning: 'Wine is the living blood of the grape; it is liable
to sickness and doomed to death' — surely a line as plangent
and eternal as ever Catullus sang.

*Since this chapter was written a war-time budget has increased
the prices of wines by 10 or 15 per cent. Heaven knows what future
war-time budgets will do to them!*

GARDENER'S CHRISTMAS

BY MILES HADFIELD

As we all know, Christmas has changed—even in so conservative a place as the garden. One may read through the
old garden books to see how gardeners and gardens spent the
season; but little is to be found, for during the days following
the winter solstice both slept. The garden lay within its
sheltering walls, against which were pressed the spidery fans
of fruit-trees. The quiet browns of the earth, with the
occasional green of a lawn, would cover the ground everywhere under the bare framework of trees. Here and there a
holly with its scarlet berries might stand shining, or the skeleton
of summer be strengthened by sombre blocks of yew. Cedars
or Scots pines also might give some massiveness among the
pattern of bare branches; but of the many conifers we know
to-day few were then planted. All was set in the English
winter landscape of rolling plough and grass, or perhaps in
later days among carefully planned park-land. Ever-present
were the bare boughs, silhouetted if the trees were separate,
formed into warm brown masses when in woods. No brilliant or fresh and tender colours were to be seen but in the faces
and clothes of men and women.

We can well imagine that precursor of the modern gardener,
the poet Shenstone, writing of this lovely, if often sombre,
scene, as he recovered from an attack of influenza (modern
experts tells us that his fashionable eighteenth-century melancholy was due to a particular susceptibility to 'the 'flu'):
'To see one's urns, obelisks, and waterfalls laid open . . . the

Naiads and Dryads exposed by that ruffian winter to universal observation, is a severity scarcely to be supported by the help of blazing hearths, cheerful companions, and a bottle of the most grateful Burgundy.'

Now all is very different. Apart from the numerous conifers and evergreens that furnish our gardens in winter, the present century has seen the introduction, mostly from China, of plants that swell the small number of winter flowerers considerably. Conifers, too, planted for timber in millions, have even changed the landscape itself. We can imagine old Shenstone to-day, his influenza cured by tablets of vitamins, cutting sprays of the winter-flowering cherry—'the jugatsu-zakura of the Japanese,' he would knowingly tell his friends.

Most of us now live in surroundings very different from even the nineteenth-century winter scenes of England drawn by Bewick or Randolph Caldecott. We are mostly suburban, with gardens of varying degrees of smallness, doing our own share of the gardening and having little in the way of heat and glass for providing an exotic Christmas display. Some may have an alpine house that will also provide December flowers; but that is a specialist's affair, and better left to the expert.

We will assume, then, that a small, sheltered, but sunny part of the garden, preferably near the house, has been chosen to grow winter-flowering shrubs and bulbs—for most winter flowers seem to be either bulbous or woody—and we will mention some that should be included in reasonable hope that they may flower at Christmas naturally and not as 'poor lingering relics of far happier hours.' They are all hardy and need shelter only against the damage of storms. All may be had from up-to-date nurserymen, but comparatively few are yet grown in the quantities that they deserve. If the ground is ready and workable they may (except the bulbs) even be planted on Christmas Day, though the more normal autumn planting is preferable.

Evergreens

First, as so many of them flower on bare branches, some evergreen backing is pleasant. There are numerous bushy conifers to choose from, varying greatly in colour, form, and texture. The larger evergreen viburnums, such as *V. rhytido-phyllum*, with its fine great leaves that will appreciate the shelter from winds, or even the common but nevertheless beautiful laurustinus (*V. Tinus*), may be used. The shelter will also protect the handsome leaves of some evergreen barberries (or mahonias), such as the early-flowering *Berberis japonica* forms. There are, too, evergreen cotoneasters that will, birds permitting, hold their scarlet berries until Christmas.

If the background is a wall, those evergreen ceanothus need-ing protection may be trained to it, or an evergreen clematis such as *C. Armandii*. In any case, *Garrya elliptica* should be included among the evergreens for its long yellow catkins that open in winter. The male form, having longer catkins, should be specified. In mild climates it grows into a very large bush, but particularly in cooler places it is often trained to a wall. In the drier parts of the country it appreciates some shade from hot sun.

Deciduous Shrubs

In front come the larger deciduous shrubs. In a sunny spot the winter-flowering cherry, *Prunus subhirtella autumnalis*, should be planted and plenty of space allowed, for it eventually makes a large bush though it can be trained as a small tree. The small pink flowers are numerous and open on fine days from autumn to spring; December is usually one of its good months. Then there is the Chinese relative of our guelder rose, *Viburnum fragrans*, with sweetly scented waxy flowers of the type seen in the laurustinus. It forms a rather narrow, straggly shrub, and does not flower very freely until well established. Fragrant, too, is the bushy honeysuckle, *Lonicera fragrantissima*, evergreen to an extent depending on the climate, with curious flowers set back to back. Very similar, with larger flowers but less scent, is *Lonicera Standishii*. The former is generally considered the better. Both are rather spreading bushes.

The witch-hazel, *Hamamelis mollis*, may wait till just after Christmas to bloom, but it must be included. The flowers are like little bunches of yellow ribbons held in a small crimson cup. It is sometimes difficult to establish if a long dry spell occurs after it is planted, but once settled it is very adaptable. This, too, is sweetly scented, finally making a rather erect shrub with open branching. The daphnes or mezereons are smaller shrubs liking their heads in the sun but their roots in a shaded place. The old pink *Daphne Mezereum* is very occasionally in flower at Christmas, though usually not till February; but its variety *grandiflora* flowers from autumn onwards. Both dislike having their sprays cut, a drawback which does not apply to any of the other shrubs mentioned. The old scrambling yellow jessamine, *Jasminum nudiflorum*, is found in most gardens, often suffering the fate of all very hardy plants, neglect. It is worthy of a periodical thinning-out after flowering. All the old wood should be cut out in a drastic manner, leaving a skeleton of vigorous shoots to be trained in. The effect on old plants is usually surprising.

For the front parts of the winter garden are the winter-flowering heaths. These are mostly hybrids of *Erica carnea*, variously coloured from rose to white. There are many named kinds from which a selection may be made to flower through-out winter; for Christmas Queen Mary and the variety *praecox* should be selected. *Erica darleyensis* ought also to be included. These, unlike most heaths, will grow in a limy or chalky soil. They need an open spot that is not overhung.

There are, of course, many other shrubs that might be included because of their coloured stems, bark, or fruit as well as those that are still uncommon and so more for the specialist, If the reader is anxious to go more deeply into a complex question full of possibilities he should study W. J. Bean's *Trees and Shrubs* and A. W. Darnell's *Winter Blossoms from the Outdoor Garden*. But the shrubs given above are perhaps the best of those which are in general cultivation. With favour‑able weather they may be expected to flower on Christmas Day, without that sad appearance of summer shrubs that in mild weather will persist until after Christmas, and so give writers of letters to the papers such pleasure.

Bulbs

Strictly speaking, most of the bulbs that we may plant among the shrubs flower just after Christmas, but some are still so little known that it may be useful to name them, an excuse being that they can be grown in pots or bowls and will then flower a little earlier and so may just qualify. After flowering they can be planted out direct, or the pots plunged in the ground until the foliage has died down, when they should be dried off and planted in the usual manner.

In the shadier parts the snowdrops will thrive. *Galanthus byzantinus* is earlier than the common kind and will flower still earlier in pots and if slightly forced. For the sunnier places there are the winter‑flowering crocuses. *Crocus Imperati*, with large flowers that are rich purple inside, and fawn covered with feathered markings on the outside, will occasionally qualify out of doors, as will *Crocus chrysanthus*. Of this, one of the most beautiful and delicate kinds, with goblet‑shaped flowers, there are several fine named varieties of different colours. It is specially good in bowls. *Crocus Sieberi* and *C. biflorus* are others that, if not flowering on Christmas Day, will encourage us by their appearance of activity and promise.

Hellebores and the Glastonbury Thorn

The Christmas rose is well known. There are several forms and *Helleborus niger* var. *altifolius* is one of the best. The hellebores (for the enthusiast there are other winter-flowerers besides the Christmas rose) are woodland plants, and so like some shade in the summer. They appreciate rich, cool soil and dislike disturbance once planted; so adequate preparations in the way of deep-digging and enriching the soil should be made before planting. They should be remembered in summer, too, when mulching, and in drought heavy watering should be done. The flowers are better if protected from severe frost and rain by a hand-light, though the plants themselves are very hardy and plenty of fresh air should be given them in fine weather.

Some gardeners might be sufficiently curious to grow the Glastonbury thorn. The legend is that Joseph of Arimathaea, failing to convert the people of Glastonbury to Christianity, asked that a miracle might happen. He drove his staff into the ground, and although it was Christmas Day the staff broke into blossom and leaf. To-day this is unromantically known as a precocious form of the common may, *Crataegus monogyna* var. *praecox*, with flowers of the true hawthorn scent opening throughout winter. It is said that its floriferousness on Christmas Day itself has decreased since the electric torch replaced the warmth of the lanterns held up by pilgrims come to view it. Plants derived from the original tree are offered by several nurserymen.

An Iris and Two Weeds

The sweet-scented winter-flowering Algerian iris known as
I. unguicularis or *I. stylosa* (the former being the right name) is
now fairly well known. It thrives on starvation, liking a
gravelly bit of soil in a sun-baked spot—if at the bottom of a
sunny wall, so much the better. It is usually planted in April.
The flowers should be pulled, not cut, from as low down as
possible, for what appears to be the flower-stem really corre-
sponds to the base of the petals. The flower-buds must be
protected from slugs.

Two weedy plants, under strictest control, may be included
in the Christmas garden. Some roots of the common coltsfoot can be potted up and kept in a cold frame so that they will
open their golden flowers even earlier than they do in sheltered
spots out of doors. Similar treatment can be given to its
continental relative, the winter heliotrope (*Petasites fragrans*),
which has dingy flowers but a very sweet scent. It is important
that this, even more than the coltsfoot, should be kept out of
the garden proper as it is likely to become ineradicable and
unrestrainable if once it finds a spot that it likes.

Cacti and Succulents

So much for gardens planned out of doors. Indoors, thanks
to the enterprise of the sixpenny stores, every one knows all
about raising bulbs in fibre (though, indeed, most of these
flower after Christmas). But few people have yet exploited
the range of cacti and succulents that may be bought at sixpence
a time. For the uninitiated, cacti may be said to be those
fleshy plants with spines or bristles, succulents those without
—at least, as far as sixpenny gardening is concerned. Either
may be bought and planted in bowls or seed-pans during late

spring and summer so that they will be established by winter. Those with leanings towards the romantic may build small and horrid deserts, those who are architecturally minded may compose exercises in form and volume, while those whose interests lie anywhere between the rococo and the surrealist can, with the aid of shells, flints, or odd stones, gratify their utmost whims by the use of these strange and often beautiful plants.

It is essential to have drainage holes in the pans used, and to fill the bottoms with crocks or washed cinders. To prevent this drainage becoming blocked some old fibrous turf or peat should be placed on top and then the plants set in soil that is mostly sand and coarse grit. It is better not to water them at all for a few days after planting, but normally during spring and summer cacti and succulents need regular watering, without allowing them to become in any way waterlogged. About August water should be decreased, and it should be withheld almost entirely during winter. Exceptions to this rule are those succulents that shrink and wither or droop their leaves —this is a sign that a little water is needed. For this reason it is better to keep succulents and cacti in different gardens; the former may also have a less arid soil and a little loam may be added.

Some, such as haworthias, gasterias, and aloes (if we are lucky enough to find out the names) prefer shade in the summer. On the other hand, plants labelled Echeveria, Mesembryanthemum, Crassula, or Kleinia are usually safe in full sun, but like plenty of water during the growing season. Some kinds refuse to change their period of growth to fit in with our summer, and grow in early winter. They can usually be distinguished easily enough by careful observation. Such will need more water at this time of year and must consequently be carefully protected from frost. When growth has stopped they must be allowed to dry off gradually so that they may have a period of rest. The hardy houseleeks (sempervivums) are best excluded from these gardens, though often recommended. They soon start growing in the warmth of a room and become drawn, quite losing the tight rosette structure that is an essential of their natural form.

Dwarf Trees and Everlastings

Christmas is also the time of dwarf trees in fancy pots. The more expensive 'Japanese' dwarf trees are best left alone unless one is willing to take the bother of studying the method of their cultivation carefully. But often seedlings of conifers, such as Lawson's cypress or Scots pine, may be picked up in shrubberies or woods and arranged in pots or bowls (the time to collect them is in spring or early autumn) according to one's taste. The vessels should have drainage holes, and the plants be watered regularly. Then when they become too large or unsightly through cramping of the roots they may be planted out and will probably grow normally into forest trees.

The making of posies of dried flowers is another Christmastide employment. Many people buy their everlastings already dried, but many kinds will do well as annuals or half-hardy annuals grown in some odd sunny corner. Their names are alarming, but a good seedsman should be able to supply satisfactory strains of Acroclinum, Ammobium, Helichrysum, Helipterum, Rhodanthe, Statice, and Xerantherum. When they come into flower the stems should be cut and hung in a dry place so that their heads fall quite perpendicularly. Then, by winter, they should be sufficiently straight and stiff to arrange without much wiring. Grasses, bulrushes, and the seedheads of honesty (Lunaria) are among the other plants that may be similarly treated. The membranaceous pieces covering the seed must be rubbed off the honesty, leaving only the shiny centre partition. Winter cherry (*Physalis*) is also easily grown —indeed, it should be placed somewhere so that it cannot damage other plants with its ramping ways.

Holiday Tasks

To conclude the preparations the gardener makes for Christmas it may be mentioned that December is not a good month for pruning holly, and that care and discretion should be used in picking berried sprays.

Turning to Boxing Day and the rest of the holidays. First, the gardener may be puzzled to know whether to plant out his Christmas presents now or keep them somewhere sheltered till later. In all but the heaviest soils and coldest places, provided the soil is workable, most trees, shrubs, and plants may be put into their permanent positions. Evergreens particularly may usually be moved with more safety now than a little later. With tender kinds some protection in the way of bracken or sacking is, of course, advisable. On the other hand, most alpine plants (usually supplied in pots) should not be planted out until later. The pots should, if possible, be plunged up to the rim in the soil or a bed of ashes, preferably in a cold frame. Nor should small plants that are likely to be lifted out of the ground after frost be planted out in the open.

Christmas time is often chosen for lopping branches off trees; it is good vigorous work to counteract what the makers of patent medicines tactfully call 'errors of diet.' With coniferous trees, most authorities agree that it is the latest period at which this work may be safely done. Large evergreens such as laurels, rhododendrons, and hollies should certainly not be touched now, but left until well on in the spring. On the other hand, ordinary deciduous trees can usually be drastically cut now, although late summer or autumn is probably better still, especially for trees such as the sycamore or birch that 'bleed' very freely.

Unfortunately there is only too much evidence that few people know the right way to remove a large branch. First, at some little distance from the main stem, a good cut is made on the underside of the branch to be removed. Then a few inches further away from the trunk the branch is sawn through until it falls. Some splitting back into the remaining snag, varying according to the type of wood, is sure to occur; but it should not reach the main stem or part which is finally to be left. If it does, then damp and disease will enter, the wound will not heal properly, and the health of the tree will finally suffer. The snag is then sawn off as nearly flush with the remaining trunk or stem as is possible. Being of little weight, it is easy to prevent any further splitting back as it falls. The more nearly flush to the main stem it is cut, the more readily will the wound heal over, leaving little trace in a year or two of the branch removed. On the other hand, if even a few inches of branch are left, this stump, besides being unsightly, will certainly rot, and through it disease may enter the main body of the tree. All wounds should be painted over with tar or white-lead paint. Cuts should be sloped so that rain will be sure to run off and lodge nowhere.

There are, too, the usual routine jobs that should be done about this time of year. Such are the clearing from hedgerows of dying matter if this is likely to infect orchards with disease, and the digging and the winter-washing of fruit and orna-mental trees. It should be remembered that the modern winter-wash burns foliage very badly, so it is advisable to keep any plants that have fine winter foliage or flowers—in fact, any of the plants of our Christmas garden—away from any fruit, ornamental cherries, or crabs that we may wish to spray. This applies particularly to hellebores, for the shade of fruit-trees appears otherwise excellent. It is, however, easy to protect small patches of plants with sacks, remembering that even in the stillest weather sprayed washes drift to a surprising extent. Pruning of fruit-trees should, if we are good gardeners and work to the experts' calendars, be completed by or at Christmas time in readiness for winter-washing.

When all is said and done, however, the Christmas garden is mostly a garden superficially asleep, though many plants, particularly those we call bulbs and many of the evergreens, are in reality quite active. In some of them changes have already taken place that will determine irrevocably certain factors of next spring's growth.

Planning and Reading

During the long dark evenings the gardener may rest and take stock of the last year, and for once, with catalogues and books before him, feel that he is not now neglecting important work by planning and dreaming for the time to come. Some of the authors from whose work entertainment as well as excellent instruction and suggestion may be expected are E. A. Bowles, Henry Bright, E. A. Bunyard, H. N. Ella-combe, Clarence Elliott, Reginald Farrer, Jason Hill, Gertrude Jekyll, A. T. Johnson, Sir Herbert Maxwell, Eden Phill-potts, Alfred Smee, and Dr Fred Stoker. There are, of course, many others, but it is always worth while searching the library shelves for one of these authors. Many plant-hunters have written accounts of their adventures, too, that are particularly interesting. They range from Robert Fortune a century ago, through Farrer, E. H. Wilson, and E. H. M. Cox, who worked in the first quarter of this century, to Kingdon Ward and others who are still active.[1]

But even as he rests and reads, let the gardener heed the

[1] A long and detailed bibliography of gardening books can be found in *The Gardener's Companion*, edited by Miles Hadfield.

advice which heads the instructions for December given in John Evelyn's old garden calendar: 'Continue your hostility against *Vermine*.' Particularly does this apply to the slug, who may be particularly active during a mild Christmas spell. In fact, during one exceptionally warm Christmas week, three tablets of meta solid fuel, very finely ground up and mixed with three handfuls of sharps (which is finer than bran and seems unattractive to birds and animals), distributed tactfully over my garden in small heaps, accounted for one thousand and forty-two slugs. One fondly imagines the devastation wrought among next year's generation that will now remain unborn.

Finally, we may conclude with Evelyn's other warning: 'Look to your *Fountain Pipes*; remember it in time, and the advice will save you both trouble and charges.'

Saws and Sayings

If you eat no beans on Christmas Eve, you will become an ass.

Tie wet strawbands around the orchard trees on Christmas Eve and it will make them fruitful.

On Christmas Eve put a stone on every tree, and they will bear the more.

Beat the trees on Christmas night, and they will bear more fruit.

If after a Christmas dinner you shake out the tablecloth over the bare ground under the open sky, crumbwort will grow on the spot.

If on Christmas Day, or Christmas Eve, you hang a wash-clout on a hedge, and then groom the horses with it, they will grow fat.

As often as the cock crows on Christmas Eve, the quarter of corn will be as dear.

If a dog howls the night before Christmas, it will go mad within the year.

CHRISTMAS GHOSTS

BY HARRY PRICE

IT was Charles Dickens who really popularized the 'Christmas ghost.' At least, it was his writings which, more than those of any other author, associated ghosts with Christmas in the minds of the reading public. Who can doubt that the immortal and repentant Scrooge in *A Christmas Carol, being a Ghost Story of Christmas*,[1] was responsible for millions of people accepting without demur the *possibility* of the beneficent influence of the dead over the living? Thackeray called this story 'a national benefit' and his words are as true to-day as they were when *A Christmas Carol* was published.

Dickens found that the story of Scrooge and his friends was to the public taste, and his next tale (written in a villa on the outskirts of Genoa) was about another Christmas ghost. This was *The Chimes: a Goblin Story of some Bells that rang an Old Year out and a New Year in*.[2] This, too, became popular, and *The Haunted Man and the Ghost's Bargain: a Fancy for Christmas Time*[3] soon followed. In 1852 appeared the first collected edition[4] of the famous 'Christmas books,' and the Christmas ghost was established for all time!

Dickens did not believe in Ghosts

Did Dickens believe in ghosts? I think it is very doubtful. Though he exploited them in his novels, he lost no opportunity in denouncing the 'spirits' of the séance-room. Between the

---

[1] London, 1843.   [2] London, 1845.
[3] London, 1848.   [4] *Christmas Books*, London, 1852.

years 1860 and 1864 a number of attacks on spiritualism appeared in *All the Year Round*, which he was then editing. These articles were not signed by Dickens, but there is little doubt that he wrote them—or at least inspired them. Such articles as 'Tom in Spirits,'[1] 'Modern Magic,'[2] 'Fallacies of Faith,'[3] 'Lufkin on Davingpodge,'[4] and others bitterly—and cleverly—attacked spiritualistic séances and the mediums of the day. In particular, he lost no opportunity in ridiculing the famous and fashionable medium, D. D. Home, who was then very much in the public eye. His article, 'The Martyr Medium,'[5] was a review of—and attack on—Home's *Incidents in my Life*[6] which every one was then reading. It is evident that in later life Dickens thought that ghosts were becoming too popular!

Though Dickens popularized Christmas ghosts, he did not invent them, and many books have been published dealing with the 'spirits' of Christmas as well as with the spirit of Christmas. It would be tedious to enumerate these works, but one little book in my library I must mention and that is *Round About our Coal-Fire: or, Christmas Entertainments; containing Christmas Gambols, Tropes, Figures, etc., with Abundance of Fiddle-Faddle-Stuff; such as Stories of Fairies, Ghosts, Hobgoblins, Witches, Bull-beggars, Rawheads, and Bloody-Bones. . . . Very proper to be read in all Families.* This blood-curdling little work was published in London just before Christmas, 1740, and was intended to be read while the family was sitting round its 'coal-fire'—then a luxury in the more humble households. Actually, the title of the book is more exciting than its contents, but the work contains many ghost stories intended to create the real Christmas atmosphere.

[1] *All the Year Round*, 8th September 1860.
[2] Ibid., 28th July 1860.   [3] Ibid., 15th September 1860.
[4] Ibid., 10th December 1864.   [5] Ibid., 4th April, 1863.
[6] London, 1863.

Why are ghost stories particularly associated with Christmas? The reason is, I think, that in the early days, Christmas was the time of year when people did not stray far from their homes. Dark nights, snowed-up roads, bad weather, difficulty with —or total lack of—transit facilities, made it almost impossible for the country people to leave their firesides during the Christ-mas season, and their amusements were dependent upon their own resources. Christmas has always been a time for story-telling, and what more natural than that these stories should deal with the unseen, the unknown, and the fearsome—'the ghosts of our own airy belief,' as Dickens says? The darkness out-side, the long nights, the howling wind or the driven snow against the window-pane—all these natural phenomena pro-vided an appropriate setting for the recital of supernatural phenomena while sitting round the 'coal-fire' or Yule log. The 'powers of darkness' reigned supreme in the winter.

Christmas Ghosts are Ancient

The association of Christmas with the supernatural can be traced right back to the dawn of Christianity. For example, to this day in Sweden the village folk scatter straw over certain rooms on Christmas Eve—a tribute to the Holy Birth and lowly stable at Bethlehem. In the Harz Mountains district of Germany, also on Christmas Eve, the wood-cutters build rough model mangers of twigs in the forests and pray for the shades of their ancestral dead. At least, they used to, the Third Reich has, I believe, frowned upon these superstitions. Other superstitions which are not exactly encouraged in Ger-many include the baking of special bread on Christmas Eve. This is—or was—sprinkled with the evening dew and the bread so treated is then supposed to have acquired miraculous and curative properties, and is afterwards used for a variety of purposes where a magical effect is desired. Similar beliefs are to this day current in various Scandinavian countries. In central Europe and the near east, vampires and were-wolves are most feared at Christmastide, and special services of protection or exorcism are still held in order that the living shall be protected from the dead. In certain villages on Christmas Eve the family of a recently deceased loved one meet just before midnight round the burial place and pray that the corpse shall be undisturbed. When twelve o'clock strikes, they sprinkle leaves of dried garlic over the grave and then adjourn to the house of the nearest relative of the deceased, where the virtues of the dear departed are extolled, liquid refreshments being handed round the while.

And now for an account of some practical Christmas ghost-hunting. I have been asked very frequently whether 'ghosts,' in the séance-room sense, or in haunted houses, are more active round about Christmas than at other times of the year. My answer is 'no.' The fact that more ghosts are seen—or alleged to be seen—in the winter months is because the nights are longer and the days are more dreary than in the summer. And more people go 'ghost-hunting' during the shorter days because, I suspect, they have nothing better to do. I remember *The Times* once had a leading article on 'A Close Season for Ghosts,' and the writer wondered what happened to them when the various psychic societies were taking their long summer holidays. Though more cases of haunted houses are reported to me during the winter, it is only because more people are 'investigating' them.

During my year's tenancy of Borley Rectory, near Sudbury, Suffolk, the 'most haunted house in England,' from May 1937 to May 1938, the quietest time was round about Christmas. The forty observers who were, successively, in charge of the place reported practically nothing during the last part of December 1937, though phenomena began to be recorded

very early in the New Year.   In fact, one of the most convincing
manifestations occurred when, with a friend, I visited the
rectory about the second week in January, 1938.   I will relate what happened.

Hunting the Borley Ghosts

Because of the dearth of phenomena during the Christmas
holidays—during which one intrepid soul spent ten days in
the house by himself!—I decided to visit the rectory in order to
ascertain whether, as was suggested, a previous 'exorcism' had
at last 'worked'—a sort of delayed action, as it were.   I
invited a young Oxford graduate to accompany me, and we
arrived at Borley (which is just within the Essex border) early
in the afternoon.   After a thorough examination of the place
and the affixing of our seals on all outside doors and windows,
we locked ourselves in and hoped for the best—or rather worst,
if the reader is afraid of ghosts.   We then prepared to make
some tea and settle down for the evening.

But I must first say a few words about the rectory itself.
The building is new and yet it is old.   This sounds para-
doxical until I mention that the present red brick structure is
less than eighty years old, though the foundations (and, I
think, part of the cellars) are those of much more ancient
buildings.   There is some ground, too, for the local belief
that originally an ancient monastery occupied part of the site.
There are also stories of an old nunnery in the immediate
vicinity, with a tunnel connecting the two.   A portion of an
underground passage is still to be seen in the farmyard adjoining
the rectory.   There was also a medieval castle near by—
besieged by Oliver Cromwell—and on the site of the present
buildings was built the chaplain's house, or manor house.
The present rectory (or what remains of it, as it was severely
damaged by fire soon after Christmas 1938) was built in 1865

by the Rev. Henry Bull, whose family owned most of the adjoining land. He had a family of fourteen children and wanted a large house. And that is why the rectory, when I rented it, had some thirty rooms in it.

These rooms, and especially the grounds, are supposed to be haunted by the spirit of a nun, among other apparitions, which are said to have been seen at different times. The nun was a young novice from the nearby nunnery who eloped with a lay brother employed at the monastery. They escaped in a black coach with two horses. Their flight was discovered; they were pursued, brought back, and received the punishment for these venial sins sometimes meted out in the old days: the girl was bricked up alive in one of the cells of the nunnery and the lay brother was hanged. A number of people—including the wife of a B.B.C. official—declare that they have seen the nun or phantom coach or both—and the 'Nun's Walk' is now the chief path through the rectory grounds. Sometimes the nun has been seen peering into the rooms of the rectory.

One of these apartments I converted into what we called the Base Room. It was really the old study, and in it I placed a table, camp-bed, lamps, chairs, stoves, etc., and a number of books. Usually my observers 'ghost-hunted' in couples, and when one was on duty in the upper part of the house, his companion would rest in the Base Room.

Well, after tea on that early January afternoon, my friend and I prepared to settle down and await darkness—and what darkness might bring. The Oxford man sat at the table and began reading a newspaper. I was stretched full length on the camp-bed and I might have been about to drop off into a doze. The door of the Base Room was wide open in order that any sound above-stairs could be heard by us. It was a very still afternoon, with a Scotch mist outside, and everything was absolutely quiet in this exceptionally quiet Essex backwater.

A Psychic Interruption

Just about five o'clock, when it was quite dark in the Base Room, my friend lit the oil lamp in order that he could continue his reading. He was sitting near the door, and I was still reclining on the camp-bed. He had hardly picked up his newspaper again, when we were startled by the sound of three short, sharp raps, repeated three times, which appeared to come from the Base Room door, which was in full view of, and quite near, my friend. The Oxford boy was a tyro at ghosthunting and it rather unnerved him for a moment. *He* could see there was nothing at or near the door. I sat up on the bed.

We waited a minute or so for a repetition of the raps. As these were not forthcoming, I jumped off the bed with the intention of exploring the passage leading to the Base Room. I had hardly crossed the room when both of us heard loud footsteps traversing the passage outside the room. They appeared to be passing our door. Before we had recovered from our surprise—if I can use so mild a term—a door slammed in the back part of the house, near the kitchen quarters.

We rushed out of the Base Room and down the long passage which led to the kitchen, but found nothing disturbed. We had carefully noted the position of each door, and none had been moved by so much as a hairbreadth. All our seals were intact and no one could have entered or left the house without our knowledge. At least, no tangible being could have done so. With our torches we then searched the whole house from attics to cellars without finding anything that would account for the almost incredible noises—incredible under the circumstances—which we had heard. There is a French proverb to the effect that a ghost was never seen by two pairs of eyes; but two pairs of ears undoubtedly heard the raps on the door and the footsteps. And there was nothing ambiguous about the slamming of that door!

It had been our intention to stay at Borley throughout that night, but my friend thought he had better be getting back to London, and as on this occasion it happened to be his car which had brought us to Borley, I, perforce, had to return with him. After some supper we packed up the odds and ends of our ghost-hunting kit and returned to town.

A Planchette Prediction fulfilled

The above adventure at Borley Rectory may appear strange to those of my readers unacquainted with this case, but I could relate a hundred even stranger occurrences there. More than fifty witnesses have testified to remarkable happenings or startling phenomena at this rectory. For half a century the place has been haunted and I have a dossier relating to this case that would fill a small trunk. It will be published in book form. As to *why* it is haunted, and the causation of the phenomena, these are questions that may be settled some day. I have certain theories of my own, which I have elaborated elsewhere.[1] But, as in the case of so many haunted houses, the phenomena appear to be cyclic and recurrent at definite intervals. I have already mentioned that Borley Rectory was burnt down soon after Christmas, 1938. Just twelve months previously, one of our observers was killing time at Borley playing with the planchette—that heart-shaped toy on wheels used for 'automatic writing.' Amongst the many 'messages' he received (all of which were preserved), one was to the effect that Borley would be burned out, the fire originating on a landing. *This prediction was fulfilled to the letter exactly one year later.*

[1] *Fifty Years of Psychical Research*, London, 1939.

I set a Trap for a Ghost

Although ghosts do not appear to be more active at Christ⁄
mas than at any other period of the year, I have investigated
alleged haunts during the Christmas holidays, sometimes with
interesting results. For example, during the Christmas vaca⁄
tion of 1925, I inquired into the phenomenon of some strange
footsteps which were heard by the tenants of a small cottage
in Surrey, and in many ways the case is unique.

The cottage itself was not haunted, but the people living in
it continually heard footsteps on the gravel path which en⁄
circled the building. The manifestations commenced as soon
as the place was occupied. During the first week, the woman
twice went to the door, thinking it was the postman, but no
one was there. The path had been newly gravelled and the
lightest step upon it could be heard within the house, which
was off the main road and quite isolated. The only occupants
of the cottage were the husband and wife, the former being
out all day.

A peculiarity of this particular 'haunt' was that the footsteps
were heard punctually at 8.30 on most mornings, but especially
towards the end of the week, though never on a Sunday.
A watch was kept in the garden from certain sheds that
commanded a view of the pathway, but the perambulating
ghost was never seen, and never heard except from within the
cottage.

Unaware that the entity never 'walked' on a Sunday, I first
visited the cottage on a Saturday night, hoping to hear the
footsteps on the following morning. Learning that this was
highly improbable, on the Sunday I busied myself with making
four wide and shallow trenches across the path. I filled these
trenches with a mixture of flour and silver sand which I made
perfectly smooth with a newspaper in the hope that the ghost's

footprints would be impressed upon it. Next morning I was up early, had breakfast, and waited for the intangible visitor. On the stroke of half past eight, the steps could be heard approaching. They appeared to come from the back of the cottage. There was nothing peculiar about the steps—it was just as if a man, with rather a firm tread, were approaching the house. I ran into the small hall and peered through the letter-box. Nothing was seen to pass, but I could hear the footsteps as they came nearer and nearer, and gradually died away. I rushed out of the cottage, but could find no one. I searched the buildings without success. The man belonging to the house had left for work soon after seven o'clock and no servant was employed. There were no animals in the immediate neighbourhood. The nearest habitation was nearly half a mile away. I was convinced that no person was playing a trick on me. I examined my trenches, but they were quite unmarked. I was disappointed that no impressions of footprints were visible—even the mark of a cloven hoof would have been acceptable! I visited the cottage three times in all, but heard the footsteps on the first occasion only. The cottage became vacant a few months after my last visit; the place was taken by two maiden ladies who turned the house into a tea garden. It did not pay, but whether the 'footsteps' or the lack of custom was responsible for their vacating the cottage, I never ascertained. But the place is still empty.

A 'Sympathetic' Ghost

Another Christmas 'ghost' I investigated turned out to be a natural phenomenon instead of a supernatural one, but as the incident was both instructive and amusing, I will relate it here.

Many years ago I was spending Christmas in a Shropshire

village. On New Year's Eve I retired to rest soon after ten o'clock, leaving my bedroom window open according to my usual custom. At about 11.45 I was awakened by the church bells ringing in the New Year. The little church was only about two hundred yards from the house in which I was staying. As I lay awake listening to them, I fancied that with their clangour I could hear sweet music coming from the dining-room, which was immediately below my bedchamber. As I listened, I could distinctly hear faint chords as from a harp or zither. Then I remembered that in the apartment below me was a piano, and it occurred to me that someone might be twanging the strings, producing a sort of *pizzicato* effect. It sounded most weird, and one could easily have imagined a ghostly harpist in the room below. I decided to investigate and made my way to the lower story. I quickly solved the mystery. Actually, the explanation was quite simple. I discovered that certain notes from the piano recurred always during a particular peal from the bells, and this gave me the clue to the 'ghostly music.' The wires of the piano were vibrating in sympathy with the noisy bells. This 'sympathetic vibration' is well known to physicists. In the same way, Caruso, the famous tenor, could emit a note that would crack a wine-glass in the immediate vicinity.

The Face at the Window

It was also in the New Year that I had a strange adventure in Austria, at the beautiful spa of Baden-bei-Wien. I was staying in Vienna at the time and read in one of the papers that much excitement prevailed in Baden owing to an alleged ghost that was haunting a cheap *pension* not far from the Theresienstrasse. I took an electric tram to Baden, where I arrived about seven o'clock in the evening. I made my way to the house, presented my card, was admitted, and heard the full story of the haunting. It appears that on the morning of the previous day, a young girl staying at the *pension* had committed suicide by throwing herself out of one of the upper windows. The body had been removed to the mortuary.

Twenty-four hours later, passers-by declared they saw her staring out of the identical window from which she had leapt to her death. Boarders in the house were convinced that they could hear screams coming from the room she had occupied. I spent some hours at the *pension* and must admit that I, too, thought I heard very faint screams coming from the girl's room. But when I entered the apartment, I could neither see nor hear anything unusual. By the time I had finished my investigation, it was very late and I was fortunate in finding a taxi to take me back to Vienna. Next day I again visited the place, and stood for some hours outside the *pension* in the hope of seeing the 'face at the window.' I was unfortunate, and saw nothing—except the gaping crowds which impeded the traffic. Like most of these local 'psychic' sensations, the Baden ghost died a natural death—if I can use such an expression—and I am still wondering whether I really heard those faint screams outside the dead girl's room. Imagination often plays a major part in these cases. Imagination or not, the proprietor of the *pension* lost all his boarders and I heard that the house had been closed.

The Girl in the Blue Room

Speaking of faces at the window reminds me that on the Sunday evening following the Borley fire, a young man from Long Melford, accompanied by a girl friend, visited the rectory in order to inspect the ruins. They made their way through the grounds to the back of the house where the best view of the damage could be obtained. It was full moon, and a bright, still evening.

Although all the upper part of Borley Rectory was burnt out, the brick gable ends are still standing. In the centre of the house is a gable which once contained the window of the Blue Room—a bedroom which figures largely in all accounts of the manifestations at Borley.

As the two young people gazed at the charred ruins in the moonlight, they saw a girl, dressed in white (or very pale blue) lean out of the Blue Room window—or what remains of it— and then fall back amongst the burnt rafters. I have inter-viewed the young man concerning this incident, and nothing can shake his conviction that both he and his companion saw this apparition—for apparition it must have been. His girl friend is equally emphatic that she saw the figure, which was perfectly visible for several seconds. Their testimony rather gives the lie to the old French saw about two pairs of eyes never seeing a ghost at the same time.

So much for 'Christmas ghosts' in haunted houses. Of the many séances I have held or attended round about Christmas-tide, most have been blank—or merely nonsensical—but those I conducted with Rudi Schneider during the period December 1929 to January 1930 were brilliant. Rudi is, of course, the famous Austrian medium whom I brought to London, and at the period I have mentioned he was definitely at the top of his form. Actually, the most brilliant séance of all during this first visit of Rudi to my laboratory was held on Monday, 23rd December 1929.

My Best Christmas Séance

The séance was held under exceptional conditions of control. Every sitter wore metallic gloves and socks which were sealed to his person. These socks and gloves formed part of an electrical circuit which lit up a row of red lamps. Every one clasped the hand of his neighbour, and every foot had to be firmly placed on one of a series of metal plates screwed to the floor. If a person failed to press the hand of his neighbour, or lifted a foot off his respective plate, a red light was instantly extinguished, thus revealing the fact that the control was broken. Rudi was not only held by two persons, one of whom was myself, but was also controlled electrically by a separate circuit. He could move neither hand nor foot without the tell-tale lights warning us that the control of him was imperfect. In addition to this electrical control, all the sitters and medium were enclosed in a large gauze cage, making it *quite impossible* for any one to cheat, or play tricks, or even move a limb, without instant detection.

A pair of heavy plush curtains (the 'cabinet') had been placed across one corner of the séance-room, within the gauze cage. Of course, the medium and his controllers sat *outside* the cabinet, which was about one metre from the nearest sitter. The switching off of the white lights automatically switched on a red one, by means of which we could see all that was going on.

I will try to describe my impressions of this séance, but words almost fail me, as it is impossible to do justice to what we all saw at this most interesting sitting. The best pheno-mena were presented in the full light of the red lamp hanging in front of the curtain opening, through which we all saw a very white delicate hand (like a woman's) steal and try to pick up a rose which a sitter was holding under the lamp. The hand emerged from the cabinet (like a timid mouse coming out of its hole) for a distance of about eight inches, but did not get within two or three inches of the sitter's hand. Virtually, the hand of the sitter was between Rudi and the phenomenon. One thinks of these things afterwards, but it is a pity that the sitter did not move his hand a little in order to meet the 'pseudopod' (literally 'false limb'), or 'terminal.' But he did make contact later. The hand was extraordinarily white — much whiter than the handkerchief over which the terminal appeared, and very much whiter than the sitter's hand and the pale yellow artificial rose which lay in his palm. All the other members of the circle commented upon this whiteness. All this was plainly visible under the naked red bulb. The sitter (who, of course, had the best view, as his eyes were but a few inches from the 'hand') thinks that the movement of the white terminal stopped at about three inches from his hand; I thought it came rather nearer, but I saw it from a different angle. Like the rest of the sitters, I saw only four fingers, long and tapering, and could see no thumb. I have simulated the experiment with my own hand, and I find that the 'hand' was visible to me for about ten seconds during emergence and withdrawal. The other sitters may have seen it for a shorter or greater period; this would depend upon where they sat and if the emergence of the hand were hidden by any part of the folds of the curtains through which the pseudopod pushed itself.

A second striking manifestation was witnessed, even while a sitter was moving the table away from the curtain: the latter did not stop swinging and billowing. This fact suggests all sorts of possibilities, but we did not have Rudi long enough to carry out the necessary experiments.

Another curious phenomenon was that the curtains, at one period of their movements, were formed into *steps* and appeared quite stiff, just as if they had been laid over a flight of stairs. I afterwards tried to simulate this movement with my hands and found it quite impossible to obtain even a similar effect. It was all very curious.

The *pièce de résistance* of this most remarkable séance was the appearance of a feminine arm and hand, complete from elbow, which slowly emerged from between the curtains, with the basket between its fingers. The basket, *in mid-air*, had already been swept into the cabinet, and to our astonishment the basket emerged from between the curtains which parted and revealed to most of the onlookers a perfectly formed woman's arm, with hand and fingers similar to those which had nearly touched a sitter's hand just previously, except that the hand appeared to possess all its fingers. It is curious how one's thoughts turn to comparisons in such circumstances. I immediately likened the arm—and especially its upward move-ments—to a swan's neck and head, in a pose similar to that which the shadowgrapher makes when he throws the picture of a swan on his screen. All the sitters agreed that it was a perfectly formed arm, like a woman's; white, with fingers; and bare from the elbow. It was a brilliant spectacle.

Other things happened that night, besides the appearance of the 'pseudopods.' I had my trouser-leg tugged twice, the small of my back thumped once, and 'something' brushed past me—almost *pushed* past me—between my chair and the bookcase against the side of which Rudi used to lean when coming out of trance. Another sitter's leg was also touched, or something brushed past it. The first time I felt the entity brush past me I said nothing, in order to see whether 'Olga' (the alleged 'spirit control' or trance personality which always speaks through Rudi's lips at these séances) had done it for my special benefit, and whether 'she' would mention the fact. 'She' did, and then I acknowledged that I had felt something brushing past. The manifestation was then repeated. In addition to the other phenomena witnessed at this Christmas séance, every one felt very cold, the temperature appearing to change several times during the sitting.

In case the reader does not appreciate the severity of the control under which we witnessed the above extraordinary manifestations, I must ask him to remember that during the whole of the period of the trance, Rudi and I were connected with four electric-light indicators which never wavered; his wrists were held in a vice-like grip by me, and his legs were pressed close against mine. His hands were also controlled by another sitter, a lady, and during every major phenomenon she informed the circle that she was verifying the position of all our limbs. The phenomena were witnessed in a much better light than usual and the trance seemed deeper. Rudi was moaning and panting alternately when 'Olga' was not speaking to us, and half the time Rudi's head was on my chest. All the other sitters were, as usual, electrically controlled. It was a brilliant evening and the phenomena were as varied and interesting as they were brilliant. If Rudi's reputation rested on nothing more than this one séance, his mediumship was proved up to the hilt. Never, in the recorded history of any psychic, have phenomena been witnessed under such a merciless triple control of medium and sitters. We waited for another half hour or so, but as no further manifestations appeared to be forthcoming, we told Rudi to 'wake up,' at the same time switching on the orange lights, which were afterwards changed for white. Rudi at last gave a yawn, stretched himself, and thus ended my most brilliant Christmas séance.

The Bell-man's Cry

From noise of scare-fires rest ye free,
From murders *Benedicite!*
From all mischances that may fright
Your pleasing slumbers in the night;
Mercy secure ye all, and keep
The goblin from ye, while ye sleep.
Past one o'clock, and almost two,
My masters all, 'Good day to you.'

ROBERT HERRICK (1591–1674).

CHESTNUTS

ROASTED BY H. H. BLANCHARD

CHRISTMAS demands its chestnuts. Turkeys, plum-puddings, and pineapples are all very well, but the moment when the roasted chestnut leaps sizzling from the grate is the peak of the festivities. Put simply, it is the halcyon moment when the well-fed ship of appetite lies calm before plunging in the winds of indigestion. Then are the old tales told. 'Chestnuts' every one, they get their annual laugh.

Now what is this strange reaction called laughter? Is it so divinely removed from the beast? When man tenses his facial muscles, bares his teeth, and emits a strange noise from his throat is he being so very different from the creature which exposes its fangs as a prelude to a bite in anger or a chew in comfort? It is a solemn thought. And the more I think of my Uncle Cuthbert the less I like it.

After all, laughter has been defined as the sound you hear when you are running after your hat. There is no denying it; most of our fun is at the expense of others. Let us take a good normal healthy bull. There is nothing funny about that— provided we do the taking. But if the bull turns round and chases us to the gate our dearest friends rock with joy.

Not all our fun is so savoured with sadism. Gusts of laughter may be caused by the mental ticklings of the high-brows or by 'nonsense' jokes. Then there is coarse humour— that essential roughage for the mind which is digested by all but the very fastidious or the very hypocritical. Chaucer, that 'well of English undefiled,' knew its value.

248

However, this is no place for exploring that avenue. Coarse humour must be one of the stones left unturned in this chapter. Like my music-hall hero, I know my duty. I may not be clever, but I am clean! Chestnuts I may be serving up, but they must not be too hot.

The Three Calamities

Birth, marriage, and death—hatch, match, and dispatch—provide much food for mirth, presumably because they are all calamities. And the greatest of these is marriage. The bullied husband can be served up as an appetizing titbit at Christmas or any other time. Over his bowed head the original apple-tree has turned to a chestnut-tree, but he remains the mug. Still, he 'can take it'—aye, and like it.

When the public dinner gets to the port stage, and the guests have eaten all that their tickets will allow, what does the funny speaker talk about? Why, the husbands who have (a) escaped from their wives, or (b) brought them with them and therefore have to behave. And when the laughter rises, chief among the chucklers are those same husbands. Like the Chinese sect, they have learnt 'to consider all things and to despise none; to laugh at everything including themselves.'

Who has not heard the seaside story of the little boy who asked mummy if he could go in to swim? 'Certainly not, my dear,' said mummy, 'it is far too cold.' 'But daddy is swimming.' 'Yes, dear, but he is insured.'

In the same class comes the police-court yarn of the old burglar up before the 'beak.' 'And so,' said the justice, 'you took these articles off the counter and left the cash in the till undisturbed.' 'Now, don't you start on that,' said the prisoner, 'my old woman's been at me abaht it something crool.'

Then there is the story of the doctor who asked his patient why he had BF76528 tattooed on his back. 'That's not tattooed, doctor,' said the mild little man, 'that's where my wife ran into me with the car when I was opening the gate.'

Another motoring story is of the husband who returned home rather shaken one evening. 'I am going to sack that chauffeur, he said, 'he almost killed me again to-day.' 'Oh, dear,' replied the wife of his bosom, 'give him another chance.'

The Children rub it in

Even the little children rub it in. There was the teacher who was explaining the difference between the stately rose and the modest violet. 'You see, children,' she said, 'a beautiful well-dressed woman walks along the street, and she is proud and does not greet anybody—that is the rose. But behind her comes a small creature with bowed head——' 'Yes, miss, I know,' interrupted little Tommy. 'That's her husband.'

Of course, now and then the men get an innings. For instance, there was the wife accompanied by her reluctant husband on a pleasure cruise. 'What would you do,' she asked, 'if I fell overboard?' 'Probably lose my head completely,' replied the brute, 'and throw you a lifebelt.'

Equally brutal was Mr Justwed. 'Henry,' said Mrs J. one moonlight night. 'There's a burglar at the silver, and one in the pantry eating my pies. Get up and call for help.' Mr Justwed (at window): 'Police! Doctor!'

Golfing husbands will appreciate the feelings of the golfer who, stalking up to another player, said: 'Confound it, sir, you nearly hit my wife.' 'Did I?' answered the culprit 'Well, have a shot at mine!'

Love laughs

So far we have only studied the story of the complete marital state. But what of the prologue? What of that honeyed period of unreality before the cold plunge into matrimony? If all the world loves a lover, it is equally true that it is prepared for kindly laughter at him. Flaming June, roses and wine, and dancing on the village green with a hey nonny, nonny no—that is the traditional setting for love-making. But Christmastide, too, provides its chances. Just think of the dangers lurking beneath the mistletoe! A violent outbreak of lipstick rash has shamed more than one bachelor into marriage after a Christmas game of postman's knock.

The trouble is that no one knows when and how the love fever will attack. Take an ordinary hearty male who enjoys juicy steaks, Rugby football, and Edgar Wallace. In a matter of hours he may be reduced to a vague creature who just toys with his breakfast toast and gapes at the grape-fruit before rushing off to write another effusion to his lady. It is all very sad. 'One must remember,' as the bishop said to the actress, 'that the love bug will bite you if you don't look out.'

Which recalls the story of the young lady wooed by an ardent youth. 'If you don't leave the house immediately,' she said, 'I'll call the whole police force to put you out.' 'Darling,' he replied, 'it would take the whole fire brigade to put me out.' Then there was the fierce toreador. 'Ah, *señorita*,' he burbled, 'to-night I will steal beneath your balcony and sing you a sweet serenade.' 'Do,' she replied, 'and I will drop you a flower.' 'Ah,' he murmured, 'in a moment of mad love?' 'No,' said she, 'in a pot.'

Motoring has given extra power to Cupid's wings. The young fellow with the two-seater rarely drives alone, while the motor cyclist with a pillion seat generally has his 'flapper bracket' occupied. Two motor cyclists were taking two girls for a quiet amble at about seventy miles an hour one Saturday, when one of the drivers made violent signals. 'Hey,' he shouted, 'your girl has fallen off.' 'Never mind,' said his pal, 'I can get another in Nottingham.' Not so casual was the young man in a car driving a girl down a lonely road. 'You look lovelier to me every minute,' he said. 'Do you know what that is a sign of?' 'I do,' she answered. 'You are about to run out of petrol.' Anyway, he was more attentive than the Scot who met a girl who was so beautiful that when he took her home in a taxi he could hardly keep his eye on the meter.

Modern young things are more calm than their vapoury grandmothers. 'Who was that man I saw you kissing last night?' a mother demanded of a modern daughter. 'Well, mother,' came the answer, 'about what time was it?' The schoolroom, too, does not escape the gentle passion. 'Willie,' asked the teacher in the grammar class, 'tell me what it is when I say "I love, you love, he loves"?' 'Well, miss,' said Willie, 'that's one of them triangles where somebody gets shot.'

Nonsense Stories

Christmas being the time of toleration, the 'nonsense' stories are permitted. Even your Aunt Veronica will become almost human if you tell her the tale of the two cemetery worms who were fighting in dead Ernest. Or, again, she may melt if you speak of the poor little ragged boy who gazed longingly at the box of soldiers marked: 'This size for 2s. 6d.' and left the shop murmuring: 'So do I.'

A real hoary old chestnut is the story of the two strangers who bumped into each other in a London bar. 'Hallo, hallo!' said A. 'Didn't I meet you last year in Singapore?' 'I'm afraid you're mistaken,' said B, 'for I've never been to

Singapore.' 'Nor have I,' replied A. 'It must have been two other men.'

Then there is the whiskered old favourite of the absent-minded man who was dining for the first time with a new acquaintance. When lettuce was handed round he seized the dish and emptied it over his head. 'My dear chap, my dear chap,' spluttered his host, 'that was lettuce.' 'Very foolish of me,' answered the guest, 'I thought it was spinach.' This piece of nonsense has split up many a home. It has even caused vegetarians to snap at each other. Personally, I will stand behind the lettuce story to the last leaf.

Of the not quite so silly variety is the yarn of the school inspector who was telling the vicar of the dull boy at the village school. 'Very funny,' said the inspector. 'I asked Tommy Green who wrote *Hamlet* and he piped up: "I didn't, sir."' Further down the street the vicar told the tale to the curate. 'Ha, ha, my dear vicar!' was the reply. 'So Tommy Green said he didn't write *Hamlet*. Very good. Very good indeed. But I'll wager he did, all the same.'

We all know that the insomniac who said he turned and twisted all night probably slept like a top. And we have all heard of the mechanical engineer who wanted to take his nose to pieces to see what made it run. But does every one know of the sweet young thing who went to the Cup Final and shamed her boy friend by asking if a football coach had four wheels?

In the nonsense class is the tale of the nervous hospital patient. 'Oh dear, sister,' he jittered, 'I'm terribly frightened. I've never had an operation before.' 'Don't worry,' said the sister, 'nor has the doctor.' And here is a chestnut which does not belong to this basket, but which I am just throwing in because I like it: *Butler* (hearing noises in the library): 'Is that you, my lord?' *Burglar:* 'Yus, mate.'

Over-the-Border Ballads

Scottish chestnuts are in a class of their own. All jokes about Scotsmen are funny, and all Scotsmen are funny about jokes. As an Englishman who has enjoyed the fullness of Scottish hospitality, I think the funniest thing about them is the way they 'get away' with the meanness myth. Non-Sassenach humour nearly always bears the stamp of Aberdeen, where a joke-making factory is kept busy all the year round. The Granite City is the place where the natives walk down the street open-mouthed if there is a nip in the air. Up there they know that rigid economy means a dead Scotsman. They tell with pride the story of the Scotsman who shouted at his unfaithful wife: 'Stand behind your lover, I am going to shoot you both.'

I like, too, the tale of the Scotsman's wife who, looking out of the window, shouted: 'Sandy, here comes company for supper!' 'Quick,' shouted Sandy, 'everybody run out on the porch with a tooth-pick!'

As ancient as the Cairngorms is the story of the two Aberdonians who met outside a 'pub' after being parted for twenty years. 'We must celebrate this,' said Angus; 'but you'll no be forgetting that I paid for the last one.' Of the same vintage is the story of the nervous train passenger and the Scot. 'Oh dear,' said the passenger, 'I'm afraid I've pulled the communication cord by mistake. What shall I do? I shall be fined £5.' 'Never mind,' said the Scot. 'Give me £3 and I'll have a fit.'

The Sporting Spirit

The Christmas spirit suffers gladly the sporting chestnut. When the fire blazes up, and glasses are kept well charged, sporting disasters are transmuted by mellowed memories into modest triumphs. Missed putts are sunk, escaped fish are brought to the gaff, and uprooted middle stumps are replanted with the bails a-wobbling. Grandpa is allowed to tell, end by end, how he won the bowls handicap, and for once no one stalks out of the room and slams the door. Poor father (handicap twenty-four) is not interrupted in his description of the only round he ever did under ninety. It is all very soothing.

Yet there is nothing to be surprised about in this toleration. For we are a wonderfully sporting nation. I say so. You say so. Everybody else says so. And if that is not proof enough we can point to the fact that we dare to make jokes about the sacred sporting spirit itself. 'Never hit a man when he's down,' a football friend used to say to me. 'Kick him, it's easier and hurts more.' Then again: 'Our club motto is "Never mind the ball, get on with the game"; and our county motto: "Kick him again, he's still breathing."'

More gentle are the cricket stories. And when there is a touring side abroad, even the chills of Christmas cannot keep your real cricketer from dreaming of the game. Up spring visions of village greens, a squat church tower, and—need I say it?—one hears again the buzz of bees in the chestnut-trees. Two old Gloucestershire cricket chestnuts are my favourites.

The first is the story of the Gloucestershire farmer who lent a field to the village club. In return he was given a place in the side. When he batted umpires turned a deaf ear to all appeals, and he never was sent back to the pavilion until his stumps were sent flying. One day a zealous new umpire appeared, and no one told him of the local rule. In came the farmer and stepped plumb in front of the wicket to take the first ball on his pads. 'How's that?' shouted the bowler. 'Hout,' said the umpire. 'Ho, hout, is it,' said the farmer. 'Then hout of my field you all go.' And out they went.

Also from the county of the Graces comes the tale of the cautious umpire. He was dragged from among the spectators, and helped into his coat with words of advice which drowned his protests. At first all went well. He counted correctly the six pebbles in his pocket as the bowler charged up to the crease, and his pipe lent him an air of wisdom. Then came a sharp appeal for a catch at the wicket. 'How's that, umpire?' shouted the bowler. The umpire just puffed at his pipe. 'How was it, umpire?' asked the fielders. But no judge could have been more impassive. 'Come along, umpire,' said the captain, 'let's know how it was.' Then the oracle took out his pipe and weighed his words. 'I bean't a-going to say neither road,' he said, 'then I shan't offend nobody.'

The Enchanted Shirt

Yet, however funny the joke, experience teaches us that laughter, like happiness, if keenly pursued may never be overtaken. It is captured without premeditation and by surprise. Of that truth Colonel John Hay's American ballad of *The Enchanted Shirt* affords an excellent example. The tale tells of how the king was sick, or said he was sick, and 'doctors came by the score,' and had their heads cut off when they failed to cure him. Then one wise leech said that the king would be well if he slept one night in the shirt of a happy man.

The courtiers hunted the realm in vain for a happy man until:

> At last they came to a village gate,
>   A beggar lay whistling there,
> He whistled and sang, and laughed and rolled
>   On the grass in the soft June air.

The courtiers felt that they had found their man, and offered him a hundred ducats for the loan of his shirt. But

> The merry blackguard lay back on the grass,
>   And laughed till his face was black,
> 'I would do it, God wot!' and he roared with the fun,
>   'But I haven't a shirt to my back.'

For the benefit of the curious, and to end the chapter on a moral note, I should add that the king grew ashamed of his useless life, went out into the world and toiled, 'the land was glad' and 'the king was well and gay.'

———

UPON the morwe, whan that it was day,
To Britaigne tooké they the righté way,—
Aurelius and this magicien bisyde,
And been descended ther they wolde abyde;
And this was, as thise bookés me remembre,
The coldé, frosty sesoun of Decembre.
  Phebus wox old, and hewéd lyk latoun,
That in his hooté declynacioun
Shoon as the burnéd gold, with stremés brighte;
But now in Capricorn adoun he lighte,
Where as she shoon ful pale, I dar wel seyn.
The bittré frostes with the sleet and reyn
Destroyéd hath the grene in every yerd:
Janus sit by the fyr with double berd,
And drynketh of his bugle horn the wyn;
Biforn hym stant brawn of the tuskéd swyn,
And 'Nowel' crieth every lusty man.

GEOFFREY CHAUCER (c. 1340–1400),
        The Frankeleyns Tale.

GAMES FOR THE PARTY

BY HUBERT PHILLIPS

Who am I ?

THIS is a 'get-together' game; it may well be the first item on the agenda. Each participant has a slip of paper pinned on his back; on this is written the name of some historical char-acter, 'Noah,' 'Napoleon,' 'Cleopatra,' 'The Man in the Iron Mask,' and so on. He is invited to discover who he is by asking questions, to which only 'Yes' or 'No' may be answered.

> 'Am I alive?'
> 'No.'
> 'A man?'
> 'No.'
> 'Did I live before 1500?'
> 'Yes.'

Only three questions may be asked at a time; the guest interrogated now asks three in his turn. Then contact should be made with someone else:

> 'I'm a woman living before 1500. Did I live before 1000?'
> 'No.'
> 'Am I French?'
> 'Yes.'
> 'Am I Joan of Arc?'
> 'Yes.'

And Joan, having discovered 'her' identity, can now devote 'herself' to being helpful to others. (Or, alternatively, 'she' may be awarded a point and given another label.)

If the guests are kept circulating, they should be on good terms with one another by the time all identities are disclosed.

What's Wrong?

An observation game. Those playing are first invited to observe carefully the details of the room they are in; then all but one of them go out. The last named now has ten minutes in which to rearrange the furniture, etc. He makes a careful note of what he has done, effecting, say, twelve or fifteen changes in all. Some should be easily spotted:

Arm-chair placed the other way round.
Bowl of flowers moved from the table to the mantelpiece.
Clock put on one hour.

Others (to make the game competitive) should be more difficult:

Poker and tongs change places.
Telephone placed the other way round on its stand.
Book which was left open at p. 128 now open at p. 178—and so on.

Now the other players come in again, and are invited to write down, within, say, five minutes, a list of the changes that have been made. A mark is given for each correct answer, and a mark deducted for each incorrect one.

Hidden Birds, etc.

We were rather horrified to learn how little George had learned about literature.

James the First was described by a famous historian as the most unpopular king of his day.

We heard of the discovery simultaneously and we both rushed to Egypt to inspect it.

Any one, reading the above sentences carefully, can discover the 'hidden birds.' They are *owl, lark, thrush.* But read the sentences aloud, and the birds become much more difficult to spot. This fact is the basis of an amusing party game.

It can be played in various ways. Thus, the host can prepare the sentences beforehand; these are then read to the assembled party, and whoever calls out the right answer first scores a point. The objection to this plan is that one or two players are generally exceptionally quick. An alternative, then, is to provide pencil and paper and ask those competing to write down what the hidden words are. They should not be allowed to write down the sentences containing them.

In a third form of the game, each player makes up a sentence; putting it, in the first instance, to the player on his left.

It is not, of course, necessary to confine oneself to 'Hidden Birds.' Thus, one can have 'Hidden Trees':

I should feel more satisfied with things in general if I had a larger income.

And now they are living in fairyland, as happy as can be.

Or 'Hidden Animals':

I left the university because I didn't want to be a research worker.

You never saw so erratic a time-keeper as the watch I bought in Belgium.

Or 'Hidden Authors':

We went for a swim in the lake at seven-thirty.

She informed the archdeacon, with many apologies, that she had now to dash away.

And so on. (The answers are on page 273.)

If players with initiative are taking part, they can think up all manner of variations.

Liars

No previous preparation is required for this game, and nothing much in the way of mental effort.

A pack of cards is shuffled and one card handed face down/wards to each player. They look at their cards, but do not show them to any one else. There should be someone with a paper and pencil to keep the score. When all are ready, the first player says: 'My card is [say] the queen of hearts.' Each of the other players now states whether, in his opinion, the first player is lying or telling the truth. The scorer should make a note of these speculations. Now the first player turns up his card. If it is the queen of hearts, those who have put him down as truthful each score one point, while he, for his part, scores one point in respect of each of those who have put him down as a liar. If his card is not the queen of hearts, the reverse, of course, is the case: those who have pronounced him a liar score, while he himself scores points at the expense of the others.

Now the same process is repeated with respect to the second player, and so the game goes on until every one has shown his card. The player with the highest aggregate of points wins.

It may appear that this game is purely guesswork, but actually quite a lot of psychology enters into it.

Coffee-pots

This is a 'conversation' game. I can perhaps best explain it by giving an example:

A is 'he' and has decided upon his 'coffee-pot.' The others in turn ask him questions—any questions they like. A's answer must be such as would normally include the *word-sound* he has selected, but instead of that *word-sound* he substitutes the word *coffee-pot*. Read carefully what follows, and see how quickly you can guess what A's 'coffee-pot' is.

A. Ready. You begin, B.

B. Did you go to the rugger match yesterday?

A. No, I went to the coffee-pot.

C. I should have thought you'd prefer the match. Why didn't you go?

A. I hadn't the coffee-pot.

D. Are you fond of the theatre, A?

A. Coffee-pot-ly!

E. What sort of plays do you like?

A. Romantic plays, with coffee-pot ladies in them.

E. Is it *light*?

A. No. (E loses one point.)

B. Have you got a good job now?

A. It's coffee-pot!

C. That's informative! What's your favourite game?

A. Coffee-pot-to!

C. Oh, *come*, A, that's taking one risk too many. Your 'coffee-pot' is *fair*.

It will be seen from this example that word-sounds should be selected which have a number of meanings. *Fair* (*fare*), given above, is a word which can be put to good use. Other examples are *post*; *mail* (*male*); *pair* (*pear, pare*); *bear* (*bare*); *pole* (*poll*); *light*; *right* (*write*), etc. Note that the answer may include variants of the 'coffee-pot'; in the example given, *coffee-pot-ly* (*fairly*); *coffee-pot-to* (*faro*), and so on.

A player should only be allowed a guess after he has himself asked a question. Wrong guesses should be penalized, and also guesses out of turn.

Blobs

This is a very popular game; the only thing against it is that it requires careful preparation. Whoever is running it should have ready a story of perhaps 1,000 to 1,500 words

containing as many recognizable errors of fact as can reasonably be crammed into a narrative. Thus, it might begin as
follows:

*About half-past six one January evening, Professor Snoggins, of
University College, Cambridge, stood by the statue of Eros in
Trafalgar Square and watched the sun setting over St Paul's. . . .*

In this short sentence there are no fewer than four absurd
statements: (1) There is no University College, Cambridge;
(2) the statue of Eros is not in Trafalgar Square; (3) the sun
sets long before half-past six; (4) in any case, it sets in the
opposite direction.

As soon as a player hears what he thinks is a mis-statement,
he shouts out 'Blob,' and the first to spot each Blob scores one
point. It is advisable, by the way, to have an official scorer
who will decide—or, at any rate, will try to decide—who has
called 'Blob' first. If a player calls 'Blob,' when, in fact,
there is no Blob, he should lose three points. This heavy
penalty should serve to bring the scorer's task within the bounds
of what is practicable.

An expert composer of Blob stories will be careful to include
a number of statements which, at first blush, seem wrong, but
which are, in fact, correct.

Word Associations

The players seat themselves in a circle, and the first of them
begins a chain of associations by mentioning any word that
comes into his head. The next player then gives a word
suggested by this first one. The third player, in his turn,
suggests an association for the second word, and so on all
round the circle. This goes on until there are, say, a couple
of dozen words altogether in the chain.

Here is an example from an actual game. There were eight players, each contributing three words:

1. Motor car	9. Horse	17. Ostrich
2. Bonnet	10. Hounds	18. Sand
3. Lady	11. Brush	19. Pyramids
4. Gentleman	12. Comb	20. Snooker
5. Pipe	13. Cock	21. Cue
6. Raleigh	14. Crow	22. Stage door
7. Queen Elizabeth	15. Nest	23. Bouquet
8. Brown Bess	16. Egg	24. Claret

When the chain is completed (in this case with 'Claret'), the players proceed to unwind it; each, that is, is supposed to remember the sequence of associations, and to be able to work backwards to the initial word. After 'Claret' comes 'Bouquet,' then 'Stage door,' then 'Cue,' and so on back to 'Motor car.' A player who has to be prompted loses a life, and the winner is he who can go on longest without making a mistake.

This game probably seems difficult to those who have not played it, but you will be surprised how easy it becomes with a little practice.

'My Aunt went to Town'

This is another 'association' game. Each player has so many lives to begin with and drops out when all his lives have been lost.

The players are seated in a circle. The first player chooses any letter he likes. Suppose it is 'S'; he starts the ball rolling by saying: 'My aunt went to town and bought [say] a siphon.' The second player now says: 'My aunt went to town and bought a siphon and [say] a sealskin coat.' The third player: 'My aunt went to town and bought a siphon, a sealskin coat, and a string of sausages.' And so it goes on, each player adding one more to the tale of 'my aunt's' purchases until someone makes a mistake and loses a life. The next player now begins another series of purchases, choosing a different letter.

Ghosts

This old favourite is perhaps the best of the *spelling* games. Players seat themselves in a circle; then one begins by naming any letter. Now each player in turn adds another letter to it, the object of the game being to go on adding letters as long as possible. Whoever ends a word loses a life.

Some agreement is necessary, however, as to what constitutes a 'word.' It is usually arranged, to begin with, that a word of *two* or *three* letters is not a word within the meaning of the rules. (Otherwise, the possibilities of the game become unduly restricted.) It is also agreed, as a rule, that plurals are barred, as also forms of a verb other than the infinitive. Also all proper names. It is just as well to appoint a referee who will adjudicate upon doubtful points.

If a player makes a mistake, it is up to the next player to challenge him; any one who interferes (other than a 'ghost') is penalized by losing a life. A player who is in a jam can often get out of his difficulties if he makes an impossible continuation with a convincing enough show of confidence. Thus we may have:

1st player	.	P
2nd player	.	L
3rd player	.	A
4th player	.	I

Now 5th player has to think hard. He will reject D, N, and T—since *plaid*, *plain*, and *plait* are all completed words—and will select, perhaps, C, for *plaice*. (He might, alternatively, try S, for *plaister*, and argue it out with the referee as to whether this word is, or is not, obsolete.) Anyway, we have:

5th player	.	C

Sixth player is now in a real quandary. *Plaice* is his only legitimate word, but if he says 'E' he loses a life anyway, so he might just as well try to save it. He therefore says, with the air of one who is carrying forward an obvious continuation, 'I' or 'H' or maybe 'A.' He *may* be challenged, in which case, of course, he can only admit defeat; but quite likely 7th player—uncertain whether 6th player has a genuine word or not—will try and carry the imposture forward, especially if 8th player is weak.

Where a player challenges, and a legitimate continuation is produced, the challenger in his turn loses a life.

A player becomes a 'ghost' when he has lost three lives (or such other number as may be mutually agreed). A 'ghost,' however, is not out of the game. He is allowed to harry the players still left in by making misleading suggestions; and if one of his suggestions is adopted, and a player loses a life in consequence, the 'ghost' gets back into the game.

When players have become really expert at 'Ghosts,' other forms of the game may be adopted. Thus, words may be spelt *backwards*. This is very difficult:

1st player	.	Y
2nd player	.	R
3rd player	.	A
4th player	.	R
5th player	.	T
6th player	.	I
7th player	.	'Challenge you!'
6th player	.	'Pituitrary!'
7th player	.	'Sorry, it isn't spelt like that.'

Referee confirms. Sixth player now loses a life.

Or, again, letters can be added *anywhere*, provided that those who interpolate them do not alter the order of the existing letters. Each player must repeat the word, so far as it has been built up; and should, of course, have a word in mind in case the next player challenges.

An example:

1st player	.	A
2nd player	.	A R
3rd player	.	I A R (liar)
4th player	.	I C A R (bicarbonate)
5th player	.	I S C A R (miscarry)
6th player	.	D I S C A R (discard)
7th player	.	D I S C H A R (discharge)
8th player	.	N D I S C H A R (undischarged)

and so on.

For this form of the game, a time-limit is desirable or unconscionable 'huddles' may result.

Proof-reading

A competitive game which calls for mental alertness. Players, working in pairs, are given sheets of paper bearing some such message as the following:

the story, every strand of it. For demo-
for lack of foresight, vitality, and moral
free nations between whom war is for
of our race, and we may well recall it
distinguishing its two main racial strains.
cracy made the federal Dominion of
the differences of thought and culture
to-day when democracy is being assailed
This is a great chapter in the history
power. Out of it has come a fraternity of
Canada with complete security for all
ever exorcised, and democracy has woven

What is this? Just twelve lines from a newspaper which

have been rearranged so that what made sense (more or less) now makes none. Here is the reconstructed passage:

> This is a great chapter in the history of our race, and we may well recall it to-day when democracy is being assailed for lack of foresight, vitality, and moral power. Out of it has come a fraternity of free nations between whom war is for ever exorcised, and democracy has woven the story, every strand of it. For democracy made the federal Dominion of Canada with complete security for all the differences of thought and culture distinguishing its two main racial strains.

The object of the game is, of course, to be the first to get the order right. To make it perfectly fair, every one should have the same passage. The lines can be cut out and pasted from several copies of the paper—rather a laborious business this—or, better, the passage, in its jumbled form, can be duplicated on a typewriter.

Adverbs

This is an amusing 'action' game requiring no previous preparation. One player goes out of the room; the others then select a suitable adverb, which has to be guessed by the player who is out. For example, 'clumsily,' 'promptly,' 'negligently,' 'enthusiastically,' 'cheerfully,' etc.

The player who is out now comes in and asks each person in the room, in turn, to perform some action or other *in the manner of the word*. Thus, he can ask the first player to light a cigarette; the second to give a dancing lesson to the third; the fourth to read a passage from a book; the fifth to pour out a glass of whisky, and so on. He is allowed three guesses as to what the adverb is which is being illustrated for his benefit.

Naturally the game is not a success unless every one co-operates to the best of his ability.

Thought Reading

Here is a very simple source of mystification. (Though naturally it will not serve to mystify those who have read this book.)

Every one sits in a circle, and one player goes out, a confederate remaining behind. The confederate then explains that the player who has left the room will come in and say who it is that the rest are thinking about, and one of those in the circle is selected for this purpose. The thought reader now comes in and is invited to discover on whom every one's thoughts are concentrated, and he goes through the motions of being suitably psychic.

Actually what happens is that the confederate unostentatiously adopts the position or gestures of the player who has been selected. The thought reader then has only to look round the room and identify his subject from his confederate's behaviour.

This performance can be repeated quite a number of times—to the growing amazement of those who are not in the secret.

'Quiz' Games

With a serious-minded party, 'Quiz' games are popular. These require pencil and paper. A quiz is just a general knowledge competition—or it can, of course, have reference to some particular branch of knowledge: history, literature, music, the stage, and so on. Be sure you do not start examining your guests unless you think they will like it! [Some examples of the quiz will be found on pages 404–440 of this book. —EDITOR.]

Less exacting than a straightforward 'Quiz' is a 'True or False?' question game. A number of factual statements are read out; all each player has to do is to list them as *true* or *false.* This gives every one a chance; since, whether one knows the answers or not, one has a fifty-fifty chance of guessing right!

Try these, for example. There are twelve statements: how many of them are true?

1. *Fuller Pilch was the name of a famous cricketer.*
2. *Rome is supposed to have been founded in 753 B.C.*
3. *By 'numismatics' is meant the study of coins.*
4. *A mile has been swum in a quarter of an hour.*
5. *Joseph Conrad's name was originally Sobieski.*
6. *Penguins inhabit the Arctic and Antarctic circles.*
7. *Mr Gladstone first became Prime Minister in 1868.*
8. *No woman can be elected to the Royal Academy.*
9. *Pewter is an alloy of tin and copper.*
10. *The University of Oxford was founded by King Edward the Confessor.*
11. *Sir John Moore was mortally wounded at Corunna.*
12. *Ruy Lopez was the name of a famous chess-player.*

(The answers are given on page 273)

Citadel

The 'citadel' is built up with matches on the top of an empty bottle, which should be placed on a flat surface in the middle of the room.

Each player in turn takes two matches and places them in position. He can arrange his matches as he likes—parallel to those last laid, at right angles, or in any other position that suits him. But if, as he is placing his matches, a match falls to the ground—either one of his, or any other—he is forthwith out of the game.

(Alternatively, each player may be given two or more 'lives.')

The last player left in is the winner. It is astonishing how many matches expert players can contribute before the 'citadel' becomes so rickety that there is nothing more to be done with it.

Concentration

This is a 'memory' game and is extraordinarily popular with young people. It requires a table and a pack of cards, though it is not, as will appear, a card game in the strict sense of the term.

The cards are well shuffled and are then laid out face downwards on the table. They must not overlap one another. When they have all been laid out each player, in turn, faces any two cards. If they are of the same denomination, e.g. two knaves, or two fours, he picks them up and places them face downwards in front of him. He can now face two more cards, and his turn will continue until he faces two cards which are not of the same denomination. These are placed face downwards again and the initiative passes to the next player.

To begin with, obviously, the game is one of pure chance, but quite soon the positions of a number of cards will have been noted and (with luck) remembered.

Towards the end of the game, 'tactics,' as well as memory, become important. Thus, if there are very few 'unknown' cards, i.e. cards that have not been faced, a good player may deliberately face a card already known to him to avoid giving vital information away.

There are two ways of playing the game, incidentally, differing according to the lay-out of the cards. If they are laid out like this:

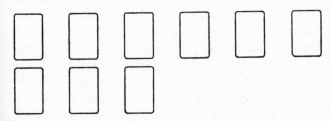

and so on, an experienced player can soon evolve a 'visual mnemonic' for remembering which card is which. If they are laid out 'higgledy-piggledy':

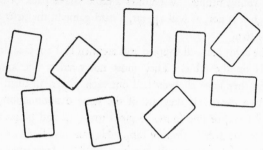

the game becomes distinctly more difficult.

The winner, of course, is he who collects the greatest number of cards.

Murder

No anthology of games, however brief, would be adequate which did not include 'Murder.'

The best number for this game is from eight to twelve. To begin with, playing cards equal to the number of players are shuffled together; these should include (say) the ace of diamonds, and the ace of spades. Whoever draws the ace of diamonds is the detective, and at once proclaims the fact; whoever draws the ace of spades is the murderer, who, of course, does not announce himself. He (and all the other players also) should put his card in his pocket and say nothing.

Now every one excepting the detective leaves the room. There should be plenty of space available for the murderer's operations (this game is pointless in a small flat); everywhere should be in total darkness. The players move about, going into whatever rooms they like, and before long—when he thinks the moment opportune—the murderer will select a victim. He should go up to the 'murderee' very quietly and whisper: 'You are dead.' The murderee should now count thirty, at the end of which time he falls to the ground uttering an ear‑piercing yell. (Meanwhile, of course, the murderer is making his 'get‑away.')

At this point, all movement must cease. The lights are turned up and every one stays where he is until the detective, emerging from his lair, has viewed the body and made such mental notes as he wishes. Now every one repairs to head‑quarters where the detective interrogates each in turn; except, of course, the corpse. Whatever questions he asks must be truthfully answered, but (*a*) he should not be given unasked‑for information, and (*b*) the murderer may lie as much as he likes. When every one has been interrogated, the detective, if he is a good detective, should be able to say who the murderer is. He is generally allowed two, or even three, guesses.

I should add that (apart from the fun of being murdered, and so forth) this game is a flop if the detective is not intelligent. A poor detective will ask a lot of aimless questions and will then just take a 'pot shot' at who the murderer is. But this is no fun really either for the questioner or for those being questioned. What the detective should properly do is to build up in his mind a visual picture of the positions of the various players at the time of the murder, checking up relentlessly on discrepancies in their statements. If he asks the right questions, and the rest co‑operate as they should, detection of even an ingenious murderer, backed up by a thumping good lie, will be a matter of certainty.

ANSWERS

HIDDEN TREES (page 260):   Elm, ash.

HIDDEN ANIMALS (page 260): Bear, cat.

HIDDEN AUTHORS (page 260): Keats, Shaw.

TRUE OR FALSE (page 270):   Statements 1, 2, 3, 7, 11, and
                            12 are true.

TWELVE TALES FOR CHRISTMAS

When they were all tired of blind-man's buff, there was a great game at snap-dragon, and when fingers enough were burned with that, and all the raisins were gone, they sat down by the huge fire of blazing logs to a substantial supper, and a mighty bowl of wassail, something smaller than an ordinary wash-house copper, in which the hot apples were hissing and bubbling with a rich look, and a jolly sound, that were perfectly irresistible.

'This,' said Mr Pickwick, looking round him, 'this is, indeed, comfort.'

'Our invariable custom,' replied Mr Wardle. 'Everybody sits down with us on Christmas eve, as you see them now—servants and all; and here we wait, until the clock strikes twelve, to usher Christmas in, and beguile the time with forfeits and old stories. Trundle, my boy, rake up the fire.'

Up flew the bright sparks in myriads as the logs were stirred. The deep red blaze sent forth a rich glow, that penetrated into the furthest corner of the room, and cast its cheerful tint on every face.

CHARLES DICKENS, *Pickwick Papers*.

TWILIGHT OF THE WISE

BY JAMES HILTON

WE were talking, on Christmas night, about other Christmas nights. I had said that twenty years ago I was in the trenches somewhere in France. 'And I,' Middleton countered, 'was somewhere in the Bavarian Alps.'

It seemed a queer place for an Englishman to have been during the war years, until he explained, with a smile: 'I was escaping. We managed it, you know—thanks to luck and Manny Stewart's German.'

I guessed then that this fellow Middleton had deliberately stayed up to talk after the others had gone to bed; he knew I had known Manny from the conversation at dinner. I had quoted one of Manny's last poems, and we had all argued about what it probably meant—all of us, that is, except Middleton, who didn't seem the kind of person to argue much about a poem, anyway.

'You must have known him well?' I suggested.

'Not exactly. But it came as a personal loss when I read of his death last year, and again to-night when you quoted that poem. I suppose an experience of the kind he and I had, even if it only lasts a few days, counts for more than years of just "knowing" somebody.'

'Maybe.'

'Ordinarily, of course, Manny and I wouldn't have had much in common—even at the prison-camp he'd been with us at least a month before I exchanged more than a few words with him. He had his own friends—chaps interested in art and books and all that. Then one day he came up to me when I was alone and said: "Is it true you nearly got away once?" It *was* true, and I told him all about it, how I'd been within a mile of the Dutch frontier when things went wrong, all because I didn't know that *Eisenstange* means a sort of iron rod. I was hiding in a railway wagon full of them . . . but that's another story. Manny laughed when I told it him. "My German's pretty good," he said. "How would you like to have another try with me?" I looked at him and I knew damn well I'd like it, and he knew I knew, too—it was a sort of sudden contact between us that didn't have to be argued about.'

'Yes,' I said. 'He made a good many of those contacts.'

'So we fixed it right away, and began to make plans. Manny thought we ought to try an escape in midwinter, because of the long nights; and he had an idea that the third week of December might be lucky for us, because even in wartime Germany the Christmas spirit had its manifestations— feasting and jollification and a general slackening of vigilance. The food shortage wasn't too bad in our part of Bavaria, and the people were a comfortable lot compared with the Prussians —as I knew myself from experience. And then, too, he thought we might try to get across the mountains instead of keeping to lowland routes—the idea, you see, being to do just what nobody would expect. Actually, we could be among the mountains within a couple of hours of leaving camp—if we dared to risk it. Do you know the Bavarian Alps? I didn't, and neither did Manny, but we had a map, and we both found we'd had plenty of pre-war climbing experience in Switzerland. It was just a matter of nerve, endurance, food-supply, and luck with the weather. Well, we thought we had the first two, and we prayed for the others. We began to hide food till we had a store; then we collected warm clothing and white coats made of bed-linen, so that we shouldn't be spotted against a snow background. Then we had to make plans for the actual escape, but I needn't tell you about these, partly because they weren't very different from those of other escapes I've read of, and also because the get-away was pretty easy. We were six thousand feet above the camp when dawn broke. We had to put on dark glasses because of the snow dazzle, and we ate chocolate and chaffed each other and stared down at the camp below—just a few littered roofs amongst the pine forests.

'Of course, by that time the hue and cry must surely have been raised, but it didn't worry us much. You can't chase two men over high alps in midwinter, and in practice you don't consider it—because you don't believe the two men would ever be such fools. *We* were, though, and we were quite happy about it. I don't believe I've ever had a feeling of such almighty ecstasy as that morning as we climbed farther and higher up the snow-slopes till we reached the steep rocks.

'The day was glorious, and we lay out in the sun during the afternoon and slept, knowing that it would be bitterly cold at night, and that we should have to keep moving all the time. We didn't talk very much, except that Manny tried to brush up my German. We climbed an icy ridge, and descended the other side. There was no trace after that of any inhabited world—the mountains enclosed us on every hand. Manny led the way, and at nightfall the moon rose, so that we went on without a halt.

'Of course we might have known that it wouldn't be all as easy as that. The next day there was no sunshine at all, and a freezing wind blew; we were utterly exhausted and slept for odd minutes in any sheltered place we could find, until our stiffening limbs awakened us. We began to walk and climb in a daze; Manny recited poetry, and I told him, I remember, about my horses and dogs at home. We were really talking to ourselves—not to each other. That night we began to realize, though neither of us put it into words, the pretty awful chance we were taking. We ate our food, primed ourselves with brandy, smoked our pipes, and drew what consolation we could from the map. It was a good map, and Manny knew exactly the place he was making for. Nevertheless, our spirits sank lower, and lowest of all during the early hours of the morning. But afterwards, when the sun came out, we grew cheerful again.

'I won't try to detail each day as it passed—partly because I can't be sure how many days did pass. During the sunshine we lived; during the cold, dark hours we slipped into a kind of coma. I think there was an exact moment when we both felt that our number was up—though whether this came on the third or the fifth or the seventh day I can't be sure. We had come to the end of our food, we were chilled and utterly wearied, and—to make things worse—the comparatively fine weather broke down and snowstorms began. I think Manny saw the future as I did, for he said once, in that wry way of his: 'I'm afraid we've been guarding against the wrong sort of danger with these white coats of ours. The trouble's going to be that we *shan't* be found, not that we *shall*.' All the same, we kept going, though I believe I was the first to collapse, and had to be given what was left of the brandy. The next thing I recollect is a clearing sky and a valley vista opening at our feet, and far down, almost as if we could have jumped on skis to it, a cluster of lights. Rather like Lauterbrunnen seen from Wengenalp, if you happen to know that.'

I said I did, and he went on: 'There was no discussion about what we should do—we had planned it so many times in our heads. We'd comforted ourselves by thinking that as soon as we came to a house we'd wait till the occupants had gone to bed, break in, and take some food. So with this new and exciting hope we staggered down the slope, running when we came to the level of the pinewoods, and checking our pace by wild grabs from tree to tree. I can remember how dark it was in those woods, and rather terrifying; we kept stumbling and

scratching our hands and faces. Then, just ahead of us—
almost as if it hadn't been there before, if you know the feeling
—we saw the lighted window of a house, shining out exactly
like a Christmas card. Yes, and smoke curling up from the
chimney. *Exactly* like a Christmas card. Warm and com-
forting and sentimental.

'But, of course, the light at the window meant that there
were still people out of bed, so there was nothing for us to do
but wait—and as it was Christmas night, we guessed we might
have to wait a long time. Still, there would be some heavy
sleeping afterwards, and that would help us. So we crouched
down on a sort of grassy ledge, rather like a golf green, where
the snow was half melted, and the moonlight lay over it like
a sort of trembling sea. I suppose it was *we* who were trembling, really—you know how it feels when you've been hurrying downhill and you come to a level stretch again—your
legs seem to sink under you. We were so exhausted we threw
ourselves on the grass and rested a minute or two, and as I
looked back at the pinewoods reaching up the side of the
mountain, I noticed a star touching the dark edge of the tree-
tops—just one little star. I'm not much of a person for
noticing things like that, but it's a queer thing—I can almost
see those woods and that star now, if I shut my eyes.

'I dare say we waited a couple of hours—it seemed twice
as long. What began to puzzle us was that there was no
sound from the house. We were quite close, and the night
was still—surely there ought to have been voices or a dog
barking or something? But there wasn't. At last Manny
whispered: "I can't stand this hanging about any longer—
I'm going to scout round!"

'We crept to the outside wall, and saw that the place was
a mountain chalet, timbered and heavily gabled. We listened
awhile but there still wasn't a sound—but I'll tell you what
there was. There was a most luscious, and to us an infuriating

smell of cooking. In the end that settled it. We groped round to the doorway, and Manny tried the handle. It turned —the door was unlocked. A gust of warm air reached us and—more overpowering than ever—a definite smell of sizzling meat and roasting poultry. I looked at Manny and my look meant: Let's take a chance. . . .

'We entered the house and tiptoed along a corridor. There was a room that had a strip of light under the door, but still no sound. Manny was trying to deduce where the larder was—we daren't strike matches. And then suddenly we heard footsteps on the inside of the lighted room, the door opened, and a young girl came walking straight into us— actually she'd have collided if we hadn't stepped away. I don't think my heart has ever jumped as much as it did at that moment. Manny had the presence of mind to say: "Guten Abend."

'The light from the doorway shone full on us then, and it suddenly occurred to me what a grim and frightening sight we must look—torn, scratched, dirty, eyes bloodshot, unshaven for days. But she didn't seem alarmed—she just said, in a tranquil voice: "You are strangers?"

'Manny answered her, and they exchanged a few sentences in such rapid German that I couldn't properly follow it. Then I realized that we were being invited into the room. . . . That room . . . I shall never forget it. . . . It dazzled me, its firelight and lamplight, for the moment; then, as I gathered my wits, I saw a table set for two and food for a banquet warming in front of the log fire. Roast chicken, slices of veal, beans, potatoes. Cheese and a bottle of wine. A little Christmas tree. . . . I just stared and stared and left Manny to do the talking. It seemed to me we'd probably have to surrender and make the best of it—we certainly weren't prepared to terrorize a girl; and for myself, the thought of immediate things that surrender would bring—food, sleep, warmth—

nearly outweighed the disappointment I knew I should feel afterwards. I wondered whether Manny felt the same, especially as the girl and he went on talking. At last she smiled and went out of the room. Then Manny turned to me and said: "It's all right. You can sit down and make yourself at home."

'I must have looked rather stupid about it, for he added: "Draw your chair to the table and don't guzzle too much all at once."

'"But — have you — told her — who — who we are?" I whispered.

'"Sssh," he answered. "I don't have to. Can't you see . . . she's blind."

'"Blind?"

'"Simply the most incredible piece of luck," he went on. "She's alone here—her father's one of the frontier guards— he's out on the mountains with a search-party. The frontier's quite close, too—that's another piece of luck. There's a whole platoon of them looking for the two escaped English-men—apparently we've been well advertised."

'I asked him who she thought we really were. He answered: "Why, part of the search-party, of course—I've explained to her that we got lost, and are dead tired and hungry. And what's more to the point, my lad, she's going to give us our Christmas dinner!"

'"But if her father returns?"

'"Then we shall just be a little less in luck, that's all."

'The girl came back then, and laid extra places at the table. She had a very serene face and beautiful hands. Now that the idea was put in my head, it seemed obvious that she was blind. Yet her movements were scarcely less quick and accurate than if she had had sight. She helped us to food and Manny carved the chicken. They talked and laughed a lot together, and though I could follow what they were saying more or less, sometimes they talked too quickly or used words I didn't understand. But the food — and the wine — and the fire! I've never had a dinner that was as good as that. I know now I never shall. . . . The girl showed us photographs of her father and her two brothers who were at the Front. We drank their healths and the healths of the German Army and —in our hearts—of the British Army, and of all brave men. Then she and Manny began an argument about the whole war business, and how damsilly it was that men should spend Christmas hunting other men over mountains instead of feasting at home. She agreed, and then added something that made my heart miss another beat. She said: "I thought at first you were the two English prisoners."

'"That would have been awkward for you," said Manny.

'"Oh, no, I expect they would have wanted food, just the same."

'"They certainly would."

'"Because, after all, there's not as much difference between English and German as between tired and hungry people and those who aren't."

'"Other people mightn't see that," said Manny, laughing.

'"They see other things instead."'

Middleton glanced round the room as if to reassure himself of privacy before he continued: 'I remember this rather strange conversation, because at the time it scared me—I thought it was just the sort of too-clever-by-half stuff that a fellow like Manny would give himself away by, instead of sticking to the proper part of the simple German soldier. Because, you see, I was getting more and more panicky over an idea that had just struck me—that the girl was leading us on with all that sort of talk, that she already suspected who we were, and was deliberately trying to keep us till her father and probably some of the other searchers came back. As soon as she next went out of the room, ostensibly to fetch another bottle of wine, I

whispered to Manny just what I felt about it. He seemed
surprised, and told me then that the girl had offered to show us
a short cut over the mountain that would lead us exactly where
he wanted to go.

'I was scared again by that. "I wouldn't trust a yard of
that short cut," I told Manny. "She's obviously going to
lead us straight into a trap." He answered, in that dreamy
way of his: "Well, you may be right. Wisdom or cleverness—
which are we up against?—that's the question, always."

'That just irritated me—it didn't seem to be the right moment
to be so damned philosophical. But he only kept on saying:
"You may be right, and I may be wrong—time will show."

'But time never did—nor anything else. Because while
we were still arguing we heard a commotion outside in the
corridor, then the girl's sudden cry amidst men's voices.
Both Manny and I took it that our number was up and that
the girl was telling them all about us. But she wasn't. We
could see what was happening through the gap in the hinge
of the door. She was crying because they had brought her
father home—on an improvised stretcher.

'Apparently he'd fallen pretty badly somewhere—had a
nasty head-wound and an arm was limp. He was in a lot of
pain, and we heard the girl imploring the men who had brought
him in—there were two of them—to hurry down to the village
and bring a doctor. And that would taken them a couple of
hours at least.

'Well, there isn't much more to tell you. Manny, as you
may or may not know, was born to be a surgeon if he hadn't
been a poet with a private income, and those soldiers hadn't
done a good job with the broken arm. Manny refixed it,
and we made the old boy as comfortable as we could before
we left. He was semi-conscious and obviously didn't care
a damn who we were—you don't, you know, if things are
hurting and somebody's helping. . . . So we said "Guten

Abend" again, and made off into the woods. We didn't find the short cut, but we did, after sundry other adventures, manage to wriggle across the frontier. And that's the end of the story. I've no doubt Manny would have told it better.'

'The odd thing is,' I said, 'that he never told it at all.'

Middleton answered after a pause: 'I wonder if he felt about it as I did afterwards—that it all happened in another sort of world? Mind you, it *did* happen—we escaped all right. That much is on record. And the roast chicken was real enough, I'll swear. And yet . . . oh, well, we were dazed with exhaustion, and sick with anxiety, and wild with hunger. And the girl was blind and her father half-crazy with pain. Things don't happen *to* you when you're like that—as Manny said, they happen *in* you.'

I agreed, and we smoked awhile, and then he went on: 'That's the worst and the best of war—you feel a brotherhood with the other side that you can't get away from, and equally that you can't give way to. I often wonder what became of the old boy—whether he got better; I hope he did. He was really quite a veteran—far too old and fat to be chasing youngsters like us over mountains. A few years after the Armistice, Manny was in Munich and tried to trace both the man and the girl, but he had no luck—couldn't even find the chalet on the hillside. Anyway, it's twenty years ago now—too late to hold an inquiry over it. But you can perhaps understand how . . . I felt . . . when you quoted that poem at dinner.'

'Oh, the poem we were all arguing about?'

'Yes. As a matter of fact, I never knew Manny had written it—poetry, I must admit, isn't much in my line. But that poem . . . well, it reminded me.'

I nodded. The volume of Manny Stewart's last poems, issued after his death, lay on the shelf at my elbow, and I reached for it, found the page, and leaned forward to catch the firelight as I read, in a sense for the first time:

> You do not know our ways are strange
>   In war-perverted brotherhood;
> How white the snow upon the range,
>   How warm the window in the wood.
> You do not know, you have not seen
> The moonlight trembling on the green;
> Nor have you watched a single star
> Rise over shades where terrors are.
> Yet in that world whose beauty lies
>   Beyond the eye and in the mind,
> Yours is the twilight of the wise,
>   And ours the noonday of the blind.

CRISP NEW BILLS FOR MR TEAGLE

BY FRANK SULLIVAN

COMING down in the elevator, Clement Teagle noticed an unwonted cordiality in Steve, the elevator boy, and Harry, the doorman, but thought nothing of it until he stopped at the bank on the corner to cash a cheque and noticed the date.

December the twenty-fourth.

'Good gosh,' Mr Teagle thought, 'I haven't bought a present for Essie yet.'

Then he remembered Steve and Harry.

His eye caught a legend on a Christmas placard on the wall. 'It is more blessed to give than to receive,' said the placard.

'Oh, yeah?' remarked Mr Teagle, who, alas, was somewhat of a cynic.

Grumbling, he tore up the cheque he had started to write, and made out another, for a larger amount.

'Will you please give me new bills?' he asked.

'Indeed I shall,' said Mr Freyer, the teller, cordially.

He counted out one hundred dollars in new bills—*crisp* new bills—and passed them over to Mr Teagle.

Then he tore up the cheque and handed the fragments to Mr Teagle.

'Don't be alarmed, Mr Teagle,' said Mr Freyer. 'The bank of the Manhattan Company wants you to accept that one hundred dollars as a slight token of its esteem, with its best wishes for a Merry Christmas. You have been a loyal depositor here these many years. You have overdrawn fewer times than most of your fellow-depositors. You never argue about your monthly statements. You never feel insulted when a new teller identifies your signature before cashing your cheque. You are the kind of depositor who makes banking a joy, and I want to take this opportunity to tell you that we fellows around here, although we are not very demonstrative about that sort of thing, love you very much. A merry Christmas to you.'

'You mean the bank is *giving* me this money?' said Mr Teagle.

'That is the impression I was trying to convey,' said Mr Freyer, with a chuckle.

'Why—uh, thanks, Mr Freyer. And—and thank the bank. This is—um—quite a surprise.'

'Say no more about it, Mr Teagle. And every Christmas joy to you, sir.'

When Mr Teagle left the bank he was somewhat perturbed, and a little stunned. He went back to the apartment to place the crisp new bills in envelopes for the boys, and as he left the elevator at his floor, Steve handed him an envelope.

'Merry Christmas, Mr Teagle,' said Steve.

'Thanks, Steve,' said Mr Teagle. 'I'll—I'll be wishing you one a little later,' he added significantly.

'You don't need to, Mr Teagle,' said Steve. 'A man like you wishes the whole world a merry Christmas every day, just by living.'

'Oh, Steve, damn nice of you to say that, but I'm sure it's not deserved,' said Mr Teagle, modestly struggling with a feeling that Steve spoke no more than the simple truth.

'Well, I guess we won't argue about *that*,' said Steve, gazing affectionately at Mr Teagle.

'I really believe that lad meant it,' thought Mr Teagle, as he let himself into the apartment. 'I really believe he did.'

Mr Teagle opened the envelope Steve had handed him. A crisp new five-dollar bill fell out.

Downstairs in the lobby, a few minutes later, Steve was protesting.

'I tell you it wasn't a mistake, Mr Teagle. I put the bill in there on purpose. For you.'

'Steve, I couldn't take——'

'But you *can* take it, and you *will*, Mr Teagle. And a very merry Christmas to you.'

'Then you accept this, Steve, and a merry Christmas to *you*.'

'Oh, no, Mr Teagle. Not this year. You have been pretty swell to we fellows all the years you've lived here. Now it's our turn.'

'You bet it is,' said Harry the doorman, joining them and pressing a crisp new ten-dollar bill into Mr Teagle's hand. 'Merry Christmas, Mr Teagle. Buy yourself something foolish with this. I only wish it could be more, but I've had rather a bad year in the market.'

'I think the boys on the night-shift have a little surprise for Mr Teagle, too,' said Steve, with a twinkle in his eye.

Just then the superintendent came up.

'Well, well, well,' he said jovially. 'Who have we got here?

Mr Teagle, it may interest you to hear that I've been having a little chat about you with a certain old gentleman with a long, snowy beard and twinkling little eyes. Know who I mean?'

'Santa Claus?' Mr Teagle asked.

'None other. And guess what! He asked me if you had been a good boy this year, and I was delighted to be able to tell him you had been, that you hadn't complained about the heat, hadn't run your radio after eleven at night, and hadn't had any late parties. Well, sir, you should have seen old Santa's face. He was tickled to hear it. Said he always knew you were a good boy. And what do you suppose he did?'

'What?' asked Mr Teagle.

'He asked me to give you this and to tell you to buy yourself something for Christmas with it. Something foolish.'

The super pressed a crisp new twenty-dollar bill upon Mr Teagle.

'Merry Christmas, Mr Teagle,' said the super.

'Merry Christmas, Mr Teagle,' said Steve the elevator boy.

'Merry Christmas, Mr Teagle,' said Harry the doorman.

'Merry Christmas,' said Mr Teagle, in a voice you could scarcely hear. Remembering that he had to buy a present for Essie, he walked out, with the air of a bewildered gazelle. He was in a very, very puzzled state of mind as he walked down East Fifty-first Street, an agitation which did not subside when the proprietor of a cigar-store on Third Avenue rushed out, pressed a box of cigars on him, cried, 'Merry Christmas, stranger!' and rushed back into his shop without another word.

To rush out of your store and give a box of cigars to a perfect stranger! And those boys at the apartment house! *And* the super!

Mr Teagle thought of the many times he had grumbled at being kept waiting a few minutes for the elevator or for a taxi. He felt ashamed. 'By George,' Mr Teagle thought, 'maybe Dickens was right.'

Mr Teagle approached the business of choosing a present for his wife in a far less carping spirit than was his Christmas wont.

'I'll get Essie something that'll knock her eye out,' he thought. 'She's a good old girl and she deserves a lot of credit for living with a grouch like me all these years. The best is none too good for her.'

Suiting the action to the word, Mr Teagle turned in at Cartier's and asked to see some square-cut emeralds. He selected one that could have done duty on a traffic light.

'I'm afraid I haven't the cash on me,' he told the clerk. 'I'll give you a cheque, and you can call the bank and verify——'

'That will not be necessary, sir,' said the clerk, with a radiant smile. 'You are Mr Clement Teagle, I believe. In that case, Cartier wishes you to accept this trinket with the Christmas greetings of the firm. We are only sorry that you did not see fit to choose a diamond stomacher. Cartier will feel honoured that one of its emeralds is adorning the finger of the wife of a man like Clement Teagle, a man four-square, a man who is a credit—— All right, all right, all *right*, Mr Teagle! Not another word, please. Cartier is adamant. You take this emerald or we may grow ugly about it. And don't lose it, sir, or I venture to say your good wife will give you Hail Columbia. Good day, sir, and God rest ye.'

Mr Teagle found himself on the street. He accosted the first passer-by.

'Excuse me, stranger, but would you mind pinching me?'

'Certainly not, certainly not,' said the stranger, cheerily. 'There. Feel better?'

'Yes. Thank you very much,' said Mr Teagle.

'Here, buy yourself something for Christmas,' said the stranger, pressing Mr Teagle's hand. Mr Teagle looked in the hand and found himself the possessor of a crisp new fifty-dollar bill.

At Fifth Avenue and Fifty-seventh Street, a Park & Tilford attendant rushed out and draped a huge basket, bedecked with ribbons and holly, on Mr Teagle's arm.

'Everything drinkable for the Yuletide dinner, with love and kisses from Park & Tilford,' whispered the clerk jovially. 'Tell your wife to be sure and put the champagne in ice early, so it will be nice and cold.'

'Oh, come on, come on,' protested the butcher at Madison Avenue and Sixty-first Street. 'Don't tell me you're too loaded down to carry a simple little turkey home, with the affectionate Christmas wishes of Shaffer's Market.'

Mr Shaffer laughed the rich laugh of the contented butcher.

'Don't take me too seriously when I say "simple little turkey,"' he said. 'That bird you got would make Roose-velt's Christmas turkey look like a humming-bird. An undernourished humming-bird. Pay for it? Certainly you won't pay for it! What do you take me for? It's Christmas. And you are Clement Teagle.'

'Am I?' said Mr Teagle, humbly.

Long before he reached home, Mr Teagle had had such a plethora of gifts pressed upon him by friendly strangers that there was nothing to do but load them into a taxi-cab. And Mr Teagle was not quite as surprised as he might have been earlier in the day when the driver refused to accept any money, but grinned and said: 'Let's just charge this trip to good old St Nick.'

'Why, Clem!' said Mrs Teagle, when, with the aid of the entire house staff, Mr Teagle had deposited his gifts in the dining-room. 'Why, Clem, I already *bought* a turkey! Clem, you've been drinking.'

'I have *not*!' Mr Teagle shouted.

Well, don't get on your high horse,' said Mrs Teagle. 'It's Christmas Eve. I don't mind. Only—you know your stomach. And you do look funny.'

'I may look funny, but I have not been drinking,' Mr Teagle insisted. 'Look! H-h-h-h-h.'

His breath was as the new-mown hay.

'See what I got you for Christmas, Essie.' Mrs Teagle opened the jewel-case and the emerald gleamed up at her. It was a moment before she could speak.

'No, Clem,' she said. 'You work too hard for your money. I don't deserve this. I won't take it from you. You've been too good to me as it is. I don't want any Christmas present from you, dear. I want to *give* you one—and oh, by the way, Clem, before I forget it, the funniest thing happened this afternoon. The income-tax man was here, the federal income-tax man. Said he just dropped in to wish you a merry Christmas. He left this cheque for your entire last year's income-tax. He said the Government wants to give it back to you as a token of affection and in recognition of your many superb qualities as a citizen and—oh, I can't remember everything he said, but he made quite a flowery speech about you, dear—— Why, Clem, what's the matter?'

Mr Teagle had burst into tears.

'A merry Christmas, Essie,' he said, through his sobs, 'and, in the language of Tiny Tim, "God bless us every one."'

A WISE MAN FROM THE EAST

BY CHARLES HEYWOOD

EVERY one in the village knew that Selina Murgatroyd was daffy except two. These two were Selina herself and Billy Murgatroyd, her husband.

Selina never tore her hair or spoke to the moon; the only proofs of her daffiness were her twisted face and her queer way of standing for a long time in silence while other people talked.

Now Billy Murgatroyd was the vicar's gardener. And by talking with his master, and reading in the old, calf-bound books which the vicar sometimes lent to him, Billy came to believe that Selina, far from being daffy, was uncommonly wise. For was not Socrates an ugly man, and silence but an uncommon kind of wisdom?

Selina herself had no time to consider whether she were daffy or no, for when she was not washing and mending and cooking in her cottage, or digging vegetables in the garden, her mind was toiling beneath a burden much heavier than the mocking of her neighbours.

Although she had been wedded for fully twenty years Selina had no children. The reason for this was not that Billy Murgatroyd had overlooked the proper duty of a hus-band. The reason was simply that Selina was afflicted like the woman Elisabeth in Scripture. And like Elisabeth she desired a child above any other blessing. She lent all her mind to praying for a child. But no child was born to her.

The cottage in which Billy and Selina Murgatroyd lived was one of two, which were joined together and in everything alike as two peas. The second cottage belonged to a man and wife whose name was Griggs. Mrs Griggs had borne a dozen children, and every year she lay-in to bear another. And since there was little room in the cottage her children lived for most of the day in the garden.

Selina Murgatroyd used to stand silently by the fence which separated her garden from the Griggses', and watch these children as they fought and played amongst themselves or chevied the hens which shared the garden with them. And although the children seldom minded their manners with her, and called her 'Daffy' to her face, she was never angry, but continued to gaze on them as kindly as though they were her own.

One winter's day Selina Murgatroyd, leaning over the fence, perceived that Mrs Griggs was soon to bear another child. And as the weather was becoming cold she broke her habitual silence and called to Mrs Griggs that she was foolish to be out of doors, for she would take a chill and harm her child. But Mrs Griggs took no heed of her, and Mr Griggs, coming out at that moment, said he wished the brat would freeze, for he had a dozen too many as it was.

Selina said no more. She knew Mr Griggs. She knew him to be a stupid man, who, being of a great size himself, hated everything that was little, even Mrs Griggs's hens.

As Christmas drew near Mrs Griggs was taken ill and had to lie in bed. So Mr Griggs was left to feed the hens. He did this with such an ill grace that the hens grew frightened of him and would not come near to take their food. Thereupon he was so angry that he threw the empty bucket at them and swore he would put their corn to better use. And next day he only gave them half a handful, which was barely enough for one of them to live on.

Selina always watched the hens being fed, and when she saw that Mr Griggs was not giving them enough to eat she went indoors and told her husband of it.

Now Billy hated to see dumb creatures treated unkindly. He was in the habit of giving a shilling every year to the National Society for the Prevention of Cruelty to Animals, and had always believed that the Germans lost the Great War because they took to eating horseflesh. So he became very sorry for Mr Griggs's unhappy hens. Unknown to Mr Griggs, or even to Selina, he bought a bag of corn, and every night he went out and sprinkled some of it in the shed where the hens slept.

On Christmas Eve the wind blew fiercely and frost gripped the soil. There were signs that snow might fall and build a Christmas scene for little boys and tramps and poets to remember.

But in spite of the cold Billy opened the door as soon as Selina was gone to bed, and set out to feed Mr Griggs's hens. When he stepped inside the hen-shed, however, he fell over a big hamper which had been put there. And he had hardly got to his feet before he heard the sound of approaching foot-steps. He quickly skipped out of the door and hid himself at the back of the shed. It was Mr Griggs who approached; Billy knew the noise of his heavy tread on the frozen ground, though he couldn't imagine what brought him to the hen-house so late.

Mr Griggs opened the door of the shed and there was a sound of shuffling inside. Then Mr Griggs began to speak.

'How are you going on, old purse-face?' he said. 'Ready to be eaten?'

There was more shuffling; and then Mr Griggs spoke again, in a quiet, sweet voice which Billy had never heard him use before.

'Here you are, purse-face,' he said, 'have a gollop at this

corn I've been saving for you. You're a real bird, you are. And I ain't going to wring your neck till morning.'

Billy, although he was puzzled to know the meaning of these words, waited to hear no more, but took advantage of Mr Griggs's conversation to creep back into his own garden.

Just as he had got through the fence he heard the door of the hen-shed slam, and Mr Griggs came walking back towards the cottage.

'Hallo, Griggs, you're out late to-night,' said Billy, in a casual tone of voice. 'How is Mrs Griggs a-going on?'

Mr Griggs paused for a moment, as though he could not think what Billy was talking about. Then he answered in a tone of disgust: 'That brat's on the way. As if twelve wasn't enough!'

Then he returned into his cottage.

When Mr. Griggs was gone Billy crept through the fence and made his way to the hen-shed once more. He could not bear to go to bed and leave the hens hungry.

He opened the door of the shed and stepped inside. The wind followed him and seemed to blow right through his clothes. He squeezed past the big basket to the back of the shed where the hens were roosting.

'You silly hens are properly in the draught,' he said, as he scattered the corn on the floor for them. 'You'd be a deal warmer if I put you in this basket.'

He stood still for a while and watched them. Then, as the wind blew fiercely through the shed again, he went to the basket and lifted up the lid, to see what was inside.

The moon came out from behind a cloud and sent a beam of light full into the hen-shed. Out of the basket appeared the head of a turkey. Billy dropped the lid quickly and stepped backwards.

'Blimey,' he said, 'it must have been you Griggs was talking to.'

He was rather scared for the moment. But soon his curiosity got the better of him. He lifted the lid of the basket again and peered at the bird thoughtfully.

'You must be a very old bird,' he said. "Tis half a shame to kill an old bird like you.'

The turkey stirred and drowsily turned its head until the moonlight was reflected in one eye. Then it winked, and opened and shut its beak several times.

Billy clearly perceived that it was trying to tell him something. He considered for a minute or two, and finally lowered the lid and carried the basket out of the shed, where he rolled it on its side and tipped the turkey out on the ground. The bird stumbled to its feet and shook its feathers.

'You're a wise old bird,' said Billy, 'and if you take my advice you'll fly away while Griggs is in bed.'

He then took the basket back into the shed and gently lifted all the hens inside it. They nestled down against one another, until they looked like a bed of feathers. Billy emptied the last of the corn on top of them and then closed the lid. When he stepped out of the shed the turkey had gone.

'I knew that was a wise old bird,' said Billy.

Christmas morning was even colder than the night before. All the fields were white with frost, and although the wind had dropped there were misty bands of cloud moving across the sky.

Selina got up early, for she had to make the cottage tidy before they went to church. When she had cleared out the grate and lit a fire and dusted the room and laid the table for breakfast she went to the door to clean the step.

She had scarcely opened it before she started back in surprise.

Upon the doorstep, wrapped in an old torn blanket, lay a newly born child. Even while Selina stood gaping it opened its mouth and began to cry.

Selina quickly took it in her arms and carried it inside the house. She laid it before the fire, and taking a thick shawl from her shoulder, wrapped it again more warmly. She then lifted it to her breast and began to rock it gently to and fro until its crying ceased.

The door opened and Billy came in. At first he saw nothing strange. He sat down at the table. Then, as he raised his head to ask when breakfast would be ready, he saw the child.

He sat still on his chair, gazing at the child.

At last he spoke:

'Where's that young un come from?' he asked.

'He was laid on the doorstep,' said Selina.

'Whose young un is he?' asked Billy.

Selina raised her eyes to the Bible on the mantelpiece, but did not reply.

Billy rose to his feet and walked over to the grate. 'I'd best get ready the breakfast,' he said.

He finished the cooking, and together they sat down to the table. Billy said nothing while he ate his breakfast, but as soon as he had finished he rose to his feet again.

'I'd best go across to the farm and get some milk for un,' he said.

He reached for his hat.

At that instant a sound of tapping came from the door. "Tis most likely Griggs,' thought Billy, and his hand trembled as he raised the latch, for suddenly he remembered what he had done the night before.

He pulled the door open.

Mr Griggs himself was nowhere to be seen. But his turkey was standing on the doorstep.

Billy's anxiety left him.

'Come in, old wise un,' he said, clicking his fingers at the turkey.

The bird walked slowly into the room.

Selina had risen to her feet and was standing behind Billy with the child in her arms. The turkey approached until Selina might have put out her hand and touched it. Then it stood still.

Several times, very rapidly, it bobbed and bowed its head. Then it raised its beak into the air and spoke in its peculiar raucous language. At last, bowing again, it turned and walked out.

Billy and Selina followed it.

As they stepped out of the door they heard a great outcry of voices in the Griggses' garden.

The turkey, which had walked a few paces down the garden path, stopped, shook its wattles, flapped its wings, and rose into the air.

Flying in a circle it mounted higher and higher until it was far above the tops of the beech trees. Then it was surrounded by a haze of falling snow, and it vanished out of sight.

'That was a live turkey, wasn't it?' said Selina, still looking up into the sky.

Billy shook his head vigorously. "Tweren't no turkey, that weren't. All the turkeys be dead and roasting on Christmas Day.'

'Then perhaps it was an eagle or a flying duck?'

'No,' said Billy, "twere too big for one of they.'

'Then like as not it was a phoenix, same as them in your old books?'

Billy shook his head again: 'There ain't no phoenixes round hereabouts,' he said.

'Then what was it?' asked Selina.

Billy reflected.

'I should say,' he said at last, 'that it be a wise man from the East. They're a queer lot in those parts, and 'tis like as not they look like turkeys.'

He nodded thoughtfully.

'And it was properly wise,' he added.

The snow began to fall around them. The child in Selina's arms whimpered. Together they returned into the warm shelter of the cottage.

THE WHITE ROAD

BY E. F. BOZMAN

'MILD weather for the time of year.'

'Yes,' I said; 'not very seasonable.'

I did not even trouble to turn round and look at the stranger who had addressed me. I remember a soft Sussex voice, strong and deep, and I have an impression of someone tall; but I had come in to have a glass of beer by myself and was not in the mood for chance conversation.

It was Christmas Eve, about nine o'clock in the evening, and the public bar at the Swan Inn was crowded. It was the first evening of my holidays and I had walked over from the farm-house where I was staying with my mother, using the inn as my objective. I had just come down from London, and was in no need of company; on the contrary, I wanted solitude. However, the landlord recognized me from previous visits and passed the time of night.

'Staying down at the farm again?' he asked.

'Yes,' I said.

'Well, we're glad to see you, I'm sure. Did you walk over?'

'Yes. I enjoy the walk. That's what I came out for.'

'And for the drink?' he suggested.

'Well, it's good beer,' I admitted, and paid for a glass for each of us. I felt rather than saw the stranger who had accosted me hovering behind me, but made no attempt to bring him in. I did not see why I should buy him a drink; and I wanted nothing from him.

'It must be pretty well three miles' walk down to where you are,' the landlord said. 'A tidy step.'

'Yes,' I said, 'a good three. Two or two and a half down to Ingo Bridge, then another mile from where the lane turns off to West Chapter.'

'Well, I suppose you know you've missed the last bus down. Must have been gone half an hour. There's only the one in from the Bridge, and that's the lot.'

'Yes, I know,' I said; 'I don't mind.'

Just then I heard the noise of the door-latch followed by a creak as the door swung open, and half turned to see the tall stranger going out. I caught a glimpse of him before he shut the door behind him.

'Who was that?' I asked the landlord.

'I didn't notice him—he must have been a stranger to me. Funny thing, now you mention it, he didn't buy a drink.'

'He seemed to be hanging round me. Cadging, I suppose.'

'You get some funny customers at this time of year.' The landlord was evidently not interested in the man. 'It'll be dark to-night, along that road,' he volunteered.

'Yes,' I said. We finished our drinks, I said good night, and made my way to the door across the smoke-laden room.

It was pitch dark outside by contrast with the glow of the inn, and as I slammed the well-used wooden door behind me the shaft of light streaming from the parlour window seemed to be my last link with civilization. The air was extraordinarily ..ld for the time of year. My way lay by a short cut across the

church fields which joined the road leading towards the sea;
a difficult way to find at night had I not known it well;
alternatively, I could have gone a longer way round, starting
in the opposite direction, and making three sides of a square
in the road which I was eventually to join by the short cut.
I knew my ground and decided on the footpath without hesitation. By the time I reached the church fields I realized that
the night was not really so dark as it had seemed to be at first,
for I could see the black tower and belfry of the church looming
against a background of lighter grey, and a glimmer of light
in one corner of the church suggested eleventh-hour preparations for the great festival. Clouds were scudding across an
unseen moon, full according to the calendar, discernible now
only secondarily by a patch of faintly diffused light towards the
south; knowing the lie of the land I could imagine the clouds
swept away and the moon hanging in its winter glory over the
cold English Channel a few miles away. Although the air
was temporarily muggy with the presage of rain, there was a
deep underlying chill in land and sea, the ingrained coldness
of the short days.

The footpath across the fields was narrow and muddy, a
single-file track. I stumbled and slithered my way along it
until I reached a narrow wooden bridge with two handrails.
Here I paused for a moment, looking at the dark swollen
stream which was just visible, black and shining, below my feet.

I was now near the point where the path joined the road,
and as I paused, my elbows leaning on the rail of the bridge,
listening to the far-reaching silence, I heard in the distance the
sound of footsteps along the road. In these days of heavy
road-traffic this old-fashioned, unmistakable sound is a rarity,
and I listened fascinated. The steady distant tread, gradually
loudening, began to grow on me, and by the time I had made up
my mind to move it was beating a rhythm in my brain. My path
now led diagonally up a sloping bank to the road, and I crept

up it silently, hearing and thinking of nothing but the approaching footsteps. The thought occurred to me that I must not let
the walker catch me up, that something important, something
connected with myself yet out of my own control, depended on
the success of my efforts, and I began to hurry. I tried to
dismiss the idea, but it would not be banished, and as I reached
the swing-gate leading out to the road the footsteps sounded
unexpectedly near. They rang on the road, and I could
hardly resist the temptation to run.

I compromised by stepping out briskly, swinging my arms.
It was ludicrous, I argued with myself; there was nothing to
be afraid of, and my own feet tried to reassure me by dimming
the sound behind me. But the pursuing footsteps would not
be drowned; they were implacable. I attempted to speed up,
without allowing myself to hurry or panic, but I could not
shake them off. They were gaining steadily on me, and as
their loudness increased tingles of fear began to go down my
spine. I could not turn round and look—could not, I realized,
because I was afraid to.

The road at this point runs between high hedges and trees
which shut out what little light was coming from the sky.
Nothing could be seen except the dark shapes of the trees, and
an occasional gleam from the black wet surface of the tarred
road. There were some outlying farm buildings and barns
immediately ahead, but no glimmer of light came from them.
The overhanging elms dripped their moisture on me from
leafless branches. No traffic was within earshot; the only
sound was of footsteps, mine and my pursuer's.

Left right, left right, left right they went behind me. The
walker had long legs. Left right, left right—the din increased
alarmingly, and I realized that I must run.

'How far now to the bridge?'

A soft voice, almost in my ear, shocked me, and yet released
the tension. I sweated suddenly and profusely.

I recognized the voice of the stranger who had addressed me in the Swan Inn. He had left just before me and must have walked round by the road, I realized, while I had taken the short cut across the fields. I could not immediately disguise my racing heart, but I managed to speak calmly, in a voice which must have sounded weak in contrast with the strong Sussex resonance of the stranger.

'About two miles,' I said.

The stranger said nothing more for the moment, but fell into step beside me, as if assuming that we were to walk together. It was not what I wanted, partly because I was ashamed of my panic of a few moments ago, and partly because I had been looking forward to walking the lonely stretch of road ahead by myself. I turned my head, but could see nothing of my companion except his tall dark form, vaguely outlined, and he must have been wearing a long coat which flapped below his knees. I was the next to break the silence.

'When we get past the farm buildings,' I said, 'and round the next corner we come to a long open stretch. It's a lovely bit of road, a special favourite of mine, absolutely deserted usually. On clear nights or days you can see the sea in the distance.'

'There's a little hill about half-way along—by an S bend.'

The stranger's remark surprised me. Why had he asked me about the way if he knew the district?

'So you know the road?' I asked querulously, as if I had been deceived.

The stranger muttered 'Years ago,' and something else I could not catch. The detail he had remembered was a significant one. The open stretch ahead of us, nearly two miles in length, promised at first sight to run straight for the sea, where it joined the main coast road; but half-way along this section of the road there was a danger spot for speeding motorists, an unexpected S bend over a little mound. Just past the bend, as the road straightened itself out again and went down the far side of the little hill, heading between low hedges for the sea, there was a notable isolated thorn-tree standing on the left of the road. Its trunk leant towards the sea, while the twigs on top of the trunk were all swept in the opposite direction, like a mat of hair, blown by the prevailing wind. From the trunk two stumpy branches sprouted, each with its bunch of twigs held out like hands; these, too, were windswept. The trunk was not gnarled and sprang strongly from the ground —no dead post, driven into the earth from above, could have achieved that appearance of strength.

I was about to refer to this tree, which was a particular landmark of mine, when we heard the sound of a distant motor. My companion seemed to be unexpectedly nervous—I could feel his anxiety. The sound increased rapidly, so different a progress from approaching feet, and before we had rounded the sharp corner leading to the open stretch of road a Southdown bus flung itself round the bend and was almost on us. The headlights flooded us, gleaming on the stranger's face, making him look pale as a ghost, and lighting the road immediately in front of us to a brilliant white.

The stranger was so dazzled by the sudden brightness that he cowered into the hedge, shielding his eyes with his hand. In an instant the bus had charged past us and round another corner, taking its lighted interior and its warm passengers with it into the enveloping darkness of the countryside.

I heard my companion murmur: 'The white road. The white road.' Something in the way he said the words brought a picture of my youth to my eyes, of a time when this same lonely road was white and dusty, with flints, and I could see myself bicycling along it, in imminent danger of punctures, hurrying to the sea. I saw the white road, the white sea road, not the black and tarred contrivance of to-day, yet the same road with the same trees and banks. It has always been a lovely country road, and it still is.

We left the farm buildings behind us and entered the lonely stretch. It was too dark for us to see a glimmer of the sea ahead or anything behind the low banked hedges on either side. A light rain began to fall, driving in our faces.

'That was the last bus,' I said, 'we'll meet no more now.'

The stranger ignored this remark, and his next words fitted in exactly with what had been in my mind when the bus distracted us.

'There's a thorn-tree, isn't there?' he said, 'just beside the road round the double corner.' He spoke as if he knew the way by heart, yet obviously he did not remember it exactly. He had not even been sure enough of himself to take the short cut by the church fields.

'Yes,' I said, 'why do you ask?'

'You've noticed it yourself?' he inquired anxiously.

'Yes.'

'And it's still there?'

'Yes, of course.' I could not for the life of me imagine what he was driving at. Yet even as I spoke the words confidently I found myself in doubt. I remembered my mother saying something about workmen on the lonely road, how they were widening it at the bend and spoiling its appearance. Like me, she had an affection for it. I had passed the spot that very evening on my way to the inn, yet when I came to think of it I could not be sure whether I had seen the tree or not. I had been preoccupied, and had not looked for it specially. But surely I would have noticed, I thought, and said aloud: 'At least it was there the last time I passed.'

'When was that?' The stranger spoke very directly and forcibly.

I was about to say this very evening, but realizing my uncertainty, said instead: 'About this time last year. I was down here for Christmas.'

'There's a story told about that tree in these parts,' he said.

'Oh,' I said; 'what do they say about it?'

'They say there was a suicide on that spot. A man from the village.' The Sussex burr was soft and confidential.

'What happened?'

'He hanged himself on the tree.'

'A man couldn't hang himself on that tree,' I said, 'it's too small.'

'There's a seven-foot clearance from the fork,' he said eagerly.

'Oh, well,' I said, 'it's a sturdy little tree. I've often noticed it, standing there all alone, holding out its branches like hands.'

'Yes,' he said, 'that's right. Like hands. And have you seen the nails? Long and curved. They haven't been cut, any more than the hair. Have you seen the hair?' His voice was strained, and I felt that he must be looking at me. I turned to read his eyes, but it was too dark to see anything but the tall shape and the long coat beside me.

'That tree didn't grow in a day,' I said.

'I don't know how old it is.' The stranger spoke apologetically. 'But it's an old story—maybe twenty, thirty, forty years old. I couldn't be sure.'

There was a pause for a few minutes. We must have covered half the mile between the farm and the tree before I spoke again.

'What's behind the story?' I asked, 'what do they say?'

'They say there was a woman in it. A dark girl, one of the coastguard's daughters down at Ingo Bridge. He was a married man, you see.'

I waited for him to go on. He spoke as if it mattered vitally to him.

'It had been going on a long time, they say. Then one night, one Christmas Eve, he left his home for good and went to the inn, and perhaps he had a drink or two there, though nobody knows that. He had made up his mind to take the girl. She was going to leave a light burning in her window, and he would see it from the distance, you see, when he turned the corner by the tree. That was to be the sign, if it was all right. Well, he left his home for good, to get that girl. But he never got her. His wife got him—by that tree.'

'I thought you said it was suicide.'

'Ah, yes, that's what they say. But it was his wife that got him.'

'You mean she followed him?'

'No, I mean that she got him there.'

We walked another two hundred yards before he added: 'I mean that he saw her there, in his mind's eye. He couldn't take the girl then. He couldn't, however much he wanted to. He couldn't because he belonged to his wife. That's what I mean when I say his wife got him.'

'It's a queer story,' I said, 'I've never heard it told before.'

'Oh, you hear it among the older men. It's common knowledge,' he said.

'It's a queer story,' I said, 'because who told it in the first place? Who was to know what was in the fellow's mind? Who was to know what actually happened?'

'He was dead, wasn't he?' The stranger spoke irritably. 'A man doesn't die in these parts without talk about it. A lot of talk.'

'But how did he die?' I insisted. 'Did he hang himself or was he murdered?'

'He was murdered.'

'What the devil do you mean?' I shouted angrily. 'Murdered, by a tree?'

The stranger clutched me by the arm. 'Have you seen the tree?' he whispered, 'have you seen it standing there year after year, leaning against the south-west wind, with the hair streaming and the hands outstretched, and the long nails growing——?'

I was suddenly aware of the loneliness of the road and of the darkness and desolation of the downs around me and the sea ahead. The stranger's next remark, though spoken in a low voice, seemed to shatter the darkness.

'By God! what's a man to do when a woman pulls at him? A dark girl. And what do men have daughters for, eh? I ask you that. Whose fault is that?' and then, as if brushing aside an imaginary criticism: 'If I were to meet that coast-guard's daughter down by the bridge to-night I'd tell her . . .'

His voice tailed off and I said nothing. The coastguards' cottages are still down by the bridge, true enough, but the coastguards have been disbanded years ago. Years ago. He must have known that.

We reached the little hill in the road, mounted it, and turned the first half of the S bend. The light rain had ceased and the clouds were thinning. We both of us knew that when we passed the next corner, the other half of the S, we should see the tree.

Just then the clouds broke suddenly and the full moon shone through. It whitened the black road, silvered the gleam of the sea ahead, and illuminated the low banks and hedges with the dark rising downs beyond. We turned the corner and both stared towards the thorn-tree.

There was nothing to be seen. No tree. Nothing. The place where the tree stood was blatantly empty, and the moon-light seemed to emphasize the barrenness, showing it up like a sore, focusing the attention. I suppose I had been un-consciously visualizing the tree as I knew it, because I was more than surprised by its absence; I was shocked, profoundly shocked, and the recollection of that absence of tree, that nothingness, is more vivid to me than my memory of the tree itself. The clouds now scudded from the moon, leaving it cold and clear and agonizingly circular in an expanse of sky. In what seemed to be a blaze of light I put my head down and ran.

I ran towards the silver sea along a white road, a ribbon road of memory, and I could believe that the dust rose under my feet and powdered my boots; though with another part of me I knew that I was wearing shoes, not boots, and was pounding down a wet tarred road. In the moonlight that road seemed white and dusty and I pattered along it with the desperate urgency of a small boy who must deliver some message or run some errand of overwhelming yet not-understood importance. I ran and I ran, urgently and desperately, thinking no more of my strange companion, yet in some way intimately associated with him.

Along the white road I ran, past the signpost at the turning to the farm, knowing yet not knowing what I should see. The clouds had gathered again, a dark pillar over the sea, and the blaze of whiteness was already dimming. There was a light in the coastguard's cottage at Ingo Bridge. I headed straight for it but did not reach it, for a woman lay across the road, an elderly woman. She must have dropped her basket as she fell, and her parcels, little objects and toys that she had bought for her grandchildren perhaps, lay scattered around her. She might have been shopping for Christmas, I thought, and had missed the last bus at Ingo Bridge; then she had tried to walk home, but her strength had failed her, and she had fallen in the road.

I ran to her side and raised her head. She was too weak to stand on her feet, and I lifted her in my arms and carried her the few yards to the coastguard's cottage where the light was still burning. For those few steps the road was white and flinty—but then it is so now; it is only a little by-road—and I found myself speaking not to an old woman who had fainted or was dying, but to a young woman.　And the words I spoke were not mine but someone else's; the words of the stranger who had accompanied me to the tree.　They were framed without my help.

'That was no murder.　That was no murder by the tree. I always belonged to you, all along, really.　I see it all now.'

The woman opened her eyes and there was an expression of love in them.　I could not say whether it was I or my stranger who spoke the next words.　They were said very gently and comfortably.

'There are things better left unsaid.　Better left; you under-stand.'

She nodded and closed her eyes, and then the stranger and the strangeness left me.

I knocked at the door of the cottage.　A man opened it, then called to his wife, a grey-haired woman dressed in black, who must have been a beautiful dark girl in her time.　I explained what had happened and they took my burden from me and laid her on their horsehair sofa.　They knew who she was, of course, for she was from the village.

But I did not know.　I could only guess.　And as I walked back in the inky blackness of an oncoming rainstorm, back to my corner, then up the lane to the farm-house where my mother was waiting up for me, I cast round in my mind for a missing fragment of knowledge, something I must know yet could not remember.

I discovered it at last accidentally, while in my mind's eye I could still see the thorn-tree, standing there, holding out its branches, its mat of twigs all set towards the north-east, and from the fork a dark form hanging, twisting slowly in a long coat, a thing with a back to its head but no face, a dark thing twisting slowly beside a long white road which stretched in a dusty ribbon to the sea.　I discovered the missing fragment of knowledge in the more exact recollection of my mother's remark, made only that very morning. 'They are widening the white road at the bend,' she had said—we always used to call it the white road between ourselves—'and this evening they are going to cut down that little old thorn-tree.'

CHRISTMAS WITH OUR BILL

BY FREDERICK H. GRISEWOOD

IT really was a ridiculous day; when you consider that Christmas was so near. The sun was quite hot, the air warm and balmy—spring might well have been round the corner instead of several months away.

Bill, whom I met on my way to the village shop which served as post office, was evidently of the same opinion. 'Nothing, don't seem right somehow these 'ere days,' he said. 'I just picked a rose in my garden. That tree 'ad ought to 'a' known better—'er 'ad ought to 'a' bin asleep a long while since, instead o' gallivantin' about like that. But it ain't only the weather as be different—things ain't what they was.'

Bill was evidently in one of his reminiscent moods, so I encouraged him to go on.

'Well, sir,' he said, 'fer one thing, us don't get what us 'ad used to get at Christmas time. In the old days it were coal an' beef fer all on us as worked on the estate. 'Ad used to come round in a waggin, an' us 'ad it reg'lar. Still, I will say as us used to work fer it. There weren't no talk o' overtime in those days. If your carter 'ad a sick mare 'e 'd sit up all night along of 'er, an' such a thing as extra payment fer it never crossed 'is mind. You see, sir,' he went on, 'us took a proper pride in our jobs those days—an' the carter 'e didn't want 'is team spoilt by a sick 'un, so o' course 'e done what 'e could to keep all 'is beasts fit. But these young lads as works now-adays—the only thing as they thinks on be their 'alf 'oliday o' Saturdays. If you take five minutes out o' a man's dinner hour now 'e 'll change you overtime fer it. Well, that's the way things goes, and if that's what they wants they can 'ave it, but it don't suit me, I can tell 'ee. All comes o' tryin' to run farmin' like a factory—that's what it is.

'Th' old Christmases were fine. Us used to go a' carol singin', and then there was the Mummers an' such like.'

But here I lost Bill and his grievances. That magic word 'Mummers' had opened the floodgates of memory. I was back in those far-off days—long before the Great War was even dreamed of—when, indeed, the Boer War was only a cloud on the horizon. I was a little boy again in a navy suit. For days there had been rumours of these strange things, Mummers. What could they be? But even Jane, the parlourmaid, who was my informant on all the important events in life, refused to tell me.

'You wait and see,' she would say. So for the time being Mummers remained a mystery.

Christmas Day came and passed, and still no sign of these queer things. And then—two nights after—just as we had finished tea—we were allowed down into the drawing-room as it was Christmas time—Jane appeared at the door and said with a knowing look in my direction: 'Please, ma'am, the Mummers are here, and we've cleared the servants' hall.'

My father was fetched from his study, and we all made our way downstairs. The cook and the other servants were there with an air of expectancy on their faces, but who could these dreadful strangers be with black faces, gleaming eyes, and outlandish dresses, who were stamping the snow from their boots in the stone passage outside? Could these frightful objects really be the Mummers? Tremblingly, I hid my face in my mother's dress. 'What's the matter?' she asked; 'you're not afraid of the Mummers, are you?' And then one of them spoke, and I withdrew my face from its hiding place and gazed in amazement. Could it be possible that concealed behind that blackened face and nightmare clothes lurked the familiar person of Bert, the boot boy? It certainly was his voice—a trifle self conscious, but unmistakably it was Bert's voice.

This put quite a different complexion on the whole affair. With renewed courage I looked about me. That familiar shuffle could only belong to one person. I should have known it in a million in spite of its owner's disguise. It was fat George, the landlord of 'The Spotted Dog.' And over there, brandishing a wooden sword, in all the finery of Bold Slasher was—yes, it was none other than dear old Joe Allen, our postman.

This was fine—this was the real thing. And so the play began. The players were introduced — each one walking round and round the room reciting his lines in his homely Oxfordshire: 'In comes I, King George, fine fellar be I. To fight for the good o' England will I try.' Bold Slasher with his challenge. The mortal combat and defeat of the challenger. The frenzied appeal for a doctor. 'Be there a doctor outside?' 'There be.' 'I'll give thee ten pun' if thou'll come.' 'Won't come for that.' 'I'll give thee five pun if thou'll come.' 'Won't come for that.' 'I'll give thee three brass fardens if thou'll come.' 'Come for that and glad o' the money. In comes I, the Doctor,' etc.

The examination of the wounded man: 'What's the matter with this 'ere man? Pain in the leg?' 'No, pain in the 'ead.' 'What's best for a pain in the 'ead?' 'Draw a tooth.' 'What, draw an arm?' 'No, draw a tooth.' The operation. Those frightful pincers. Were they really going to pull out one of Joe's teeth?

This was too much. I started up from my chair, but Ernest, the pseudo-doctor, grinned all over his black face and gave me a portentous wink. The pincers were inserted; every one pulled—once, twice, three times—and there, gripped firmly in the jaws of the murderous instrument, was an enormous tooth, which Ernest displayed in triumph. So Bold Slasher was made whole again and lived to fight another day.

What a splendid climax, and how we applauded—nor did the fearsome apparition of Beelzebub—'On my shoulder I carries my club'—evoke any feeling from me beyond that of wonder that our usually mild gardener could transform himself into such a demon.

Then there were songs from the company, congratulations, much shaking of hands and drinking of beer—and——

Here I came back to earth again to hear Bill saying: 'An' one o' they young rapscallions clumb up into the branches o' Hassams' oak and very nigh startled old Polly Chivers out o' 'er senses. You knows as they says as that there oak be 'aunted. A lot o' nonsense, I sez.' 'You don't believe in ghosts then, Bill?' I asked, pulling myself together. 'Ghosts,' said Bill, and I wish I could portray the scorn in his voice. 'I don't set no store by they—why, ol' Ted as lived next door to me 'e 'ad used to see 'em every Saturday night. 'It at 'em wi' a stick, that he did—reg'lar.'

And with that he turned and trudged slowly towards 'The Spotted Dog.'

HOW SANTA CLAUS CAME TO
SIMPSON'S BAR

BY FRANCIS BRET HARTE

IT had been raining in the valley of the Sacramento. The
North Fork had overflowed its banks, and Rattlesnake Creek
was impassable. The few boulders that had marked the
summer ford at Simpson's Crossing were obliterated by a vast
sheet of water stretching to the foot-hills. The up-stage was
stopped at Grangers; the last mail had been abandoned in the
tules, the rider swimming for his life. 'An area,' remarked the
Sierra Avalanche, with pensive local pride, 'as large as the
state of Massachusetts is now under water.'

Nor was the weather any better in the foot-hills. The mud
lay deep on the mountain road; wagons that neither physical
force nor moral objurgation could move from the evil ways
into which they had fallen, encumbered the track, and the way
to Simpson's Bar was indicated by broken-down teams and
hard swearing. And farther on, cut off and inaccessible, rained
upon and bedraggled, smitten by high winds and threatened
by high water, Simpson's Bar, on the eve of Christmas Day,
1862, clung like a swallow's nest to the rocky entablature and
splintered capitals of Table Mountain, and shook in the blast.

As night shut down on the settlement, a few lights gleamed
through the mist from the windows of cabins on either side
of the highway now crossed and gullied by lawless streams and
swept by marauding winds. Happily most of the population
were gathered at Thompson's store, clustered round a red-hot
stove, at which they silently spat in some accepted sense of

social communion that perhaps rendered conversation unnecessary. Indeed, most methods of diversion had long since been exhausted on Simpson's Bar; high water had suspended the regular occupations on gulch and on river, and a consequent lack of money and whisky had taken the zest from most illegitimate recreation. Even Mr Hamlin was fain to leave the Bar with fifty dollars in his pocket—the only amount actually realized of the large sums won by him in the successful exercise of his arduous profession. 'Ef I was asked,' he remarked somewhat later—'ef I was asked to pint out a purty little village where a retired sport as didn't care for money could exercise hisself, frequent and lively, I'd say Simpson's Bar; but for a young man with a large family depending on his exertions, it don't pay.' As Mr Hamlin's family consisted mainly of female adults, this remark is quoted rather to show the breadth of his humour than the exact extent of his responsibilities.

Howbeit, the unconscious objects of this satire sat that evening in the listless apathy begotten of idleness and lack of excitement. Even the sudden splashing of hoofs before the door did not arouse them. Dick Bullen alone paused in the act of scraping out his pipe, and lifted his head, but no other one of the group indicated any interest in, or recognition of, the man who entered.

It was a figure familiar enough to the company, and known in Simpson's Bar as 'The Old Man.' A man of perhaps fifty years; grizzled and scant of hair, but still fresh and youthful of complexion. A face full of ready but not very powerful sympathy, with a chameleon-like aptitude for taking on the shade and colour of contiguous moods and feelings. He had evidently just left some hilarious companions, and did not at first notice the gravity of the group, but clapped the shoulder of the nearest man jocularly, and threw himself into a vacant chair.

'Jest heard the best thing out, boys! Ye know Smiley, over yar—Jim Smiley—funniest man in the Bar? Well, Jim was jest telling the richest yarn about——'

'Smiley's a —— fool,' interrupted a gloomy voice.

'A particular —— skunk,' added another in sepulchral accents.

A silence followed these positive statements. The Old Man glanced quickly around the group. Then his face slowly changed. 'That's so,' he said reflectively, after a pause, 'certingly a sort of a skunk and suthin' of a fool. In course.' He was silent for a moment as in painful contemplation of the unsavouriness and folly of the unpopular Smiley. 'Dismal weather, ain't it?' he added, now fully embarked on the current of prevailing sentiment. 'Mighty rough papers on the boys, and no show for money this season. And to-morrow's Christmas.'

There was a movement among the men at this announcement, but whether of satisfaction or disgust was not plain. 'Yes,' continued the Old Man in the lugubrious tone he had, within the last few moments, unconsciously adopted—'yes, Christmas, and to-night's Christmas Eve. Ye see, boys, I kinder thought—that is, I sorter had an idee, jest passin' like, you know—that maybe ye'd all like to come over to my house to-night and have a sort of tear round. But I suppose, now, you wouldn't? Don't feel like it, maybe?' he added with anxious sympathy, peering into the faces of his companions.

'Well, I don't know,' responded Tom Flynn with some cheerfulness. 'P'r'aps we may. But how about your wife, Old Man? What does *she* say to it?'

The Old Man hesitated. His conjugal experience had not been a happy one, and the fact was known to Simpson's Bar. His first wife, a delicate, pretty little woman, had suffered keenly and secretly from the jealous suspicions of her husband, until one day he invited the whole Bar to his house to expose her infidelity. On arriving, the party found the shy, *petite* creature quietly engaged in her household duties, and retired abashed and discomfited. But the sensitive woman did not easily recover from the shock of this extraordinary outrage. It was with difficulty she regained her equanimity sufficiently to release her lover from the closet in which he was concealed, and escape with him. She left a boy of three years to comfort her bereaved husband. The Old Man's present wife had been his cook. She was large, loyal, and aggressive.

Before he could reply, Joe Dimmick suggested with great directness that it was the 'Old Man's house,' and that, invoking the Divine Power, if the case were his own, he would invite whom he pleased, even if in so doing he imperilled his salva⁄tion. The Powers of Evil, he further remarked, should con⁄tend against him vainly. All this delivered with a terseness and vigour lost in this necessary translation.

'In course. Certainly. Thet's it,' said the Old Man with a sympathetic frown. 'Thar's no trouble about *thet*. It's my own house, built every stick on it myself. Don't you be afeard o' her, boys, She *may* cut up a trifle rough—ez wimmin do—but she'll come round.' Secretly the Old Man trusted to the exaltation of liquor and the power of courageous example to sustain him in such an emergency.

As yet, Dick Bullen, the oracle and leader of Simpson's Bar, had not spoken. He now took his pipe from his lips. 'Old Man, how's that yer Johnny gettin' on? Seems to me he didn't look so peart last time I seed him on the bluff heavin' rocks at Chinamen. Didn't seem to take much interest in it. Thar was a gang of 'em by yar yesterday—drownded out up the river—and I kinder thought o' Johnny, and how he'd miss 'em! Maybe now, we'd be in the way ef he wus sick?'

The father, evidently touched not only by this pathetic picture of Johnny's deprivation, but by the considerate delicacy of the speaker, hastened to assure him that Johnny was better and that a 'little fun might 'liven him up.' Whereupon Dick arose, shook himself, and saying: 'I'm ready. Lead the way, Old Man: here goes,' himself led the way with a leap, a characteristic howl, and darted out into the night. As he passed through the outer room he caught up a blazing brand from the hearth. The action was repeated by the rest of the party, closely following and elbowing each other, and before the astonished proprietor of Thompson's grocery was aware of the intention of his guests, the room was deserted.

The night was pitchy dark. In the first gust of wind their temporary torches were extinguished, and only the red brands dancing and flitting in the gloom like drunken will-o'-the-wisps indicated their whereabouts. Their way led up Pine-Tree Cañon, at the head of which a broad, low, bark-thatched cabin burrowed in the mountain-side. It was the home of the Old Man, and the entrance to the tunnel in which he worked when he worked at all. Here the crowd paused for a moment, out of delicate deference to their host, who came up panting in the rear.

'P'r'aps ye'd better hold on a second out yer, whilst I go in and see that things is all right,' said the Old Man, with an indifference he was far from feeling. The suggestion was graciously accepted, the door opened and closed on the host, and the crowd, leaning their backs against the wall and cowering under the eaves, waited and listened.

For a few moments there was no sound but the dripping of water from the eaves, and the stir and rustle of wrestling boughs above them. Then the men became uneasy, and whispered suggestion and suspicion passed from the one to the other. 'Reckon she's caved in his head the first lick!' 'Decoyed him inter the tunnel and barred him up, likely.' 'Got him down and sittin' on him.' 'Prob'ly biling suthin' to heave on us: stand clear the door, boys!' For just then the latch clicked, the door slowly opened, and a voice said: 'Come in out o' the wet.'

The voice was neither that of the Old Man nor of his wife. It was the voice of a small boy, its weak treble broken by that preternatural hoarseness which only vagabondage and the habit of premature self-assertion can give. It was the face of a small boy that looked up at theirs—a face that might have been pretty, and even refined, but that it was darkened by evil knowledge from within, and dirt and hard experience from without. He had a blanket around his shoulders, and had evidently just risen from his bed. 'Come in,' he repeated, 'and don't make no noise. The Old Man's in there talking to mar,' he continued, pointing to an adjacent room which seemed to be a kitchen, from which the Old Man's voice came in deprecating accents. 'Let me be,' he added querulously, to Dick Bullen, who had caught him up, blanket and all, and was affecting to toss him into the fire. 'Let go o' me, you damned old fool, d' ye hear?'

Thus adjured, Dick Bullen lowered Johnny to the ground with a smothered laugh, while the men, entering quietly, ranged themselves around a long table of rough boards which occupied the centre of the room. Johnny then gravely proceeded to a cupboard and brought out several articles, which he deposited on the table. 'Thar's whisky. And crackers. And red herons. And cheese.' He took a bite of the latter on his way to the table. 'And sugar.' He scooped up a mouthful *en route* with a small and very dirty hand. 'And terbacker. Thar's dried appils too on the shelf, but I don't admire 'em. Appils is swellin'. Thar,' he concluded, 'now wade in, and don't be afeard. *I* don't mind the old woman. She don't b'long to *me*. S'long.'

He had stepped to the threshold of a small room, scarcely larger than a closet, partitioned off from the main apartment, and holding in its dim recess a small bed. He stood there a moment looking at the company, his bare feet peeping from the blanket, and nodded.

'Hallo, Johnny! You ain't goin' to turn in agin, are ye?' said Dick.

'Yes, I are,' responded Johnny decidedly.

'Why, wot's up, old fellow?'

'I'm sick.'

'How sick?'

'I've got a fevier. And childblains. And roomatiz,' returned Johnny, and vanished within. After a moment's pause, he added in the dark, apparently from under the bed-clothes—'And biles!'

There was an embarrassing silence. The men looked at each other and at the fire. Even with the appetizing banquet before them, it seemed as if they might again fall into the despondency of Thompson's grocery, when the voice of the Old Man, incautiously lifted, came deprecatingly from the kitchen.

'Certainly! Thet's so. In course they is. A gang o' lazy, drunken loafers, and that ar Dick Bullen's the ornariest of all. Didn't hev no more *sabe* than to come round yar with sickness in the house and no provision. Thet's what I said: "Bullen," sez I, "it's crazy drunk you are, or a fool," sez I, 'to think o' such a thing. Staples," I sez, "be you a man, Staples, and 'spect to raise hell under my roof and invalids yin' round?" But they would come—they would. Thet's wot you must 'spect o' such trash as lays round the Bar.'

A burst of laughter from the men followed this unfortunate, exposure. Whether it was overheard in the kitchen, or whether the Old Man's irate companion had just then exhausted all other modes of expressing her contemptuous indignation, I cannot say, but a back door was suddenly slammed with great violence. A moment later and the Old Man reappeared, haply unconscious of the cause of the late hilarious outburst, and smiled blandly.

'The old woman thought she'd jest run over to Mrs

McFadden's for a sociable call,' he explained, with jaunty indifference, as he took a seat at the board.

Oddly enough it needed this untoward incident to relieve the embarrassment that was beginning to be felt by the party, and their natural audacity returned with their host. I do not propose to record the convivialities of that evening. The inquisitive reader will accept the statement that the conversa׳ tion was characterized by the same intellectual exaltation, the same cautious reverence, the same fastidious delicacy, the same rhetorical precision, and the same logical and coherent dis׳ course somewhat later in the evening, which distinguish similar gatherings of the masculine sex in more civilized localities and under more favourable auspices. No glasses were broken in the absence of any; no liquor was uselessly split on the floor or table in the scarcity of that article.

It was nearly midnight when the festivities were interrupted. 'Hush,' said Dick Bullen, holding up his hand. It was the querulous voice of Johnny from his adjacent closet: 'Oh, dad!'

The Old Man arose hurriedly and disappeared in the closet. Presently he reappeared. 'His rheumatiz is coming on agin bad,' he explained, 'and he wanted rubbin'.' He lifted the demijohn of whisky from the table and shook it. It was empty. Dick Bullen put down his tin cup with an embarrassed laugh. So did the others. The Old Man examined their contents and said hopefully, 'I reckon that's enough; he don't need much. You hold on all o' you for a spell, and I'll be back'; and vanished in the closet with an old flannel shirt and the whisky. The door closed but imperfectly, and the following dialogue was distinctly audible:

'Now, sonny, whar does she ache worst?'

'Sometimes over yar and sometimes under yer; but it's most powerful from yer to yer. Rub yer, dad.'

A silence seemed to indicate a brisk rubbing. Then Johnny:

'Hevin' a good time out yer, dad?'

'Yes, sonny.'

'To-morrer's Chrismiss—ain't it?'

'Yes, sonny. How does she feel now?'

'Better. Rub a little furder down. Wot's Chrismiss, anyway? Wot's it all about?'

'Oh, it's a day.'

This exhaustive definition was apparently satisfactory, for there was a silent interval of rubbing. Presently Johnny again:

'Mar sez that everywhere else but yer everybody gives things to everybody Chrismiss, and then she jist waded inter you. She sez thar's a man they call Sandy Claws, not a white man, you know, but a kind o' Chinemin, comes down the chimbley night afore Chrismiss and gives things to chillern—boys like me. Puts 'em in their butes! Thet's what she tried to play upon me. Easy now, pop, whar are you rubbin' to—thet's a mile from the place. She jest made that up, didn't she, jest to aggrewate me and you? Don't rub thar. . . . Why, dad!'

In the great quiet that seemed to have fallen upon the house the sigh of the near pines and the drip of leaves without was very distinct. Johnny's voice, too, was lowered as he went on: 'Don't you take on now, fur I'm gettin' all right fast. Wot's the boys doin' out thar?'

The Old Man partly opened the door and peered through. His guests were sitting there sociably enough, but there were a few silver coins and a lean buckskin purse on the table. 'Bettin' on suthin'—some little game or 'nother. They're all right,' he replied to Johnny, and recommenced his rubbing.

'I'd like to take a hand and win some money,' said Johnny reflectively after a pause.

The Old Man glibly repeated what was evidently a familiar formula, that if Johnny would wait until he struck it rich in the tunnel he'd have lots of money, etc.

'Yes,' said Johnny, 'but you don't. And whether you strike it or win it, it's about the same. It's all luck. But it's mighty cu'ro's about Chrismiss—ain't it? Why do they call it Chrismiss?'

Perhaps from some instinctive deference to the overhearing of his guests, or from some vague sense of incongruity, the Old Man's reply was so low as to be inaudible beyond the room.

'Yes,' said Johnny, with some slight abatement of interest, 'I've heerd o' *him* before. Thar, that'll do, dad. I don't ache near so bad as I did. Now wrap me tight in this yer blanket. So. Now,' he added in a muffled whisper, 'sit down yer by me till I go asleep.' To assure himself of obedience, he disengaged one hand from the blanket and, grasping his father's sleeve, again composed himself to rest.

For some moments the Old Man waited patiently. Then the unwonted stillness of the house excited his curiosity, and without moving from the bed he cautiously opened the door with his disengaged hand, and looked into the main room. To his infinite surprise it was dark and deserted. But even then a smouldering log on the hearth broke, and by the upspringing blaze he saw the figure of Dick Bullen sitting by the dying embers.

'Hallo!'

Dick started, rose, and came somewhat unsteadily toward him.

'Whar's the boys?' said the Old Man.

'Gone up the cañon on a little *pasear*. They're coming back for me in a minit. I'm waitin' round for 'em. What are you starin' at, Old Man?' he added with a forced laugh; 'do you think I'm drunk?'

The Old Man might have been pardoned the supposition, for Dick's eyes were humid and his face flushed. He loitered and lounged back to the chimney, yawned, shook himself, buttoned up his coat and laughed. 'Liquor ain't so plenty as that, Old Man. Now don't you git up,' he continued, as the Old Man made a movement to release his sleeve from Johnny's hand. 'Don't you mind manners. Sit jest whar you be; I'm goin' in a jiffy. Thar, that's them now.'

There was a low tap at the door. Dick Bullen opened it quickly, nodded 'Good night' to his host, and disappeared. The Old Man would have followed him but for the hand that still unconsciously grasped his sleeve. He could have easily disengaged it; it was small, weak, and emaciated. But per-haps because it *was* small, weak, and emaciated, he changed his mind, and, drawing his chair closer to the bed, rested his head upon it. In this defenceless attitude the potency of his earlier potations surprised him. The room flickered and faded before his eyes, reappeared, faded again, went out, and left him—asleep.

Meantime Dick Bullen, closing the door, confronted his companions. 'Are you ready?' said Staples. 'Ready,' said Dick; 'what's the time?' 'Past twelve,' was the reply; 'can you make it?—it's nigh on fifty miles, the round trip hither and yon.' 'I reckon,' returned Dick shortly. 'Whar's the mare?' 'Bill and Jack's holdin' her at the crossin'.' 'Let 'em hold on a minit longer,' said Dick.

He turned and re-entered the house softly. By the light of the guttering candle and dying fire he saw that the door of the little room was open. He stepped toward it on tiptoe and looked in. The Old Man had fallen back in his chair, snor-ing, his helpless feet thrust out in a line with his collapsed shoulders, and his hat pulled over his eyes. Beside him, on a narrow wooden bedstead, lay Johnny, muffled tightly in a blanket that hid all save a strip of forehead and a few curls damp with perspiration. Dick Bullen made a step forward, hesitated, and glanced over his shoulder into the deserted room. Everything was quiet. With a sudden resolution he parted his huge moustaches with both hands and stooped over the sleeping boy. But even as he did so a mischievous blast, lying in wait, swooped down the chimney, rekindled the hearth, and lit up the room with a shameless glow from which Dick fled in bashful terror.

His companions were already waiting for him at the crossing. Two of them were struggling in the darkness with some strange misshapen bulk, which as Dick came nearer took the semblance of a great yellow horse.

It was the mare. She was not a pretty picture. From her Roman nose to her rising haunches, from her arched spine, hidden by the stiff *machillas* of a Mexican saddle, to her thick, straight, bony legs, there was not a line of equine grace. In her half blind but wholly vicious white eyes, in her protruding underlip, in her monstrous colour, there was nothing but ugliness and vice.

'Now then,' said Staples, 'stand cl'ar of her heels, boys, and up with you. Don't miss your first hold of her mane, and mind ye get your off stirrup *quick*. Ready!'

There was a leap, a scrambling struggle, a bound, a wild retreat of the crowd, a circle of flying hoofs, two springless leaps that jarred the earth, a rapid play and jingle of spurs, a plunge, and then the voice of Dick somewhere in the darkness, 'All right!'

'Don't take the lower road back onless you're hard pushed for time! Don't hold her in downhill. We'll be at the ford at five. G' lang! Hoopa! Mula! Go!'

A splash, a spark struck from the ledge in the road, a clatter in the rocky cut beyond, and Dick was gone.

.   .   .   .   .   .

Sing, O Muse, the ride of Richard Bullen! Sing, O Muse, of chivalrous men! the sacred quest, the doughty deeds, the battery of low churls, the fearsome ride and gruesome peril, of the Flower of Simpson's Bar! Alack! she is dainty, this

Muse! She will have none of this bucking brute and swaggering, ragged rider, and I must fain follow him in prose, afoot!

It was one o'clock, and yet he had only gained Rattlesnake Hill. For in that time Jovita had rehearsed to him all her imperfections and practised all her vices. Thrice had she stumbled. Twice had she thrown up her Roman nose in a straight line with the reins, and, resisting bit and spur, struck out madly across country. Twice had she reared, and, rearing, fallen backward; and twice had the agile Dick, unharmed, regained his seat before she found her vicious legs again. And a mile beyond them, at the foot of a long hill, was Rattlesnake Creek. Dick knew that here was the crucial test of his ability to perform his enterprise, set his teeth grimly, put his knees well into her flanks, and changed his defensive tactics to brisk aggression. Bullied and maddened, Jovita began the descent of the hill. Here the artful Richard pretended to hold her in with ostentatious objurgation and well-feigned cries of alarm. It is unnecessary to add that Jovita instantly ran away. Nor need I state the time made in the descent; it is written in the chronicles of Simpson's Bar. Enough that in another moment, as it seemed to Dick, she was splashing on the overflowed banks of Rattlesnake Creek. As Dick expected, the momentum she has acquired carried her beyond the point of balking, and, holding her well together for a mighty leap, they dashed into the middle of the swiftly flowing current. A few moments of kicking, wading, and swimming, and Dick drew a long breath on the opposite bank.

The road from Rattlesnake Creek to Red Mountain was tolerably level. Either the plunge in Rattlesnake Creek had dampened her baleful fire, or the art which led to it had shown her the superior wickedness of her rider, for Jovita no longer wasted her surplus energy in wanton conceits. Once she bucked, but it was from force of habit; once she shied, but it was from a new, freshly painted meeting-house at the crossing of the country road. Hollows, ditches, gravelly deposits, patches of freshly springing grasses, flew from beneath her rattling hoofs. She began to smell unpleasantly, once or twice she coughed slightly, but there was no abatement of her strength or speed. By two o'clock he had passed Red Mountain and begun the descent to the plain. Ten minutes later the driver of the fast Pioneer coach was overtaken and passed by a 'man on a Pinto hoss'—an event sufficiently notable for remark. At half past two Dick rose in his stirrups with a great shout. Stars were glittering through the rifted clouds, and beyond him, out of the plain, rose two spires, a flagstaff, and a straggling line of black objects. Dick jingled his spurs and swung his *riata*, Jovita bounded forward, and in another moment they swept into Tuttleville, and drew up before the wooden piazza of 'The Hotel of All Nations.'

What transpired that night at Tuttleville is not strictly a part of this record. Briefly I may state, however, that after Jovita had been handed over to a sleepy ostler, whom she at once kicked into unpleasant consciousness, Dick sallied out with the bar-keeper for a tour of the sleeping town. Lights still gleamed from a few saloons and gambling-houses; but, avoiding these, they stopped before several closed shops, and by persistent tapping and judicious outcry roused the proprietors from their beds, and made them unbar the doors of their magazines and expose their wares. Sometimes they were met by curses, but oftener by interest and some concern in their needs, and the interview was invariably concluded by a drink. It was three o'clock before this pleasantry was given over, and with a small waterproof bag of indiarubber strapped on his shoulders Dick returned to the hotel. But here he was waylaid by Beauty— Beauty opulent in charms, affluent in dress, persuasive in speech, and Spanish in accent! In vain she repeated the invitation in *Excelsior*, happily scorned by all Alpine-climbing youth, and rejected by this child of the Sierras—a rejection softened in this instance by a laugh and his last gold coin. And then he sprang to the saddle and dashed down the lonely street and out into the lonelier plain, where presently the lights, the black line of houses, the spires, and the flagstaff sank into the earth behind him again and were lost in the distance.

The storm had cleared away, the air was brisk and cold, the outlines of adjacent landmarks were distinct, but it was half past four before Dick reached the meeting-house and the crossing of the county road. To avoid the rising grade he had taken a longer and more circuitous road, in whose viscid mud Jovita sank fetlock deep at every bound. It was a poor preparation for a steady ascent of five miles more; but Jovita, gathering her legs under her, took it with her usual blind, unreasoning fury, and a half-hour later reached the long level that led to Rattlesnake Creek. Another half-hour would bring him to the creek. He threw the reins lightly upon the neck of the mare, chirruped to her, and began to sing.

Suddenly Jovita shied with a bound that would have unseated a less practised rider. Hanging to her rein was a figure that had leaped from the bank, and at the same time from the road before her arose a shadowy horse and rider. 'Throw up your hands,' commanded the second apparition, with an oath.

Dick felt the mare tremble, quiver, and apparently sink under him. He knew what it meant and was prepared.

'Stand aside, Jack Simpson. I know you, you d—d thief! Let me pass, or——'

He did not finish the sentence. Jovita rose straight in the air with a terrific bound, throwing the figure from her bit with a single shake of her vicious head, and charged with deadly malevolence down on the impediment before her. An oath, a pistol-shot, horse and highwayman rolled over in the road, and the next moment Jovita was a hundred yards away. But the good right arm of her rider, shattered by a bullet, dropped helplessly at his side.

Without slacking his speed he shifted the reins to his left hand. But a few moments later he was obliged to halt and tighten the saddle-girths that had slipped in the onset. This in his crippled condition took some time. He had no fear of pursuit, but looking up he saw that the eastern stars were already paling, and that the distant peaks had lost their ghostly whiteness, and now stood out blackly against a lighter sky. Day was upon him. Then completely absorbed in a single idea, he forgot the pain of his wound, and mounting again dashed on toward Rattlesnake Creek. But now Jovita's breath came broken by gasps, Dick reeled in his saddle, and brighter and brighter grew the sky.

Ride, Richard; run, Jovita; linger, O day!

For the last few rods there was a roaring in his ears. Was it exhaustion from loss of blood, or what? He was dazed and giddy as he swept down the hill, and did not recognize his surroundings. Had he taken the wrong road, or was this Rattlesnake Creek?

It was. But the brawling creek he had swum a few hours before had risen, more than doubled its volume, and now rolled a swift and resistless river between him and Rattlesnake Hill. For the first time that night Richard's heart sank within him. The river, the mountain, the quickening east, swam before his eyes. He shut them to recover his self-control. In that brief interval, by some fantastic mental process, the little room at Simpson's Bar and the figures of the sleeping father and son rose upon him. He opened his eyes wildly, cast off his coat, pistol, boots, and saddle, bound his precious pack tightly to his shoulders, grasped the bare flanks of Jovita with his bared knees, and with a shout dashed into the yellow water. A cry rose from the opposite bank as the head of a man and horse struggled for a few moments against the battling current, and then were swept away amidst uprooted trees and whirling driftwood.

The Old Man started and woke. The fire on the hearth was dead, the candle in the outer room flickering in its socket, and somebody was rapping at the door. He opened it, but fell back with a cry before the dripping, half-naked figure that reeled against the doorpost.

'Dick?'

'Hush! Is he awake yet?'

'No—but, Dick——?'

'Dry up, you old fool! Get me some whisky, *quick*!' The Old Man flew and returned with—an empty bottle! Dick would have sworn, but his strength was not equal to the occasion. He staggered, caught at the handle of the door, and motioned to the Old Man.

'Thar's suthin' in my pack yer for Johnny. Take it off. I can't.'

The Old Man unstrapped the pack, and laid it before the exhausted man.

'Open it, quick!'

He did so with trembling fingers. It contained only a few poor toys—cheap and barbaric enough, goodness knows, but bright with paint and tinsel. One of them was broken; another, I fear, was irretrievably ruined by water; and on the third—ah me! there was a cruel spot.

'It don't look like much, that's a fact,' said Dick ruefully. . . . 'But it's the best we could do. . . . Take 'em, Old Man, and put 'em in his stocking, and tell him—tell him, you know—hold me, Old Man——' The Old Man caught at his sinking figure. 'Tell him,' said Dick, with a weak little laugh—'tell him Sandy Claus has come.'

And even so, bedraggled, ragged, unshaven, and unshorn, with one arm hanging helplessly at his side, Santa Claus came to Simpson's Bar and fell fainting on the first threshold. The Christmas dawn came slowly after, touching the remoter peaks with the rosy warmth of ineffable love. And it looked so tenderly on Simpson's Bar that the whole mountain, as if caught in a generous action, blushed to the skies.

OH, WHAT A HORRID TALE!

BY P. S.

COME, friends, gather round the fireside, and listen to the sad but seasonable tale of Ernie the Actor.

Ernie was one of those actors who only find fame at Christmas. He could rule a Christmas pantomime like Robey or Little Tich, but between seasons he was lucky if he got a month's engagement with a concert-party. Sad, but true! However, he worked hard, lived soberly, and would doubtless have lasted to a ripe and insignificant old age, had not the course of his life been strangely altered by his marrying a Mrs Tonks, a widow with four young children and an eye for the pay-packet.

Mrs Tonks had booked a seat for *Cinderella*, to comfort herself for the recent death of her first husband. She liked a joke as well as the next woman, and she liked a good cry too. Ernie made her laugh so much that, being at once so happy and so sad, she fell in love with him. Ernie fell more in love with her four children than with Mrs Tonks; but nevertheless they got married. Now, Ernie took his work so seriously that he could hardly cease being funny, even when he was off the stage. His wife used to find his cross-talk and gags a great solace in her domestic worries; and the children were always happy when Ernie was at home, because his antics kept them laughing all the time.

As the years went by, however, the children needed more and more food, and more and more clothes, while Mrs Ernie asked for more and more of Ernie's money. Ernie's engagements, on the other hand, became fewer and fewer, and he found it less and less easy to earn enough money to pay the larger and larger bills.

The strain of working too hard and always being anxious for the future told at last on Ernie's temper. He began to dislike returning home, after a tiring round of the managers' offices, only to be treated by his family as a joke. One day he brought his fist down on the breakfast-table with a bang, and said: 'I won't be a laughing-stock any longer, I won't; I won't; I won't.' And, putting his hat on his head, he announced that he was going to apply for a straight part, and act the clown no more.

It was not easy to persuade the managers that he meant what he said. Most of them laughed, offered him a cigarette, and exclaimed: 'Jolly good joke, ha!' But one of them jestingly offered him the part of the Demon King in *Aladdin*, at a little second-rate theatre in Staffs, for a salary which was half his former wage. Ernie accepted it.

'Well, you don't expect *me* to spend Christmas Day in the workhouse, do you?' said Mrs Ernie, when he told her the news. And without more ado she departed with the children to stay at Chorlton - cum - Hardy with her married sister. But the pantomime ran for nine weeks, and the local dramatic critic wrote that 'no more terrifying Demon King has ever walked the boards of the "Alexandra."' When the last performance was ended Ernie was paid a bonus. He packed his belongings and took the first train to Chorlton-cum-Hardy, that he might tell his wife of his success.

His welcome, however, was not so happy as he expected. When he put his head round the door he was greeted, not by cries of pleasure or yet of laughter, but by startled faces and a shriek of horror. Ernie pretended not to notice it; but in the weeks that followed it became clear that every one was afraid of him. The children wept if he took them on his knee, and even Mrs Ernie, who was so buxom and handy with a rolling-pin, would shrink away when he approached.

Ernie was quite unable to account for this. It pained him more than any mockery could do, for he was naturally a gentle man. After some months he began to feel that his having played the Demon King had something to do with it. And now he often wished that he were Buttons or the Broker's Man once more, so that he could move them to laughter instead of fear.

When the time came for him to make his contract for the next year's pantomime, he decided that he would be Demon King no longer. He even refused the parts of the Giant in *Jack and the Beanstalk* and the Wicked Uncle in *Cinderella*, for which good and comfortable salaries were offered.

He no longer wished to frighten people.

The managers, very naturally, considered him daft to refuse good offers, and he would have gone without any engagement at all had not 'Puss' in a touring company of *Dick Whittington and his Cat* fallen from the balustrade of the dress circle and lost its ninth (and last) life. Almost in despair, for there were only four days till the first performance, the manager offered the part to Ernie. Ernie accepted it.

He had never played an animal part before, but he very quickly learned what to do. He scratched, miaowed and purred to a nicety.

It was very pleasant to feel once more the affection of an audience instead of its hatred. Before the season was finished

Ernie had become a favourite with actors and public alike. But what made him happiest of all was that his own family's fear of him suddenly departed. Mrs Ernie began to put her arms round his neck and caress him with every token of kind, ness, while the children no longer dreaded his touch, but climbed about him and played all sorts of loving games with him.

Ernie was affected almost to tears by this love and tenderness, and thereafter he lived very happily for several years, continuing to play the 'Puss' at every Christmas pantomime. He only suffered two discomforts. One was that he was expected— and indeed compelled—to sit and sleep upon the mat, in, stead of an arm-chair or his bed. The other was that Mrs Ernie forbade him to have a drop of beer or stout or whisky, but insisted that he should always drink milk.

After he had played Whittington's Cat or Puss-in-Boots at almost every reputable theatre in the provinces, the time came when Ernie was no longer as supple in his limbs as a first-class cat should be. Giving long thought to the matter he finally made up his mind that he ought to take another part before people began to say: 'Poor old Ernie isn't as nimble as he used to be.' And after talking with his agent he con-tracted to play a part which entailed much less activity and effort than did that of 'Puss,' namely the title role in *Mother Goose*.

Unfortunately Ernie's new salary was much less than that which he had earned before. Mrs Ernie had some hard things to say when he told her about this, and blamed him very much for giving up his old part. But Ernie took a great pride in his calling, and informed her in no uncertain tones that there is more honour in competently laying a golden egg than in being but a lame companion to Dick Whittington. This difference of opinion led to the first dispute between husband and wife since the days of the Demon King.

The first rehearsals of *Mother Goose* went well—so well that Ernie begged his wife to come with the children to see the dress rehearsal, which was to take place on Christmas Day. But Mrs Ernie refused, and when the day came Ernie left their lodgings to a volley of recrimination from his better-or-worse.

The performance went from start to finish without a hitch—a most unusual happening in a pantomime. As Ernie returned to the lodgings he felt that he had never given a better performance in his whole career, and he regretted more than ever that none of his family had been present to see his triumph.

When he arrived he found that his wife and the children had gone to bed; so he sat down before the fire in the sitting-room, as was his wont, and soon fell asleep.

Mrs Ernie rose from her bed on the next morning in an evil temper. She was still furious about her husband's preference for Art over Money, and she was disappointed at having been unable to afford a turkey for the children's Christmas dinner.

She came downstairs and opened the door of the sitting-room. To her surprise Ernie was not there. But in front of the fire, preening its feathers, was a fat, grey goose.

With a cry of delight Mrs E. ran into the kitchen and fetched a carving-knife.

The children enjoyed their dinner that day more than on any other Boxing Day. And they all agreed that if there is one fowl more tender and delicious than a turkey it is a nice fat goose.

MADAM CROWL'S GHOST

BY J. SHERIDAN LE FANU

I'M an old woman now; and I was but thirteen my last birthday, the night I came to Applewale House. My aunt was the housekeeper there, and a sort of one-horse carriage was down at Lexhoe to take me and my box up to Applewale.

I was a bit frightened by the time I got to Lexhoe, and when I saw the carriage and horse, I wished myself back again with my mother at Hazelden. I was crying when I got into the 'shay'—that's what we used to call it — and old John Mulbery that drove it, and was a good-natured fellow, bought me a handful of apples at the 'Golden Lion,' to cheer me up a bit; and he told me that there was a currant-cake, and tea, and pork chops, waiting for me, all hot, in my aunt's room at the great house. It was a fine moonlight night and I eat the apples, lookin' out o' the shay winda.

It is a shame for gentlemen to frighten a poor foolish child like I was. I sometimes think it might be tricks. There was two on 'em on the tap o' the coach beside me. And they began to question me after nightfall, when the moon rose, where I was going to. Well, I told them it was to wait on Dame Arabella Crowl, of Applewale House, near by Lexhoe.

'Ho, then,' said one of them, 'you'll not be long there!'

And I looked at him as much as to say: 'Why not?' for I had spoke out when I told them where I was goin', as if 'twas something clever I had to say.

'Because,' says he—'and don't you for your life tell no one, only watch her and see—she's possessed by the devil, and more than half a ghost. Have you got a Bible?'

'Yes, sir,' says I. For my mother put my little Bible in my box, and I knew it was there: and by the same token, though the print's too small for my ald eyes, I have it in my press to this hour.

As I looked up at him saying 'Yes, sir,' I thought I saw him winkin' at his friend; but I could not be sure.

'Well,' says he, 'be sure you put it under your bolster every night, it will keep the ald girl's claws aff ye.'

And I got such a fright when he said that, you wouldn't fancy! And I'd a liked to ask him a lot about the ald lady, but I was too shy, and he and his friend began talkin' together about their own consarns, and dowly enough I got down, as I told ye, at Lexhoe. My heart sank as I drove into the dark avenue. The trees stands very thick and big, as ald as the ald house almost, and four people, with their arms out and finger-tips touchin', barely girds round some of them.

Well, my neck was stretched out o' the winda, looking for the first view o' the great house; and, all at once we pulled up in front of it.

A great white-and-black house it is, wi' great black beams across and right up it, and gables lookin' out, as white as a sheet, to the moon, and the shadows o' the trees, two or three up and down upon the front, you could count the leaves on them, and all the little diamond-shaped winda-panes, glimmer-ing on the great hall winda, and great shutters, in the old fashion, hinged on the wall outside, bolted across all the rest o' the windas in front, for there was but three or four servants and the old lady in the house, and most o' t' rooms was locked up.

My heart was in my mouth when I sid the journey was over, and this, the great house afore me, and I sa near my aunt that

I never sid till noo, and Dame Crowl, that I was come to wait upon, and was afeard on already.

My aunt kissed me in the hall, and brought me to her room. She was tall and thin, wi' a pale face and black eyes, and long thin hands wi' black mittins on. She was past fifty, and her words was short; but her word was law. I hev no complaints to make of her; but she was a hard woman, and I think she would hev bin kinder to me if I had bin her sister's child in place of her brother's. But all that 's o' no consequence noo.

The squire—his name was Mr Chevenix Crowl, he was Dame Crowl's grandson—came down there, by way of seeing that the old lady was well treated, about twice or thrice in the year. I sid him but twice all the time I was at Applewale House.

I can't say but she was well taken care of, notwithstandin', but that was because my aunt and Meg Wyvern, that was her maid, had a conscience, and did their duty by her.

Mrs Wyvern—Meg Wyvern my aunt called her to herself, and Mrs Wyvern to me—was a fat, jolly lass of fifty, a good height and a good breadth, always good-humoured, and walked slow. She had fine wages, but she was a bit stingy, and kept all her fine clothes under lock and key, and wore, mostly, a twilled chocolate cotton, wi' red, and yellow, and green sprigs and balls on it, and it lasted wonderful.

She never gave me nout, not the vally o' a brass thimble, all the time I was there; but she was good-humoured, and always laughin', and she talked no end o' proas over her tea; and, seeing me sa sackless and dowly, she roused me up wi' her laughin' and stories; and I think I liked her better than my aunt—children is so taken wi' a bit o' fun or a story— though my aunt was very good to me, but a hard woman about some things, and silent always.

My aunt took me into her bedchamber, that I might rest

myself a bit while she was settin' the tea in her room. But first she patted me on the shouther, and said I was a tall lass o' my years, and had spired up well, and asked me if I could do plain work and stitchin'; and she looked in my face, and said I was like my father, her brother, that was dead and gone, and she hoped I was a better Christian, and wad na du a' that lids.

It was a hard sayin' the first time I set my foot in her room, I thought.

When I went into the next room, the housekeeper's room— very comfortable, yak (oak) all round—there was a fine fire blazin' away, wi' coal, and peat, and wood, all in a low together, and tea on the table, and hot cake, and smokin' meat; and there was Mrs Wyvern, fat, jolly, and talkin' away, more in an hour than my aunt would in a year.

While I was still at my tea my aunt went upstairs to see Madam Crowl.

'She's agone up to see that old Judith Squailes is awake,' says Mrs Wyvern. 'Judith sits with Madam Crowl when me and Mrs Shutters'—that was my aunt's name—'is away. She's a troublesome old lady. Ye'll hev to be sharp wi' her, or she'll be into the fire, or out o' t' winda. She goes on wires, she does, old though she be.'

'How old, ma'am?' says I.

'Ninety-three her last birthday, and that's eight months gone,' says she; and she laughed. 'And don't be askin' questions about her before your aunt—mind, I tell ye; just take her as you find her, and that's all.'

'And what's to be my business about her, please ma'am?' says I.

'About the old lady? Well,' says she, 'your aunt, Mrs Shutters, will tell you that; but I suppose you'll hev to sit in the room with your work, and see she's at no mischief, and let her amuse herself with her things on the table, and get her food or drink as she calls for it, and keep her out o' mischief, and ring the bell hard if she's troublesome.'

'Is she deaf, ma'am?'

'No, nor blind,' says she; 'as sharp as a needle, but she's gone quite aupy, and can't remember nout rightly; and Jack the Giant Killer, or Goody Twoshoes will please her as well as the king's court, or the affairs of the nation.'

'And what did the little girl go away for, ma'am, that went on Friday last? My aunt wrote to my mother she was to go.'

'Yes; she's gone.'

'What for?' says I again.

'She didn't answer Mrs Shutters, I do suppose,' says she. 'I don't know. Don't be talkin'; your aunt can't abide a talkin' child.'

'And please, ma'am, is the old lady well in health?' says I.

'It ain't no harm to ask that,' says she. 'She's torflin' a bit lately, but better this week past, and I dare say she'll last out her hundred years yet. Hish! Here's your aunt coming down the passage.'

In comes my aunt, and begins talkin' to Mrs Wyvern, and I, beginnin' to feel more comfortable and at home like, was walkin' about the room lookin' at this thing and at that. There was pretty old china things on the cupboard, and pictures again the wall; and there was a door open in the wainscot, and I sees a queer old leathern jacket, wi' straps and buckles to it, and sleeves as long as the bed-post, hangin' up inside.

'What's that you're at, child?' says my aunt, sharp enough, turning about when I thought she least minded. 'What's that in your hand?'

'This, ma'am?' says I, turning about with the leathern jacket. 'I don't know what it is, ma'am.'

Pale as she was, the red came up in her cheeks, and her eyes flashed wi' anger, and I think only she had half a dozen steps to take, between her and me, she'd a gov me a sizzup.

But she did give me a shake by the shouther, and she plucked the thing out o' my hand, and says she: 'While ever you stay here, don't ye meddle wi' nout that don't belong to ye,' and she hung it up on the pin that was there, and shut the door wi' a bang and locked it fast.

Mrs Wyvern was liftin' up her hands and laughin' all this time, quietly in her chair, rolling herself a bit in it, as she used when she was kinkin'.

The tears was in my eyes, and she winked at my aunt, and says she, dryin' her own eyes that was wet wi' the laughin': 'Tut, the child meant no harm—come here to me, child. It's only a pair o' crutches for lame ducks, and ask us no questions mind, and we'll tell ye no lies; and come here and sit down, and drink a mug o' beer before ye go to your bed.'

My room, mind ye, was upstairs, next to the old lady's, and Mrs Wyvern's bed was near hers in her room and I was to be ready at call, if need should be.

The old lady was in one of her tantrums that night and part of the day before. She used to take fits o' the sulks. Sometimes she would not let them dress her, and other times she would not let them take her clothes off. She was a great beauty, they said, in her day. But there was no one about Applewale that remembered her in her prime. And she was dreadful fond o' dress, and had thick silks, and stiff satins, and velvets, and laces, and all sorts, enough to set up seven shops at the least. All her dresses was old-fashioned and queer, but worth a fortune.

Well, I went to my bed. I lay for a while awake; for a' things was new to me; and I think the tea was in my nerves, too, for I wasn't used to it, except now and then on a holiday, or the like. And I heard Mrs Wyvern talkin', and I listened with my hand to my ear; but I could not hear Mrs Crowl, and I don't think she said a word.

There was great care took of her. The people at Applewale knew that when she died they would every one get the sack; and their situations was well paid and easy.

The doctor come twice a week to see the old lady, and you may be sure they all did as he bid them. One thing was the same every time; they were never to cross or frump her, any way, but to humour and please her in everything.

So she lay in her clothes all that night, and next day, not a word she said, and I was at my needlework all that day, in my own room, except when I went down to my dinner.

I would a liked to see the ald lady, and even to hear her speak. But she might as well a bin in Lunnon a' the time for me.

When I had my dinner my aunt sent me out for a walk for an hour. I was glad when I came back, the trees was so big, and the place so dark and lonesome, and 'twas a cloudy day, and I cried a deal, thinkin' of home, while I was walkin' alone there. That evening, the candles bein' alight, I was sittin' in my room, and the door was open into Madam Crowl's chamber, where my aunt was. It was then, for the first time, I heard what I suppose was the ald lady talking.

It was a queer noise like, I couldn't well say which, a bird, or a beast, only it had a bleatin' sound on it, and was very small.

I pricked my ears to hear all I could. But I could not make out one word she said. And my aunt answered:

'The evil one can't hurt no one, ma'am, bout the Lord permits.

Then the same queer voice from the bed says something more that I couldn't make head nor tail on.

And my aunt med answer again: 'Let them pull faces, ma'am, and say what they will; if the Lord be for us, who can be against us?'

I kept listenin' with my ear turned to the door, holdin' my breath, but not another word or sound came in from the room.

In about twenty minutes, as I was sittin' by the table, lookin' at the pictures in the old *Aesop's Fables*, I was aware o' something moving at the door, and lookin' up I sid my aunt's face lookin' in at the door, and her hand raised.

'Hish!' says she, very soft, and comes over to me on tiptoe, and she says in a whisper: 'Thank God, she's asleep at last, and don't ye make no noise till I come back, for I'm goin' down to take my cup o' tea, and I'll be back i' noo—me and Mrs Wyvern, and she'll be sleepin' in the room, and you can run down when we come up, and Judith will gie ye yaur supper in my room.'

And with that away she goes.

I kep' looking at the picture-book, as before, listenin' every noo and then, but there was no sound, not a breath, that I could hear; an' I began whisperin' to the pictures and talkin' to myself to keep my heart up, for I was growin' feared in that big room.

And at last up I got, and began walkin' about the room, lookin' at this and peepin' at that, to amuse my mind, ye'll understand. And at last what sud I do but peeps into Madam Crowl's bedchamber.

A grand chamber it was, wi' a great four-poster, wi' flowered silk curtains as tall as the ceilin', and foldin' down on the floor, and drawn close all round. There was a lookin'-glass, the biggest I ever sid before, and the room was a blaze o' light. I counted twenty-two wax candles, all alight. Such was her fancy, and no one dared say her nay.

I listened at the door, and gaped and wondered all round. When I heard there was not a breath, and did not see so much as a stir in the curtains, I took heart, and I walked into the room on tiptoe, and looked round again. Then I takes a keek at myself in the big glass; and at last it came in my head: 'Why couldn't I ha' a keek at the ald lady herself in the bed?'

Ye'd think me a fule if ye knew half how I longed to see

Dame Crowl, and I thought to myself if I didn't peep now I might wait many a day before I got so gude a chance again.

Well, my dear, I came to the side o' the bed, the curtains bein' close, and my heart a'most failed me. But I took courage, and I slips my finger in between the thick curtains, and then my hand. So I waits a bit, but all was still as death. So, softly, softly I draws the curtain, and there, sure enough, I sid before me, stretched out like the painted lady on the tomb-stean in Lexhoe Church, the famous Dame Crowl, of Apple-wale House. There she was, dressed out. You never sid the like in they days. Satin and silk, and scarlet and green, and gold and pint lace; by Jen! 'twas a sight! A big powdered wig, half as high as herself, was a-top o' her head, and, wow! — was ever such wrinkles? — and her old baggy throat all powdered white, and her cheeks rouged, and mouse-skin eyebrows, that Mrs Wyvern used to stick on, and there she lay grand and stark, wi' a pair o' clocked silk hose on, and heels to her shoon as tall as nine-pins. Lawk! But her nose was crooked and thin, and half the whites o' her eyes was open. She used to stand, dressed as she was, gigglin' and dribblin' before the lookin'-glass, wi' a fan in her hand, and a big nose-gay in her bodice. Her wrinkled little hands was stretched down by her sides, and such long nails, all cut into points, I never sid in my days. Could it ever a bin the fashion for grit fowk to wear their finger-nails so?

Well, I think ye'd a bin frightened yourself if ye'd a sid such a sight. I couldn't let go the curtain, nor move an inch, not take my eyes off her; my very heart stood still. And in an instant she opens her eyes, and up she sits, and spins herself round, and down wi' her, wi' a clack on her two tall heels on the floor, facin' me, ogglin' in my face wi' her two great glassy eyes, and a wicked simper wi' her old wrinkled lips, and lang fause teeth.

Well, a corpse is a natural thing, but this was the

dreadfullest sight I ever sid. She had her fingers straight out pointin' at me, and her back was crooked, round again wi' age. Says she:

'Ye little limb! What for did ye say I killed the boy? I'll tickle ye till ye're stiff!'

If I'd a thought an instant, I'd a turned about and run. But I couldn't take my eyes off her, and I backed from her as soon as I could; and she came clatterin' after, like a thing on wires, with her fingers pointing to my throat, and she makin' all the time a sound with her tongue like zizz-zizz-zizz.

I kept backin' and backin' as quick as I could, and her fingers was only a few inches away from my throat, and I felt I'd lose my wits if she touched me.

I went back this way, right into the corner, and I gev a yellock, ye'd think saul and body was partin', and that minute my aunt, from the door, calls out wi' a blare, and the ald lady turns round on her, and I turns about, and ran through my room, and down the back stairs, as hard as my legs could carry me.

I cried hearty, I can tell you, when I got down to the house-keeper's room. Mrs Wyvern laughed a deal when I told her what happened. But she changed her key when she heard the ald lady's words.

'Say them again,' says she.

So I told her.

'Ye little limb! What for did ye say I killed the boy? I'll tickle ye till ye're stiff.'

'And did ye say she killed a boy?' says she.

'Not I, ma'am,' says I.

Judith was always up with me, after that, when the two elder women was away from her. I would a jumped out at winda, rather than stay alone in the same room wi' her.

It was about a week after, as well as I can remember, Mrs Wyvern, one day when me and her was alone, told me a thing about Madam Crowl that I did not know before.

She being young, and a great beauty, full seventy years before, had married Squire Crowl of Applewale. But he was a widower, and had a son about nine year old.

There never was tale or tidings of this boy after one mornin'. No one could say where he went to. He was allowed too much liberty, and used to be off in the mornin', one day, to the keeper's cottage, and breakfast wi' him, and away to the warren, and not home, mayhap, till evening, and another time down to the lake, and bathe there, and spend the day fishin' there, or paddlin' about in the boat. Well, no one could say what was gone wi' him; only this, that his hat was found by the lake, under a haathorn that grows thar to this day, and 'twas thought he was drowned bathin'.' And the squire's son, by his second marriage, by this Madam Crowl that lived sa dreadful lang, came in for the estates. It was his son, the ald lady's grandson, Squire Chevenix Crowl, that owned the estates at the time I came to Applewale.

There was a deal o' talk lang before my aunt's time about it; and 'twas said the stepmother knew more than she was like to let out. And she managed her husband, the ald squire, wi' her whiteheft and flatteries. And as the boy was never seen more, in course of time the thing died out of fawks' minds.

I'm goin' to tell ye noo about what I sid wi' my own een.

I was not there six months, and it was winter time, when the ald lady took her last sickness.

The doctor was afeard she might a took a fit o' madness, as she did, fifteen years before, and was buckled up, many a time, in a strait-waistcoat, which was the very leathern jerkin I sid in the closet, off my aunt's room.

Well, she didn't. She pined, and windered, and went off, torflin', torflin', quiet enough, till a day or two before her flittin', and then she took to rabblin', and sometimes skirlin' in the bed, ye 'd think a robber had a knife to her throat, and she used to work out o' the bed, and not being strong enough, then, to walk or stand, she'd fall on the flure, wi' her ald wizened hands stretched before her face, and skirlin' still for mercy.

Ye may guess I didn't go into the room, and I used to be shiverin' in my bed wi' fear, at her skirlin' and scrafflin' on the flure, and blarin' out words that id make your skin turn blue.

My aunt, and Mrs Wyvern, and Judith Squailes, and a woman from Lexhoe, was always about her. At last she took fits, and they wore her out.

T' sir (parson) was there, and prayed for her; but she was past praying with. I suppose it was right, but none could think there was much good in it, and sa at lang last she made her flittin', and a' was over, and old Dame Crowl was shrouded and coffined and Squire Chevenix was wrote for. But he was away in France, and the delay was sa lang, that t' sir and doctor both agreed it would not du to keep her langer out o' her place, and no one cared but just them two, and my aunt and the rest o' us, from Applewale, to go to the buryin'. So the old lady of Applewale was laid in the vault under Lexhoe Church; and we lived up at the great house till such time as the squire should come to tell his will about us, and pay off such as he chose to discharge.

I was put into another room, two doors away from what was Dame Crowl's chamber, after her death, and this thing happened the night before Squire Chevenix came to Applewale.

The room I was in now was a large square chamber, covered wi' yak panels, but unfurnished except for my bed, which had no curtains to it, and a chair and a table, or so, that looked nothing at all in such a big room. And the big looking-glass, that the old lady used to keek into and admire herself from head to heel, now that there was no mair o' that wark, was put out of the way, and stood against the wall in my room, for there was shiftin' o' many things in her chambers ye may suppose, when she came to be coffined.

The news had come that day that the squire was to be down next morning at Applewale; and not sorry was I, for I thought I was sure to be sent home again to my mother. And right glad was I, and I was thinkin' of a' at hame, and my sister, Janet, and the kitten and the pymag, and Trimmer the tike, and all the rest, and I got sa fidgety, I couldn't sleep, and the clock struck twelve, and me wide awake, and the room as dark as pick. My back was turned to the door, and my eyes toward the wall opposite.

Well, it could na be full quarter past twelve, when I sees a lightin' on the wall befoore me, as if something took fire behind, and the shadas o' the bed, and the chair, and my gown, that was hangin' from the wall, was dancin' up and down, on the ceilin' beams and the yak panels; and I turns my head ower my shouther quick, thinkin' something must a gone afire.

And what sud I see, by Jen! but the likeness o' the ald beldame, bedizened out in her satins and velvets, on her dead body, simperin', wi' her eyes as wide as saucers, and her face like the fiend himself. 'Twas a red light that rose about her in a suffin' low, as if her dress round her feet was blazin'. She was drivin' on the right for me, wi' her ald shrivelled hands crooked as if she was goin' to claw me. I could not stir, but she passed me straight by, wi' a blast o' cald air, and I sid her, at the wall, in the alcove as my aunt used to call it, which was a recess where the state bed used to stand in ald times, wi' a door open wide, and her hands gropin' in at somethin' was there. I never sid that door befoore. And she turned round to me, like a thing on a pivot, flyin' (grinning), and all at once the room was dark, and I standin' at the far side o' the bed; I don't know how I got there, and I found my tongue at last, and if I did na blare a yellock, rennin' down the gallery, and almost pulled Mrs Wyvern's door off t' hooks, and frightened her half out o' her wits.

Ye may guess I did na sleep that night; and wi' the first light, down wi' me to my aunt, as fast as my two legs cud carry me.

Well, my aunt did na frump or flite me, as I thought she would, but she held me by the hand, and looked hard in my face all the time. And she telt me not to be feared; and says she:

'Hed the appearance a key in its hand?'

'Yes,' says I, bringin' it to mind, 'a big key in a queer brass handle.'

'Stop a bit,' says she, lettin' go ma hand, and openin' the cupboard door. 'Was it like this?' says she, takin' one out in her fingers and showing it to me, with a dark look in my face.

'That was it,' says I, quick enough.

'Are ye sure?' she says, turnin' it round.

'Sart,' says I, and I felt I was gain' to faint when I sid it.

'Well, that will do, child,' says she, saftly thinkin', and she locked it up again.

'The squire himself will be here to-day, before twelve o'clock, and ye must tell him all about it,' says she, thinkin', 'and I suppose I'll be leavin' soon, and so the best thing for the present is, that ye should go home this afternoon, and I'll look out another place for you when I can.'

Fain was I, ye may guess, at that word.

My aunt packed up my things for me, and the three pounds that was due to me, to bring home, and Squire Crowl himself came down to Applewale that day, a handsome man, about thirty years old. It was the second time I sid him. But this was the first time he spoke to me.

My aunt talked wi' him in the housekeeper's room, and I don't know what they said. I was a bit feared on the squire, he bein' a great gentleman down in Lexhoe, and I darn't go near till I was called. And says he, smilin':

'What's a' this ye a sen, child? It mun be a dream, for ye

know there's na sic a thing as a bo or a freet in a' the world. But whatever it was, ma little maid, sit ye down and tell us all about it from first to last.'

Well, so soon as I med an end, he thought a bit, and says he to my aunt:

'I mind the place well. In old Sir Oliver's time lame Wyndel told me there was a door in that recess, to the left, where the lassie dreamed she saw my grandmother open it. He was past eighty when he telt me that, and I but a boy. It's twenty year sen. The plate and jewels used to be kept there, long ago, before the iron closet was made in the arras chamber, and he told me the key had a brass handle, and this ye say was found in the bottom o' the kist where she kept her old fans. Now, would not it be a queer thing if we found some spoons or diamonds forgot there? Ye mun come up wi' us, lassie, and point to the very spot.'

Loath was I, and my heart in my mouth, and fast I held by my aunt's hand as I stept into that awesome room, and showed them both how she came and passed me by, and the spot where she stood, and where the door seemed to open.

There was an ald empty press against the wall then, and shoving it aside, sure enough there was the tracing of a door in the wainscot, and a keyhole stopped with wood, and planed across as smooth as the rest, and the joining of the door all stopped wi' putty the colour o' yak, and, but for the hinges showed a bit when the press was shoved aside, ye would not consayt there was a door there at all.

'Ha!' says he, wi' a queer smile, 'this looks like it.'

It took some minutes wi' a small chisel and hammer to pick the bit o' wood out o' the keyhole. The key fitted, sure enough, and, wi' a strang twist and a lang skreeak, the boult went back and he pulled the door open.

There was another door inside, stranger than the first, but the lacks was gone, and it opened easy. Inside was a narrow floor and walls and vault o' brick; we could not see what was in it, for 'twas dark as pick.

When my aunt had lighted the candle the squire held it up and stept in.

My aunt stood on tiptoe tryin' to look over his shouther, and I did na see nout.

'Ha! ha!' says the squire, steppin' backward. 'What's that? Gi' ma the poker—quick!' says he to my aunt. And as she went to the hearth I peeps beside his arm, and I sid squat down in the far corner a monkey or a flayin' on the chest, or else the maist shrivelled up, wizened ald wife that ever was sen on yearth.

'By Jen!' says my aunt, as, puttin' the poker in his hand, she keeked by his shouther, and sid the ill-favoured thing, 'hae a care, sir, what ye 're doin'. Back wi' ye, and shut to the door!'

But in place o' that he steps in saftly, wi' the poker pointed like a swoord, and he gies it a poke, and down it a' tumbles together, head and a', in a heap o' bayans and dust, little meyar an' a hatful.

'Twas the bayans o' a child; a' the rest went to dust at a touch. They said nout for a while, but he turns round the skull as it lay on the floor.

Young as I was I consayted I knew well enough what they was thinkin' on.

'A dead cat!' says he, pushin' back and blowin' out the can'le, and shuttin' to the door. 'We 'll come back, you and me, Mrs Shutters, and look on the shelves by and by. I 've other matters first to speak to ye about; and this little girl's goin' hame, ye say. She has her wages, and I mun mak' her a present,' says he, pattin' my shoulder wi' his hand.

And he did gimma a goud pound, and I went aff to Lexhoe about an hour after, and sa hame by the stage-coach, and fain was I to be at hame again; and I never saa ald Dame Crowl o' Applewale, God be thanked, either in appearance or in dream, at-efter. But when I was grown to be a woman my aunt spent a day and night wi' me at Littleham, and she telt me there was na doubt it was the poor little boy that was missing sa lang sen that was shut up to die thar in the dark by that wicked beldame, whar his skirls, or his prayers, or his thumpin' cud na be heard, and his hat was left by the water's edge, whoever did it, to mak' belief he was drowned. The clothes, at the first touch, a' ran into a snuff o' dust in the cell whar the bayans was found. But there was a handful o' jet buttons, and a knife with a green handle, together wi' a couple o' pennies the poor little fella had in his pocket, I suppose, when he was decoyed in thar, and sid his last o' the light. And there was, amang the squire's papers, a copy o' the notice that was prented after he was lost, when the old squire thought he might a run away, or bin took by gipsies, and it said he had a green-hefted knife wi' him, and that his buttons were o' cut jet. Sa that is a' I have to say consarnin' ald Dame Crowl, o' Applewale House.

THE CHRISTMAS CARD

BY JAMES BRIDIE

ONCE upon a time there was a stout little knight who lived in Alpaca Square—a round peg in a Square hole, he used laughingly to say to his guests at dinner. As he grew wealthier and wealthier he moved into Eaton Square. He didn't like Eaton Square at all (who would?), but he was a man who liked to keep his guests amused. It had to be some sort of Square. It would be unfair and perhaps dangerous to print his name, so I shall call him Sir James Watson, and his wife, Lady Watson. Lady Watson's hair was, at the time the story opens, of bright copper colour brindled with, perhaps, slightly less artificial bands of pure white. She was many years younger than her husband in fact and in spirit, a lover of balls, routs, and assemblies, and a laugher of gay laughter. As she went from room to room of her large house, one would have thought that an Italian soprano was practising. She had another note in her voice that sounded like a file, but she seldom employed that note except in the privacy of her own bedroom when Sir James came in to kiss her good morning before going out to make money at his office.

They had married latish in life. Sir James (as I prefer to call him) had wooed and won her as a corollary of a situation few ladies can resist. In the knightliest possible fashion, he had rescued her from a caitiff of the same degree whose name was Sir Isadore Waldteufel. Like some Old Lochinvar he had seized his bride from the very steps of the altar, or worse. I should give you more in the way of detail, but I am afraid that you would recognize that celebrated cause or seek the files of the newspapers for it. It was in all the papers.

This was all very well; but, when a romance begins so auspiciously as that I wish I were in a position to describe to you, to provide a series of mounting climaxes is a very difficult job. Without them the dread anticlimax is sure to set in, sooner or later. To a spirit like that of Lady Watson, an anti-climax is as abhorrent as a vacuum is to her Mother Nature.

She was a true child of Nature and, in a sense, of Bohemia. She liked happy faces around her in large numbers and loud noises and continuous enrapturing movement. It was other-wise with her chubby husband. He also, it is true, liked happy faces; but he preferred them in small doses. He liked his noises quiet and select. The gentle rhythmic movements made by a fat man with a cat on his lap sleeping in an arm-chair before a large fire were movement enough for him. He was looking forward with a certain warmth of pride to his seventieth birthday.

Lady Watson was passionately fond of dancing, but so was not he. Lady Watson was fond of gin mixed with Bacardi and Cointreau. He preferred whisky for most occasions or, after dinner, a rather heavy and sticky opaque kind of port wine of which he was very proud. Lady Watson liked young men with curly hair, loud laughs, and prominent front teeth. Sir James didn't. Lady Watson liked her motor cars to be shaped like torpedoes or sharks. Sir James liked them like hearses. Sir James liked jokes that took a long time to tell. Lady Watson liked short jokes. Sir James liked Mendelssohn's *Songs without Words*, the Barcarolle from *Tales of Hoffmann*, and one or two pieces by Grieg. These tunes made Lady Watson scream and turn off the gramophone. Lady Watson liked dressing up. Hard collars cut Sir James's neck and stiff shirt fronts pressed into his abdomen and gave him indigestion. Lady Watson liked playing contract bridge and making a great song about it, though, indeed, she played abominably. Sir James had not been averse to a rubber of whist in his day, but he was not heart-broken to find that nobody played that game in the year in which this story is taking such an unconscionable time in opening.

On November the twenty-first, in nineteen hundred and thirty-four, Lady Watson had gone out to the play. Her escort was a young fellow whose deep, abiding, and hereditary sense of honour was attested by the designation 'The Honourable,' whenever his name appeared in print, which it did many times, often with the word Goofy in brackets and inverted commas between his Christian name and his surname. The play they went to see had been written by James Bridie and they talked all through it, for they had much in common, this ripe and handsome matron and that innocent and lively young man. After the play they went behind the scenes and Lady Watson kissed the leading lady and told her she was marvellous, which was perfectly true. They then went to a dancing club and ate a hearty meal, during and after which they walked about in each other's embrace, threading their way with much grace and skill through a mob behaving in a like fashion. They got to their respective homes at about three in the morning.

While all this was going on, the cat, Riza Khan, sat on the lap of its master, Sir James Watson, or on what was left of that lap, which was not a great deal. Riza Khan's golden eyes were closed, but the blue eyes of Sir James were open and staring into the fire. He was thinking that it would soon be Christmas and that he would like to send Lady Watson a Christmas card.

The word 'send' might imply that he hoped or intended to be at some distance from Lady Watson when Christmastide came round, but this was not the chain of thought that had led him to this curious idea. While he was stroking the silvery back of Riza Khan a difference bewteen ladies and cats occurred to him. Cats, he thought, are prepared to put up a show of affection where their affections are not engaged. This, he imagined, was seldom true of ladies. At least, he corrected himself, for any extended period; for Lady Watson *had*, over a period of several weeks, shown some sort of interest in him and even laughed at his little jokes. That was some time ago—ten or fifteen years—shortly after they first met. It was a long time since he had so much as made her laugh. Lately she had not laughed *at* him. She seemed to find him tiresome. He was sorry. His strong card was making people laugh. He was a funny-looking little ticket.

Sir James Watson thought: 'Why, bless my heart, I can do most things I set out to do in a determined way. And surely it is a little thing to make her ladyship laugh. She has a very strong sense of humour and laughs quite frighteningly at

a great many things. I am determined to make her laugh.
I shall give myself till Christmas time. That is nearly a month.
More than a month.'

The trouble was that, in his sad mood, he could not think
of anything funny; and when an idea did come to him he
could not disguise from himself the fact that it was not so much
funny as *outré*. Yet many a time and oft Lady Watson had
laughed at things which were not so much funny as *outré*.
One afternoon at a sherry party a lord had persuaded Goofy
that if he held a glass full of sherry hard against the roof with
a curtain pole the molecular attraction and the contraction of
the surface air would cause the glass to stick to the roof.
Goofy had stood for half an hour holding his end of the
curtain pole and Lady Watson had laughed herself quite sick;
for, of course, everybody knows that a glass will not stick to
the roof in these circumstances. The only feelings aroused in
Sir James Watson's bosom were feelings of pity for Goofy;
but then he did not laugh at things that were *outré*, only at
things that were funny.

The idea that came to him was that, instead of giving Lady
Watson a costly present this Christmas, he would send her a
Christmas card. If this didn't succeed of its purpose, he would
at least save money, for he always gave Lady Watson very
costly presents indeed. He thought he would get someone to
design a very comical Christmas card for him and then he
thought that wouldn't be fair. If the card amused Lady
Watson it would be the work of the artist that would get the
credit. He decided to design the Christmas card himself.

He put Riza Khan gently on to the rug and began to wander
round the house looking for material on which to jot down his
preliminary sketch. He wandered from room to room.
He could not help feeling that the rooms, which had been
decorated (or, if you prefer it, undecorated) by a famous and
costly firm, were perhaps more notable as works of art than as

places in which a person could live. Except for one room they looked like brand-new railway station lavatories. The one room was furnished and decorated as the subjects of Good Queen Victoria were supposed to furnish their rooms. Lady Watson used to take her guests into it and they would all laugh merrily and say it was sweet. Well, Sir James Watson had been a subject of Good Queen Victoria himself and could not remember ever having lived in a room like that. . . . Still, it was full of a number of things and it had made Lady Watson laugh, which was more than he could do.

At the far end of the Victorian Room there was an oblong object covered with a rusty bed-sheet. Sir James Watson recognized it as the portrait of Lady Watson which was being made by an artist in Lady Watson's spare time. Sir James Watson had painted in water-colours several very nice pictures of the Lake District when he was a young man, but he had never painted in oils and sometimes thought he would like to try. He went up to the artist's picture and turned aside the bed-sheet wrapping. He remembered the artist saying to Lady Watson that he definitely must paint her in the Victorian Room; and, though Lady Watson, like a true child of Bohemia, much preferred to have her portrait taken in a real artist's studio, she consented. She had been afraid during the evening, from his reactions to her skilful hintings, that the artist might not paint her at all. That would have been terrible; because this particular artist was the only artist nobody sneered at who did portraits that did not look like mad prize potatoes in a snowstorm. Lady Watson liked her pictures like that, but there is a point at which every one must draw the line, and she drew it at having her figure distorted and her features put out of drawing and her neck stretched, and her very careful complexion rendered like tinned salmon that has been cooled a long time in the deep-delved earth.

Sir James Watson thought that the portrait, in its unfinished state, was not unlike what he thought she had been like when he first rescued her from Sir Isadore Waldteufel's clammy clutch. He also peered into the portrait very carefully to see how it was done. He thought that he could paint in oils too, that there was nothing really in it. He thought that he would paint his Christmas card in oils. He thought that he would make it of enormous size and put into it not robins and church⁄ steeples merely, but anything that came into his head. He thought that he would at least manage to compose something *outré*. He went to bed feeling happier than he had felt for many a day.

By the following afternoon he had begun his Christmas card. He found a large attic above the servants' bedrooms. It was full of a great deal of rubbish and of that delightful dust that lies in attics and is the softest of all created or collected things. Sir James Watson and some of the pleasantest of his servants cleared the attic. Sir James Watson himself worked the vacuum cleaner. This gave him great pleasure, as to whom would it not? At intervals he ran downstairs to the telephone and gave orders and yet further orders to a firm of purveyors of artists' materials. By the afternoon he had set up his easel and was preparing his canvas with the help of the artists' material man who had brought the stuff round. They both consulted a very good book on the subject and by the time the north light which illumined the attic was fading, they had covered the canvas very evenly with the particular kind of white paint recommended by the book. At that point Sir James Watson recollected with a start that he had not seen Lady Watson all day. He cleaned himself with turpen⁄ tine, put on a black jacket, a grey necktie, and merino trousers, and went downstairs to his wife's boodwar with a cunning look on his round face.

Lady Watson happened to be in. She was busy polishing her finger⁄nails with a thing for polishing finger⁄nails, for she was very careful about her personal appearance. She was none of your careless sluts or trollops was Lady Watson.

She gave Sir James Watson a suspicious look as he came in, though what she had to be suspicious about, the Lord knows. The look of innocent cunning on Sir James Watson's face was no more sinister than a beam of sunlight filtered through a cupboard keyhole lighting up a Danish cheese. Yet the subtle alteration caused by the appearance of any sort of expression at all on that countenance which had once beamed upon her with love divine, woke a faint misgiving in Lady Watson's bosom.

She said: 'What have you been doing?'

He said: 'Nothing.'

She said: 'I wish you would get some sort of hobby. You are getting on in life and people like that go mad when they have nothing to do.'

He said: 'Yes. I suppose they do. But there is always the office.'

She said: 'I am sick to death of you being Something in the City. It used to be quite a respectable thing to be; but now the very phrase connotes an outrageous blend of imbecility and knavery. Why don't you go into politics, or buy Leeds University, or write your autobiography or something?'

He said: 'Because I don't want to do any of these things, my dear.'

She said: 'You think of nobody but yourself. Does it never occur to you that I might like to be a viscountess?'

He said: 'Would you?'

She said: 'Not particularly, but one likes to provide for one's old age. Now run along. Perhaps you don't realize it, but I require some rest. I am going to lie down for an hour.'

He said: 'Are you dining at home to-night?'

She said: 'No.'

He went away thinking that it was rather clever of her to

spot that he wanted a hobby. Perhaps that was what he had needed all these years. He certainly felt happier now that he had got one.

He changed into an old flannel suit and a Harris tweed jacket and joined Riza Khan by the fireside.

Next day he got to work on his Christmas card in earnest. He had not slept much because he could not hit on a design. But, in the morning in his bath, he thought: 'Why have a design at all?' The canvas was large. It measured fifteen feet by twelve feet. It was as big as the screen in Sir James Watson's nursery before he had become Sir James and received his monarch's accolade on that sovereign's birthday. That screen was the most beautiful work of art young James Watson (as he then was) had ever seen. It was made of papier mâché on a wooden frame. Loving hands had stuck all over it figures cut from illustrated papers and scraps. The scraps were mostly in low relief and painted in bright colours. They represented humming-birds, cockatoos, bunches of flowers, gipsies, soldiers in uniform, plates of fruit, tambourines, clowns, the heads of cherubim, and true lovers' knots in scarlet, blue, and orange coloured ribbons. When the surface of the screen had been filled with these things and portraits of Queen Victoria and Mr Gladstone affixed to the middle of each section, the whole was spread with thick and shiny varnish and the effect was superb. Sir James Watson decided to paint his Christmas card in a thousand little bits just as they came into his head. In the issue it would look like a carnival or his nursery screen and nothing could be more delightful.

There was this in it, that the work would take some time and there was very little time to lose. It was now the twenty-third of November, only thirty-two days till Christmas, if he worked on the Sabbath. He reflected, however, that he had really nothing else to do. True, there was the City; but the City had got on without him before he was born and would get on without him after he was dead. Besides, the peculiar thing about money is that after you have made a certain amount it goes on making itself in quite sufficient quantities to meet the simple needs of such people as Sir James and Lady Watson, with a little over to invest in organizations that were only too delighted to make more still without any call upon the exer, tions of Sir James and his lady. Sir James paid handsomely a number of men and women who were prepared to take even this simple matter of investment off his shoulders, and his visits to the City were, perhaps, less the formidable forays of a merchant prince than an old josser seeking a palliative for his loneliness.

His club in St James's would not miss him for a month or so. The members seldom spoke to one another and one bald man more or less asleep in a saddle-backed chair made little difference to a club of its distinction. As for Lady Watson, she did, indeed, from time to time, ask him where he had been and what he had been doing with himself; but, like Jesting Pilate, she seldom waited for a reply.

He took off his coat, rolled up his sleeves, fastened a bath, towel round his neck, and began to prepare his palette. He squeezed out of his tubes serpent after serpent, gaudy and fresh in colour, intoxicating in smell. He could have gone on doing that all day, but he thought of the briefness of time that was his portion, heaved a sigh, and mounted a small library ladder to begin, methodically enough, on the top left-hand corner.

With a brush loaded with prussian blue he made a curving gesture at his canvas and a start was made. The record of his gesture was like a beak of a toucan, so he painted a toucan, an interesting and not too difficult fowl. He perched it upon what he intended for a branch, but it turned out to be the Forth Bridge in burnt sienna. He placed a vermilion wart on the toucan's forehead and began a new piece while the toucan dried sufficiently to put in a background of lemon yellow. This time he began with the background and made a sky by mixing chinese white with ultramarine, and a royal blue sea. Beyond this he painted a chrome yellow land with a magenta and purple jungle growing out of it and then he went back and finished the toucan's sky, joining it to the ocean sky with a rather bulbous drawing of Wren's master⁄piece (St Paul's Cathedral) in crimson lake. When the sea was dry he put a schooner and some waves on it, and when the jungle was dry he filled it with flying birds of many colours. To use up these colours, he painted Joseph in his grand coat on the steps of the cathedral being welcomed by the sub⁄dean in lamp⁄black. He painted a train of Joseph's camels moving along a chrome desert in front of the sea. Behind them a line of pilgrims taking the Golden Road to Samarkand, clothed to their feet and easy to draw. Farther along he put the gilt minarets of Bagdad which they had just left. A chimney⁄stack divided the olive Mesopotamian sky from that he had set above the ocean. A grove of palm⁄trees surmounted by flying kites took him to the top right⁄hand corner, and darkness fell on Eaton Square. There was now a frieze above the virgin stretch of canvas and it looked awful. Sir James Watson did not, however, despair. He climbed down his ladder and down the attic stairs and had a bath and a glass of sherry. He was ahead of schedule.

In bed at night he had only to close his eyes to see the wonderful things. He saw whorls of vivid peacock blue shot with silver stars. He saw dark velvet green poplar⁄trees under innumerable scarlet moons. He saw glittering fish and stately dragons and bright⁄eyed birds. He saw spray and beech hedges and rose petals on the snow. He tried to remember all these things to put on his Christmas card, but he fell asleep and forgot them. He remembered, however, a flight of flamingoes and it went into the picture.

So the days went by. Sir James Watson became more

inventive and speculative in the things he put into his picture. The wart on the toucan's forehead made him think of Oliver Cromwell, 'under whose warts beat a heart primed with true religious sentiment'; and he drew the Lord Protector and his primed heart. This led to 'Where is your father, boy?' and Japhet in search of a father. He had very vague recollections of that book, but he painted Japhet and many of the imagined incidents of his search. This led on to Shem and Ham and the final discovery of Noah twined in his vine and surrounded by wondering (if destructive) Little Foxes. The Little Foxes (who spoil our vines) made a charming excuse for a hunt in full cry and many of the beauties of the Handley Cross country-side. He painted then a picture of the first hunt he had seen when he had fallen in love afar off with a girl of five on a Shetland pony. Since that day she had had four husbands, including a member of the Russian imperial family, and she was now a wizened harridan and a tormentor of the poor. He drew her four husbands. The Russian he drew performing a Caucasian dance, surrounded by wild Cossacks in furry hats.

Odd, forgotten incidents and sights began to appear in his picture. His enormous nurse with an apron over her crinoline loomed through the steam of his bath before the fire. A long-dead dog barked at an impudent rabbit. A bearded gardener dug in a kitchen garden. A sailor unfastened his wooden leg and made it dance by itself. A canary drank out of a dribbling tap. The sea washed right up on to the floor of a summer-house. An errand-boy stole a packet of gelatine sweeties shaped like lions, elephants, tigers, and babies. A snowball struck a clergyman in the eye. A bus-driver coughed over his horses going down High Holborn. A hansom cab drove Sir James Watson to the dentist's and the dentist gave him a shilling for being brave. A missel thrush looked out of its nest with an angry eye. The glories of Edgbaston,

Birmingham, where Aunt Alicia lived, were suitably suggested, as was the top of a haystack in the hot sunshine and a
water wheel and a fast mill lode where a man had once been
drowned. There was a curious bit showing a boy relieving
the tedium of a sermon by doing acrobats along the nave and
swinging on the chandelier.

From this point, architecture and landscape began to take
up the rest of the Christmas card. Fields with giraffes and
leopards as well as cows began to appear with woods, mountains, and caverns measureless to man. Cataracts roared down
gullies past castles and huts, cathedrals, public houses, and
shops. More fantastic buildings with ladies looking out of
the windows at soldiers marching past to the tap of the drum
found their way into the picture. There was an exciting
mixture of perspectives, but in odd places a sort of distance grew.

Sir James Watson, as time hurried on, began to work at
night, by the light of an oil lamp. He found that the parts
he painted thus looked different in daylight, but this was all
to the good. His sleeping time dwindled to four hours every
night, and twice, in the week before Christmas, he did not go
to bed at all.

By the twenty-second of December the canvas was full.

Sir James Watson sat looking at it for a whole day before
he began to varnish it. He felt very much astonished at himself, as well he might. It was a great feat for a man who had
painted nothing for fifty years and then only in water-colour,
to complete a picture a hundred and eighty square feet in size.
Nay, more, it was a very satisfying picture. A stranger, seeing
it for the first time, might well have been puzzled as to what it
was all about. But to know at a glance what a picture is all
about is not essential to the enjoyment of it. The totality of
Sir James Watson's picture was satisfying as a crazy quilt is
satisfying. There was warmth and movement in it. There
were startling associations of discordant colour. There was

a strange sense of life in it, as there is in a jam-pot containing worms for bait.

To one person at least, Sir James Watson himself, every square inch was packed with significance.

There was no beginning and end about the picture. There was no orderly pattern. But it had its key-point where a road suddenly began to go beside a river, through a mountain pass and up to a far-away town in a blue mist high up the mountain side. It was in this part of the picture that Sir James Watson had been most successful in conveying distance, and he could not keep his eyes off it.

When the varnish was dry, Sir James Watson took the canvas off the frame and rolled it up, for he could not get such a large picture otherwise through the exiguous trap-door of the attic. He took it down to a room on the second floor which was seldom visited by any member of his household and never by Lady Watson. There he had it remounted and framed in a gilt frame. To the foot of the frame he had attached a gilt label on which was written in Gothic letters:

A MERRY CHRISTMAS TO LADY WATSON FROM
SIR JAMES WATSON

He then covered the picture with a brown cloth and awaited the day. He hardly knew what to hope from Lady Watson. He felt pretty certain that she would be surprised and that would be, at least, something.

On Christmas Eve he was neither, as the Scots say, to hold nor to bind. Lady Watson was spending this phase of the great religious festival in the 'Hell Hole,' quietly, with a few friends. The 'Hell Hole' is, I think, off Oxford Street and specializes in bottle parties and a Malayan orchestra.

Sir James Watson was too restless to sit at home by the fireside, so he went to his club and talked to one of the waiters whose name was Hogge. Hogge's wife was ill and Sir James was sorry to hear it, for Hogge was a dismal enough person by nature without having illness in the house on top of it all. Hogge had been a soldier in the Great War and had been buried by a shell-burst at Ypres. This had left him with a peculiar twitching of the left side of his face.

He told Sir James Watson about his wife's eight operations. He was not usually so communicative, but Sir James Watson was the only member in the club on that night and Hogge felt that it was his bounden duty to entertain him by all the means in his power. So he came and went, telling a fresh instalment of his wife's sad history at each visit to Sir James Watson's table and, later, to his chair in the library. In addition to the pleasures of conversation with Hogge, Sir James Watson had treated himself to two Coronas and three glasses of port after dinner. He went home by taxi at half-past eleven and went to bed. Sir James Watson slept.

When I tell you what happened on Christmas Day you can believe me or not as you like. Before you dismiss it all as a fiction, think for a little. When a man, for the first time for many a year, suddenly does a piece of creative work, phenomenal things happen to him and to it. His work is apt to possess him, to master him, to dissolve his identity in its own. Any amount of experience of material facts will not help us to explain this mastery and this solution.

Sir James Watson's creation was something new. What happened to Sir James Watson must be judged as something new. Old standards do not apply to it.

He hung holly and mistletoe on his veiled Christmas card and, calling up all his rusty determination, induced Lady Watson to come to the room to see it. He unveiled the picture with a tremulous flourish. Lady Watson screwed in an eye-glass to look at it and this dialogue followed:

'Whose is it?'

'It is yours, my dear. It is a sort of a Christmas card.'

'No, no.   I mean who did it?'

'I did.'

'*You* did?   You painted that thing?'

'Yes.'

'That's what comes of having no hobbies.   You must see a psychotherapist at once.   I'll tell Miss Smith to ring up Dr Liebestraum.'

That was all.   She did not laugh.   It was something, however, that she took it seriously.   She went into the Victorian Room and rang for Miss Smith, the secretary.   Although her car was waiting in the Christmas rain, she took time to give Miss Smith certain instructions.

Upstairs Sir James Watson was still looking at his picture. In that moment he loved it more than he loved Lady Watson. His eyes were fixed on the part in which he had most successfully conveyed distance.   Without any real intention of doing anything at all, he slowly stepped over the gilt border and into his picture.   His eyes still sought his cunningly conveyed distance as he walked slowly up the road that led to the mountain pass.

When Dr Liebestraum arrived he was nowhere to be found. Lady Watson caused Miss Smith to call WHItehall 1212 in vain.   The picture was dismantled, rolled, and returned to the attic where it was born.   Nobody ever saw Sir James Watson again.

A CURIOUS MISTAKE

AFTER 'BEACHCOMBER'

A MAN with red eyes and a shaking hand went into a bank in Kensington the other day, and asked the first disengaged clerk for a pint of beer.

'This is not a public house,' said the clerk. 'It is a bank.'

'That doesn't matter,' said the man; 'I'll have a ham sandwich with it.'

'But this is a bank. You can't get a drink here,' said the clerk.

'That's what I said,' replied the man, 'unless it's Boxing Day.'

'It *is* Boxing Day,' said the clerk, clutching at a straw.

'Oh,' said the man, 'that's different.'

And out he went.

THE PICKWICK CLUB ON THE ICE

BY CHARLES DICKENS

'Now,' said Wardle, after a substantial lunch, with the agreeable items of strong beer and cherry-brandy, had been done ample justice to; 'what say you to an hour on the ice? We shall have plenty of time.'

'Capital!' said Mr Benjamin Allen.

'Prime!' ejaculated Mr Bob Sawyer.

You skate, of course, Winkle?' said Wardle.

'Ye-yes; oh, yes,' replied Mr Winkle. 'I—I—am *rather* out of practice.'

'Oh, *do* skate, Mr Winkle,' said Arabella. 'I like to see it so much.'

'Oh, it is *so* graceful,' said another young lady.

A third young lady said it was elegant, and a fourth expressed her opinion that it was 'swan-like.'

'I should be very happy, I'm sure,' said Mr Winkle, reddening; 'but I have no skates.'

This objection was at once overruled. Trundle had a couple of pair, and the fat boy announced that there were half a dozen more down stairs: whereat Mr Winkle expressed exquisite delight, and looked exquisitely uncomfortable.

Old Wardle led the way to a pretty large sheet of ice; and the fat boy and Mr Weller having shovelled and swept away the snow which had fallen on it during the night, Mr Bob Sawyer adjusted his skates with a dexterity which to Mr Winkle was perfectly marvellous and described circles with his left leg, and cut figures of eight, and inscribed upon the ice, without once stopping for breath, a great many other pleasant and astonishing devices, to the excessive satisfaction of Mr Pickwick, Mr Tupman, and the ladies: which reached a pitch of positive enthusiasm, when old Wardle and Benjamin Allen, assisted by the aforesaid Bob Sawyer, performed some mystic evolutions, which they called a reel.

All this time, Mr Winkle, with his face and hands blue with the cold, had been forcing a gimlet into the soles of his feet, and putting his skates on, with the points behind, and getting the straps into a very complicated and entangled state, with the assistance of Mr Snodgrass, who knew rather less about skates than a Hindoo. At length, however, with the assistance of Mr Weller, the unfortunate skates were firmly screwed and buckled on, and Mr Winkle was raised to his feet.

'Now, then, sir,' said Sam, in an encouraging tone; 'off with you, and show 'em how to do it.'

'Stop, Sam, stop!' said Mr Winkle, trembling violently, and clutching hold of Sam's arms with the grasp of a drowning man. 'How slippery it is, Sam!'

'Not an uncommon thing upon ice, sir,' replied Mr Weller. 'Hold up, sir!'

This last observation of Mr Weller's bore reference to a demonstration Mr Winkle made at the instant, of a frantic desire to throw his feet in the air, and dash the back of his head on the ice.

'These—these—are very awkward skates; ain't they, Sam?' inquired Mr Winkle, staggering.

'I'm afeerd there's a orkard gen'l'm'n in 'em, sir,' replied Sam.

'Now, Winkle,' cried Mr Pickwick, quite unconscious that there was anything the matter. 'Come; the ladies are all anxiety.'

'Yes, yes,' replied Mr Winkle, with a ghastly smile. 'I'm coming.'

'Just a goin' to begin,' said Sam, endeavouring to disengage himself. 'Now, sir, start off!'

'Stop an instant, Sam,' gasped Mr Winkle, clinging most affectionately to Mr Weller. 'I find I've got a couple of coats at home that I don't want, Sam. You may have them, Sam.'

'Thank 'ee, sir,' replied Mr Weller.

'Never mind touching your hat, Sam,' said Mr Winkle, hastily. 'You needn't take your hand away to do that. I meant to have given you five shillings this morning for a Christmas-box, Sam. I'll give it you this afternoon, Sam.'

'You're wery good, sir,' replied Mr Weller.

'Just hold me at first, Sam; will you?' said Mr Winkle. 'There—that's right. I shall soon get in the way of it, Sam. Not too fast, Sam; not too fast.'

Mr Winkle stooping forward, with his body half doubled up, was being assisted over the ice by Mr Weller, in a very singular and un-swan-like manner, when Mr Pickwick most innocently shouted from the opposite bank:

'Sam!'

'Sir?'

'Here. I want you.'

'Let go, sir,' said Sam. 'Don't you hear the governor a callin'? Let go, sir.'

With a violent effort, Mr Weller disengaged himself from the grasp of the agonized Pickwickian, and, in so doing, administered a considerable impetus to the unhappy Mr Winkle. With an accuracy which no degree of dexterity or practice could have insured, that unfortunate gentleman bore swiftly down into the centre of the reel, at the very moment when Mr Bob Sawyer was performing a flourish of unparalleled beauty. Mr Winkle struck wildly against him, and with a loud crash they both fell heavily down. Mr

Pickwick ran to the spot. Bob Sawyer had risen to his feet, but Mr Winkle was far too wise to do anything of the kind, in skates. He was seated on the ice, making spasmodic efforts to smile; but anguish was depicted on every lineament of his countenance.

'Are you hurt?' inquired Mr Benjamin Allen, with great anxiety.

'Not much,' said Mr Winkle, rubbing his back very hard.

'I wish you'd let me bleed you,' said Mr Benjamin, with great eagerness.

'No, thank you,' replied Mr Winkle hurriedly.

'I really think you had better,' said Allen.

'Thank you,' replied Mr Winkle; 'I'd rather not.'

'What do *you* think, Mr Pickwick?' inquired Bob Sawyer.

Mr Pickwick was excited and indignant. He beckoned to Mr Weller, and said in a stern voice: 'Take his skates off.'

'No; but really I had scarcely begun,' remonstrated Mr Winkle.

'Take his skates off,' repeated Mr Pickwick firmly.

The command was not to be resisted. Mr Winkle allowed Sam to obey it in silence.

'Lift him up,' said Mr Pickwick. Sam assisted him to rise.

Mr Pickwick retired a few paces apart from the bystanders; and, beckoning his friend to approach, fixed a searching look upon him, and uttered in a low, but distinct and emphatic tone, these remarkable words:

'You're a humbug, sir.'

'A what?' said Mr Winkle, starting.

'A humbug, sir. I will speak plainer, if you wish it. An impostor, sir.'

With those words, Mr Pickwick turned slowly on his heel, and rejoined his friends.

While Mr Pickwick was delivering himself of the sentiment just recorded, Mr Weller and the fat boy, having by their joint endeavours cut out a slide, were exercising themselves thereupon, in a very masterly and brilliant manner. Sam Weller, in particular, was displaying that beautiful feat of fancysliding which is currently denominated 'knocking at the cobbler's door,' and which is achieved by skimming over the ice on one foot, and occasionally giving a postman's knock upon it with the other. It was a good long slide, and there was something in the motion which Mr Pickwick, who was very cold with standing still, could not help envying.

'It looks a nice warm exercise that, doesn't it?' he inquired of Wardle, when that gentleman was thoroughly out of breath, by reason of the indefatigable manner in which he had converted his legs into a pair of compasses, and drawn complicated problems on the ice.

'Ah, it does indeed,' replied Wardle. 'Do you slide?'

'I used to do so on the gutters, when I was a boy,' replied Mr Pickwick.

'Try it now,' said Wardle.

'Oh do, please, Mr Pickwick!' cried all the ladies.

'I should be very happy to afford you any amusement,' replied Mr Pickwick, 'but I haven't done such a thing these thirty years.'

'Pooh! pooh! Nonsense!' said Wardle, dragging off his skates with the impetuosity which characterized all his proceedings. 'Here; I'll keep you company; come along!' And away went the goodtempered old fellow down the slide, with a rapidity which came very close upon Mr Weller, and beat the fat boy all to nothing.

Mr Pickwick paused, considered, pulled off his gloves and put them in his hat: took two or three short runs, baulked himself as often, and at last took another run, and went slowly and gravely down the slide, with his feet about a yard and a quarter apart, amidst the gratified shouts of all the spectators.

'Keep the pot a bilin', sir!' said Sam; and down went Wardle again, and then Mr Pickwick, and then Sam, and then Mr Winkle, and then Mr Bob Sawyer, and then the fat boy, and then Mr Snodgrass, following closely upon each other's heels, and running after each other with as much eagerness as if all their future prospects in life depended on their expedition.

It was the most intensely interesting thing, to observe the manner in which Mr Pickwick performed his share in the ceremony; to watch the torture of anxiety with which he viewed the person behind, gaining upon him at the imminent hazard of tripping him up; to see him gradually expend the painful force he had put on at first, and turn slowly round on the slide, with his face towards the point from which he had started; to contemplate the playful smile which mantled on his face when he had accomplished the distance, and the eagerness with which he turned round when he had done so, and ran after his predecessor: his black gaiters tripping pleasantly through the snow, and his eyes beaming cheerfulness and gladness through his spectacles. And when he was knocked down (which happened upon the average every third round), it was the most invigorating sight that can possibly be imagined, to behold him gather up his hat, gloves, and handkerchief, with a glowing countenance, and resume his station in the rank, with an ardour and enthusiasm that nothing could abate.

The sport was at its height, the sliding was at the quickest, the laughter was at the loudest, when a sharp smart crack was heard. There was a quick rush towards the bank, a wild scream from the ladies, and a shout from Mr Tupman. A large mass of ice disappeared; the water bubbled up over it; Mr Pickwick's hat, gloves, and handkerchief were floating on the surface; and this was all of Mr Pickwick that anybody could see.

Dismay and anguish were depicted on every countenance, the males turned pale, and the females fainted, Mr Snodgrass and Mr Winkle grasped each other by the hand, and gazed at the spot where their leader had gone down, with frenzied eagerness: while Mr Tupman, by way of rendering the promptest assistance, and at the same time conveying to any persons who might be within hearing, the clearest possible notion of the catastrophe, ran off across the country at his utmost speed, screaming 'Fire!' with all his might.

It was at this moment, when old Wardle and Sam Weller were approaching the hole with cautious steps, and Mr Benjamin Allen was holding a hurried consultation with Mr Bob Sawyer, on the advisability of bleeding the company generally, as an improving little bit of professional practice—it was at this very moment, that a face, head, and shoulders emerged from beneath the water, and disclosed the features and spectacles of Mr Pickwick.

'Keep yourself up for an instant—for only one instant!' bawled Mr Snodgrass.

'Yes, do; let me implore you—for my sake!' roared Mr Winkle, deeply affected. The adjuration was rather unnecessary; the probability being, that if Mr Pickwick had declined to keep himself up for anybody else's sake, it would have occurred to him that he might as well do so, for his own.

'Do you feel the bottom there, old fellow?' said Wardle.

'Yes, certainly,' replied Mr Pickwick, wringing the water from his head and face, and gasping for breath. 'I fell upon my back. I couldn't get on my feet at first.'

The clay upon so much of Mr Pickwick's coat as was yet visible, bore testimony to the accuracy of this statement; and as the fears of the spectators were still further relieved by the fat boy's suddenly recollecting that the water was nowhere more than five feet deep, prodigies of valour were performed to get him out. After a vast quantity of splashing, and cracking, and struggling, Mr Pickwick was at length fairly extricated from his unpleasant position, and once more stood on dry land.

'Oh, he 'll catch his death of cold,' said Emily.

'Dear old thing!' said Arabella. 'Let me wrap this shawl round you, Mr Pickwick.'

'Ah, that 's the best thing you can do,' said Wardle; 'and when you 've got it on, run home as fast as your legs can carry you, and jump into bed directly.'

A dozen shawls were offered on the instant. Three or four of the thickest having been selected, Mr Pickwick was wrapped up, and started off, under the guidance of Mr Weller: presenting the singular phenomenon of an elderly gentleman, dripping wet, and without a hat, with his arms bound down to his sides, skimming over the ground, without any clearly defined purpose, at the rate of six good English miles an hour.

But Mr Pickwick cared not for appearances in such an extreme case, and urged on by Sam Weller, he kept at the very top of his speed until he reached the door of Manor Farm, where Mr Tupman had arrived some five minutes before, and had frightened the old lady into palpitations of the heart by impressing her with the unalterable conviction that the kitchen chimney was on fire—a calamity which always presented itself in glowing colours to the old lady's mind, when anybody about her evinced the smallest agitation.

Mr Pickwick paused not an instant until he was snug in bed. Sam Weller lighted a blazing fire in the room, and took up his dinner; a bowl of punch was carried up afterwards, and a grand carouse held in honour of his safety. Old Wardle would not hear of his rising, so they made the bed the chair, and Mr Pickwick presided. A second and a third bowl were ordered in; and when Mr Pickwick awoke next morning, there was not a symptom of rheumatism about him: which proves, as Mr Bob Sawyer very justly observed, that there is nothing like hot punch in such cases; and that if ever hot punch did fail to act as a preventive, it was merely because the patient fell into the vulgar error of not taking enough of it.

RING OUT, WILD BELLS

BY D. B. WYNDHAM LEWIS

NOTHING could be more festive than the breakfast room at Merryweather Hall this noontide of 29th December. On the hearth a huge crackling fire bade defiance to the rain which lashed the tall french windows. The panelled walls were gay with holly and mistletoe and paper decorations of every hue. On the long sideboard were displayed eggs in conjunction with ham, bacon, and sausages, also boiled and scrambled; kedgeree, devilled kidneys, chops, grilled herrings, sole, and haddock, cold turkey, cold goose, cold grouse, cold game pie, cold ham, cold beef, brawn, potted shrimps, a huge Stilton, fruit of every kind, rolls, toast, tea, and coffee, all simmering on silver heaters or tempting the healthy appetite from huge crested salvers. Brooding over all this with an evil leer, the butler, Mr Banks, looked up to see a youngish guest with drawn and yellow face, shuddering violently.

'Breakfast, sir?' asked Banks, rubbing his hands.

The guest, a Mr Reginald Parable, nodded and held out his palm. Banks shook into it two tablets from a small bottle.

'They're all in the library,' said Banks, pouring half a tumbler of water. 'Cor, what they look like—well,' said Banks, chuckling, 'it's just too bad.'

Mr Parable finished breakfast in one swallow and went along to the library. In every arm-chair, and lying against each other on every settee, eyes closed, faces worn with misery, each wearing a paper cap from a cracker, lay Squire Merry-weather's guests. The squire believed in a real old-fashioned Christmas, and for five days now his guests had tottered, stiff with eating, from table to chair, only to be roused by the jovial squire with a festive roar ten minutes later.

The countryside was under water; and as nobody could go out from morning to night, Squire Merryweather could, and did, devise every kind of merrie old-time entertainment for his raving guests.

Thunderous distant chuckles as Mr Parable wavered into the only unoccupied corner of a huge leather settee announced that the squire had been consulting his secret store of books of merriment once more. And even as Mr Parable hastily turned to feign epilepsy in his corner, Squire Merryweather bustled in.

'Morning,' said a weak voice, that of Lord Lymph.

'Wake all these people up,' said the squire.

When everybody was awake the squire said: 'Colonel Rollick has five daughters, Gertrude, Mabel, Pamela, Edith, and Hilda. Mabel is half the age that Gertrude and Edith were when Hilda and Mabel were respectively twice and one-and-a-half times as old as Pamela will be on 8th May 1940. Wait a minute—that's right, 8th May. Every time the colonel takes his five daughters to town for the day it costs him three pounds fifteen and eightpence-halfpenny in railway fares, first return. One Christmas night Colonel Rollick says to his guests: "Let's play rectangles." "I don't know how it's played," says old Mrs Cheeryton, who happens to be present. "Why," says the colonel, "like this: we get the Ague-Browns to drop in, and form ourselves into four units, the square on the hypotenuse of which is equal to the sum of the squares on the——"'

At this point a lovely, lazy, deep-voiced blonde, Mrs Wallaby-Threep, roused herself sufficiently to produce a dainty pearl-handled revolver from her corsage and fire at Squire Merryweather twice, missing him each time.

'Eh? Who spoke?' asked the squire abruptly, without raising his eyes from *Ye Merrie Christmasse Puzzle-Booke*.

'Tiny Tim,' replied Mrs Wallaby-Threep, taking one more shot. This time, however, she missed as before.

'You probably took too much of a pull on the trigger,' murmured the rector with a deprecating smile. The squire was patron of the living and he felt a duty towards his guests.

'I'll get him yet,' said Mrs Wallaby-Threep.

'CHARADES!' shouted Squire Merryweather suddenly, waving a sprig of holly in his right hand.

'Again?' said a querulous Old Etonian voice. It was that of Mr Egbert Frankleigh, the famous gentleman-novelist, who wanted to tell more stories. Since Christmas Eve there had been five story-telling sessions, each guest supplying some tale of romance, adventure, mystery, or plain boredom. After every story the squire had applauded loudly and called for wassail, frumenty, old English dances, and merry-making —even after two very peculiar stories about obsessional neuroses told by two sombre young Oxford men, Mr Ebbing and Mr Crafter, both of whom took hashish with Avocado pears, wore black suède shoes, and practised Mithraism.

'Charades!' roared Squire Merryweather, tucking his book under his arm and rubbing his hands with a roar of laughter. 'Hurrah! Come along, everybody. Jump to it, boys and girls! This is going to be fun! Two of you, quick!'

A choking snore from poor old Lady Emily Wainscot, who was quite worn out (she died the following week, greatly regretted), was the only reply. Fourteen pairs of lack-lustre-ringed-with-blue eyes stared at him in haggard silence.

'Eh? What?' asked the squire, more bewildered than hurt.

'You said *charades*, sir?' said Mr Ebbing. 'We shall be delighted to assist!'

Booming like a happy bull, the squire flung an arm round each of the two young men and danced them out of the room.

'Me for the hay,' said Mrs Wallaby-Threep, snuggling into a cushion and closing her eyes. The rest of the company were not slow to follow suit. Very soon all were asleep, and snoring yelps and groans filled the library of Merryweather Hall.

It was bright, sunshiny daylight when the banging of the gong by the second footman roused the squire's guests from nearly twenty-four hours of deep, refreshing sleep. The sardonic Banks stood before them. He seemed angry, and addressed himself to Lord Lymph.

'I just found the squire's body in a wardrobe trunk, my lord.'

'In a *trunk*, Banks?'

'That's all right,' said Lady Ura Treate, yawning. 'It's an old Oxford trick. Body in a trunk. All these neurotics do it. Where *are* those two sweet chaps, Banks?'

'They've hopped it, my lady.'

'Well, that's all right, Banks,' said Freddie Slouche. 'Body in trunk. Country-house mystery. Quite normal.'

As he spoke, the guests, chattering happily, were already streaming out to order the packing and see to their cars. In a few moments only Banks and Mr Parable were left in the room. Banks seemed aggrieved.

'It's all pretty dam fine, Mr Whoosis, but who gets it in

the neck when the cops get down? Who'll be under suspicion as per usual? Who always is? The butler! Me!'

'Just an occupational risk,' said Mr Parable, politely.

'It would be if I wasn't a bit smart,' said Banks.

Mr Parable nodded and hurried out as the servants began
looting the hall.

———

This jovial little story concludes our TWELVE TALES FOR CHRIST-
MAS. *It is now time to break away from idle tale-telling, and
invigorate the mind with a stiff course of puzzles, problems, and
quizzes. In passing, I must make it clear that Colonel Crackanthorpe, whom you are about to meet, is not related to the late Squire
Merryweather.* EDITOR.

PUZZLES AND PROBLEMS

BY CALIBAN

CHRISTMAS at Colonel Crackanthorpe's is apt to be a strenuous affair. The colonel, who was once in the Sappers, likes nothing better than a good problem, and he takes care to gather round him others of similar tastes. Last year, when the port began to circulate, there was circulated with it a sheet of puzzles which the colonel had had duplicated. 'Something for you to get your teeth into, boys,' was Crackanthorpe's bluff explanation. 'They're not very difficult, but it's fun to try to do them against time. There's a box of cigars for the lad who first solves them correctly.'

Strange to say, no one made any protest. Pencils and paper were distributed, and Crackanthorpe's five guests got to work.

These were the puzzles which the colonel had provided for them. The answers will be found on page 396.

1. The School Expedition

Our school expedition this year cost £18 1s. 8¾d. The quotation was so much a head, and we got specially cheap rates because there were over a hundred in the party.

What was the actual number?

2. The Marathon Race

'At the end of the first quarter of an hour,' writes Longlegs, 'I was exactly 100 yards ahead of Thruster. He covers twice as many miles in an hour as I cover yards in a second.'

Find Longlegs's speed in yards per second.

3. *Windows*

Sir Draftover Grabbe, Chancellor of the Exchequer, conceived the unoriginal plan of imposing a tax on windows. A window having 12 square feet of glass paid a tax of £2 3s.; a 24-square-foot window paid £3 1s.; a 48-square-foot window paid £4 17s.

What do you suppose was the basis of the tax?

4. *Cubes*

I have just asked a carpenter to supply me with two wooden cubes. The sides of both are an exact number of inches in length. The larger cube exceeds the smaller in volume by 3,185 cubic inches.

Can you deduce their respective sizes?

5. *Noticed by Ned*

'I've noticed,' said my ingenious young friend, Nosy Ned, 'that, if digits are represented by certain letters, the square of AT is LARD and the square of TA is BAND.

'Peculiar, isn't it?'

'Not particularly,' I said. 'But it's quite interesting to deduce what figures your letters stand for.'

Can you do this?

6. *Extraordinary*

'This is, you know, a most extraordinary thing,' said Jones. 'Out of thirteen in our household, two have drawn tickets in the sweep. And their two tickets are respectively numbered 153 and 846.'

'I don't see anything extraordinary in that,' said Brown.

Do you?

7. *Tricolour*

A number of identical wooden cubes are to be painted red, white, and blue. Each face of each cube is to be painted in one only of these colours, and each cube is to have at least one face of each colour.

How many cubes can be produced which are distinguishable from one another?

8. *Cash Distribution*

'We distributed £2 among the boys and girls at the orphanage. Each boy got the same amount—1s. 5d.—and each girl got the same amount too.'

'How much did each girl get?'

'I forget. But it was an exact number of pennies; I remember that.'

There are seven boys at the orphanage.

How many girls are there?

9. *Football*

Three football teams—the Villa, the Lodge, and the Towers—formed themselves into a miniature league. Each team played two matches against each of the others. No two matches produced the same result, eleven goals in all being scored. The Villa scored four goals in all, but did not lose any of their matches. The Lodge, owing to poor shooting, did not score a single goal.

Can you complete the League Table below?

	P.	W.	D.	L.	Gls.	Pts.
Villa . .	4			0		4
Towers . .	4					
Lodge . .	4	0			0	

o

10. *Holidays*

'The order in which you girls take your holidays,' said Mr Green to his five clerks, 'will be determined by lot. We'll write down on a slip of paper every possible sequence, and the office boy will draw one out of a hat.'

'It'll take us all day to get the slip written out,' objected one of the girls.

'Nonsense,' answered Green sharply. 'I forgot to mention, you know, that Miss Black is to have one of the three middle periods; so also is Miss White.'

How many slips of paper went into the hat?

11. *Balls in a Bag*

Here is a simple, but perhaps somewhat puzzling, exercise in what is sometimes called inverse probability. I have nine coloured balls in a bag; some are blue, some white, some red. I draw out three balls at random. I am twice as likely to draw out one ball of each colour as to draw out two blue balls and a red one, and also twice as likely to draw out one ball of each colour as to draw out two red balls and a white one.

How many balls of each colour are in the bag?

12. *Billiards*

Three competitors—Smith, Brown, and Jones—have entered for a billiards tournament. It will be on a knock-out basis, so there will be a bye in the first round. The award of the bye will be determined by lot.

According to the experts, Smith will win against Brown in two games out of three. Similarly, Brown will win against Jones in two games out of three. Against Jones, Smith will win three games out of four.

What are the players' respective chances of winning?

Professor De Brane was the first to solve the twelve puzzles, his time being forty-three minutes. 'Seventeen minutes under bogey,' said the colonel. 'I call that pretty good, De Brane.

'Now,' he went on, when he had handed over twenty-five Coronas to the gratified professor, 'we've a couple of days' leisure ahead of us. My suggestion, chaps, is that each of us should think up a couple of really nice problems. Not too difficult, you know, but something really original and stimulating. We'll produce these, say, at lunch-time to-morrow. Then each of us will have ten puzzles to amuse himself with in the intervals between meals. We can run a modest sweepstake—say a quid or so a head—and compare our results on Monday night. That'll be four quid for the most successful solver, and two quid for the runner-up.'

This suggestion was seconded by Dean Potter and enthusiastically endorsed by the others. And I think you will agree, if you look at the twelve problems that follow, that the spirit of Colonel Crackanthorpe's intentions was very conscientiously carried out!

Mr Howe Strange won the first prize in the sweep; while the colonel—to the general satisfaction—ran second.

COLONEL CRACKENTHORPE'S PROBLEMS

Athletics : The Simian League

'This year,' said Orang, the hon. secretary of the Simian League, 'the number of clubs in our league has been increased.'

'More work for you,' I said.

'Definitely. Each club in our league plays home and away matches with each of the others. So that this year the total of matches played is increased by a number equal to sixteen times the number of clubs added to the league.'

I went into the question more closely, and made another interesting discovery: that the number of matches played last year, plus the number to be played this year, totalled four less than would have been played this year had yet one more club been added to the league.

How many clubs are there in the Simian League? Answer, page 397.

Athletics : The Old Boys fight back

A feature of the school year at Westchester is the annual athletics contest between the School and the Old Boys.

The contest is divided into two halves, each comprising an equal number of events, and this year its outstanding feature was the fight put up by the Old Boys in the second half. Points are scored in respect of the competitors placed first, second, third, and fourth in each event. At the end of the first half the Old Boys had scored 47 points only and were thus 26 points in arrears. In each of three events only one of their representatives had been placed—these competitors taking, respectively, first, second, and third places—while in each of the others they had taken first and third places.

The second half was exciting. In each of the first three races two Old Boys were placed—taking second and third place on each occasion. But in each of the remaining events Old Boys occupied the first three places.

What was the result of the contest? Answer, page 397.

DEAN POTTER'S PROBLEMS

Ages : Miranda turns the Tables

'I suppose, Miranda,' I said, 'that you're quite a whale on algebra now you've passed the School Certificate. I hear you got a credit in mathematics.'

'I surely did,' said Miranda. 'In fact, I can turn the tables on you. I made up a problem about our ages—mine and Stella's and Eva's and Lucinda's and Dorothea's—and father was completely stumped by it, though he's every bit as clever as you are.'

She showed me her problem, which ran as follows: 'The sum of our ages is five times my age. (By "age," throughout this problem, is meant "age in years.") When Stella is three times my present age, the sum of my age and Dorothea's will be equal to the sum of the present ages of the five of us. Eva's age will be three times her present age and Lucinda's age will be twice Stella's present age, plus one year.'

How old is Miranda? Answer, page 398.

Ages : Five Years

I said to Katia: 'What have you been doing at school?'
'Harmonic mean,' said Katia.
'Interested?'
Katia pouted. 'I think it's rather silly.'
'How so, Katia?'
'Why,' said Katia, 'I was working out the harmonic mean of our ages—Kitty's and Karen's and mine. (I'm the eldest, you know.) Then I worked out what their harmonic mean would be in five years' time. And, do you know, the second mean exceeds the first, not, as I'd expect it to do, by 5 years, but by 5 years and 95/143 of a year.'

I smiled. 'There are,' I began, 'more things in heaven and earth——' But Katia cut me short: 'I know that one.'

How old is Katia? Answer, page 398.

JUDGE GAVELKIND'S PROBLEMS

Squares: Fabrics from Jugginpore

'See these pieces of fabric?' asked Tomkins. 'They come from Jugginpore. Each of them is an exact number of feet square.'

'How much do they cost?'

'A shilling a square foot.'

'You 've got—how many?'

'A dozen of them,' said Tomkins. 'Each year I buy two. And, do you know, I 've made it a rule to spend, each year, twice as much as the year before. But I shan't do that next year, because it isn't possible. No single fabric, you see, costs as much as £10.'

How many different-sized fabrics does Tomkins's collection include? Answer, page 399.

Squares : The Praying-mats

'Each of the embroidered praying-mats is so many feet square. And they cost—let me see—two shillings a square foot.'

'My dear Mabel, do you mean to tell me that you paid twenty pounds or so for a praying-mat?'

'Oh no, dear; none of them cost as much as that. Let me see, we bought two each; didn't we, Ethel?'

'That 's right,' said Ethel. 'You spent ten pounds more than I did.'

'So I did,' said Mabel.

'But I got larger mats than you did. Didn't I, Charles?'

'Didn't you what, darling?'

'Get larger mats than Ethel.'

'Of course you did. You 've just been telling Amy, you spent ten pounds more.'

'They needn't both of them have been larger,' said little Frank, who had been listening. 'If you 'd laid out your money differently, mamma, Ethel's mats would both have been larger than the smaller of yours.'

'Quite right,' said Charles. 'Unless, of course, Ethel had also laid out *her* money differently. There seem to have been all sorts of possibilities.'

'That's right,' said Mabel. 'Coming along to see the praying-mats, Amy?'

What size mats had Mabel and Ethel bought? *Answer, page* 399.

ADMIRAL MAINBRACE'S PROBLEMS

Elementary Ciphers : Clarissa's Homework

'I can't do my homework,' said Clarissa.

'Let's have a look at it.'

'It's in code, to start off with,' said Clarissa. 'The word FACTORS is the key, if that conveys anything to you. But what I have to do is not only to decode the problem, but also to find the answer to it.'

'Hand it over,' I said.

This was Clarissa's problem:

J Z O V K	O B T U W	P C W Q Q
M Y K O N	O W M Y N	B Q K O V
N J E Y Z	L Y M Y W	Q B T N J
M Y W M W	O C N E W	Q M J K L
M N P Q Z	Q M E N M	Y Z P V Q
M Y W Q B	T N J M Y	W M E W C
D W C N E	W Q M J K	L M N P Q

What is the answer to it? *Answer, page* 400.

Elementary Ciphers : The Pietas Code

'My old schoolmaster, Dunderhead,' said Juggins, 'was great on codes and ciphers. As a tribute to his memory, I've evolved a simple code. That's one reason why I call it the "Pietas."'

'How does it work?' I asked.

'I'll give you an example of it. Here's a Pietas message.'

He handed me a slip of paper. 'Don't forget this,' he added. 'You ignore the sixth letter throughout.'

This was the message:

D I T N R   S S O H E
S D T N E   A U E H D
M R T A A   E E T D R

Can you decode it?   Answer, page 401.

Calculation of Chances : Uncle Podger

My Uncle Podger is an inveterate gambler.

When I last went to see him he had five metal disks laid out face downwards in front of him.

'Like to take a chance?' he asked. 'Each disk has on its face one of the digits 1 to 9. No two the same digit. You buy a chance and this is what you do. You select three disks, and multiply together the digits that they bear. Then you multiply together the two remaining digits. Finally you add the two products, and their sum is the number of pennies you get.'

'How much does a chance cost?' I asked.

'Sixteen and eightpence.'

'And how much can I get in return?'

'The most you can get is twenty-seven shillings and three-pence.'

'I'll take a chance,' I said.

What is Podger's expectation of gain or loss?   Answer, page 401.

Calculation of Chances : Elocutionary

'Six of my children,' said Mr Spoutforth Glibly, 'have entered for an elocution contest. There are so many prizes for boys and so many for girls. And it is possible—though only just possible—for my family to carry off all the prizes.'

'Indeed!' I said. 'And how many competitors are there altogether?'

'Twenty. Over half of them girls.'

'Twenty,' I said. 'Glibly, I know your methods. You're going to ask me in a minute to work out how many of the twenty are boys and how many are girls. Having first, I suppose, given me the odds against your family taking all the prizes.'

Glibly laughed. 'Such odds,' he said, 'can only be calcu-lated on the very arbitrary assumption that all the boys com-peting are equally likely to get a prize and that all the girls are equally likely to get a prize. I've worked them out. And I'll tell you something very peculiar. If one of the girls competing withdrew, and a boy were entered in her place, the odds against my family's scooping the pool would remain exactly the same.'

How many boys, and how many girls, are competing, and how many of each sex are the offspring of Spoutforth Glibly? Answer, page 402.

PROFESSOR DE BRANE'S PROBLEMS

Post-Mortem

Here is a study in the exploration of the seemingly in-consequent.

'I don't know if there's a problem in this,' writes 'Enquirer,' 'but it seems to me there might be. I caught the last bus home the other night and there was only one seat unoccupied. All the other passengers, I gathered, had been taking part in a partnership bridge drive. Each pair had had to play five rubbers, and each pair—to the great jubilation of the party—had won every rubber played. This fact, though remarkable, was not nearly so remarkable as other facts which subsequently emerged.

'The first of these was that each pair, in addition to winning all its rubbers, had won the same amount in cash. I gathered that a rubber was not "won" unless the winning pair won by over 50 points, and that cash settlement, as in most clubs, was on the basis of so much per hundred, calculated to the nearest hundred. In this drive the basis of payment had been:

For the first rubber	.	1s. per 100
„ second „	.	2s. „
„ third „	.	3s. „
„ fourth „	.	4s. „
„ fifth „	.	5s. „

The second remarkable fact was that each pair, in addition to winning the same amount in cash, had averaged the same amount per hundred points won. I gathered also that no two pairs had "clocked up" the total amount won in precisely the same way, while every method of "clocking up" this total, consistent with the number of pairs in the party, had been utilized.

'There was also much hilarity in connection with a sweep, the prize in which went to the pair who had won most in the last two rubbers. This prize went to two brothers named Deuceace, and I dare say it will interest you to try and work out what their winnings on these last two rubbers were.'

After pondering the contents of 'Enquirer's' letter I sent him the following wire:

'How many seats were there on the bus?'

And I received the following somewhat tantalizing reply:

'The number of seats on the bus was equal to the number of shillings which the Deuceace brothers won in the last three rubbers.'

What were the successive scores of the five rubbers won by the brothers Deuceace? Answer, page 403.

Weasel's Blank Cheque

This is another study in the exploration of the apparently inconsequent.

Some eight years after his marriage, I went to stay with Weasel. He has several children, no two of whom were born within twelve months of one another. He showed me a letter from his father-in-law, a retired professor of mathematics. It was accompanied by a blank cheque.

'Look at this,' said Weasel. 'The old fellow's nuts. Help me to fill in the cheque, will you?'

This was the text of his father-in-law's letter:

'MY DEAR CHARLIE,

'If you fill in the enclosed correctly—in accordance with the instructions that follow—it will be honoured by my bank. If not, it won't.

'I want you to imagine that the cheque, which is for an exact number of pounds, is to be divided among certain of your children. Not all. Each boy among the recipients is to get (you must assume) either £1 or a multiple of £1; each girl is to get either £1 or a multiple of £1. But two recipients belonging to the same sex may not receive similar amounts.

'Moreover, if you have made the right assumptions, you will find that the number of ways in which the boys' share of the cheque can be partitioned among those participating, plus the number of ways in which the girls' share can be partitioned among those participating, is equal to three times the total number of participants; while the number of pounds for which the cheque is to be made out is equal to four times the total number of participants. And I think, my dear Charlie, that that is all you need to know.

'Yours to a surd,

'EUCLIDES POPFORTH.'

For what amount did we fill in Weasel's cheque? Answer, page 403.

ANSWERS TO CALIBAN'S PUZZLES AND PROBLEMS

1. THE SCHOOL EXPEDITION. 179. The rate per head was 2s. 0¼d.

2. THE MARATHON RACE. Five yards per second.

3. WINDOWS. A payment of 25s., plus 1s. 6d. for every square foot of window.

4. CUBES. The sides of the cubes are respectively 17 inches and 12 inches.

5. NOTICED BY NED.   AT = 37   LARD = 1369.
                     TA = 73   BAND = 5329.

6. EXTRAORDINARY. $\frac{2}{13}$ expressed as a decimal fraction is ·153846̇.

7. TRICOLOUR. Twenty-nine. Six cubes have four faces of one colour; eighteen have three faces of one colour; five have two faces of each colour.

8. CASH DISTRIBUTION. Nineteen.

9. FOOTBALL.

	P.	W.	D.	L.	Gls.	Pts.
Villa	4	2	2	0	4 2	6
Towers	4	2	1	1	7 3	5
Lodge	4	0	1	3	0 6	1

10. HOLIDAYS. Thirty-six.

11. BALLS IN A BAG. Four red, three blue, two white.

12. BILLIARDS. The respective chances are: Smith, 61/108; Brown, 31/108; Jones, 16/108.

THE SIMIAN LEAGUE

Let number of clubs last year $= a$, and number added this year $= b$.

Matches played last year $= a(a-1)$, this year $(a+b)(a+b-1)$.

Then $(a+b)(a+b-1) - a(a-1) = 16b$.

$$\text{i.e.} \qquad b^2 + 2ab - b = 16b$$

$$\therefore \qquad b + 2a - 17 = 0 \quad (\text{or } b = 0)$$

$$\therefore \qquad b = 17 - 2a.$$

Also $(a+b+1)(a+b) - (a+b)(a+b-1) - a(a-1) = 4$.

$$\text{i.e. } -a^2 + 3a + 2b = 4.$$

Substitute $(17 - 2a)$ for b.

$$-a^2 - a + 30 = 0$$

$$\therefore a = 5 \text{ or } -6.$$

Positive root only is permissible, and $b = 7$.

$$\therefore \textit{Number of clubs last year} = 5$$
$$\textit{this year} = 12.$$

THE OLD BOYS FIGHT BACK

The Old Boys won by 125 points to 115.

Let a, b, c, and d be the number of points scored for 1st, 2nd, 3rd, and 4th places.

If there are 5 (the minimum) events in each half, then $a + b + c + d = 24$, and

$$3a + b + 3c = 47$$
$$2a + 4b + 2c + 5d = 73.$$

Eliminating a and c,
$$2b + 3d = 25,$$

from which the only reasonable values of b and d are 8 and 3. The only possible values of a and c are then 9 and 4. These values of a, b, c, and d give the above result.

If it is assumed that there are 6 or 8 events in each half, similar equations may be worked out, but they fail to give possible values for a, b, c, and d.

MIRANDA TURNS THE TABLES

Let M, E, L, D, S be the ages of Miranda, Eva, Lucinda, Dorothea, and Stella respectively. Then we have the equations:

$$M + E + L + D + S = 5M \qquad (a)$$
$$M + (3M - S) + D + (3M - S) = 5M \qquad (b)$$
$$E + (3M - S) = 3E \qquad (c)$$
$$L + (3M - S) = 2S + 1 \,(d)$$

(c) gives $2E = 3M - S$

(d) gives $L = 3S - 3M + 1$

(b) gives $D = 2S - 2M$

So, substituting in (a)

$$2M + 3M - S + 6S - 6M + 2 + 4S - 4M + 2S = 10M$$

i.e. $11S + 2 = 15M$

This equation is satisfied by S = 8; M = 6

S = 23; M = 17, etc.

Since Miranda has just taken School Certificate, the required solution is that which makes her 17 years old. *Miranda is therefore* 17.

FIVE YEARS

Beginning with the formula:

$$\frac{n}{b} = \frac{1}{a} + \frac{1}{b} + \frac{1}{c}$$

and knowing that 143 is the denominator of the difference between b_1 and b_2, we may therefore put:

$$\frac{3 \times 11 \text{ or } 13}{?} = \frac{bc + ac + ab}{abc},$$

which means that when b_1 and b_2 are in their lowest terms their denominators will be 11 and 13. Assuming for the moment that 11 is the denominator of b_1 and that N_2 and N_2 are the numerators of b_1 and b_2 respectively, then:

$$\frac{N_2}{13} - \frac{N_1}{11} = \frac{810}{143}.$$

It is found after experiment that 180 and 90 are the only satisfactory values for N_2 and N_1 respectively. This means that
the L.C.M. of the three ages is 30 and is 60 after five more years.

The only age basis consistent with these figures is $5 : 10 : 15$.

Katia is therefore 15 years old.

FABRICS FROM JUGGINPORE

An easy problem.   We have to find the series:

$$a + b + c + d + e + f,$$

where $b = 2a$, $c = 2b$, etc.; a, b, c, d, e, f each equals $m^2 + n^2$;
and neither m nor n exceeds 14.

The only possible series is:

$$1^2 + 2^2 = 5$$
$$1^2 + 3^2 = 10$$
$$2^2 + 4^2 = 20$$
$$2^2 + 6^2 = 40$$
$$4^2 + 8^2 = 80$$
$$4^2 + 12^2 = 160$$

Hence Tomkins's collection includes seven different sizes of fabrics.

THE PRAYING MATS

Let a and b be the sizes in feet of the mats bought by Mabel
and e and d the sizes of those bought by Ethel.   Then we have
the equation: $(a^2 + b^2) - (c^2 + d^2) = 100$.

On the footing that neither a, b, c, nor d exceeds 14 and that *a* and *b* are both larger than *c* and *d*, there are the following alternative solutions, viz.:

a and *b* =		*c* and *d* =	
7 and 8		2 and 3	
6 and 9		1 and 4	
5 and 10		3 and 4	
8 and 9		3 and 6	
13 and 14		11 and 12	
8 and 11		6 and 7	

One only of those solutions (the last) allows both Mabel and Ethel alternative ways of laying out their money. Therefore, Mabel's mats were 8 *and* 11 *feet square* and Ethel's mats 6 *and* 7 *feet square*.

CLARISSA'S HOMEWORK

Using for the decode:

F A C T O R S B D E G H I
J K L M N P Q U V W X Y Z

The problem is read to be:
'Find a number less than one thousand of which the sum of the ten lowest factors is two-thirds the sum of the twelve lowest factors.'

Solution is 840.

Lowest factors are 1, 2, 3, 4, 5, 6, 7, 8, 10, 12, 14, 15, of which the sum of the first ten is 58 and the sum of the first twelve is 87.

THE PIETAS CODE

The basis of the Pietas Code is PI·ETA—the sixteenth and
seventh letters of the Greek alphabet. Transposing the letters
by cyclic elimination, taking the sixteenth and seventh alternately, and ignoring each sixth letter in the final transposition,
one gets the message: A THUNDERSTORM IS THREATENED.

UNCLE PODGER

We require in the first place five different digits such that the
maximum possible value of the sum of the product of three
of them and the product of the remaining two is 327. The
five digits must be 3, 4, 5, 7, and 9.

There are ten different amounts possible in return for picking
three of Podger's five disks. These amounts are:

$$3 \quad 4 \quad 5 + 7 \quad 9 = 123 \text{ pence}$$
$$3 \quad 4 \quad 7 + 5 \quad 9 = 129 \text{ ,,}$$
$$3 \quad 4 \quad 9 + 5 \quad 7 = 143 \text{ ,,}$$
$$3 \quad 5 \quad 7 + 4 \quad 9 = 141 \text{ ,,}$$
$$3 \quad 5 \quad 9 + 4 \quad 7 = 163 \text{ ,,}$$
$$3 \quad 7 \quad 9 + 4 \quad 5 = 209 \text{ ,,}$$
$$4 \quad 5 \quad 7 + 3 \quad 9 = 167 \text{ ,,}$$
$$4 \quad 5 \quad 9 + 3 \quad 7 = 201 \text{ ,,}$$
$$4 \quad 7 \quad 9 + 3 \quad 5 = 267 \text{ ,,}$$
$$5 \quad 7 \quad 9 + 3 \quad 4 = 327 \text{ ,,}$$

The average return is therefore 187 pence = 15s. 7d.

As the cost of a chance is 16s. 8d., Podger's expectation is a
gain of 1s. 1d.

Ans. 1s. 1d. gain.

ELOCUTIONARY

Six boys and 14 girls competed of whom 2 were sons and 4 were daughters of Mr Glibly.

Method : Let a, b represent Glibly's sons and daughters. A, B, the total boys and girls respectively.

Then $A + B = 20$, $A < B$ and $a + b = 6$.

Then, if $_A C_a$ is the number of combinations of A things taken a at a time, the chance of any set of 'a' boys winning all the prizes is:

$$\frac{1}{_A C_a} \text{ or } \frac{1}{_{(A+1)} C_a} \text{ if there are A + 1 boys.}$$

Similarly the chance of any set of 'b' girls is:

$$\frac{1}{_B C_b} \text{ or } \frac{1}{_{(B-1)} C_b} \text{ if there are B - 1 girls.}$$

The chance therefore of 'a' boys and 'b' girls winning together is:

$$\frac{1}{_A C_a} \times \frac{1}{_B C_b} \text{ or } \frac{1}{_{(A+1)} C_a} \times \frac{1}{_{(B-1)} C_b}$$

but, we are told, these chances are equal, so that:

$$\frac{_{(A+1)} C_a}{_A C_a} = \frac{_B C_b}{_{(B-1)} C_b}$$

By inspection, the only values (within the limits) that satisfy this are (1) $a = 2$, $b = 4$ and (2) $a = 4$, $b = 2$.

(1) gives $A = 6$, $B = 14$; (2) gives $A = 13$, $B = 7$. But $A < B$ and (1) alone gives an acceptable answer.

POST MORTEM

The successive scores of the rubbers won by the Deauceace brothers were :

$$300, 100, 100, 300, 200$$

This gives an aggregate win of

$$3 + 2 + 3 + 12 + 10 = 30s.,$$

and 30s. can be won in 12 ways in all. There were 25 seats on the bus (3 + 12 + 10)—one occupied by 'Enquirer' and 24 by the 12 pairs of bridge players.

This problem conforms to no definite (mathematical) type. It can only be solved by (intelligent) trial and error.

WEASEL'S BLANK CHEQUE

The cheque was filled in for £20.

From the wording of the problem, there cannot be more than six children who rank for shares.

As there were at least 2 sharers of each sex, at least 4 children (2 m., 2 f.) must have shared in the gift. Thus the initial possibilities are:

£16 divided between 4 (2 + 2) children.
£20 „ „ 5 (2 + 3) children.
£24 „ „ 6 (2 + 4 or 3 + 3) children.

No method of dividing a total sum of £16, split into 2 portions, among two groups of 2 children, so that the members of each group get differing amounts, offers a sum of the variant possibilities in both groups totalling 4 × 3. (The maximum is 7.)

Division of £24 between groups of 2 and 4 or 3 and 3 children offers a wide range of possibilities, but none of which the sum of the 2 group totals amounts to 6 × 3 = 18.

If £20 be divided, £16 between 3, and £4 between 2 children, the variant ways of doing this within the above conditions are 14 + 1 = 15, i.e. 3 times the number of children getting a share.

CHRISTMAS QUIZ

BY INSTRUCTOR-CAPTAIN R. WEATHERHEAD

THIS makes no pretence of being a compendium of 'General Knowledge.' Readers are entreated to bear in mind that there are some subjects that do not lend themselves as well to this particular game as others, that there are some subjects of which the compiler knows nothing, and some for which he cares nothing; that there are some for which he has a weakness, and some—or, at any rate, items—for which he would like to do a little propaganda.

But no deep knowledge is required in any subject; only an average person's interest; and many questions are made very easy on purpose. A somewhat flippant tone is, it is hoped, not incompatible with a deep reverence for the subject spoken of.

There is really only one rule; but that is important. The questions are arranged in sets of twelve; and the twelve answers to any set of questions must all be different. If, as sometimes happens, you want to give the same answer to two of the questions, both answers may be correct in themselves, but you may be sure that there is an alternative reply to one of them.

Apart from this, there is, here and there, more than one answer to a question; and alternatives that seem reasonable are given in the answers, which will be found on pages 440–459.

Finally, the writer would like to say, in excuse and self-defence, that the composition of the sets of questions comes almost entirely out of his own head; and that a third of these papers were used at tea-party competitions (with prizes!), way back in 1922, long before he ever heard that games of this sort interested America, or the readers of the *Daily Express*.

Men as Beasts

We find the names of animals very useful in describing the natures of men. As thus: (*a*) Directly, as nouns for: (1) A surly male. (2) A spiteful female. (3) A silly girl. (4) A sweet girl. (5) A very superior golfer. (6) A very inferior cricketer.

(*b*) As verbs or adjectives, to define: (7) Bolting one's food greedily. (8) Pretending, shamming. (9) Following persistently.

(*c*) In similes, to indicate: (10) Unusual force or power. (11) Exceptional courage. (12) Making very little noise.

Trees

From what tree do we notably obtain: (13) Ships' timbers. (14) Dining-room tables. (15) Elegant wardrobes. (16) The victor's wreath. (17) The schoolmaster's friend. (18) Cricket bats. (19) Lead pencils. (20) A cure for colds. (21) A nut oil. (22) A pleasing sugar. (23) Long bows. (24) Spear shafts.

Operas

Who composed these operas: (25) The Magic Flute. (26) Carmen. (27) Samson and Delilah. (28) Falstaff. (29) La Tosca. (30) The Rose-Cavalier. (31) The Huguenots. (32) Orpheus. (33) Lucia di Lammermoor. (34) Romeo and Juliet. (35) The Barber of Seville. (36) Pagliacci.

Battles

Name a famous battle in which:

(37) A king of England was taken prisoner.

(38) A king of France was taken prisoner.

(39) A king of England was slain.

(40) A king of Scotland was slain.

(41) A king of England fought in person for the last time.

(42) The victor called the result 'a crowning mercy.'

(43) The vanquished said: 'Tout est perdu fors l'honneur.'

(44) Both generals were killed.

(45) The beaten side was utterly destroyed, and for ever famous.

(46) It was said: 'The guard dies, but does not surrender.'

(47) An interested spectator said: 'C'est magnifique, mais ce n'est pas la guerre.'

(48) The defeated sent home the dispatch: 'The ships are lost; Mindarus is dead; the men are starving; we don't know what to do.'

Old Testament Animals

What person in the Old Testament had a strange or dramatic experience concerned with: (49) Lions. (50) Bears. (51) A donkey. (52) A ram. (53) A kid. (54) Kine—fourteen. (55) Bees. (56) Serpents. (57) Quails. (58) Ravens. (59) A dove. (60) A marine monster.

Familiar Expressions

What is the historical origin of these expressions in common use: (61) Crossing the Rubicon. (62) As rich as Croesus. (63) The sword of Damocles hangs over his head. (64) A Parthian shot. (65) A Job's comforter. (66) Taking his ewe lamb. (67) Killing the fatted calf. (68) The writing on the wall. (69) Without the Pale. (70) Burning his boats. (71) Gone west. (72) A band of brothers.

Classical Sayings

What Greek (73 to 78), or Roman (79 to 84) said:

(73) 'This child is greater than any man in Greece, for the Athenians command the Greeks, I command the

Athenians, his mother commands me, and he commands his mother.'

(74) 'I am not the general. Nicias is.'

(75) Being told that his countrymen had condemned him to die: 'But I will show them that I am alive.' (And did.)

(76) Having drunk the fatal cup of hemlock, tossing out the dregs as an oblation: 'This to the gentle Critias.'

(77) Having drunk the cup of hemlock, as his last words: 'I owe a cock to Asclepius, do not forget to pay it.'

(78) 'The sea, the sea!'

(79) 'Go and tell him that you have seen the exile—sitting on the ruins of Carthage.'

(80) 'More men worship the rising than the setting sun.'

(81) 'No friend ever did me so much good, or enemy so much harm, but I repaid him with interest.' (For his own epitaph.)

(82) 'It is not the sleek and fat men that I fear, but the pale and lean.'

(83) 'Varus, give me back my legions.'

(84) 'What an artist dies in me.'

Captains and Kings

These passages from poems, all by different authors, refer in turn to three famous statesmen, three indifferent kings, three great captains, and three noble benefactors of their kind. Who are they?

(85) . . . our chief of men, who through a cloud,
    Not of war only, but detractions rude,
    Guided by faith and matchless fortitude,
    To peace and truth thy glorious way hast ploughed.

(86) A fiery soul, which, working out its way,
    Fretted the pygmy body to decay,
    And o'er-informed the tenement of clay.

(87) Now is the stately column broke,
The beacon-light is quenched in smoke,
The trumpet's silver sound is still,
The warder silent on the hill.

(88) He nothing common did, or mean,
Upon that memorable scene,
But with his keener eye
The axe's edge did try;
Nor called the gods with vulgar spite
To vindicate his helpless right,
But bowed his comely head
Down, as upon a bed.

(89) Here lies our sovereign lord the king,
Whose word no man relies on;
He never said a foolish thing,
Nor ever did a wise one.

(90) An old, mad, blind, despised, and dying king—

(91) And, pleased the Almighty's orders to perform,
Rides in the whirlwind and directs the storm.

(92) With neck out-thrust, you fancy how,
Legs wide, arms locked behind,
As if to balance the prone brow
Oppressive with its mind.

(93) Our greatest, yet with least pretence,
Great in council and great in war,
Foremost captain of his time,
Rich in saving common sense,
And, as the greatest only are,
In his simplicity sublime.

(94) The bloody writing is for ever torn,
And thou henceforth shalt have a good man's calm,
A great man's happiness; thy soul shall find
Repose at length, firm friend of human kind.

(95) A lady with a lamp shall stand
   In the great history of the land,
      A noble type of good,
      Heroic womanhood.

(96) O God, the cleanest offering
   Of tainted earth below,
      Unblushing to Thy feet we bring—
      A leper white as snow.

Surnames

Add surnames to: (97) Sir Isaac. (98) Sir Joshua. (99)
Sir Christopher. (100) Sir Timothy. (101) Sir Humphry.
(102) Sir Ian. (103) Sir Hamilton. (104) Sir Cloudesley.
(105) Sir Stamford. (106) Sir Augustus. (107) Sir Evelyn.
(108) Sir Elijah.

Ships

What are these ships famous for: (109) Téméraire. (110)
Arethusa. (111) Shannon. (112) Merrimac. (113) Ala-
bama. (114) Maine. (115) Birkenhead. (116) Victoria.
(117) Titanic. (118) Sidney. (119) Monmouth. (120)
Invincible.

Churchmen

For what are these English divines best remembered:
(121) Bede. (122) Anselm. (123) Nicholas Breakspear.
(124) Wycliffe. (125) William of Wykeham. (126) Tyn-
dale. (127) Colet. (128) Donne. (129) Richard Hooker.
(130) Laud. (131) Bishop Butler. (132) Newman.

Sweethearts and Comrades

Who was the sweetheart or the dear comrade of: (133) Paris.
(134) Perseus. (135) Pyramus. (136) Pericles. (137) Paolo.
(138) Pelleas. (139) Peirithous. (140) Patroclus. (141)
Pylades. (142) Pythias. (143) Pelopidas. (144) Palemon.

Zoology

A. *Who was it that*

(145) Went for a ride on a tiger.

(146) Bought a python from a man,
　　　　And kept it for a pet.

(147) Having eloped together and being anxious to get
　　　married asked: 'Dear Pig, are you willing
　　　　　　　　To sell for one shilling
　　　　　　　　Your ring,' etc.

(148) Said of the leopard:
　　　　　　　'Cet animal est très méchant,
　　　　　　　Quand on l'attaque il se défend.'

(149) Turning to his horse, he said:
　　　　　'I am in haste to dine;
　　　　'Twas for your pleasure you came here,
　　　　　You shall go back for mine.'

(150) Tells us that
　　　　　'A lion never will attack
　　　　　A white if he can get a black.
　　　　　And as there were a lot of these
　　　　　We could afford with perfect ease
　　　　　　To spare one here and there.
　　　　　It made us more compact; and then,
　　　　　It's *right* to spare one's fellow-men.'

B. *Why is it that*

(151) The friendly cow, all red and white,
　　　　I love with all my heart.

(152) I shoot the hippopotamus with bullets made of
　　　platinum.

(153) The Polar Bear is unaware
　　　　Of cold that cuts me through.

(154) The Walrus and the Carpenter 'wept like anything.'

C.

(155) What was the duet sung by the Gryphon and the
Mock Turtle?

(156) The wound it seemed both sore and sad
  To every Christian eye,
 And while they swore the dog was mad,
  They swore the man would die.
 But soon a wonder came to light
  Which showed the rogues they lied.
    What was that?

Delicacies

What delectable article of food or drink is recalled by the
places: (157) Colchester. (158) Tiptree. (159) York.
(160) Bournville. (161) Jamaica. (162) Plymouth. (163)
Smyrna. (164) Jaffa. (165) Syra. (166) Everton. (167)
Reading. (168) Oxford.

Shakespeare's Plays

What play of Shakespeare is about, or contains: (169)
Witches. (170) Fairies. (171) An island. (172) A forest.
(173) Twin brothers. (174) Twin brother and sister.

A sensational scene: (175) At a wedding. (176) At a play.
(177) In a court of law. (178) In a bedroom. (179) In a
family vault. (180) At a funeral.

Chivalry and Magic

Name the famous English poem, or its author, which tells of:
(181) How a 'gentle knight was pricking on the plaine,' and
of other knights and ladies. (182) A knight's journey, in the
face of evil omens, to a Dark Tower. (183) A knight be-
guiled by a sorceress in the guise of a wandering maiden.
(184) How a pure maiden praying in the forest for her true
knight met there a strange lady, 'beautiful exceedingly.'

(185) How a lady caused the death of her false knight by burning his image in wax. (186) How a knight and a lady drank unwittingly a fatal potion, and of their great love resulting. (187) How a queen was accused of deceiving her husband with the chiefest of his knights. (188) How a maiden, immured in a tower, gazed out on a passing knight, and brought a curse upon her. (189) How a lady, wedded to a man of the sea, deserted him and her mermaiden children, and returned to the land again. (190) How a maid disappeared into Fairyland, returned, and went back there again. (191) How two maidens, sisters, bought luscious fruits of evil fairy merchants. (192) How a great lady sold her soul to demon merchants for bread for her starving peasants.

Two Men, Same Name

These are pairs of men who have the same surnames (perhaps differing slightly in the spelling), and the familiar Christian name in common, and who are, or were, celebrated in some way or other. Give both names. They may, or may not, be related.

(193) Chief minister to a great queen; and chief minister to another great queen. (194) A medieval preacher and rebel; and a great amateur golfer. (195) A Tudor statesman, beheaded; and an admiral of the fleet and O.M. (196) A pioneer of the steam-engine; and a great Irish three-quarter. (197) One of Nelson's captains; and a great modern novelist. (198) Prime Minister to a king of England; and Prime Minister to the same king. (199) A great adventurer; and a distinguished modern literary critic. (200) A witty and provocative writer; and ditto. (201) A great novelist; and a publisher. (202) A distinguished English architect; and a famous American general. (203) A living British statesman; and an American novelist. (204) A famous old English lyric poet; and an American novelist.

Biblical Slayers

Who was slain, or caused to be slain, in the Old Testament by: (205) Moses. (206) Ehud. (207) Saul. (208) David. (209) Absalom. (210) Omri. (211) Jephthah. (212) Joab. (213) Jehu. (214) Jael. (215) Jezebel. (216) Judith.

Rivals

With whom do we associate, as his rival or complement in life or fame: (217) Themistocles. (218) Hannibal. (219) Sulla. (220) Louis XI. (221) Francis I. (222) Cortez. (223) Turenne. (224) Marlborough. (225) Pitt. (226) Castlereagh. (227) Talleyrand. (228) Cavour.

Familiar Quotations in Prose

Who started us all saying:
(229) God tempers the wind to the shorn lamb.
(230) To love her was a liberal education.
(231) Vice itself lost half its evil by losing all its grossness.
(232) He that hath wife and children hath given hostages to fortune.
(233) Necessity, the mother of invention.
(234) His death eclipsed the gaiety of nations.
(235) A sea of upturned faces.
(236) Bread is the staff of life.
(237) Government of the people, by the people, for the people.
(238) The better part of valour is discretion.
(239) When found, make a note of.
(240) It is only a step from the sublime to the ridiculous.

Titles and Nicknames

Who was called: (241) The king-maker. (242) The wisest fool in Christendom. (243) The Great Commoner. (244) The First Gentleman of Europe. (245) The Father of his Country. (246) The Pilot who weathered the storm. (247) Le Grand Monarque. (248) Le Bien-Aimé. (249) Le Petit Caporal. (250) Le brave des braves. (251) L'enfant chéri de la victoire. (252) Sans peur et sans reproche.

Colours in Titles

Fill up the colours in the titles of the following novels or plays:
(253) Under the . . . Robe.
(254) The Woman in . . . .
(255) A Study in . . . .
(256) The . . . Hat.
(257) A pair of . . . Eyes.
(258) The . . . Diamond.
(259) The . . . Land.
(260) The Young Person in . . . .
(261) The . . . Sunbonnet.
(262) The . . . Azaleas.
(263) The Dancer in . . . .
(264) A . . . Eye or So.

Trios

Complete the triumvirate, or whatever it is: (265) Shem. (266) Tom. (267) Pip. (268) Shadrach. (269) Pompey. (270) Athos. (271) Vardon. (272) Mulvaney. (273) Ananias. (274) The Sketch. (275) Charlotte (Brontë). (276) Ormonde (the great three-year-olds of 1886).

Take your Choice

Name three out of the
(277–9) 'Seven Wonders of the World.'
(280–2) 'Seven Cities of Asia.'
(283–5) The Muses.
(286–8) The Signs of the Zodiac.

Names for Kings

What nicknames or epithets have been given to these English monarchs: (289) Henry I. (290) Richard I. (291) John. (292) Edward I. (293) Richard III. (294) Henry VIII. (295) Elizabeth. (296) Charles I. (297) Charles II. (298) George III. (299) William IV. (300) Edward VII.

A Mixed Bag

What were, or are : (301) Urim and Thummim. (302) Abana and Pharphar. (303) A deoch and dorris. (304) The Curse of Scotland. (305) An Austin Seven. (306) A Silver King. (307) A Mme Édouard Herriot. (308) A March Brown. (309) A right-and-left. (310) A pig's ear. (311) 5XX Daventry. (312) A Williams's Bon Chrétien.

Couples

State briefly who were these couples of persons, whose names always go together: (313) Mutt and Jeff. (314) Liddell and Scott. (315) Burke and Hare. (316) Codlin and Short. (317) Sacco and Vanzetti. (318) Hengist and Horsa. (319) Fafner and Fasolt. (320) John Doe and Richard Roe. (321) Lambert Simnel and Perkin Warbeck. (322) Rosencrantz and Guildenstern. (323) Rothermere and Beaverbrook. (324) Potash and Perlmutter.

Animals Named

What were these animals, and for what famed: (325) Bucephalus. (326) Rosinante. (327) Rikkitikkitavy. (328) Black Beauty. (329) The spaniel, John. (330) Grane. (331) Bagheera. (332) Rintintin. (333) 'My horse, Capilet.' (334) Moby Dick. (335) Winnie the Pooh. (336) Tylette.

National Heroes

What man is regarded as the national hero, against aggression or tyranny, of: (337) AngloSaxon England. (338) Early Ireland. (339) Medieval Scotland. (340) Medieval Wales. (341) Medieval France. (342) Medieval Switzerland. (343) Medieval Spain. (344) Ireland of the English Revolution. (345) Ireland of the '98. (346) Union of Italy. (347) Republican Rome. (348) The Athenian Democracy (two men).

A Day in London

With what form of entertainment, refreshment, or service do you connect these places in London: (349) Hamley. (350) Bumpus. (351) Hartnell. (352) Poole. (353) Lincoln & Bennett. (354) Cartier. (355) Truefitt. (356) Scott. (357) Keith Prowse. (358) Hatchett. (359) Hatchard. (360) Hachette.

Strange Phenomena in O.T.

With what Old Testament character are these strange phenomena associated: (361) The sun standing still. (362) The shadow on the dial moving backward. (363) Fire coming down from heaven. (364) Fire without burning. (365) Immunity from fire. (366) Calling the dead to life. (367) Reappearance as a ghost. (368) Entertaining angels unawares. (369) A freshwater cure for disease. (370) Disease by word of mouth. (371) Feeding like a beast. (372) Strange writing appearing on the wall.

Famous Pictures

Who painted these pictures: (373) Mona Lisa. (374) Sacred and Profane Love. (375) The Marriage at Cana of Galilee. (376) The Coming of Spring. (377) The Lesson in Anatomy. (378) The Laughing Cavalier. (379) The Blue Boy. (380) The Duchess of Milan. (381) Ulysses defying Polyphemus. (382) Beata Beatrix. (383) The Carpenter's Shop. (384) Carnation, Lily, Lily, Rose.

Light Verse

Give the proper names and titles for X and Y in the following:

(385) I am X.
  All there is to know I know it.
  I am Y.
  And what I don't know isn't knowledge.

(386) X had a love for Y
  Such as words could never utter.
  Would you know how first he met her?
  She was cutting bread and butter.

(387) The king to X sent a troop of horse,
  For Tories know no argument but force.
  With equal skill to Y books he sent,
  For Whigs admit no force but argument.

(388) While X informs the Scottish youth
  That parsons seldom tell the truth,
  Y cries
  That history is a pack of lies.

(389) X and Y
  Cupid's darts never feel.
  How different from us,
  Y and X.

(390) Says gorging X to guzzling Y,
    'I am extremely hungaree.'
    To gorging X says guzzling Y,
    'We've nothing left, us must eat we.'

(391) Will there never come a season
    Which shall rid us from the curse
    Of a prose which knows no reason
    And an unmelodious verse:

    .   .   .   .   .

    When the X cease from Y
    And the Z W no more.

(392) When they told X
    That he didn't know how to cooee,
    He replied, 'Perhaps I mayn't,
    But I do know how to paint.'

(393) In Lilac Street, where I was born,
    Two X reside,
    And one of them is pale and worn,
    While one is puffed with pride.

(394) Here lies X,
    Who to heaven might have gone,
    But didn't, when he heard the news
    That the place was run by Jews.

(395) No one can say of X
    'The sort of chap that lives in London.'

(396) X suffered fearful loss
    By putting money on a horse.
    Which he believed, if it were pressed,
    Would run far faster than the rest:
    For someone who was in the know
    Had confidently told him so.
    But on the morning of the race
    It only took the seventh place.

Technical Terms in Sport

In what sport or game do we speak of a: (397) Spinnaker. (398) Ruff. (399) Chukka. (400) Stymie. (401) Flush. (402) Capot. (403) Tufter. (404) Pitcher. (405) Wrench. (406) Googly. (407) Let. (408) Winger.

Birthplaces and Residences

What famous person was associated by birth or residence with: (409) 'Scio's rocky isle.' (410) Tarsus. (411) Macedon. (412) Monmouth. (413) Hawarden. (414) Abbotsford. (415) Gadshill. (416) Strawberry Hill. (417) Kelmscott. (418) Twickenham. (419) Apsley House. (420) The Pines, Putney.

Mathematics and Science

Of what branch of mathematics or science is this a feature: (421) Tapping rocks with little hammers. (422) Working out the ages of X and Y (and possibly Z). (423) Studying various systems of pulleys. (424) Intricate dealings with small 'd's.' (425) Gazing at heaps of stones, and reflecting how nice they must have looked once. (426) The Pons Asinorum. (427) Where 'g' has a lot to say for itself. (428) Making pictures to show how A increases (or decreases), in proportion to the rise (or fall) of B. (429) 'Shooting the sun.' (430) Mixing up things: 'Which being of the dangerous sort, Exploded with a loud report.' (431) Water, water, every, where—not necessarily undrinkable. (432) Looking at Betelgeuse and Benetnasch.

Dying Sayings

What famous English man or woman said at the point of, or at the moment of, a violent death:

(a) On the scaffold.

(433) (Removing his beard from the block) 'Pity that should be cut that has never committed treason.'

(434) (Spanning it with her hands) 'Such a little neck.'

(435) 'What matter how lies the head, so long as the heart be right.'

(b) *At the stake.*

(436) 'We shall this day light such a candle by God's grace in England as I trust shall never be put out.'

(437) 'This was the hand that wrote it, therefore it shall suffer first punishment.'

(c) *Dying of wounds received in battle.*

(438) 'Thy necessity is greater than mine.'

(439) 'Here die I . . . with a joyful and quiet mind, for that I have ended my life as a true soldier ought to do that hath fought for his country, queen, religion, and honour.'

(440) 'O Lord save my country, O Lord, be merciful to . . .

(441) 'Then I die happy.'

(442) 'I hope England will be satisfied: I hope my country will do me justice.'

(443) (Expecting shipwreck) 'We are as near to heaven by sea as by land.'

(444) (Sighting the unexpected enemy) 'Now the Lord receive our souls, for our bodies are Prince Edward's.'

Numbers

What was the number of: (445) The Muses. (446) The Graces. (447) The Valkyries (*Wagner*). (448) The Major Prophets. (449) The Major Planets (with earth). (450) The Deadly Sins. (451) The Labours of Hercules. (452) The number of days in Leap Year. (453) The Sundays after Epiphany. (454) The 'classic' races (horse). (455) The operas of Wagner. (456) The number sacred to the stethoscope.

Assassinated

These celebrated men all had the misfortune to die by the hands of murderers. Name them:

An English	(457) Prime Minister.
	(458) General.
	(459) Actor.
A French	(460) King.
	(461) Admiral.
	(462) President.
A United States	(463) President.
	(464) President (another).
	(465) President (yet another).
An Irish	(466) Chief Secretary.
	(467) Popular leader.
	(468) Cabinet Minister.

A Lot of

How should you properly define it, when you meet a largish collection of: (469) Elephants. (470) Sheep. (471) Wolves. (472) Bees. (473) Partridges. (474) Wild geese. (475) Snipe. (476) Peacocks. (477) Ordinary men. (478) Fair Ladies. (479) Convicts. (480) Angels.

Gilbert and Sullivan

Who, in the Gilbert and Sullivan operas: (481) Declared he was an intellectual chap, and thought of things that would astonish you. (482) Preferred when there was any fighting to lead his regiment from behind. (483) Possessed, at one period of his successful career, only a couple of shirts and a collar or two and a ring that looked like a ruby. (484) Was by an accident apprenticed to a pirate instead of to a pilot. (485) Was

generally considered such a disagreeable man. (486) Was a
dealer in magical spells. (487) Believed that as he took his
flowery way every one would say: 'What a particularly pure
young man that pure young man must be.' (488) Was taken
from the county jail by a set of curious chances. (489–90)
Agreed together to tell a tale of cock, tell a tale of bull.
(491) Never (well, hardly ever), said a big big D. (492) Confessed after his complete reformation (rather overdone, in fact),
that he once was a very abandoned person, making the most
of evil chances.

Dear Old Friends : The Ho⟋He⟋To's

What ancient Greek author wrote: (493) Anecdotes of the
Great, and strange stories of primitive peoples. (494) Talks
with the great Talker. (495) All about the 'wine⟋dark sea,'
and 'rosy⟋fingered Dawn.' (496) Though not a naturalist,
plays about frogs and wasps and birds. (497) In terrible
Greek of a terrible war. (498) Love in red⟋hot fragments.
(499) An adventure full of parasangs. (500) As a Greek sort
of bardic Bernard Darwin, a Plum Warner on Pegasus, a
Wallis Myers cum William Morris. (501) Heated orations.
(502) A work beloved, not necessarily in the original, by
dramatic critics. (503) Witty, irreverent dialogues. (504)
'He that fashioned the garland of poets,' and in it set 'from his
own muse some early white violets.'

Inventors and Discoverers

With what invention or scientific discovery are these famous
names associated: (505) Kepler. (506) Roger Bacon.
(507) Galileo. (508) Harvey. (509) Newton. (510) Watt.
(511) Napier. (512) Jenner. (513) Pasteur. (514) Lister.
(515) Edison. (516) Curie.

War Sayings

With what general, war, or battle, are these famous sayings associated:

(517) The scourge of God.

(518) Let the boy win his spurs.

(519) His baptism of fire.

(520) I will die in the last ditch.

(521) War is hell.

(522) Trust in God, and keep your powder dry.

(523) An army marches on its stomach.

(524) General Janvier and General Février.

(525) The whole line will advance.

(526) Veni, vidi, vici.

(527) The whole earth is the sepulchre of brave men.

(528) Return with your shields or on them.

Anecdotes of Kings

What English monarch is recalled by a story about : (529) Fair Rosamond. (530) Roses. (531) An oak. (532) Wash. (533) Cakes. (534) Lampreys. (535) Sea-shore. (536) Arrow. (537) An incorruptible Chief Justice. (538) His minstrel's voice. (539) 'The little gentleman in brown velvet.' (540) Death.

'I have supp'd Full with Horrors'

Name the famous play, or its author, that treats of:

(541) A woman murders her husband on his return home from his great war.

(542) A woman murders her children, and the bride by whom her husband is proposing to replace her.

(543) A man murders his wife and then commits suicide.

(544) The murder of an English king by order of his wife.

(545) A woman and her lover get her husband murdered by two ruffians, but are brought to justice.

(546) The murder of an Italian great lady (and her family), by order of her brothers.

(547) The trial of an Italian count for wife-murder.[1]

(548) The murder of an incestuous Italian count by his children.

(549) A man discovers that his wife is his own mother.

(550) A woman falls in love with her stepson.

(551) The fatal passion of a brother and sister.

(552) A woman and her lover go out to commit suicide in the same way and place as his wife had done it.

Poets and the Moon

What poet sings thus about the moon:

(553) The moving moon went up the sky,
      And nowhere did abide;
    Softly she was going up,
      And a star or two beside.

(554) Till a silence fell with the waking bird,
      And a hush with the setting moon.

(555) The moon doth with delight
    Look round her when the heavens are bare.

(556) In the moonlight the shepherds,
    Soft lull'd by the rills,
    Lie wrapt in their blankets
    Asleep on the hills.

(557) And haply the Queen-Moon is on her throne,
      Cluster'd around by all her starry Fays.

[1] This is not a play but a long poem; only it fits in here so well.

(558)   I walk unseen
        On the dry smooth/shaven green,
        To behold the wand'ring moon,
        Riding near her highest noon.

(559) Of this green and darkling spot,
        Latticed from the moon's beams,
        Perchance a distant dreamer dreams.

(560) That orbèd maiden with white fire laden,
           Whom mortals call the moon,
        Glides glimmering o'er my fleece/like floor,
           By the midnight breezes strewn.

(561) Lady, by yonder blessed moon I swear,
        That tips with silver all these fruit/tree tops. . .

(562) The sun was gone now; the curled moon
           Was like a little feather
        Fluttering far down the gulf.

(563) I saw the new moon late yestreen
           Wi' the auld moon in her arm.

(564) The moon was shining sulkily,
           Because she thought the sun
        Had got no business to be there
           After the day was done.

Persons' Names for Things—Modern

Give the name of the man of quite modern times from whom
is derived each of these words in common use, as expressing:
(565) A species of boot. (566) A species of intoxicating
drink. (567) A species of two / wheeled horse vehicle.
(568) A species of quick/firing gun. (569) A species of shell.
(570) A species of raincoat. (571) A process of editing certain

books so as to render them suitable pabulum for the young and innocent. (572) A process of hypnotic suggestion. (573) A process of reducing or keeping down one's weight. (574) A process of improving the surface of roads. (575) A process of isolating or 'sending to Coventry.' (576) A guardian of our laws and public morals.

What are in Sport?

Explain shortly what are, or were, and in relation to what sport or game they are famous: (577) The Soarer. (578) The Croucher. (579) The Quorn. (580) The 'Alps.' (581) The Prophet. (582) The Chains. (583) The Dedans. (584) The Portland. (585) The Long Reach. (586) The Rowley Mile. (587) The Blues. (588) The Babes.

Poets and Ladies

What poet specialized in singing the praises (not necessarily to the exclusion of all others) of a lady called: (589) Heliodora. (590) Lesbia. (591) Corinna. (592) Beatrice. (593) Laura. (594) Stella. (595) Lucasta. (596) Julia. (597) Celia. (598) Mary. (599) Lucy. (600) Rose.

Killed in Battle

What gallant soldier fell at the battle of: (601) Amphipolis. (602) Mantinea. (603) The Metaurus. (604) Evesham. (605) Ravenna. (606) Lützen. (607) Ticonderoga. (608) Marengo. (609) Aspern-Essling. (610) Ciudad Rodrigo. (611) Waterloo. (612) Chancellorsville.

Political Sayings

Name the statesman who invented, or made popular, these sayings or catchwords:

(613) Take away that bauble.

(614) They are ringing the bells now; they will soon be wringing their hands.

(615) I know that I can save this country, and that no one else can.

(616) England has saved herself by her courage and she will save Europe by her example.

(617) I have called in the New World to redress the balance of the Old.

(618) Peace with honour.

(619) Intoxicated with the exuberance of his own verbosity.

(620) A cold and calculated lie.

(621) A terminological inexactitude.

(622) Wait and see.

(623) Ninepence for fourpence.

(624) My spiritual home.

Dates

What feasts, or great events, are celebrated or commemorated on these days: (625) 30th January. (626) 17th March. (627) 23rd April. (628) 24th May. (629) 18th June. (630) 4th July. (631) 15th July. (632) 4th August. (633) 12th August. (634) 21st October. (635) 11th November. (636) 30th November.

Fiction

What person, in a famous novel in English, was remarkable for : (637) Maintaining a persistently hopeful view of his future. (638) Eventually marrying the mother of his first love. (639) Declared that his foot was upon his native heath and his name was Macgregor. (640) Asked his friend: 'Am I no a bonny fechter?' (641) Was fond of describing his battles in Flanders. (642) Prided himself on his knowledge of the correct deportment of 'elegant females' when proposed to.

(643) Was always talking about an imaginary lady-friend.
(644) Had a partiality for old port, taken advantage of by his
prospective son-in-law. (645) Swanking about a 'barouche-
landau.' (646) Advised his son to beware of widows.
(647) Was arrested on Stonehenge for murder. (648) Firmly
married a diffident gentleman from the Five Towns.

Aquarium

(649) I sent a message to the fish:
    I told them 'This is what I wish.'
    The little fishes of the sea
    They sent an answer back to me.
    The little fishes' answer was . . .?

(650) What did Smee find inside the mouth of the crocodile,
    and how did he explain its presence to Starkey?

(651) On June the seventh, after dark,
    A young and very hungry shark
        Came crawling up the side.
    It ate . . . and . . .;   *Who were the victims?*

(652) 'Will you walk a little faster?' said a whiting to a
    snail;   *Why?*

(653) On Peter's portion oysters grew—a delicacy rare.
    But oysters were a delicacy Peter couldn't bear.
    On Somers' side were turtle, on the shingle lying thick,
    Which Somers couldn't eat, because it always made
        him sick.

*What constrained these two men, sharing a desert island between
    them, to waste its dainties thus?*

(654) Lithe limbs curling free as a creeper
     That creeps in a desolate place,
To enrol and envelop the sleeper
     In a silent and stealthy embrace;
Cruel beak craning forward to bite us,
     Our juices to drain and to drink,
Or to whelm us in waves of Cocytus,
        Indelible ink!

The poem Octopus, *of which this is a verse, is a parody of ?*

(655) She sighed, 'It is fit fit fitter
     He should love my glit glit glitter,
        Than his heart fling away
        On the butterflies gay,
Or the birds that twit twit twitter.'

Where does this ditty of The Amorous Goldfish *come from?*

(656) Yet you balanced an eel on the end of your nose,
     Do you think at your age it was right?

Who performed this feat?

(657)   All along the backwater
       Through the rushes tall,
       Ducks are a dabbling,
       Up tails all!
       Ducks' tails, drakes' tails,
       Yellow feet a quiver,
       Yellow bills all out of sight
       Busy in the river!

Who sang this Ducks' Ditty?

(658) I wind about, and in and out,
     With here a blossom sailing,
And here and there a lusty trout,
     And here and there a grayling.

Who speaks?

(659) Beyond the shadow of the ship
    I watched the water-snakes:
    They moved in tracks of shining white,
    And when they rear'd, the elfish light
    Fell off in hoary flakes.
Who is the speaker?

(660) But more than mundane weeds are there,
    And mud, celestially fair,
    Fat caterpillars drift around
    And Paradisal worms are found . . .
    And, in that heaven of all their wish,
    There shall be no more land, say fish.
Who wrote this picture of a fish's heaven?

Boths in Families

Give the family name of: (661) Brother and sister, both poets (great). (662) Husband and wife, both poets (great) (663) Two sisters, both novelists. (664) Two brothers, both novelists. (665) Father and daughter, both novelists. (666). Husband and wife, both novelists. (667) Three brothers, all novelists. (668) Father and two sons, all actors. (669) Parents, son, and daughter, all actors. (670) Two sisters, both actors. (671) Two brothers, both singers. (672) Husband and wife, both singers.

Flowers

What flower is by nature, art, or chance, associated in the mind with the idea of: (673) England; home; and beauty. (674) Sleep. (675) Conservative leanings. (676) France. (677) Modesty. (678) Remembrance. (679) Japan. (680) Holland. (681) First signs of spring. (682) Wordsworth— 10,000 of them. (683) Sweet-smelling bags. (684) 'Wan that hang the pensive head.'

An Alphabet

Who are, or were, in fact or fiction?:

(685) Anthony Absolute.

(686) Betty Balfour.

(687) Charles Conder.

(688) Daniel Deronda.

(689) Edward Elgar.

(690) Frank Fairleigh.

(691) George Graves.

(692) Harold Hilton.

(693) Isaac Isaacs.

(694) Jack Jones.

(695) Kubla Khan.

(696) Lotte Lehmann.

(697) Maurice Maeterlinck.

(698) Newman Noggs.

(699) Oliver Onions.

(700) Percy Perrin.

(701) Ronald Ross.

(702) Sacheverell Sitwell.

(703) Thomas Traherne.

(704) Vesta Victoria.

(705) Walt Whitman.

(706) Xer⁄Xes.

(707) Y.Y. [pen⁄name]

(708) Z.Z. [pen⁄name]

Familiar Quotations in Verse

Who first started us all saying :

(709) Fools rush in where angels fear to tread.

(710) God made the country, and man made the town.

(711) Music hath charms to soothe a savage breast.

(712) Compound for sins they are inclined to
By damning those they have no mind to.

(713)   Where ignorance is bliss,
'Tis folly to be wise.

(714) Casting a dim religious light.

(715) In the spring a young man's fancy lightly turns to
thoughts of love.

(716) 'Tis distance lends enchantment to the view.

(717) A thing of beauty is a joy for ever.

(718) And all went merry as a marriage-bell.

(719)   And still the wonder grew
That one small head could carry all he knew.

(720) The still sad music of humanity.

Dear Old Friends : The Hic-Haec-Hoc's

What ancient Latin author wrote:

(721) How 'Omnia Gallia' is, as the Irishman put it,
quartered into three halves.

(722) Shocking scandals about gods and goddesses.

(723) At great length about old age.

(724) Of 'the gods who haunt
The lucid interspace of world and world.'

(725) The history of Rome in umpty books (but still
unfinished).

(726) A beano at a profiteer's.

(727) Elegant verses about Lalage (sweetly smiling, sweetly
speaking), and other fair ladies.

(728) A work that Mr David Garnett would, no doubt,
have entitled 'Gentleman into Ass.'

(729) Satires, not always translatable.

(730) 'At pius Aeneas,' and so on.

(731) Bovrilled history.

(732) 'That "Ave atque Vale" of the poet's hopeless woe,
Tenderest of Roman poets nineteen hundred years ago.'

Famous Songs

What war, battle, or outbreak is recalled by, or celebrated in, these songs: (733) The Song of Taillefer. (734) Lilliburlero. (735) Bonny Dundee. (736) Malbrouck s'en va t en guerre. (737) Charley is my Darling. (738) The Marseillaise. (739) The Wearing of the Green. (740) Farewell and Adieu to you, fair Spanish ladies. (741) Maryland, my Maryland. (742) The Watch on the Rhine. (743) The Absent minded Beggar. (744) Keep the Home Fires burning.

Coins

Of what country are, or were, these coins or money tokens: (745) Anna. (746) Drachma. (747) Guilder. (748) Krone. (749) Lira. (750) Maravedi. (751) Medjidie. (752) Reis. (753) Rouble. (754) Tael. (755) Thaler. (756) Yen.

Astronomical

A. *Name the planet that :*
   (757) Is nearest the sun.
   (758) Is only visible about dawn or twilight.
   (759) Has famous moons.
   (760) Has famous rings.

B. *Name the star that is :*
   (761) Called the Dog Star.
   (762) The brightest star invisible in England.

C. *Name the constellation that :*
   (763) Looks like a plough.
   (764) Has a great 'belt.'

D. *Name the best known :*
   (765) Cluster of small stars.
   (766) Variable star.
   (767) Comet.
   (768) Summer shower of meteors.

Poems on Birds

What bird is spoken of in the following:
(769) . . . with lively din
    Scatters the rear of darkness thin.

(770) . . . he sings each song twice over,
    Lest you should think he never could recapture
    The first fine careless rapture.

(771) The wrinkled sea beneath him crawls;
    He watches from his mountain walls,
    And like a thunderbolt he falls.

(772) . . . on every tree
    Mocks married men, for thus sings he.

(773) . . . did ever chaunt
        So sweetly to reposing bands
    Of travellers in some shady haunt
        Among Arabian sands.

(774) . . . did follow
    And every day for food or play
        Came to the mariners' hollo.

(775) Proud Maisie is in the wood
        Walking so early;
    . . . sits on the bush
        Singing so rarely.

(776) . . . all that ever was
    Joyous and clear and fresh, thy music doth surpass.

(777) . . . what a boy you are;
    How you do go it!
Blowing your bugle to that one sweet star—
    How you do blow it!

(778) . . . doth to the moon complain
    Of such as, wandering near her secret bower,
    Molest her ancient solitary reign.

(779) Ye 'll sit on his white hause bane,
    And I 'll pick out his bonny blue een:
    Wi' ae lock of his gowden hair
    We 'll theek our nest when it grows bare.

(780) We saw . . . gathering in the sky,
    And in the osier isle we heard them noise.

Tales and Legends of Animals

A. What animals correspond to the 'were wolf' of European legend and superstition in: (781) Malaya. (782) Japan. (783) Nigeria.

B. What poet: (784) Used to keep tame hares, and write letters about them. (785) Wrote a poem about the drowning of a pet cat in a bowl of goldfishes. (786) Called a mouse a 'wee, sleekit, cow'rin, tim'rous beastie.' (787) Kept a wombat (and other strange creatures) in his Chelsea garden.

C. (788) What Roman general had a tame fawn? (789) Why were geese much respected in Rome? (790) What did the Roman admiral say when he threw overboard the sacred fowls (who were off their feed)? (791) What animal is the clever 'Brer Rabbit,' as is were, of Malay States fable? (792) What animal, according to the showman, gets its name, partly on account of its immense pecooniary value and partly 'cos of being mentioned in Holy Writ?

What the D——?

What do these queer names suggest to you: (793) Atahualpa. (794) Borogove. (795) Gazeka. (796) Gugnunc. (797) Iddon. (798) Jix. (799) Kilimanjaro. (800) Minnehaha. (801) Pobble. (802) Tarazed. (803) Thark. (804) Tishy.

Women and Murder

What relation or connection did each of these ladies (real and imaginary) perhaps kill, help to kill, or encourage the killing of: (805) Althaea. (806) Electra. (807) Jocasta. (808) Madeline Smith. (809) Constance Kent. (810) Edith Thompson. (811) Goneril. (812) Hetty Sorel. (813) Tess Durbeyfield. (814) Queen Mary. (815) Mary Queen of Scots. (816) Catherine de' Medici (a miss-fire).

Fleet Street Gossip

We know that our conversation is largely in Latin and French phrases. This dialogue will sound much more natural and English when you translate the bits in inverted commas: (817) Well, Jones has given the papers a 'dainty morsel.' (French.) (818) Old Jones! 'Wonderful to relate.' (Latin.) (819) They gave him 'a nasty time of it' in the witness-box. (F.) (820) Oh, we must take the reports 'with a grain of salt.' (L.) (821) Yes, but 'he who excuses himself accuses himself.' (F.) (822) I suppose he was 'in his senses'? (L.) (823) 'Between ourselves,' Mrs —— (F.) (824) Ah, 'the source and origin'! (L.) (825) Exactly. 'Hence these tears.' (L.) (826) So, this was only 'just by way of something to do.' (F.) (827) That's it. 'For lack of better.' (F.) (828) Dear, dear! What an 'unfortunate occurrence'! (F.)

The Goldens

Explain briefly—all are terrestrial: (829) The Golden Gate. (830) The Golden Horn. (831) The Golden Fleece. (832) The Golden Calf. (833) The Golden Hind. (834) The Golden Ass. (835) The Golden Image. (836) The Golden Bough. (837) The Golden Legend. (838) The Golden Vanity. (839) The Golden Treasury. (840) The Golden City.

Artists

Name the artist famous for, or in connection with: (841) The Parthenon. (842) The Sistine Chapel at Rome. (843) The Cathedral Tower at Florence. (844) St Paul's Cathedral. (845). The Burghers of Calais Group. (846) Portraits of Spanish grandees. (847) Portraits of the Court of Charles I. (848) Portraits of the Court of Charles II. (849) Portraits of Lady Hamilton. (850) Pictures of well-nourished young girls with lambs and things. (851) Liverpool Cathedral. (852) The Cenotaph at Whitehall.

The Soul of Wit

Who were the authors of these epigrams:

(853) On parent knees, a naked new-born child,
      Weeping thou sat'st, while all around thee smil'd;
      So live, that sinking in thy last long sleep,
      Calm thou mayst smile while all around thee weep.

(854) Nature and Nature's laws lay hid in night;
      God said, 'Let Newton be,' and all was light.

(855) It did not last: the Devil, howling 'Ho!
      Let Einstein be!' restored the *status quo*.

(856) The Devil, having nothing else to do,
  Went off to tempt My Lady Poltagrue.
  My lady, tempted by a private whim,
  To his extreme annoyance, tempted him.

(857) Venus, take my votive glass;
  Since I am not what I was,
  What from this day I shall be,
  Venus, let me never see.

(858) Jealous, I own it, I was once,
  That wickedness I here renounce.
  I tried at wit . . . it would not do . . .
  At tenderness . . . that failed me too.
  Before me on each path there stood
  The witty and the tender Hood.

(859) I, rapt in scrutiny as Night unbars
  The thick and mazy glories of the stars,
  Though earth on Earth, no more am linked to her,
  But sit in Jove's own hall a banqueter.

(860) Thou wert the morning star among the living,
  Ere thy fair light had fled;
  Now, having died, thou art as Hesperus giving
  New splendour to the dead.

(861) The sun may set and rise;
  But we, contrariwise,
  Sleep after our short light
  One everlasting night.

(862) May! Be thou never graced with birds that sing,
  Nor Flora's pride!
  In thee all flowers and roses spring.
  Mine only died.

(863) A shipwrecked seaman, buried on this coast,
       Bids you set sail;
   Full many a gallant ship, when we were lost,
       Weathered the gale.

(864)   TO THE BABE NIVA

Niva, Child of Innocence,
   Dust to dust *we* go:
Thou, when Winter wooed thee hence,
   Wentest snow to snow.

Sayings of Frenchmen

To whom are these famous sayings attributed:

A. *Of French kings:*

(865) 'Well, then kill them all, that not a single man may
be left to reproach me.' (866) Looking down on the dead
body of his hated subject, just killed by his order: 'My God,
how tall he is!' (867) 'Paris is worth a Mass.' (868) L'État
c'est moi.' (869) 'Après moi le déluge.' (870) After his
trial, to his advocate: 'What am I to do for all these poor
clerks who laboured so hard for me. I have nothing.' (The
fine answer was: *Embrassez-les.*)

B. *Of French women:*

(871) They asked the queen, when the ship was likely to
be a wreck, if they should arouse her children. 'No,' said she,
'you shall not wake them, nor dress them, Let them go to
God sleeping.' (872) 'Most noble Dauphin, I have come
on the part of God to help you, you and your kingdom.'
(873) 'O Liberty, what crimes are committed in thy name!'
(On her way to execution.)

C. *Of men of the Revolution:*

(874) 'If there had been no God, we should have been
obliged to invent Him.' (875) 'Il nous faut de l'audace,
et encore de l'audace, et toujours de l'audace.' (876) 'A whiff
of grape-shot.'

What Happened At?

What important events give fame to these otherwise not very important places: (877) Appamatox. (878) Baylen. (879) Domremy. (880) Lexington. (881) Plataea. (882) Sarajevo. (883) Saratoga. (884) Tilsit. (885) Torbay. (886) Varennes. (887) Valmy. (888) Vereeniging.

ANSWERS TO THE CHRISTMAS QUIZ

MEN AS BEASTS

(1) Bear. (2) Cat. (3) Goose. (4) Duck. (5) Tiger. (6) Rabbit. (7) Wolf. (8) Fox. (9) Dog. (10) Horse. (11) Lion. (12) Mouse.

TREES

(13) Oak. (14) Mahogany. (15) Walnut. (16) Bay. (17) Birch. (18) Willow. (19) Cedar. (20) Eucalyptus. (21) Beech. (22) Maple. (23) Yew. (24) Ash.

OPERAS

(25) Mozart. (26) Bizet. (27) Saint-Saëns. (28) Verdi. (29) Puccini. (30) Strauss. (31) Meyerbeer. (32) Gluck. (33) Donizetti. (34) Gounod. (35) Rossini. (36) Leon-cavallo.

BATTLES

(37) Lewes. (38) Poictiers. (39) Bosworth, or Hastings. (40) Flodden. (41) Dettingen. (42) Worcester. (43) Pavia (Francis I). (44) Quebec. (45) Thermopylae. (46) Waterloo (saying doubtful). (47) Balaclava (Charge of Light Brigade). (48) Cyzicus (the Spartan dispatch).

OLD TESTAMENT ANIMALS

(49) Daniel. (50) Elisha. (51) Balaam. (52) Abraham. (53) Jacob. (54) Joseph. (55) Samson. (56) Aaron. (57) Moses. (58) Elijah. (59) Noah. (60) Jonah.

FAMILIAR EXPRESSIONS

(61) Caesar's decisive act of rebellion against the Roman Senate was when he crossed the boundary river Rubicon, in north of Italy. (62) A king in Asia Minor in early Greek history, of fabulous wealth. (63) The tyrant of Syracuse had a sword suspended by a thread over Damocles' head at a banquet, to show him that being a tyrant was not such fun as he thought. (64) The Parthian horsemen shot their arrows with greatest effect in flight. (65) The friends who came to sympathize with Job in his troubles only aggravated them. (66) The prophet's parable of the Poor Man and the Rich, by which he denounced David for his treatment of Uriah. (67) The parable of the Prodigal Son and his great welcome home by his father. (68) The fatal, mysterious writing, fore-telling the downfall of Babylonian Empire. (69) The Pale was ring of defence containing the Anglo-Irish settlements near Dublin. Without were the native 'savages.' (70) Cortez in invading Mexico burnt his boats that his men might not retreat. (71) Perhaps a Newgate phrase for the road to execu-tion at Tyburn: perhaps from setting of sun. (72) Phrase used by Nelson of his captains, but originated in Henry V's great speech before Agincourt (Shakespeare).

CLASSICAL SAYINGS

(73) Themistocles. (74) Cleon. (75) Alcibiades. (76) Theramenes. (77) Socrates. (78) The Greek army of Xenophon. (79) Marius. (80) Pompeius Magnus. (81) Sulla. (82) Julius Caesar. (83) Tiberius. (84) Nero.

CAPTAINS AND KINGS

(85) Cromwell (*Milton*). (86) Shaftesbury (*Dryden*). (87) William Pitt (*Scott*). (88) Charles I (*Marvell*). (89) Charles II (*Rochester*). (90) George III (*Shelley*). (91) Marlborough (*Addison*). (92) Napoleon (*Browning*). (93) Wellington (*Tennyson*). (94) Thomas Clarkson (*Wordsworth*). (95) Florence Nightingale (*Longfellow*). (96) Father Damien (*Father Tabb*).

SURNAMES

(97) Newton. (98) Reynolds. (99) Wren. (100) O'Brien. (101) Davy. (102) Hamilton. (103) Harty. (104) Shovell. (105) Raffles. (106) Harris. (107) Wood. (108) Impey.

SHIPS

(109) 'The Fighting Téméraire,' of Turner's painting. (110) 'The Saucy Arethusa,' frigate in old song. (111) Duel with U.S.A. 'Chesapeake.' (112) Duel with Northern States ironclad, 'Monitor.' (113) Southern States privateer, built in England, sunk by Northern States 'Kearsage.' (114) U.S.A. battleship, sunk off Cuba, starting war with Spain. (115) Troopship sunk at sea; fine conduct of troops. (116) Flagship of Sir George Tryon commanding Mediterranean Fleet, sunk in collison. (117) Atlantic liner, sunk by iceberg. (118) Australian cruiser, sank German 'Emden.' (119) British cruiser, sunk at Coronel. (120) British battleship, sunk at Jutland, flying flag of Admiral Hood.

CHURCHMEN

(121) First English historian. (122) Great archbishop under Henry I. (123) Only English pope. (124) Great preacher and Bible-reader. (125) Founded Winchester College. (126) Translated Bible into English. (127) Dean of

St Paul's; great scholar and preacher. (128) Dean of St
Paul's; great scholar and poet. (129) Wrote *Ecclesiastical
Polity*. (130) Archbishop under Charles I; beheaded.
(131) Wrote Butler's *Analogy*. (132) Leader of Oxford
Movement; went over to Rome; wrote *Apologia*.

SWEETHEARTS AND COMRADES

(133) Helen. (134) Andromeda. (135) Thisbe. (136)
Aspasia. (137) Francesca. (138) Melisande, or Etarre.
(139) Theseus. (140) Achilles. (141) Orestes. (142) Damon.
(143) Epaminondas. (144) Arcite.

ZOOLOGY

(145) 'There was a young lady of Riga,' etc.
(146) 'I had an aunt in Yucatan,
    Who,' etc.
      (*More Beasts for Worse Children*, by H. Belloc.)
(147) The Owl and the Pussy-cat.
             (*Nonsense Rhymes*, by E. Lear.)
(148) A French showman in a long rhyme about his
    animals. Author unknown; dates back to 1826.
(149) John Gilpin to his horse.
(150) *The Modern Traveller*, by H. Belloc.
(151) 'She gives me cream with all her might,
    To eat with apple tart.'
    (*A Child's Garden of Verses*, by R. L. Stevenson.)
(152) 'Because if I use leaden ones, his hide is sure to
    flatten 'em.'
      (*The Bad Child's Book of Beasts*, by H. Belloc.)
(153) 'For why, he has a coat of hair.
    I wish I had one too!'   (As in 152.)
(154) 'To see Such quantities of sand.'
(155) 'Soup of the Evening, Beautiful Soup.'

(156) 'The man recovered of the bite.
          The dog it was that died.'
                    (*Elegy on a Mad Dog,* by O. Goldsmith.)

DELICACIES

(157) Oysters. (158) Jam. (159) Ham. (160) Chocolate and cocoa. (161) Rum. (162) Gin. (163) Figs. (164)
Oranges. (165) Turkish delight. (166) Toffee. (167) Biscuits.
(168) Marmalade.

SHAKESPEARE'S PLAYS

(169) Macbeth. (170) A Midsummer Night's Dream.
(171) The Tempest. (172) As You Like It. (173) A Comedy
of Errors. (174) Twelfth Night. (175) Much Ado about
Nothing. (176) Hamlet. (177) The Merchant of Venice.
(178) Othello, or Cymbeline. (179) Romeo and Juliet.
(180) Julius Caesar, or Richard III.

CHIVALRY AND MAGIC

(181) Spenser, 'The Faerie Queene.' (182) Browning,
'Childe Roland.' (183) Keats, 'La Belle Dame sans Merci.'
(184) Coleridge, 'Christabel.' (185) D. G. Rossetti, 'Sister
Helen.' (186) Swinburne, 'Tristram and Iseult.' (187)
William Morris, 'Defence of Guinevere.' (188) Tennyson,
'The Lady of Shalott.' (189) Arnold, 'The Forsaken Mer-
man.' (190) James Hogg, 'Kilmeny.' (191) Christina
Rossetti, 'Goblin Market.' (192) W. B. Yeats, 'The Countess
Cathleen.'

TWO MEN, SAME NAME

(193) Robert Cecil. (194) John Ball. (195) Edward
Seymour. (196) George Stephenson. (197) Thomas Hardy.
(198) William Pitt. (199) Walter Raleigh. (200) Samuel
Butler. (201) Walter Scott. (202) Thomas Jackson. (203)
Winston Churchill. (204) Robert Herrick.

BIBLICAL SLAYERS

(205) The Egyptian taskmaster. (206) Eglon. (207) Agag. (208) Uriah or Goliath. (209) Amnon. (210) Zimri. (211) His daughter. (212) Absalom. (213) Ahaziah, or Jezebel, or Jehoram. (214) Sisera. (215) Naboth. (216) Holofernes.

RIVALS

(217) Aristides. (218) Scipio Africanus Major. (219) Marius. (220) Charles the Bold, of Burgundy. (221) Charles V, of Spain. (222) Pizarro. (223) Condé. (224) Prince Eugene. (225) Fox. (226) Canning. (227) Metternich, or Fouché. (228) Mazzini, or Victor Emmanuel.

FAMILIAR QUOTATIONS IN PROSE

(229) Sterne. (230) Steele. (231) Burke. (232) Bacon. (233) Farquhar. (234) Johnson. (235) Scott. (236) Swift. (237) Lincoln. (238) Shakespeare (Falstaff). (239) Dickens (Captain Cuttle). (240) Napoleon (probably nor original).

TITLES AND NICKNAMES

(241) The Earl of Warwick. (242) James I. (243) William Pitt, the Elder. (244) The Prince Regent, (George IV). (245) George Washington. (246) William Pitt, the Younger. (247) Louis XIV. (248) Louis XV. (249) Napoleon. (250) Marshal Ney. (251) Marshal Masséna. (252) The Chevalier Bayard.

COLOURS IN TITLES

(253) Red. (254) White. (255) Scarlet. (256) Green. (257) Blue. (258) Black. (259) Purple. (260) Pink. (261) Lilac. (262) Crimson. (263) Yellow. (264) Grey.

TRIOS

(265) Ham and Japheth. (266) Dick and Harry. (267) Squeak and Wilfred. (268) Meshach and Abed-nego. (269) Caesar and Crassus. (270) Porthos and Aramis. (271) Braid and Taylor. (272) Learoyd and Ortheris. (273) Azarias and Misael. (274) The Tatler and The By-stander. (275) Emily and Anne. (276) Minting and The Bard.

TAKE YOUR CHOICE

(277-9) *The Seven Wonders of the World :* The Hanging Gardens of Babylon. The Pyramids. The Pharos of Alex-andria. The Mausoleum of Halicarnassus. The Temple of Diana at Ephesus. The Colossus of Rhodes. The Statue of Zeus by Phidias.

(280-2) *The Seven Cities of Asia :* Ephesus. Pergamos. Sardis. Thyatira. Smyrna. Philadelphia. Laodicea.

(283-5) *The Nine Muses :* Calliope. Clio. Erato. Euterpe. Melpomene. Polyhymnia. Terpsichore. Thalia. Urania.

(286-8) *The Twelve Signs of the Zodiac :* Aries. Taurus. Gemini. Cancer. Leo. Virgo. Libra. Scorpio. Sagittarius. Capricornus. Aquarius. Pisces.

NAMES FOR KINGS

(289) Beauclerc. (290) Cœur-de-lion. (291) Lackland. (292) Longshanks. (293) Crookback. (294) Bluff King Hal. (295) Good Queen Bess, or Gloriana, or the Virgin Queen. (296) The Martyr. (297) Old Rowley. (298) Farmer George. (299) The Sailor King. (300) The Peace-maker.

A MIXED BAG

(301) Part of the Jewish high priest's breastplate. (302) Rivers of Damascus. (303) A final potation. (304) The nine of diamonds. On the back of this card the order for

the massacre of Glencoe is said to have been written. (305) Species of motor-car. (306) Species of golf ball. (307) Rose. (308) Fishing fly. (309) A kill of birds with both barrels. (310) A glass of beer. (311) Station for broadcasting. (312) A species of pear.

COUPLES

(313) Comic couple on drawn films. (314) Compiled Greek lexicon. (315) Murderers and body-snatchers. (316) 'Codlin's the friend, not Short.' Showman in Dickens's *Old Curiosity Shop*. (317) Found guilty of murder in U.S. riots. (318) Early Saxon invaders of Britain. (319) Giants in Wagner's *Rhinegold*. (320) Names used in legal documents. (321) Pretenders to the throne of Henry VII. (322) Inseparable courtiers in *Hamlet*. (323) Pluralist newspaper owners. (324) Comic Jew partners in American plays.

ANIMALS NAMED

(325) Alexander's horse. (326) Don Quixote's horse. (327) Mongoose in *The Jungle Book*. (328) Autobiographical horse in famous story. (329) Dog in Galsworthy's *Country House*. (330) Brünnhilde's horse. (331) Black panther in *The Jungle Book*. (332) Great film-actor dog. (333) Offered by Sir Andrew Aguecheek to get out of his duel with Viola. (334) Whale hunted by Captain Ahab in novel. (335) Teddy-bear friend of Christopher Robin. (336) Cat in *The Blue Bird*.

NATIONAL HEROES

(337) Alfred the Great. (338) Brian Boru. (339) William Wallace. (340) Llewellyn the Great, or Owen Glendower. (341) Bertrand de Guesclin. (342) William Tell. (343) The Cid. (344) Sarsfield. (345) Robert Emmet, or Lord Edward Fitzgerald. (346) Garibaldi. (347) Brutus. (348) Harmodius and Aristogeiton.

A DAY IN LONDON

(349) Toys. (350) Books. (351) Ladies' gowns, etc. (352) Men's tailor. (353) Men's hats. (354) Jewellers. (355) Hairdresser. (356) Fish lunch, crabs, etc. (357) Theatre tickets. (358) Restaurant. (359) Books (mostly English). (360) Books (mostly French).

STRANGE PHENOMENA IN O.T.

(361) Joshua. (362) Hezekiah. (363) Elijah. (364) Moses. (365) The three Jews (see Ans. 268). (366) Elisha. (367) Samuel. (368) Abraham. (369) Naaman. (370) Gehazi. (371) Nebuchadnezzar. (372) Belshazzar.

FAMOUS PICTURES

(373) Leonardo da Vinci. (374) Titian. (375) Paul Veronese. (376) Botticelli. (377) Rembrandt. (378) Franz Hals. (379) Gainsborough. (380) Holbein. (381) Turner. (382) Rossetti. (383) Millais. (384) Sargent.

LIGHT VERSE

(385) 'I am the reverend Dr Jowett.'
      'I am the Master of Balliol College.'
(386) 'Werther had a love for Charlotte.'
(387) Oxford. Cambridge.
(388) Froude. The Rev. Canon Kingsley.
(389) 'Miss Buss and Miss Beale.' (Principals of Chelten-
      ham Ladies' College.)
(390) Jack. Jimmy. (Thackeray.)
(391) 'When the Rudyards cease from kipling
      And the Haggards ride no more.' (J. K. Stephen.)
(392) Cimabue. (E. C. Bentley.)
(393) Two clergymen. (The Vicar and The Rector.
      A. P. Herbert.)

(394) G. K. Chesterton. (Humbert Wolfe.)
(395) Mr Blunden. ('Tally Ho.' J. J. Morton.)
(396) Lord Hippo. ('More Peers.' H. Belloc.)

TECHNICAL TERMS IN SPORT

(397) Yachting. (398) Bridge. (399) Polo. (400) Golf.
(401) Poker. (402) Piquet. (403) Stag-hunting. (404) Base-
ball. (405) Coursing. (406) Cricket. (407) Lawn tennis.
(408) Rugby football.

BIRTHPLACES AND RESIDENCES

(409) Homer. (410) St Paul. (411) Alexander. (412)
Henry V. (413) Gladstone. (414) Sir Walter Scott. (415)
Dickens. (416) Horace Walpole. (417) William Morris.
(418) Pope. (419) Wellington. (420) Swinburne.

MATHEMATICS AND SCIENCE

(421) Geology. (422) Algebra. (423) Statics. (424) Differ-
ential calculus. (425) Archaeology. (426) Geometry.
(427) Dynamics. (428) Graphs. (429) Navigation. (430)
Chemistry. (431) Hydraulics. (432) Astronomy.

DYING SAYINGS

(433) Sir Thomas More. (434) Lady Jane Grey. (435)
Sir Walter Raleigh. (436) Latimer. (437) Cranmer. (438)
Sir Philip Sidney. (439) Sir Richard Grenville. (440)
Hampden. (441) Wolfe. (442) Sir John Moore. (443)
Sir Humphrey Gilbert. (444) Simon de Montfort.

NUMBERS

(445) Nine. (446) Three. (447) Nine. (448) Four.
(449) Eight. (450) Seven. (451) Twelve. (452) Three
hundred and sixty-six. (453) Six. (454) Five. (455) Eleven.
(456) Ninety-nine.

ASSASSINATED

(457) Mr Percival.   (458) Sir Henry Wilson.   (459) William Terriss.   (460) Henry III, or Henry IV.   (461) Coligny.   (462) Carnot.   (463) Lincoln.   (464) Garfield. (465) McKinley.   (466) Lord Frederick Cavendish.   (467) Michael Collins.   (468) Kevin O'Higgins.

A LOT OF

(469) Herd.   (470) Flock.   (471) Pack.   (472) Swarm. (473) Covey.   (474) Gaggle.   (475) Wisp.   (476) Muster. (477) Crowd.   (478) Bevy.   (479) Gang.   (480) Host.

GILBERT AND SULLIVAN

(481) Private Willis, in *Iolanthe*.   (482) Duke of Plaza-Toro, in *Gondoliers*.   (483) The Judge, in *Trial by Jury*. (484) Frederick, in *The Pirates of Penzance*.   (485) King Gama, in *Princess Ida*.   (486) John Wellington Wells, in *The Sorcerer*.   (487) Bunthorne, in *Patience*.   (488) Koko, in *The Mikado*.   (489-90) Jack Point, the jester, and Wilfred Shadbolt, the jailer, in *Yeoman of the Guard*.   (491) The Captain of *H.M.S. Pinafore*.   (492) Sir Rupert Murgatroyd, in *Ruddigore*.

DEAR OLD FRIENDS: THE HO-HE-TO'S

(493) Herodotus.   (494) Plato.   (495) Homer.   (496) Aristophanes.   (497) Thucydides.   (498) Sappho.   (499) Xenophon. (500) Pindar.   (501) Demosthenes.   (502) Aristotle.   (503) Lucian.   (504) Meleager.

INVENTORS AND DISCOVERERS

(505) Motion of celestial bodies.   (506) Gunpowder. (507) Telescope.   (508) Circulation of the blood.   (509)

Gravitation. (510) Power of steam. (511) Logarithms.
(512) Vaccination. (513) Treatment of rabies. (514) Anti-
septics. (515) Telephone. (516) Uses of radium.

WAR SAYINGS

(517) Attila the Hun. (518) Edward III of Black Prince
at Crécy. (519) Napoleon III of Prince Imperial in 1870.
(520) William III. (521) General Sherman. (522) Oliver
Cromwell. (523) Napoleon. (524) Russian general in
Crimean War. (525) Wellington at Waterloo. (526) Julius
Caesar. (527) Pericles at Athens. (528) To the Spartan
warriors.

ANECDOTES OF KINGS

(529) Henry II. (530) Henry VI. (531) Charles II.
(532) John. (533) Alfred the Great. (534) Henry I.
(535) Canute. (536) Harold, or William II. (537) Henry V.
(538) Richard I. (539) William III. (540) Queen Anne.

'I HAVE SUPP'D FULL WITH HORRORS'

(541) *Agamemnon*, Aeschylus. (542) *Medea*, Euripides.
(543) *Othello*, Shakespeare. (544) *Edward II*, Marlowe.
(545) *Arden of Feversham*, Anon. (546) *The Duchess of Malfi*,
Webster. (547) *The Ring and the Book*, Browning. (548) *The
Cenci*, Shelley. (549) *Oedipus Tyrannus*, Sophocles. (550)
Phèdre, Racine. (551) *'Tis Pity she's a Whore*, Ford. (552)
Rosmersholm, Ibsen.

POETS AND THE MOON

(553) Coleridge, *The Ancient Mariner*. (554) Tennyson,
Maud. (555) Wordsworth, *Ode on Intimations, etc.* (556)
Arnold, *Empedocles on Etna*. (557) Keats, *Ode to a Nightingale*.
(558) Milton, *Il Penseroso*. (559) W. de la Mare, *The Sunken*

Garden. (560) Shelley, *The Cloud*. (561) Shakespeare, *Romeo and Juliet*. (562) D. G. Rossetti, *The Blessed Damozel*. (563) Anonymous, *Ballad of Sir Patrick Spens*. (564) Lewis Carroll, *Walrus and Carpenter*.

PERSONS' NAMES FOR THINGS: MODERN

(565) Wellington. (566) Bass, or Guinness (and there are others). (567) Hansom. (568) Gatling, or Maxim. (569) Shrapnel. (570) Burberry, or Macintosh. (571) Bowdler. (572) Mesmer. (573) Banting. (574) Macadam. (575) Boy-cott. (576) Peel (Peeler).

WHAT ARE IN SPORT?

(577) Horse won Grand National, in 1896. (578) Nick-name of Gilbert Jessop, the cricketer. (579) Famous hunt. (580) Famous 'carry' at Hoylake golf course. (581) Daniel, famous Rugger player and coach. (582) Boggy bit of ground on Exmoor where Devon and Somerset staghounds hunt. (583) Term for part of a (real) tennis court. (584) Club in London, Mecca of bridge. (585) Part of a course on Cam at Cambridge. (586) Part of race-course at Newmarket. (587) Post-Great-War dance, now demoded. (588) Nickname for lawn tennis couple.

POETS AND LADIES

(589) Meleager. (590) Catullus. (591) Ovid. (592) Dante. (593) Petrarch. (594) Sidney. (595) Lovelace. (596) Herrick. (597) Carew. (598) Burns, or Cowper. (599) Wordsworth. (600) Austin Dobson.

KILLED IN BATTLE

(601) Brasidas. (602) Epaminondas. (603) Hasdrubal. (604) Simon de Montfort. (605) Gaston de Foix. (606)

Gustavus Adolphus. (607) Lord Howe. (608) Desaix. (609) Lannes. (610) Crauford. (611) Picton. (612) Stone/ wall Jackson.

POLITICAL SAYINGS

(613) Cromwell. (614) Walpole. (615) Chatham. (616) Pitt. (617) Canning. (618) Disraeli. (619) Lord Randolph Churchill. (620) Balfour. (621) Winston Churchill. (622) Asquith. (623) Lloyd George. (624) Lord Haldane.

DATES

(625) Execution of Charles I. (626) St Patrick. (627) Shakespeare and St George. (628) Empire Day. (629) Battle of Waterloo. (630) Declaration of Independence. (631) St Swithin. (632) England entered Great War. (633) Grouse shooting begins. (634) Battle of Trafalgar. (635) Armistice Day. (636) St Andrew.

FICTION

(637) Mr Micawber. (638) Henry Esmond. (639) Rob Roy. (640) Alan Breck. (641) Uncle Toby. (642) Rev. Mr Collins. (643) Mrs Gamp. (644) Rev. Dr Middleton. (645) Mrs Elton. (646) Tony Weller. (647) Tess of the Durbervilles. (648) Hilda Lessways.

AQUARIUM

(649) 'We cannot do it, sir, because——' (*Through the Looking/glass.*) (650) Captain Hook's hook. The clock had run down at last. (651) 'The chaplain and the mate.' (*The African Traveller.*) (652) 'There's a porpoise close behind us, and he's treading on my tail.' (653) 'Etiquette'; as the title of this Bab Ballad says: 'they had not been intro/ duced.' (654) Swinburne's 'Dolores,' by A. C. Hilton. (655) The musical comedy *The Geisha*. It was sung by Marie

Tempest. (656) Old Father William—Alice's. (657) Rat, in Kenneth Grahame's *The Wind in the Willows*. (658) 'The Brook,' by Tennyson. (659) 'The Ancient Mariner,' by Coleridge. (660) Rupert Brooke.

BOTHS IN FAMILIES

(661) Rossetti. (662) Browning. (663) Brontë. (664) Kingsley. (665) Thackeray. (666) A. and E. Castle, or Askews, or Williamsons. (667) A. C., E. R., and Hugh Benson. (668) Irving. (669) Fred Terry, Julia Neilson, and Neilson Terry. (670) Vanbrugh, or Terry, or Jeans. (671) Jean and Édouard de Reszke. (672) Clara Butt and Kennerly Rumford.

FLOWERS

(673) Rose. (674) Poppy. (675) Primrose. (676) Lily. (677) Violet. (678) Rosemary. ('That's for remembrance.') (679) Chrysanthemum. (680) Tulip. (681) Snowdrop, or crocus. (682) Daffodil. ('I wandered lonely as a cloud.') (683) Lavender. (684) Cowslip. (Milton's 'Lycidas.')

AN ALPHABET

(685) Character in Sheridan's *Rivals*. (686) Screen star. (687) Famous painter (especially for his fans). (688) Character in George Eliot's book. (689) Great English composer. (690) Hero of sporting novel by Frank Smedley. (691) Comic actor of to-day. (692) Great amateur golfer. (693) Distinguished Australian lawyer. (694) Celebrated Labour M.P., or Welsh novelist and playwright. (695) Eastern potentate (see poem). (696) Great opera singer. (697) Famous Belgian author. (698) Old clerk in Dickens's *Nicholas Nickleby*. (699) Distinguished English novelist. (700) Famous Essex cricketer. (701) Distinguished authority

on tropical diseases. (702) Well-known writer of prose and verse. (703) Poet of seventeenth century. (704) Music-hall artiste. (705) American poet. (706) King of Persia. (707) Robert Lynd (in *New Statesman*). (708) Louis Zangwill.

FAMILIAR QUOTATIONS IN VERSE

(709) Pope. (710) Cowper. (711) Congreve. (712) *Hudibras*, Butler. (713) Gray. (714) Milton. (715) Tennyson. (716) *Pleasures of Hope*, Campbell. (717) Keats. (718) Byron. (719) Wordsworth. (720) Goldsmith.

DEAR OLD FRIENDS: THE HIC-HAEC-HOC'S

(721) Caesar. (722) Ovid. (723) Cicero. (724) Lucretius. (725) Livy. (726) Petronius. (727) Horace. (728) Apuleius. (729) Juvenal. (730) Virgil. (731) Tacitus. (732) Catullus.

FAMOUS SONGS

(733) Hastings. (734) Revolution of 1689: expulsion of James II. (735) Revolution of 1689: Killiecrankie. (736) Campaigns of Marlborough. (737) 'The Young Pretender,' 1745. (738) French Revolution. (739) Irish Rebellion of 1798. (740) Peninsular War. (741) American Civil War, Southern States song. (742) Franco-German War, 1870, German song. (743) Boer War. (744) The 1914–18 War.

COINS

(745) India. (746) Greece. (747) Holland. (748) Denmark and Scandinavia. (749) Italy. (750) Spain. (751) Turkey. (752) Portugal. (753) Russia. (754) China. (755) Germany. (756) Japan.

ASTRONOMICAL

(757) Mercury. (758) Venus. (759) Jupiter. (760) Saturn. (761) Sirius. (762) Canopus. (763) The Great Bear. (764) Orion. (765) The Pleiades. (766) Algol. (767) Halley's Comet. (768) The Persides.

POEMS ON BIRDS

(769) The cock, *Milton*. (770) 'That's the wise thrush,' *Browning*. (771) The eagle, *Tennyson*. (772) 'The cuckoo, then,' *Shakespeare*. (773) No nightingale,' *Wordsworth*. (774) The albatross, *Coleridge*. (775) 'Sweet Robin,' *Scott*. (776) The skylark, *Shelley*. (777) The blackbird, *T. E. Brown*. (778) 'The moping owl,' *Gray*. (779) The twa corbies, *Old Ballad*. (780) The swallow, *Meredith*.

TALES AND LEGENDS OF ANIMALS

(781) Tiger. (782) Fox. (783) Hyena. (784) Cowper. (785) Gray. (786) Burns. (787) Rossetti. (788) Sertorius. (789) They saved the Capitol from the night attack of the Gauls by their screeching. (790) 'If they will not eat, let them have a drink.' (791) The mouse-deer. (792) The 'rhino,' 'serious.'

WHAT THE D——!

(793) Peruvian king in time of Pizarro. (794) 'A thin shabby-looking bird with its feathers sticking out all round.' (795) Queer pet, invented by George Graves in *The Little Michus*. (796) Club formed by admirers of 'Wilfred.' (797) Lancashire county cricketer. (798) Pet name for Sir W. Joynson Hicks (Lord Brentford). (799) Great mountain in Central Africa. (800) Girl in 'Hiawatha.' Also falls

on river. (801) 'That had no toes.' See Edward Lear. (802) Star, of three in Aquila forming a line. (803) Name of Aldwych Theatre fame. (804) Comic race horse, became a by word for always losing races.

WOMEN AND MURDER

(805) Son. (806) Mother. (807) Self. (808) Not proven— fiancé. (809) Stepbrother. (810) Husband. (811) Sister. (812) Baby. (813) Lover. (814) Female cousin. (815) Male cousin (he was her husband, too). (816) Son in law. (Henry of Navarre. But she may have wanted him to escape the massacre of St Bartholomew).

FLEET STREET GOSSIP

(817) Bonne bouche. (818) Mirabile dictu. (819) Un mauvais quart d'heure. (820) Cum grano salis. (821) Qui s'excuse s'accuse. (822) Compos mentis. (823) Entre nous. (824) Fons et origo. (825) Hinc illae lacrimae. (826) Pour passer le temps. (827) Faute de mieux. (828) Contretemps.

THE GOLDENS

(829) Harbour mouth at San Fransisco. (830) At Con stantinople. (831) Taken by Jason and the Argonauts. (832) Worshipped by Children of Israel. (833) Drake's ship round the world. (834) Famous Graeco Roman romance by Apuleius. (835) Set up by Nebuchadnezzar for worship. (836) Sir J. Frazer's book on primitive religions. (837) Poem by Longfellow. (838) Name of ship in old song of 'the Midland Sea.' (839) Collection of English songs and lyrics. (840) El Dorado: fabled city of the Incas.

ARTISTS

(841) Phidias. (842) Michelangelo. (843) Giotto. (844) Sir Christopher Wren. (845) Rodin. (846) Velasquez. (847) Van Dyck. (848) Sir Peter Lely. (849) Romney. (850) Greuze. (851) Sir Gilbert Giles Scott. (852) Sir Edwin Lutyens.

THE SOUL OF WIT

(853) Sir William Jones. (854) Pope. (855) J. C. Squire (an impromptu reply to No. 854). (856) Hilaire Belloc. (857) Prior. (858) Landor. (859) Richard Garnett (after Ptolemy). (860) Shelley (after Plato). (861) Sir Walter Raleigh (after Catullus). (862) William Browne of Tavistock. (863) H. Wellesley (after Theodorides). (864) Father Tabb.

SAYINGS OF FRENCHMEN

(865) Charles IX. (866) Henry III (of the Duke of Guise). (867) Henry IV. (868) Louis XIV. (869) Louis XV. (870) Louis XVI. (871) Queen of Louis IX (returning from Crusade). (872) Joan of Arc. (873) Madame Roland. (874) Robespierre. (875) Danton. (876) General Bonaparte.

WHAT HAPPENED AT?

(877) Surrender of Southern army under General Lee, ending American Civil War. (878) Surrender of General Dupont with French army encouraging Spain in Peninsular War. (879) Birth of Joan of Arc. (880) First clash of insurgents with British troops in American Revolution. (881) Final defeat of Persians in Greece. (882) Murder of Austrian Archduke, causing 1914–18 War. (883) Surrender of General Burgoyne to American insurgents, encouraging

France and Spain to declare war on Great Britain. (884) Alliance of Napoleon and Tsar after battle of Friedland. (885) Landing of William of Orange. (886) Flight of Louis XVI from France, arrested. (887) French revolutionary army wins first, unexpected, success against Allies. (888) Signing of Peace Treaty after Boer War.

TWELVE X-WORDS FOR XMAS

BY HUBERT PHILLIPS

I

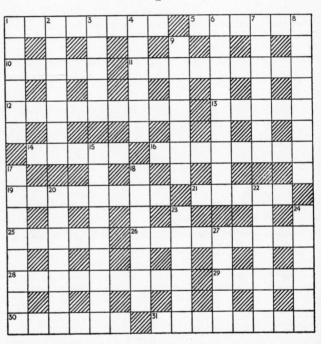

Across

1. Figure which suggests that the writer's implement is labelled (8).
5. A not quite precise summary (6).
10. Abroad is different (5).
11. The professor's first lecture (9).
12. Subordinate hiding in the heather? (9).
13. He deserves one, no doubt! (5).
14. A statute for shoppers? (5).
16. Beastly suggestion of a chap who isn't harassed? (8).
19. Sane clam (anag.) (8).
21. The whole is composed of the reversed parts (5).
25. The dance enjoins pallor, apparently (5).
26. The world can hardly be his oyster, since he's evidently swallowed it (9).
28. I seem to be incompetent about my twisted lip (9).
29. Void, containing a nurse-maid (5).
30. Sent on poetically (6).
31. How to make the most of one's wits? (8).

Down

1. For cocktail-bar or Zoo (6).
2. The day touches its high-spot (7).
3. Appropriate transformation of one of King Lear's daughters? (5).
4. Spirited end of the beginning (6).
6. Solomon's advice to the herald? (9).
7. Is this where a 'Red' would dig up his means of transport? (7).
8. Leg-wear (two words; 4, 4).
9. His job is unpleasant, but at least he knows the ropes (7).
15. Tore chain to be solitary (9).
17. Use a tram (anag.) (8).
18. Theme of a Weyman romance (two words: 3, 4).
20. Plaything for the Muses? (7).
22. Designed to protect the pilot of a bombing-plane? (two words: 3, 4).
23. Ulysses didn't care two 'hoots' for them (6).
24. Uninhibited ending with a city (6).
27. If the abstraction is implied (5).

II

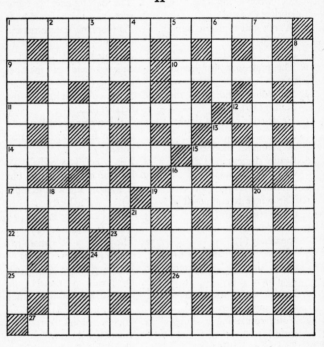

Across

1. One misses a bust (anag.) (14).
9. City famous for its Loop (7).
10. Occupied by George at the opera? (7).
11. Free from reverie (10).
12. The man from Utica (4).
14. Chaos (two words: 3, 5).
15. Barefoot (6).
17. They wax and wane (6).
19. In love with Bianca (8).
22. Profound vegetable (4).
23. Suggestion that the men all wore tails (three words: 2, 5, 3).
25. This still is confiscable (7).
26. Knowledge systematized (7).
27. Enough (five words: 2, 4, 2, 1, 5).

Down

1. Book-keeper's haunch? (14).
2. Weld sin for fraud (7).
3. Provoke (10).
4. A mystery of history (two words: 4, 4).
5. This lay is silent (6).
6. 'One over the eight' (4).
7. Subject-matter of a comment (7).
8. Source of a number of tracts (two words: 6, 8).
13. Feature of the seashore (10).
16. Salt to us (anag.) (8).
18. Ornamental floor-polishers? (7).
20. Cobweb's mistress (7).
21. Jarred (6).
24. Found in the breech of a rifle (4).

III

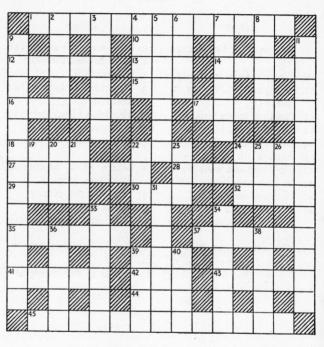

Across

1. 'Murder most foul' (13).
10. What is there in money? (3).
12. Appeal to a dying fruit? (5).
13. Young lady in plaid attire (3).
14. Educate (5).
15. Such service is valueless (3),
16. Legal summary (6).
17. Lamentation (6).
18. I have left Spain (4).
22. Negordyh (3).
24. An old-fashioned oath (4).
27. Here a king kept court (7).
28. In spite of 23? (7).
29. Tennysonian heroine (4).
30. Flower upset for a root (3).
32. The beautiful youth lacks nous (4).
35. Musicianly weapons? (6).
37. Island in Asia (6).
39. Endless fable (3).
41. The belted warrior (5).
42. Myself (3).
43. Curtail the kingdom for the physicist (5).
44. Unexpected development in Sparta (3).
45. The game is played with a prolate spheroid (two words: 5, 8).

Down

2. Out of this nettle? (5).
3. Untoward gesture from a poet? (6).
4. Ground (4).
5. State which includes an empire (7).
6. Low tide (4).
7. Adds up (6).
8. The little beast's all right to begin with (5).
9. Second in Scone (anag.) (13).
11. Great Britain and Ireland (two words: 6, 7).
19. Legendary piper (3).
20. My friend in Amiens (3).
21. 'Who was alive and is dead' (3).
22. A humble dwelling (3).
23. Fleshy tissue (3).
24. A letter from Greece (3).
25. 'Reeking tube' (3).
26. Do your stuff, Mr Garrick (3).
31. Oral leg (anag.) (7).
33. Mightier than the sword's point (two words: 3, 3).
34. Splash with paint (6).
36. Valediction (5).
38. Serve (5).
39. Falls in the fall (4).
40. Shakespearian injunction (two words: 2, 2).

IV

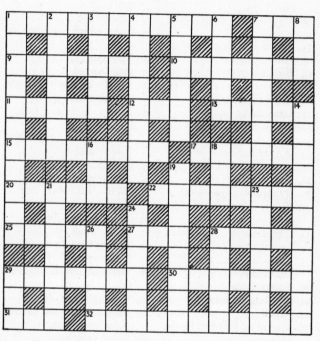

Across

1. Meg and her sisters (two words: 6, 5).
7. Unit in Stonehaven (3).
9. Chef's orchid (7).
10. A source of light if cruel (7).
11. Solid objects of worship (5).
12. Ardent spirit (3).
13. Wine-bags (5).
15. A donkey—or just young Edward? (8).
17. Born sailor—one of four? (6).
20. Peculiarities of speech (6).
22. Agreement about slaves (8).
25. Two of a kind (5).
27. Appears on the surface (3).
28. Fur coats appeal to them (5).
29. A notion from Venice (7).
30. Featured in the Book of Numbers? (7).
31. Leviathan among birds (3).
32. Anglers fire for the army (two words: 5, 6).

Down

1. Has Cupid lost his way? (four words: 4, 2, 1, 4).
2. Necessary to a leg-pull? (7).
3. Still makes melody (5).
4. Argumentative mathematician (8).
5. Solemn fruits (6).
6. Little devils? (5).
7. Order to remove the sundaes? (7).
8. Borrowed by Antony? (3).
14. Something exceptional among lyrics (three words: 4, 2, 5).
16. Engineer's pet? (3).
18. High priest (3).
19. Lame Bess for the meet (8).
21. So silly (7).
23. 7 across less one (7).
24. A place in the sun? (6).
26. Less foolish (5).
28. Paradise for brewers? (5).
29. Melody (3).

V

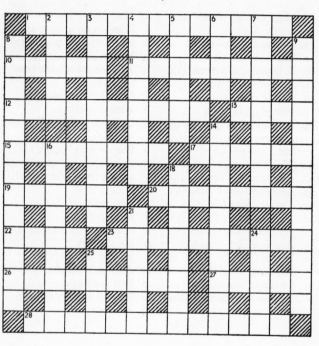

Across

1. Scene of a wicked uncle's villainy (three words: 5, 2, 6).
10. Pronouncement by vocal confectioner? (5).
11. Clean chit for specialization (9).
12. Doctor's identification of an organ? (10).
13. Goddess in the raw (4).
15. Terrors of the highway (two words: 4, 4).
17. Here are forged the bonds of matrimony (6).
19. A soldier from the hills (6).
20. Chip lard—for pickling? (8).
22. Unfilial gesture by Goneril and Regan? (4).
23. The Scot law (anag.) (two words: 6, 4).
26. He voices his praise (9).
27. A successful forward (at Rugby) might perhaps be so described (5).
28. Set in sham past—far too often! (13).

Down

2. The home of Rigel and Betelgeuse (5).
3. Name still proudly borne (10).
4. Makes most noise in the bathroom? (8).
5. Derived from milk (6).
6. Daughters of Mnemosyne (4).
7. Its basis is sound co-operation (9).
8. No, not the Royal Academy (two words: 7, 6).
9. Appurtenances of romantic drama (three words: 5, 3, 5).
14. Brings into being (10).
16. Is this where the belated letter-writer lost his race against time? (three words: 2, 3, 4).
18. Is it a raw flower? (8).
21. Praying insect (6).
24. Black republic (5).
25. Singular scene of knightly combat (4).

VI

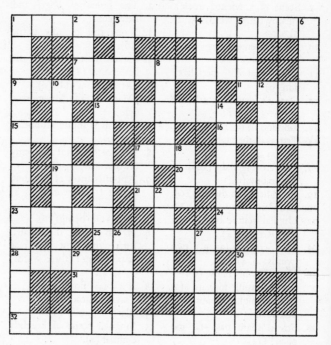

Across

1. Possessory formula (five words: 2, 4, 3, 2, 4).
7. See mishap (anag.) (9).
9. A ruler is able (4).
11. Christmas produces a comedian (4).
13. There's a Pole in the closet (7).
15. Incision (5).
16. Danced by Henry Cotton? (5).
17. Grandson of Rehoboam (3).
19. Ready for the lists (5).
20. Not much longer than an inch (5).
21. What Bill hopes to become (3).
23. Darker shade (5).
24. My lot was knightly (5).
25. Employ after faulty pose (7).
28. My age is mean but not sordid (4).
30. 'Rolling rapidly' (4).
31. Roast line (anag.) (9).
32. 'Hear my cry' is its beginning (three words: 5, 5, 5).

Down

1. His wife was an amateur pastry-cook (four words: 3, 4, 2, 6).
2. The stronghold is a snuggery (4).
3. Drive out (5).
4. The unconverted? (5).
5. Injunction to the scrum (4).
6. County delicacy (10, 5).
8. They are found among all classes (5).
10. Tread lads (anag.) (9).
12. Response to a trunk call? (9)
13. Shift (7).
14. Just around (7).
17. Maid in a dairy (3).
18. An Irishman in difficulties (3).
22. My half has out-lived me (5).
26. Vulgar corpse (5).
27. Begin with a saint (5).
29. From the mathematician's garden? (4).
30. Is doubly divine (4).

VII

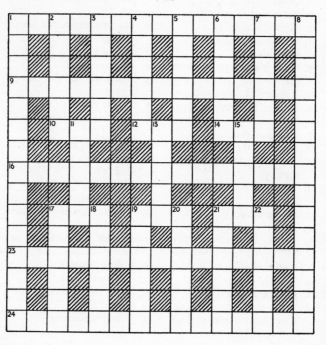

Across

1. Homely advice to the globe trotter? (three words: 3, 7, 5)
9. In a brain sat a bat (anag.) (15).
10. You will find me in Bratislava (3).
12. My bus was Charon's father (3).
14. Alternatively, 21 down (3).
16. Could the young George Washington, paradoxically, have been thus characterized (five words: 3, 4, 2, 2, 4).
17. One of Clive Newcome's friends was this size (3).
19. Often partnered by bill (3).
21. Found in all the best circles (3).
23. Trial scene (two words: 11, 4).
24. Diapason is style (anag.) (15).

Down

1. An incorruptible footballer? (15).
2. His regrets are often conventional (6).
3. Horatio's morn wore this mantle (6).
4. Vocal quality (6).
5. Inborn (6).
6. Adult provender? (6)
7. They're grand in Michigan (6).
8. A scene of planned activity (two words: 9, 6).
11. Contend verbally (5).
13. Hamlet's friend without his half-hose (5).
15. My burn was a battleground (5).
17. Nobs, or knobs (6).
18. 10, or maybe 15, turns up (6).
19. This is where they take the count (6).
20. My sheet is folded 5, so to speak (6).
21. Daughter of Hyperion (6).
22. Odd coppers? (6).

VIII

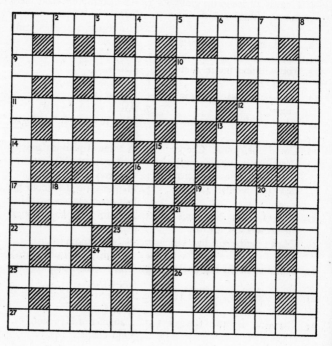

Across

1. It occurs in December (three words: 3, 7, 5).
9. Fitted date pad (7).
10. A girl in a veil (7).
11. For the careful motorist (two words: 5, 5).
12. Millions are seeking it (4).
14. I have left the revised edition (6).
15. His friend courted the mistress; he, the maid (8).
17. Gone, Anne? So one figures (8).
19. Acceptable form of payment (two words: 2, 4).
22. Workers in pleasant surroundings (4).
23. Emphatic declaration by hero of 8? (four words: 1, 4, 2, 3).
25. 'Here's yet some liquor left' (two words: 2, 5).
26. Byron's daughter (7).
27. Dramatic announcement of a felicitous event (four words: 3, 2, 3, 7).

Down

1. Litters on a train (anag.) (15).
2. Forward—from Calais (two words: 2, 5).
3. Dramatic dismissal of the maid? (10).
4. The mad dog gets up again, swearing (6).
5. Unaccompanied lay trios (8).
6. A rascal in church? (4)
7. Scene of a Browning soliloquy (7).
8. Why the old-fashioned suitor sought out his girl's father (five words: 2, 3, 3, 3, 4).
13. He wields a knife (10).
16. My dream was musical (8).
18. Many (three words: 3, 1, 3).
20. In France, a forbidding weapon would be almost gay enough (7).
21. Mother—alas!—turns up for the salute (6).
24. Amusing birds (4).

IX

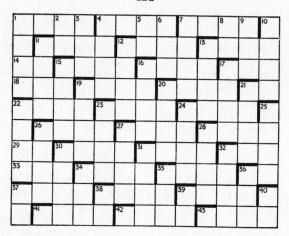

Across

1. You want me to be shaw (4)
4. Current in Germany (4).
7. Downtrodden fish? (4)
11. Beloved department? (4).
12. To be thrown with us (4).
13. Fruit seen double? (4).
14. Only with 8 down (2).
15. Macbeth's three sisters were (4).
16. Butcher's bird? (4).
17. This cuts no ice with me (3).
18. Secret (3).
19. Vicar of Bray? (4).
20. Vulgar prison (4).
21. My tail is clear (2).

Down

1. A kiss for the conductor? (4).
2. My sin was card/sharping (2).
3. Dum's replica (3).
4. I wander in earlier Rome (4)
5. Divide with 20 down (2).
6. A stream in the sky (3).
7. Bobtailed? (4).
8. See 14 (2).
9. 19 across has two (3).
10. The price of *bijouterie* (4).
11. See 29 (4).
12. Comes after a van (4).
13. Even at the tables (4).
15. The Speaker's is singular (4).
16. Dry (4).

Across—continued

22. Found in quite a wide area (4).
23. You could not catch my ward napping (4).
24. Ketch's concern (4).
26. Oh, to be in the Forum! (4).
27. Thin with 39 across (4).
28. Booty (4).
29. 11 down before 40 (2).
30. Rope for a tar (4).
31. Ante up! (4).
32. Interesting discovery in Caledonia (3).
33. Feudal commander with 34 down (3).
34. Chick peas or misery (4).
35. 'The little archer?' Not exactly! (4).
36. With 37 down, a daughter of the gods (2).
37. Irish king (4).
38. Osculation goes astray? (4).
39. See 27 across (4).
41. Separation suggested by a mutiny of the Nore (4).
42. Sturdy actor? (4).
43. What pen, perhaps, owes to sword (4).

Down—continued

17. My nest is afloat (4).
19. Product of 42? (4).
20. See 5 (4).
21. Precious word of comradeship? (4).
22. The pupils are within (4).
23. Singular parliamentary interjection (4).
24. She turns up to eat? (4).
25. The curve provokes an exclamation? (4).
26. An appeal to 9 (4).
27. Well concealed—and in doing the lady a kindness, too! (4).
28. A sad reverse for the late journalist (4).
30. Overblown rose? (4).
31. The chieftain emerges from the mud (4).
32. The realtor's contribution to harmony? (4).
34. See 33 (3).
35. 5 and 20 down a carrier (3).
36. For courage, you have nothing on me (3).
37. See 36 (2).
38. Indifferent with 14 (2).
39. { Reward } (2).
40. { Reward } (2).

X

Across

1. They are fond of their insides (14).
14. Secreted in a brown paper parcel (3).
15. Has rings but no bracelet (6).
17. Lower inversion (5).
18. *rev.* Half empty (3).
19. Taps (7).
20. Peculiar cult (4).
21. Tailless oriental potentate (4).
22. Overheard in seaside lodgings? (5).
23. Hood sang of one (5).
24. My pole becomes amphibious (3).
25. *rev.* Money for a nabob (4).
27. Torture tortured (7).
28. Is a unit of empire (7).
29. Bup (3).
30. Attained perhaps by translation (3).
31. End of the 'long, long trail' (3).
32. A letter for Xenophon (3).
33. Nest of song-birds (5).
35. All a god (3).
36. I come out nicely (5).
37. Vitally without 45 (5).
38. Fruit with no degree (4).

Down

1. His fellows received an epistle (8).
2. Give Rima her coat and reorganize (8).
3. List (8).
4. *rev.* Condition before 32 *rev.* (2).
5. Knock a town for appetite (8).
6. A little flower has lost my Latin bone (4).
7. I make a note of a lap-dog for the ring (8).
8. It's just inside (8).
9. Tending towards nudism? (6).
10. These were famous games (8).
11. The historian has forsaken us (5).
12. Originating in a tusk (8).
13. He was not quite a gentleman (8).
16. Rat's more upright half (3).
19. *rev.* Means of distortion (6).
26. Just twist a continent's tail (4).
27. 11 now loses sex-appeal (3).
30. Sartorial superfluity with 4 (3).
34. My sun can disinfect (2).

XI

Across

1. 'For us to levy power —— to the enemy is all impossible' (14).
14. Herne's served as a rendezvous (3).
15. Painless end with articled continent (4).
17. *rev.* Went after a reorganization (3).
18. *rev.* You want the half-moon for Brigham Young (4).
19. Tangled yarns to keep the rain out? (5).
20. An opening (4).
21. Mingle with 40 for a reception (2).
22. Mother has left town (3).
23. My return is welcomed by football-fans (5).
24. She is in a sorry plight (3).
25. Should one thus address a goddess? (3).
26. Somewhat confused tale-teller (5).
28. Juno's were coupled and inseparable (5).
31. Affliction (3).
32. That of Naples was hid with English gilt (4).
33. Unweighted regicide (3).
34. Casca was (4).
35. Sought for by 12 (2).
36. *rev.* All the hearts before 35 (2).
37. My date is found in Tanganyika (3).

38. Cain and Abel after 11 (2).
39. I have four 36's (4).
40. Snatched from a tame elephant? (3).
41. Salisbury found my savours uncleanly (14).

Down

1. 'A man faithful and honourable' (8).
2. Cuttings from Shakespeare? (7).
3. What a state to be in! (8).
4. Ammunition for 16? (4).
5. Mendacious but not at home? (8).
6. 'Set less than thou ——' (8).
7. *rev.* Unmerciful less less (4).
8. His 'scourge is weigh'd' (8)
9. For cricketers and such poor fish (4).
10. Another one has turned up! (8).
11. See 38 (2).
12. They hint that the little archer fibs (8).
13. Struggle for type in the case-room? (8).
16. Reshape me: you may find my hill on the map (7).
21. *rev.* Cut out (5).
27. The daughter of my grandmother is in sorry plight (4).
29. Often before decamp (4).
30. None and I are pink (4).

XII

Across

1. Doomed to die at Easter (13).
13. Shape of an ulnar (7).
14. *rev.* Heart of the Hoosier State (3).
16. My sons occur in sequence (3).
17. One of the porch boys (5).
18. Likewise following 8 rev. (2).
19. You must get on to make the gateway (6).
20. *rev.* Understanding from a plover (3).
21. Accommodation in dis-array (4).
22. *rev.* Wild ass (6).
24. His cities were fenced (2).
25. My king has five claws on each foot (3).
26. *rev.* Fixed stakes (8).
27. Fine muslin without its stamp (5).
30. I transferred from a be-gonia (3).
31. Untarred obsolete army (4).
32. My attributes are nominal (4).
33. No advantage to any one (5).
35. 34 (2).
36. Carboniferous end pin doodler (13).

Down

1. For the clergy (8).
2. Honegger opera (8).
3. Flowery injunction to wintry skies? (8).
4. City of many quakes (5).
5. Sore (5).
6. Proverbially proletarian (two words: 4, 3).
7. One of the 'slings' of out-rageous fortune (6).
8. See 18 (2).
9. *rev.* Roller's objective (3).
10. Lattice, not for lettuce (8).
11. He was shown how to find out directions by indirec-tions (8).
12. Victim of unrequited love? (8).
15. *rev.* He is of mixed parent-age (7).
19. Where chaps go all Bo-hemian (6).
23. Crumbled cake (5).
28. Conductor with 34 *rev.* (3).
29. A useful connection (3).
34. See 28 (2).

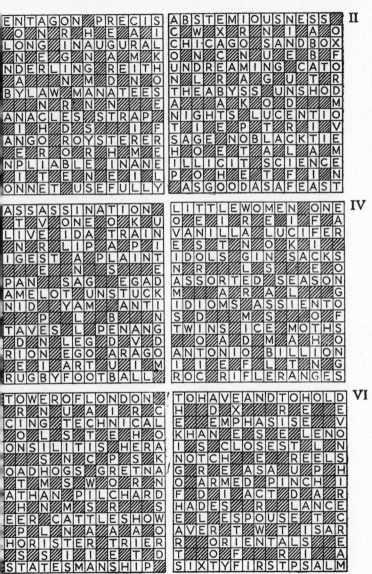

VII

```
S E E B R I T A I N F I R S T
T D U I N O A E
R I S M N R P N
A N T I S A B B A T A R I A N
I O E R T G D E S
G R A T E R E E O S S
H R A I
T O O G O O D T O B E T R U E
F U I E E
O B E L C O O A R C V
R O A E C U H A
W E S T M I N S T E R H A L L
A S I S A O N L
R E N U V R G E
D I S P A S S I O N A T E L Y
```

VIII

```
T H E L O N G E S T N I G H
R N U O A O
A D A P T E D L A V I N
N V G D I E D
S P A R E P A R T S W O F
L N N M A S L
I N T O E D G R A T I A
T R T Y E
E N N E A G O N I N C A S
R O L Y S C S
A N T S I M E A N I T S I
A G A L L E
I N F L A S K A L L E G R
O E M E A E A
N O W W E A R E M A R R I E
```

IX

```
B R A D E L B E S O L E P
U C H E R D I S C P E A R
S O E E R Y S K U A C R I
S L Y M O K E S T I R O X
I D E A H E R E D R O P O
R E S S E D E C I S W A G
I C S T A Y E T N A A L E
S H O G R A M T E L L H E
B O R U S K I S M A T E E
E R E N O T R E E W O R D
```

X

```
G A S T R O P H I L I T E S
A R C S A T U R N E S A B A
L O H S P I G O T S T C U L
A M E E A S I D E S H I R T
T A D S C A L T R O M T N E
I T U N I S I A N N I S E E
A I L E T A S C A L A P A N
N C E L Y I T A L Y N A N A
```

XI

```
P R O P O R T I O N A B L E
O A K E U T H T F E M R O M
L S L A T E R I F T O E V B
O H A S L O O P E S H D E A
N E H T Y S W A N S A I L T
I R O N I R E I D U L L I T
U S M A N O S D E C K E E L
S L A U G H T E R H O U S E
```

XII

```
P A S Q U E F L O W E R S
A N N U L A R A I D S E A
S T O I C S O P R O P Y L
T I W T E T N R E G A N O
O G D O R E D A S I L A P
R O R G A N E G O M I L I
A N O U N D E U C E E D A
L E P I D O D E N D R O N
```

NOTES ON No. X.—*Across:* 18, Hol/low; 21, Amee/r; 27, anag. of Torm... 29, Pub. *rev.*; 38, N(i)cely; 37, (V)ital(l)y; 38, (B.A.)nana.

Down: 2, Rima/coat, anag.; 5, Rap/a/city; 6, (My/os)otis; 7, Pug/I... 9, Less/on; 11, 27, Tac/it/us; 13, 'The Young Visiters'; 16, Rod... 34, Ly/sol.

CHRISTMAS ROUND THE WORLD

In Bethlehem

EVER since sunset people have been crowding into the great Church of the Nativity in Bethlehem to kneel at the very place where Our Lord was born. Palestinians in their picturesque clothes—the women wearing the high pointed 'coif' said to be a legacy from the Crusades: the men with large yellow turbans and cloaks of black or brown camel hair: monks and nuns of every religious order: members of the British community—civilians, soldiers, and police: foreign visitors and pilgrims from America and various European countries: all these came last night to pay their homage at the manger.

The famous Basilica built by the Emperor Constantine in the fourth century has been little changed since those early days. It is probably the oldest church in the world still in Christian use, and almost certainly covers the site assigned by tradition to the birth of Our Lord. After crouching low to enter the tiny door—only four feet high—at the western end, the visitor pauses awhile in the dim light to gaze at the double column of marble pillars, at the wooden roof whose beams were sent from England by King Edward IV, and finally at the gilded 'IKONOSTASIS' at the east end of the church.

The crowd moves slowly eastwards: behind the high altar, steep, winding steps on either side lead to the grotto, and down these steps the pilgrims pass, beneath the living rock of the cave, their heads almost touching the overhanging roof. Here is the site, marked by a silver star, of the birth of Jesus: here, too, is the site of the manger, where the Holy Babe lay, 'because there was no room for them in the inn.'

IGOR VINOGRADOFF, *Broadcast*, 1937.

Shepherds' Midnight Mass, Provence

Picture in the desolate and chaotic countryside—which inspired Dante with the Inferno of his *Divine Comedy*—a crowd of worshippers winding their way up to the little church on the heights of Les Baux. On either side strange rocky formations, woven into fantastic patterns, even stranger under the moon-light. The muffled tone of the voices, and the lanterns which are carried, all add to the impressiveness of the scene.

Among the many onlookers who have come from afar or from the neighbouring towns, one notices the attractive coifs and shawls of the girls from Arles. The tolling bell calls them up the steep hill, and suddenly at a turning the splendour of the illuminated church appears. Now the well-lit Roman porch appears distinctly and soon they enter the church of Les Baux. The candles twinkle, the arches resound to the music of the organ. Near by, in one of the small chapels, carved in the rock, is the crib, a very crowded crib, indeed, as crowded as the church, for around the Child, the Virgin, St Joseph, the saints, the bishops, the kings, the ass, the ox, the camels, stand a mass of small figures representing shep-herds, peasants, people of all trades, dressed in their best clothes. These little persons are peculiar to Provence; carved in wood or made of plaster, they are called 'santons,' little saints, and at Christmas adorn not only the cribs in the churches but also in most homes. They form a procession similar to that we are going to witness, a ceremony which has remained unchanged through the ages.

At the offertory, whilst the procession is being formed in the church, the call of the angel is heard from behind the altar, a shepherd replies with a tune in F minor, very slow and stirring. Each verse of that song ends to the accompaniment of the fife and Provençal drum with a rigadoon in F major. After this duet the shepherds with their cloaks of rough serge, the shepherdesses, their hair covered with a coloured ribbon, wrapped in coats of printed calico and guided by the angel, proceed towards the altar to the tune of a slow march played at the back of the church by fife and drums. They are preceded by a cart decorated with many-coloured candles and drawn by a ram covered with a gold embroidered coat. Inside, on a carpet of red wool, lies a lamb. When the head shepherd reaches the altar, he takes the lamb in his arms, and is admitted into the presence of the child Jesus, represented by a priest. He bows gravely and, looking straight in front of him, tells in the language of Provence the story of the journey he has just made across the hills with his companions to pay homage to the Redeemer. This ended, he kisses the feet of the child, walks back two steps, bows again, turns slowly towards his shepherdess, who bows likewise and to whom he gives the lamb. She walks towards the altar and offers the lamb with the same ceremony, then passes it on to the next shepherd, and this goes on until the last shepherd replaces the lamb in the cart.

During the service, the head shepherd kneels in front of the altar with the lamb in his arms. At the supreme moment of the mass, the elevation of the host, you hear not the usual ringing of a bell—but the bleating of the lamb. All this takes place gravely, with little gesture, in quietness and peaceful contemplation. Under the low arches of the old church, one seems to be brought back to past centuries. Then heads are raised and the famous Provençal carols are sung.

IGOR VINOGRADOFF, *Broadcast*, 1937.

A Gond Village in India

It is a quarter-past eight in the evening here and a calm, starry night, warm as your English June. I have travelled down to Bombay to speak to you from the Gond village where I live. It is three days' journey by bullock cart from the nearest town. It lies among the eastern spurs of the sacred Maikal Hills, the ancient home of the great sages of India, now peopled by some of the most primitive members of the human family. At this moment, a huge log fire is blazing there in front of a tiny mud chapel of St Francis. Round the fire gathers a varied company—two or three hundred wild and glorious children of the forest, bright-eyed and beautiful. There are the naked Baigas, sons of the Earth Mother, the blacksmith Agarias, romantic, music-loving Pardhans, and the royal Gonds, once kings and princes, with long, black hair, peacock feathers nodding in their turbans. And here, sitting apart, is a pathetic group of lepers. And there is a Mussulman, a Brahmin, an 'untouchable,' an Englishman, an Indian Christian, bound by service into one family—symbol of what might be through-out the world if the message of the Christ-child was taken to our hearts. For though only two of the company are Christians all are held together by that Christmas love which teaches that a thing has only to be human to be precious, and that where poverty is, there Christ would desire to be. For always the Gonds are hungry. Annadeo, God of Food, they say, has left the forest for the cities, where he makes men fat. But at Christmas, at least, the God of Food returns, and all the children, and the lepers, and as many animals as will come, have a great feast. As I speak more and more people will be gathering from their tumbledown mud huts, and soon they will begin to dance the Karma, famous dance of the new birth of trees. All through this holy night they dance till the dawn comes, and they sing an old, old song which might have a Christmas meaning, for while in the chapel rises the strain of 'While shepherds watch'd their flocks by night,' the roar of the drum answers, and the dancers cry:

> 'O sleeper, rise, if thou wouldst see
> At midnight the tree burst into flower.'

Broadcast, 1935.

Feast of the Lanterns, Senegal

A few minutes after I had ridden up, sounds of music were heard, and a crowd of blacks came to the door, carrying the model of a ship made of paper, and illuminated within; and hollowed pumpkins also lighted up for the occasion. Then they sang some of our dear old Christmas carols.

You can imagine with what feelings I listened to those simple words, sung by negresses who knew not a phrase of English besides. You can imagine what recollections they called up, as I sat under an African sky, the palm-trees rustling above my head, and the crocodiles moaning in the river beyond. . . .

Next day, sadness and sentiment gave way, for a while at least, to more prosaical feelings. When Mr Reade sat down to his Christmas dinner, he must have wished with Macbeth: 'May good digestion wait on appetite,' as he contemplated the fare awaiting discussion, and to which a boar's head grinned a welcome. Snails from France, oysters torn from trees, gazelle cutlets, stewed iguana, smoked elephant, fried locusts, manati-breasts, hippopotamus steaks, boiled alligator, roasted crocodile eggs, monkeys on toast, land crabs and Africa soles, carp, and mullet—detestable in themselves, but triumphant proof of the skill of the cook—furnished forth the festival-table, in company with potatoes, plantains, pineapples, oranges, papaws, bananas, and various fruits rejoicing in extraordinary shapes, long native names, and very nasty flavours; and last, but not least, palm-cabbage stewed in white sauce, 'the ambrosia of the gods,' and a bottle of good Bordeaux at every man's elbow.

When evening came, Mr Reade and a special friend sought the river. The rosy wine had rouged our yellow cheeks, and we lay back on the cushions and watched the setting sun with languid, half-closed eyes. Four men, who might have served as models to Apelles, bent slowly to their stroke, and murmured forth a sweet and plaintive song. Their oars, obedient to their voice, rippled the still water, and dropped from their blades pearls, which the sun made rubies with its rays. Two beautiful girls, who sat before us in the bow, raised their rounded arms and tinkled their bracelets in the air. Then, gliding into the water, they brought us flowers from beneath the dark bushes, and kissed the hands which took them, with wet and laughing lips. Like a dark curtain, the warm night fell upon us; strange cries roused from the forest; beasts of the waters plunged around us, and my honest friend's hand pressed mine. And Christmas Day was over.

A CONTRIBUTOR TO *Chambers' Journal*, 25th Dec. 1869.

A Child in Hungary

I was a small boy of six with flowing flaxen curls. Twelve days before Christmas my mother had gone to Budapest to purchase Christmas gifts. The day before Christmas I rushed to the hall as I heard bells tinkling in the chestnut alley before the gate. From a sledge alighted the slender figure of my mother, wrapped in heavy furs. From a second sledge a footman took trunks, boxes, and parcels—no end of parcels! The parcels were taken to the large state-room with the oak-panelled fire-place and the family pictures on the wall. I knew the Christmas tree stood in there, for I had seen it being taken in. But I was not allowed to enter the room.

As we were having tea, the clattering of shoes sounded up in the hall; little bells tinkled. The butler opened the door. A group of strangely disguised peasant lads and girls stepped over the threshold, four boys and three girls—the 'Bethlehem players.' They were: Herod, the king; Joseph; the runner or messenger; two angels with white muslin wings; two shepherds.

Herod was dressed up like a Hungarian hussar, with red trousers and a blue dolman. A curved sword hung by his side, boots with long spurs covered his feet. Joseph had a large wooden sword, like that of a headsman. The runner had a long stick; tiny bells were fastened to the top of it.

The 'Bethlehem,' a light church-like wooden structure, decorated with long paper-chains, was taken in by the two angels. A candle burned in it, lighting up the walls of the 'Bethlehem,' the tiny holy pictures on its walls, the carved, wooden animals around the stall, the Child in the manger. The runner bowed and addressed my mother in rhymes, asking permission for his party to bless the house. My mother replied: 'Stay, this is God's house!'

The 'Bethlehem' was placed upon two chairs. The two shepherds lay down before it while the others sang.

The shepherds knelt down and offered the Child a tiny cheese and lamb. Then all rose and sang together, announcing the birth of Jesus in a stable, in a manger, amidst cattle where 'the mouths of calves were his warming stove.' Herod, the king, solemnly blessed our house.

My mother gave the players sweets and cakes and hot punch, and slipped a small purse filled with copper coins into the runner's hand. They said good-bye and pressed the door handle. . . . The runner dashed ahead to find a new house where they would be let in.

On Christmas Day—the old Hungarian minstrels' day— groups of minstrel boys and girls from the village knocked at our gate. The minstrels are fairly grown-up lads and girls; they go together in little groups of four or five.

They make a strange noise with their instruments, imitating all kinds of animals. Their quaint instruments are: a stick with a chain, a pipe, and an iron pot covered with a pig's bladder. The bladder is perforated and a reed is stuck into it.

If they draw a wet finger across the reed it gives a queer, droning sound.

The minstrels came in singing:

> 'Get up, farmer, get up,
> God has descended on your house
> With His legions and His army . . .'

Then the leader of the minstrels started 'telling' of a wondrous ox in the barn with cracknels on his horns, coins in his ears; his tail is filled with walnuts, on the tuft of his tail hangs a bottle of fiery Tokay wine!

In the afternoon the sledge was harnessed and we all drove to the roadside chapel near the vineyards, where the 'Bethlehem players' were to perform. As we alighted, the children came in procession with banners and holy pictures. 'The angels' placed a beautiful 'Bethlehem' upon the altar, and there they acted the games of Bethlehem with the old traditional songs and Hungarian tunes.

The chorus urges the shepherds to go to Bethlehem: 'You will find in the manger—covered with chaff—a tiny Child—O hallelujah!'

At the end of the performance Joseph appeared, saying: 'Give a few pennies to Joseph, the bell-ringer, for candles!' My mother gave me some coins, which I poured into the wallet that hung at the side of Joseph, the bell-ringer.

COUNT ALFRED HESSENSTEIN.

Contrasts of an Empire, 1932

Halifax, Nova Scotia. In the beautiful Cape Breton country, peopled by descendants of the Scottish highlands, the psalms will rise in the Gaelic tongue, and native bards will recall the stories of an older land. In the hundred fishing villages, tucked into the cliffs of our granite coast, the fishermen have left their boats at anchor and in the white-walled cottages they will sing old songs and carols brought from the Basque country and Brittany or from Somerset two centuries ago.

Vancouver. Behind us the mountains which encircle Vancouver are still lost in darkness, though a faint radiance announces that the dawn is on the way. From a high window we are looking down upon the city, upon empty streets, upon lawns and squares where the gaily illuminated Christmas trees are glowing softly. Dots of red and green lights in the harbour, with its eighty miles of water frontage, show where ships are riding at anchor—ships for Great Britain, for Australia, for China, for Japan, laden with British Columbia fir and cedar, with salmon, with fruit from the Okanagan, with grain from the prairies.

A Wine Farm in South Africa. In front of me—I am actually standing on the stoep—is a large courtyard. Three sides of it are flanked by the homestead—all dazzling white in the brilliant South African sunshine; but shadowed here and there by tall oaks which have stood sentinel since they were planted there in the time of Simon van der Stell. Masses of blue hydrangeas reflect the blue of the sky above. On the fourth side terraces go down to the vineyards which stretch as far as the eye can see. There is a faintly sweet smell in the air which comes from the ripening fruit, and, overhead, the doves are making friendly noises.

Montreal. This afternoon, the slopes of Mount Royal will be alive with a gay throng. Throughout the winter the mountain is our chief playground. Toboggans slide merrily down the steep descents, skiers fly through the air from high jumps, or sweep in long graceful curves down the snowy slopes. Bright coloured caps and sashes make a vivid picture against the glistening snow and dark evergreens.

Winnipeg. At the eastern rim of the prairies a golden sun is climbing upward, the snow is sparkling like a million dia‑monds, the tang of frost in the air makes one glad to be alive —that same frost which gives us the gorgeous tints of our autumn landscapes, and hardens our wheat and our men. All over the snowy plain, at intervals of half a mile or more, spirals of blue smoke are curling upwards in the clear, frosty morning air.

Wellington. We are welcoming Boxing Day in New Zea‑land, whilst in the homeland you are still enjoying Christmas cheer. With us the skies are bright and the fields are green. It is the busy season for our industries. Throughout the country flocks are being mustered and stripped of their golden fleece; butter and cheese factories are working at high pressure; and our orchards are once again coming into fruitful profusion.

Broadcast, 1932.

Goodwill in Poland

With us in Poland Christmas Eve and not Christmas Day is the important occasion. Imagine yourselves, therefore, yesterday evening in a village on the slopes of one of the Tatra mountains. It is cold. The high mountain peaks, the slopes and the valleys, the luscious pine woods and the fields are covered with a thick blanket of snow. But for the thatched roof the little white cottage would be scarcely visible in the failing light, against the snowy waste.

With the first star of the evening—the star of the East— the family forgather in the living room, all decked up, round a huge deal table in the middle, with a Christmas tree in the corner. The whole household, the family and farmhands, assemble, each in his or her place round the table. Under the table‑cloth hay is spread out to remind them of the hay

in which Jesus lay in the manger. All present, masters and
servants, break and eat the blessed wafer and exchange wishes
for a merry Christmas. And then they sit down to the great
evening meal. If they can afford it, twelve courses are served
—in remembrance of the twelve apostles. Almond soup,
many kinds of sweetwater fish, pickled cabbage with mush-
rooms, pastry with poppy seed, and the famous *kootyah*, a
mixture of popped wheat, honey, and poppy seed, are the
usual dishes. No meat is eaten, for it is a day of fast.

One empty seat at the table is always left in case an unknown
traveller should appear to share the meal. Towards the end
of the meal, the little coloured candles are being lit on the
Christmas tree, and the meal over, every one gathers round it
to sing the famous Polish Christmas carols. The children
find their Christmas presents under the tree and every one is
happy and full of joy. Soon voices are heard outside the
warm cottage. A light appears faintly through the window.
It is a group of poor village boys who have come with the
Star of Bethlehem—the paper star with a lighted candle inside,
borne on a long pole—to sing and to partake of the good things
which the household have not been able to finish. The
Polish carols are old, quaint songs that have come down through
the ages. They are naïve, but often very touching by their
downright directness.

> 'God is born,
> All power is a-trembling!'

the boys sing, announcing the glad tidings. Or they are full
of resentment at the fall of man and they love to sing:

> 'O wretched Eve! O miserable Eve!
> Why hast thou eaten that apple?'

From Christmas Eve to Twelfth Night another group of
village boys carry, from cottage to cottage, their stage-theatre
and puppets and perform the drama of Nativity; the homage

of kings and shepherds, the wicked Herod and Judas, who move in funny jerks across the stage to the accompaniment of a primitive dialogue. The show always ends with ugly Herod and accursed Judas being dragged away by the Devil into the very depths of hell.

IGOR VINOGRADOFF, *Broadcast*, 1937.

Three Christmas Day Workers

A Miner in Wales. I am standing half a mile underground. I am at the bottom of the downcast shaft of the Bedwas Navigation Colliery. It's the deepest shaft working in Wales. There are only three of us down below to-day—not counting the horses and the rats. One is the pump man. I expect you can hear one of his pumps working. And here comes the cage. Now my mate and I are going off to inspect the workings. They have got to be watched whether it's Christmas or no. You're nice and comfortable in front of a big fire, I hope. Perhaps the coal in it came from here. A Nadolig llawen i holl lowyr y byd.

A Tollkeeper on Sydney Harbour Bridge. Don't think this bridge is falling down. That noise is the Hornsby train going over on the left there. Trams cross on the right; p'raps you 'll hear one in a minute. Trams and trains aren't my worry; my job's taking the toll from cars. But there's plenty of *them*, even with so many away on holidays.

Here's a car coming now, so I 'll have to go in a sec. Quite a lot happens up here, hundred an' fifty feet over the water; must 'a' been quieter here once!

Right oh! No need to toot, I'm coming.

A Life-saver on Bondi Surf Beach. Can't stay long—pretty busy—bit of undertow running. It's hard to keep the crowd between the flags. Drag gets worse further along. Feller in

trouble there bit earlier. Two of 'em too far over now.
(*Blows whistle.*) Confound them. (*Whistle again.*) That's
better. Not really dangerous. Great beach and fine surf.
Fellers right out are regulars—don't worry—swim like fish—
wait for big shoots. See, they're catching this 'un. Got
it—be beached in a minute. Good surf to-day—don't the
crowd enjoy it? Jus' listen to 'em.

Broadcast, 1934.

Christmas Day in the Workhouse

The bell rang and we scrambled out of bed, leaving
our warm blankets reluctantly, and went downstairs to collect
our clothes. When we were dressed we heard the tramp major
call out: 'Come and get it,' which meant that our breakfast
was ready. Making the traditional jokes about getting eggs
and bacon, we got into line and filed up to the hatchway,
where we each grabbed a pint mug of tea, two slices of bread,
and a piece of margarine, the usual spike breakfast, and found
seats at the bare but clean scrubbed tables.

After eating we sat back smoking, waiting for the taskmaster to come in and give us our jobs for the day. A sailor,
with whom I had palled up, had a concertina, and as I always
carry my mouth-organ, we gave the dossers a bit of music.

Presently the taskmaster came in with his book and began
to call out our names, and gave us different jobs to do, such as
scrubbing out the wards and stoking the furnaces. When he
came to the sailor's name he said: 'You're a sailor aren't you?
All right, I want you . . . and you,' he said, pointing to me.
Wondering what was coming we stood to one side until he had
finished giving jobs to the others. Then he closed his book
and told us to go with him. We went with him across the
yard to the regular workhouse quarters and he took us into the
dining-room, where we saw a lot of holly and paper decorations
on the tables.

'I want you men to fix this stuff up,' he said, 'but we've left it a bit late and you'll have to get a move on. Colonel Gethering is giving a dinner to the inmates and he likes the place to look a bit Christmasy.'

'Do we come in on the grub?' asked the sailor.

'Oh, yes, it's for everybody,' the master replied. 'All the casuals come in.'

'Right, Bonzo,' said the sailor. 'Let's get stuck in.'

We set to work with a will, and in about three hours we had the place looking quite festive. When we had finished we went back to the casual ward where we found the dossers in a state of high excitement, and doing themselves up for the great occasion.

At two o'clock the tramp major came in and said: 'Grub up, boys. Put on your bibs and tuckers.' We went with him to the workhouse dining-room, where the tables were now spread with white table-cloths and laid out for dinner. The regulars were already sitting down and looked at us with curiosity as we filed in and sat together at the end of one of the tables.

The attendants came in bearing piled-up plates of roast beef, baked potatoes and greens, and we set to with regular tramps' appetites. After that we had a big slab of Christmas pudding, and when I thought we had eaten as much as we could hold they brought round some nuts, and much to my surprise, half an ounce of tobacco for each of us.

When we had lit up the master came in with a stout, ruddy-faced man in plus-fours. The master made a speech and told us we owed our dinner to Colonel Gethering and called for three cheers for our host. Then the colonel got up and said: 'I don't suppose you men want to listen to any speech of mine, so I'll just say that I've had a damned good dinner myself, and I didn't see why you shouldn't get one, too. Happy Christmas, everybody.' And with that he went out.

Left to ourselves we relaxed and smoked happily, talking about the good feed we had just had, comparing spikes, and swapping experiences. Then one of the dossers called out: 'What about a song, sailor?' and Joe said: 'What shall we give 'em, Bonzo?'

We played a few dance tunes, but by and by we drifted into the regular tramp songs such as:

> Rejoice and be glad,
> For the springtime has come;
> And we'll throw down our shovels
> And go on the bum.

with the chorus:

> Hallelujah! I'm a bum,
> Hallelujah! Bum again.
> Hallelujah! Give us a handout,
> To revive us again.

JOHN WORBY.

Rome

There is a crib, striving to outdo its neighbours, in every church in Rome. That in the Ara Coeli is the most famous. The great flight of steps leading up to the old temple of Jupiter has since yesterday been crowded with street merchants, crying their sacred wares: 'Bambinello di cera, un baiocco!' and with crowds that seethe about them like an ant-hill. They are thronging to see the figure of the Christ-child that was carved from a tree on the Mount of Olives by a Franciscan and coloured by St Luke while the friar slept; there the Bambino lies crowned in His glory, covered with emeralds and dia-monds and pearls. And there, the day long, the children have preached before the crib, with utter absence of self-conscious-ness. Sometimes these young preachers tend to be too lengthy, and others waiting their turn pull at their skirts to remind them that they are not the only orators who want to tell the story of

Bambino Gesù to the world. Sometimes three will speak together, telling in trialogue of the Child in the crib, and the Madonna and St Joseph, and why He is born in such a poor little shelter as a stable, and so on. All the speakers deliver their discourses with a great deal of animation and dramatic action, for Italian children are born orators,. and never at a loss for words. And grouped around are the parents and elder brothers and sisters of the little preachers.

IGOR VINOGRADOFF, *Broadcast*, 1937.

With the Gipsies

An old gipsy friend of mine belongs to one of the Heredia clan of gipsies, who spend their time wandering about Spain from Castile down into Andalusia. On one occasion some years back, I met him on the outskirts of Granada, and spent Christmas night with him.

In South Spain, Christmas among the gipsies used to be a period of *juergas* or sprees. My friend brought me to a cave in the Barranco del Abogao, where we joined a throng of gipsies, who spend their time singing *polos* and *soleares*. In the middle of the cave stood a big barrel of red wine from which the host drew countless *canas*. Christmas in Spain among the gipsies is but the beginning of a period of jollification which lasts through the New Year until the Feast of Kings.

Some gipsies possess a deep emotional power in their singing. I have heard *saetas* sung by gipsy singers in Holy Week, and *villancicos* at Christmas time, which brought tears to my eyes. The tendency of the gipsies is to graft some of the ancient pagan customs they have collected on to the Christian rites.

Take the English gipsies. They used to call Christmas the *Boro divvus* or great day. On that day the gipsies would always burn an ashwood fire. Leland, the noble old Romany Rye, once asked them why. 'We do it,' said they, 'because people say Our Saviour was born on the Great Day, in the field out in the country, like us Romanys, and he was brought up by an ash fire. The ivy, the holly, and the pine trees never said a word when he was hiding himself, and so they keep life all winter and look green all year. But the ash, like the strong tree (oak) turned against him where he was hiding, so they have to remain dead through the winter, and so we gipsies always burn an ash fire every Great Day. For the Saviour was born in the open field like a gipsy and rode on an ass like one of us, and went round the land a-begging his bread like a "Rom," and he was always a poor wretched man like us.'

It is curious to note some of the Christmas witchcraft observed by the wandering folk. When Christmas time comes, the gipsies go out into the woods and get sticks from an oak, beech, or ash, which they put outside the house door. In the evening the mother of the family scatters straw on the floor, puts the table on it, and sets fruit and nuts on it—but no animal fats. After supper she walks around the house three times, followed by the children, imitating the clucking of a hen to which the children answer shrilly by imitating chickens. Then in the night all the gipsy family leave the house and scatter through the neighbourhood trying to steal something. They do not steal valuable things—as a rule, a piece of wood or twigs. When they bring back the stolen object to the house they throw it on the floor saying: 'Let nobody know that I have been stealing to-night.' As the piece of wood burns in the fire, they pray that as the fire burns brightly so may they steal cleverly.

There are Christmas Day customs which must be followed by the gipsies. At dawn the father of the family must go to the well and bring a jugful home. He leaves it in front of the door, then a youth must knock at the door, asking: 'Are you at home, master?' When he is admitted he must bring with him the jug of water and Yule logs. He must also have a few coins in his pocket, which will symbolize wealth in the coming year. Then he puts the logs on the fire, and when the sparks fly up, he says: 'As many sparks, so may my cattle, swine, sheep, thrive in good health.'

We next come to the more uproarious part of the ritual. The visitor kneels by the fire, and the hostess brings to him a cushion to sit on, but when he tries to sit down she pulls it and he falls on his back. This painful process is repeated three times, and the woman says the following words in a low voice: 'As I deceive you, so may I deceive the *gorgio* (non-gipsies).' At last the guest is allowed to sit on the cushion, and he is given sugar and water, black coffee, and cakes. He will share the Christmas feast with the family.

In some parts of Serbia there are strange gipsy customs connected with New Year's Eve. It is called the Little Christmas. The father of the family goes out at midnight secretly, and breaks a twig from a fruit-bearing tree. He ties a money bag to this twig and returns home when he knows every one is in bed. He knocks at the door and waits for somebody to say 'Come in.' As he closes the door, he says: 'Give, O God, health for many years to our children.' While repeating these words, he goes over to his wife and children and strikes them with the money bag. Finally he takes the twig from the bag, stirs the fire with it, and sticks it into a hole in the wall of the house.

Dr Petróvic, an authority on the Gipsies of Serbia, says that the twig symbolizes good harvest in the coming year and the money bag means wealth. He also says that those magic ceremonies are performed not only by the nomadic gipsies, but also by artisans and musicians who no longer steal. These customs have thus been inherited from the time when all lived in tents, and the moral is that a gipsy always remains a gipsy— you can't change him!

WALTER STARKIE.

Connemara

'Every day is Christmas day with her,' says the Connemara mother, as she proudly boasts how her daughter is thriving in America. Such is her idea of supreme luxury.

At the Christmas market a few days ago the *vanathee* ('woman of the house') has been busy 'buying the Christmas,' as the saying goes, and as every door is left open during the Holy Season, the villagers move freely from home to home, and vie with one another in open-hearted hospitality. Homeless and hungry wayfarers are also welcome to a Christmas drink and a seat by the fire.

A fiddler or a concertina-player is seated on the hob (the Sassenach calls it the ingle-nook) and there is a non-stop succession of Irish dances to the strains of *The Middhereen Rhu* (*The Little Red Fox*), *Nora Creina*, *Pop goes the Weasel,* and *Miss McCloud's Reel*. The rhythmic beat of the feet of the dancing bouchals and colleens is punctuated every now and then by a chorus of wild whoops like war-cries—the safety valve of sheer exuberance of spirits.

In the intervals between the dances the revellers listen intently to the *seannachie*, or traditional story-teller, as he spins his folk-tales or tells of the benevolent whims or impish pranks of the fairies, or the 'good people,' as they are called. For, the 'good people,' or the 'gentry,' as they are also known, are in jubilant mood during the feast of the Nativity, like all the visible and invisible forces of nature.

And so while the flames of the bog-deal swirl amid eddying coils of smoke up the chimney, the *seannachie* tells about the Christmas revels of *sheeogues*, *pookhas*, and *cluricanns*, and that cantankerous little brat, the leprechaun, whose crock of gold is as elusive as the winning ticket for the Irish sweep.

But there are no evil spirits—no dhouls ('the demons of Connemara') allowed to walk the earth during this season of peace and goodwill—they are strictly confined to the infernal regions.   The banshee never keens during the Holy Season, and the spells of witches, red-headed women, squint-eyed women, and of those baleful ones endowed with the evil eye are equally impotent at Christmas.

IGOR VINOGRADOFF, *Broadcast*, 1937.

The Chinese New Year

On the last day of the old year, accounts are settled, debts cancelled, and books carefully balanced in every mercantile establishment from the largest merchants or bankers down to the itinerant vendors of cooked food and vegetable-mongers.

It is considered disgraceful, and almost equivalent to an act of bankruptcy, if all accounts are not settled the last day of the old year; consequently it frequently happens that articles of ornament or curiosity can be purchased at low rates in the last week of the year from the desire of merchants to sacrifice their stock rather than go without ready money.   In all courts the official seals are locked in strong-boxes till the holiday is at an end.

On the last day of the old year is observed the ancient custom of surrounding the furnace. A feast is spread in great form before males in one room, females in another; under-neath the table exactly in the centre is placed a brazier filled with lighted wood or charcoal; fireworks are discharged, gilt paper burned, and the feast eaten, the younger sons serving the head of the house.   After the repast there is more burning of gilt paper, and the ashes are divided, while still smouldering, into twelve heaps, which are anxiously watched. The twelve heaps are each allotted to a month, and it is believed that from the length of time it takes each heap to die completely out, can be predicted the changes of rain or drought which will be of benefit to the crops or the reverse.

H. C. SIRR, *China and the Chinese.*

A Dinner to the Birds

One of the prettiest of Christmas customs is the Norwegian practice of giving on Christmas Day a dinner to the birds. On Christmas morning every gable, gateway, or barn-door is decorated with a sheaf of corn fixed on the top of a tall pole, wherefrom it is intended that the birds should make their Christmas dinner. Even the peasant contrives to have a handful set by for this purpose, and what the birds do not eat on Christmas Day remains for them to finish at their leisure during the winter.

W. F. DAWSON, *Christmas, Its Origin and Associations.*

CAROLS AND CHRISTMAS SONGS

WHAT sweeter music can we bring
Than a carol, for to sing
The birth of this our Heavenly King?
Awake the voice! awake the string!
Heart, ear, and eye, and everything,
Awake! the while the active finger
Runs division with the singer.

ROBERT HERRICK.

Man, be merry
As birds on berry,
And all thy care let away.

ANON.

A BABE IS BORN

TRADITIONAL: FIFTEENTH CENTURY.

A Babe is born all of a may,
  To bring salvation unto us.
To Him we sing both night and day
  Veni Creator Spiritus.

At Bethlehem, that blessed place,
  The Child of bliss then born He was;
And Him to serve God give us grace,
  O Lux beata Trinitas.

There came three kings out of the East,
  To worship there that King so free;
With gold and myrrh and frankincense,
  A solis ortus cardine.

The shepherds heard an angel's cry,
  A merry song that night sang he,
'Why are ye so sore aghast?'
  Jam lucis orto sidere?

The angel came down with a cry,
  A fair and joyful song sang he,
All in the worship of that Child,
  Gloria tibi Domine.

GOD REST YOU MERRY, GENTLEMEN

TRADITIONAL.

God rest you merry, gentlemen,
 Let nothing you dismay,
For Jesus Christ our Saviour
 Was born upon this day;
To save us all from Satan's **pow'r**
 When we were gone astray.
  O tidings of comfort and joy!

In Bethlehem in Jewry
 This blessèd Babe was born
And laid within a manger,
 Upon this blessèd morn;
The which His mother Mary
 Did nothing take in scorn,
  O tidings of comfort and joy!

From God our heavenly Father
 A blessèd angel came,
And unto certain shepherds
 Brought tidings of the same,
How that in Bethlehem was born
 The Son of God by name.
  O tidings of comfort and joy!

'Fear not,' then said the angel,
  'Let nothing you affright,
This day is born a Saviour,
  Of virtue, power, and might;
So frequently to vanquish all
  The friends of Satan quite.'
    O tidings of comfort and joy!

The shepherds at those tidings
  Rejoicèd much in mind,
And left their flocks a-feeding
  In tempest, storm, and wind,
And went to Bethlehem straightway
  This blessèd Babe to find.
    O tidings of comfort and joy!

But when to Bethlehem they came,
  Whereat this Infant lay,
They found Him in a manger
  Where oxen feed on hay;
His mother Mary kneeling
  Unto the Lord did pray.
    O tidings of comfort and joy!

Now to the Lord sing praises,
  All you within this place,
And with true love and brotherhood
  Each other now embrace;
This holy tide of Christmas
  All others doth deface.
    O tidings of comfort and joy!

THE FIRST NOWELL

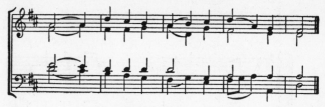

TRADITIONAL: SIXTEENTH CENTURY.

The first nowell the angel did say
Was to certain poor shepherds in fields as they lay;
In fields where they lay, keeping their sheep,
In a cold winter's night that was so deep.
   Nowell, nowell, nowell, nowell!
   Born is the King of Israel.

They lookèd up and saw a star,
Shining in the east, beyond them far,
And to the earth it gave great light,
And so it continued both day and night.

And by the light of that same star,
Three wise man came from country far;
To seek for a king was their intent,
And to follow the star wheresoever it went.

This star drew nigh to the north-west,
O'er Bethlehem it took its rest,
And there it did both stop and stay,
Right over the place where Jesus lay.

Then did they know assuredly
Within that house the King did lie:
One entered in then for to see,
And found the Babe in poverty.

Then entered in those wise men three,
Full reverently upon their knee,
And offered there, in His presence,
Their gold, and myrrh, and frankincense.

Between an ox-stall and an ass
This Child truly there born He was;
For want of clothing they did Him lay
All in the manger, among the hay.

Then let us all with one accord,
Sing praises to our Heavenly Lord,
That hath made Heaven and earth of naught,
And with His blood mankind hath bought.

If we in our time shall do well,
We shall be free from death and hell;
For God hath preparèd for us all
A resting-place in general.

IN DULCI JUBILO

FOURTEENTH CENT.: HARM. BARTHOLOMEW GESIUS, 1601.

In dulci jubilo
Now sing with hearts aglow!
   Our delight and pleasure
Lies *in praesepio,*
   Like sunshine is our treasure
Matris in gremio.   Alpha es et O!

O Jesu, parvule,
For Thee I long alway;
   Comfort my heart's blindness,
O Puer optime,
   With all Thy loving-kindness,
O Princeps gloriae.   Trahe me post te!

O Patris caritas!
O Nati lenitas!
   Deeply were we stainèd
Per nostra crimina;
   But Thou for us hast gainèd
Coelorum gaudia.   O that we were there!

Ubi sunt gaudia
In any place but there?
   There are angels singing
Nova cantica,
   And there the bells are ringing
In Regis curia.   O that we were there!

* The small notes in the last two bars are added to preserve the usual version of the tune.

O COME, ALL YE FAITHFUL

EIGHTEENTH CENTURY.

O come, all ye faithful,
Joyful and triumphant,
O come ye, O come ye to Bethlehem;
Come and behold Him,
Born the King of angels:
   O come, let us adore Him,
   O come, let us adore Him,
   O come, let us adore Him,
    Christ the Lord.

Sing, choirs of angels,
Sing in exultation,
Sing, all ye citizens of heaven above;
'Glory to God
In the highest':

Yea, Lord, we greet Thee,
Born this happy morning;
Jesu, to Thee be glory given;
Word of the Father,
Now in flesh appearing:

     Tr. FREDERICK OAKELEY (1802–80).

THE CARNAL AND THE CRANE

TRADITIONAL: ARR. R. VAUGHAN WILLIAMS.

As I passed by a river-side,
  And there as I did rein,
In argument I chanced to hear
  A carnal[1] and a crane.

The carnal said unto the crane,
  'If all the world should turn,
Before we had the Father,
  But now we have the Son.

[1] *Carnal* is assumed to derive from the French *corneille*, a crow.

'From whence does the Son come?
  From where and from what place?'
He said: 'In a manger,
  Between an ox and ass.'

'I pray thee,' said the carnal,
  'Tell me before thou go,
Was not the mother of Jesus
  Conceived by the Holy Ghost?'

'She was the purest virgin,
  And the cleanest from sin;
She was the handmaid of our Lord,
  And mother of our King.'

'Where is the golden cradle
  That Christ was rockèd in?
Where are the silken sheets
  That Jesus was wrapt in?'

'A manger was the cradle
  That Christ was rockèd in;
The provender the asses left,
  So sweetly He slept on.'

HARK! THE HERALD ANGELS SING

FELIX MENDELSSOHN-BARTHOLDY (1809–47).

Hark! the herald angels sing,
Glory to the new-born King;
Peace on earth and mercy mild;
God and sinners reconciled.
Joyful all ye nations rise;
Join the triumph of the skies;
With th' angelic host proclaim,
Christ is born in Bethlehem.
    Hark! the herald angels sing,
    Glory to the new-born King.

Christ, by highest heaven adored,
Christ, the everlasting Lord,
Late in time behold Him come,
Offspring of a virgin's womb.
Veiled in flesh the Godhead see;
Hail th' incarnate Deity,
Pleased as man with man to dwell,
Jesus, our Emmanuel!

Hail the heaven-born Prince of Peace!
Hail the Sun of Righteousness!
Light and life to all He brings,
Risen with healing in His wings.
Mild He lays His glory by;
Born that man no more may die;
Born to raise the sons of earth;
Born to give them second birth.

CHARLES WESLEY, GEORGE WHITEFIELD,
and MARTIN MADAN.

WHILE SHEPHERDS WATCH'D

ESTE'S PSALTER, 1592.

While shepherds watch'd their flocks by night,
   All seated on the ground,
The angel of the Lord came down,
   And glory shone around.

'Fear not,' said he; for mighty dread
   Had seized their troubled mind;
'Glad tidings of great joy I bring
   To you and all mankind.

'To you in David's town this day
   Is born of David's line
A Saviour, who is Christ the Lord;
   And this shall be the sign:

'The heav'nly Babe you there shall find
   To human view display'd,
All meanly wrapp'd in swathing bands,
   And in a manger laid.'

Thus spake the seraph; and forthwith
   Appear'd a shining throng
Of angels praising God, who thus
   Address'd their joyful song:

'All glory be to God on high,
   And to the earth be peace;
Good will henceforth from Heav'n to men
   Begin and never cease.'

               NAHUM TATE (1652–1715).

WINTER'S SNOW

JOHN GOSS (1800-80).

524

See amid the winter's snow,
Born for us on earth below,
See the tender Lamb appears,
Promised from eternal years.

Hail, thou ever blessed morn!
Hail, redemption's happy dawn!
Sing through all Jerusalem,
Christ is born in Bethlehem.

Lo, within a manger lies
He who built the starry skies;
He, who throned in height sublime,
Sits amid the cherubim.

Say, ye holy shepherds, say,
What your joyful news to-day;
Wherefore have ye left your sheep
On the lonely mountain steep?

'As we watched at dead of night,
Lo, we saw a wondrous light;
Angels singing peace on earth,
Told us of a Saviour's birth.'

Sacred Infant, all divine,
What a tender love was Thine;
Thus to come from highest bliss
Down to such a world as this.

Teach, O teach us, Holy Child,
By Thy face so meek and mild,
Teach us to resemble Thee,
In Thy sweet humility.

E. CASWALL (1814–78).

CHRISTIANS, AWAKE

JOHN WAINWRIGHT (d. 1768).

Christians, awake, salute the happy morn,
Whereon the Saviour of the world was born,
Rise to adore the mystery of love,
Which hosts of angels chanted from above;
With them the joyful tidings first begun
Of God incarnate and the Virgin's Son.

Then to the watchful shepherds it was told,
Who heard the angelic herald's voice, 'Behold,
I bring good tidings of a Saviour's birth
To you and all the nations upon earth;
This day hath God fulfilled His promised word;
This day is born a Saviour, Christ the Lord.'

He spake; and straightway the celestial choir
In hymns of joy, unknown before, conspire;
The praises of redeeming love they sang,
And heaven's whole orb with Hallelujahs rang;
God's highest glory was their anthem still,
Peace upon earth, and unto men good will.

To Bethlehem straight the enlightened shepherds ran,
To see the wonder God had wrought for man,
And found, with Joseph and the blessèd Maid,
Her Son, the Saviour, in a manger laid;
They to their flocks, still praising God, return,
And their glad hearts within their bosoms burn.

Like Mary, let us ponder in our mind
God's wondrous love in saving lost mankind;
Trace we the Babe, who has retrieved our loss,
From His poor manger to His bitter cross;
Tread in His steps, assisted by His grace,
Till man's first heavenly state again takes place.

Then may we hope, the angelic hosts among,
To sing, redeemed, a glad triumphal song;
He that was born upon this joyful day
Around us all His glory shall display;
Saved by His love, incessant we shall sing
Eternal praise to heaven's Almighty King.

JOHN BYROM (1692–1763).

I SAW THREE SHIPS

TRADITIONAL.

I saw three ships come sailing in
  On Christmas day, on Christmas day;
I saw three ships come sailing in
  On Christmas day in the morning.

And what was in those ships all three
  On Christmas day, on Christmas day . . .

Our Saviour Christ and His lady,
   On Christmas day, on Christmas day . . .

Pray whither sailed those ships all three
   On Christmas day, on Christmas day . . .

O they sailed into Bethlehem
   On Christmas day, on Christmas day . . .

And all the bells on earth shall ring
   On Christmas day, on Christmas day . . .

And all the angels in heaven shall sing
   On Christmas day, on Christmas day . . .

And all the souls on earth shall sing
   On Christmas day, on Christmas day . . .

Then let us all rejoice amain!
   On Christmas day, on Christmas day . . .

GOOD KING WENCESLAS

SPRING CAROL: *Tempus adest floridum*

Good King Wenceslas look'd out
  On the feast of Stephen,
When the snow lay round about,
  Deep and crisp and even.
Brightly shone the moon that night,
  Though the frost was cruel,
When a poor man came in sight,
  Gathering winter fuel.

'Hither, page, and stand by me,
  If thou know'st it, telling,
Yonder peasant, who is he?
  Where and what his dwelling?'
'Sire, he lives a good league hence,
  Underneath the mountain;
Right against the forest fence,
  By Saint Agnes' fountain.'

'Bring me flesh and bring me wine,
  Bring me pine-logs hither;
Thou and I will see him dine,
  When we bear them thither.'
Page and monarch, forth they went,
  Forth they went together;
Through the rude wind's wild lament,
  And the bitter weather.

'Sire, the night is darker now,
And the wind blows stronger;
Fails my heart, I know not how,
I can go no longer.'
'Mark my footsteps, good my page,
Tread thou in them boldly;
Thou shalt find the winter's rage
Freeze thy blood less coldly.'

In his master's steps he trod,
Where the snow lay dinted;
Heat was in the very sod
Which the saint had printed.
Therefore, Christian men, be sure,
Wealth or rank possessing,
Ye who now will bless the poor,
Shall yourselves find blessing.

J. M. NEALE (1818–66).

THE SEVEN JOYS OF MARY

TRADITIONAL.

The first good joy that Mary had,
  It was the joy of one;
To see the blessèd Jesus Christ
  When he was first her son:

  When he was first her son, good man:
    And blessèd may he be,
  Praise Father, Son, and Holy Ghost,
    To all eternity.

The next good joy that Mary had,
  It was the joy of two;
To see her own son, Jesus Christ,
  To make the lame to go:

The next good joy that Mary had,
  It was the joy of three;
To see her own son, Jesus Christ,
  To make the blind to see:

The next good joy that Mary had,
  It was the joy of four;
To see her own son, Jesus Christ,
  To read the Bible o'er:

The next good joy that Mary had,
  It was the joy of five;
To see her own son, Jesus Christ,
  To bring the dead alive:

The next good joy that Mary had,
  It was the joy of six;
To see her own son, Jesus Christ,
  Upon the crucifix:

The next good joy that Mary had,
  It was the joy of seven;
To see her own son, Jesus Christ,
  Ascending into heaven:

THREE KINGS OF ORIENT

J. H. HOPKINS.

All : We three kings of Orient are,
Bearing gifts we traverse afar,
Field and fountain, moor and mountain,
Following yonder star.

> *O star of wonder, star of night,*
> *Star with royal beauty bright,*
> *Westward leading, still proceeding,*
> *Guide us to thy perfect light.*

Melchior : Born a king on Bethlehem's plain,
Gold I bring, to crown Him again,
King for ever, ceasing never,
Over us all to reign.

Caspar : Frankincense to offer have I,
Incense owns a Deity nigh,
Prayer and praising, all men raising,
Worship Him, God most high.

Balthazar : Myrrh is mine, its bitter perfume
Breathes a life of gathering gloom;
Sorrowing, sighing, bleeding, dying,
Sealed in the stone-cold tomb.

All: Glorious now behold Him arise,
King and God and sacrifice,
Alleluia, alleluia;
Earth to the heavens replies.

JOHN HENRY HOPKINS (1820–91).

THE CHERRY TREE CAROL

TRADITIONAL.

* This note is required for verses 3, 4, 5 and 7.

Joseph was an old man,
  An old man was he,
When he married Mary,
  In the land of Galilee.

Joseph and Mary walked
  Through an orchard green,
Where was cherries and berries
  As thick as might be seen.

O then bespoke Mary,
  Her sweet lips so mild,
'Pluck me a cherry, Joseph,
  For I am with child.'

O then bespoke Joseph
  With answer unkind,
'Let him pluck thee a cherry
  That brought thee with child.'

O then bespoke the Baby
  Within His mother's womb,
'Bow down then the tallest tree,
  For My mother to have some.'

The uppermost sprig then
  Bowed down to her knee,
'Thus you may see, Joseph,
  These cherries are for me.'

'O eat your cherries, Mary,
  O eat your cherries now,
O eat your cherries, Mary,
  That grow upon the bough.'

THE HOLLY AND THE IVY

TRADITIONAL.

The Holly and the Ivy,
   When they are both full grown,
Of all the trees are in the wood,
   The Holly bears the crown.

   O the rising of the sun,
      And the running of the deer,
   The playing of the merry organ,
   Sweet singing in the choir.

The Holly bears a blossom
   As white as any flower;
And Mary bore sweet Jesus Christ
   To be our sweet Saviour.

The Holly bears a berry
   As red as any blood;
And Mary bore sweet Jesus Christ
   To do poor sinners good.

The Holly bears a prickle
   As sharp as any thorn;
And Mary bore sweet Jesus Christ
   On Christmas in the morn.

The Holly bears a bark
   As bitter as any gall;
And Mary bore sweet Jesus Christ
   For to redeem us all.

The Holly and the Ivy
   Now both are full well grown:
Of all the trees are in the wood
   The Holly bears the crown.

THE MOON SHINES BRIGHT

TRADITIONAL: BELLMAN'S SONG.

The moon shines bright, and the stars give a light
  A little before the day,
Our mighty Lord He looked on us,
  And bade us awake and pray.

Awake, awake, good people all,
  Awake, and you shall hear,
Our Lord, our God, died on the Cross,
  For us He loved so dear.

O fair, O fair Jerusalem,
  When shall I come to thee?
When shall my sorrows have an end
  The joy that I may see?

542

The fields were green as green could be,
   When from His glorious seat
Our Lord, our God, He watered us
   With His heavenly dew so sweet.

And for the saving of our souls
   Christ died upon the cross.
We ne'er shall do for Jesus Christ,
   As He hath done for us.

The life of man is but a span,
   And cut down in its flower,
We're here to-day, to-morrow gone,
   The creatures of an hour.

Instruct and teach your children well,
   The while that you are here;
It will be better for your soul,
   When your corpse lies on the bier.

To-day you may be alive and well,
   Worth many a thousand pound;
To-morrow dead and cold as clay,
   Your corpse laid underground.

With one turf at thine head, O man,
   And another at thy feet:
Thy good deeds and thy bad, O man.
   Will all together meet.

My song is done, I must be gone,
   I can stay no longer here;
God bless you all, both great and small,
   And send you a joyful new year.

THE WASSAIL SONG

TRADITIONAL: SEVENTEENTH CENTURY.

* This note is required for verses 2, 3, 4, 5, 6, and 8.

Here we come a-wassailing
   Among the leaves so green;
Here we come a-wandering,
   So fair to be seen:

> *Love and joy come to you*
> *And to you your wassail too,*
> *And God bless you, and send you*
> *A happy new year;*
> *And God send you a happy new year.*

Our wassail-cup is made
   Of the rosemary tree,
And so is your beer
   Of the best barley:

We are not daily beggars
   That beg from door to door,
But we are neighbours' children
   Whom you have seen before:

Good master and good mistress,
   As you sit by the fire,
Pray think of us poor children
   Who are wandering in the mire:

We have a little purse
   Made of ratching leather skin;
We want some of your small change
   To line it well within:

Call up the butler of this house,
   Put on his golden ring;
Let him bring us a glass of beer,
   And better we shall sing:

Bring us out a table,
  And spread it with a cloth;
Bring us out a mouldy cheese,
  And some of your Christmas loaf:

God bless the master of this house,
  Likewise the mistress too;
And all the little children
  That round the table go:

                              TRADITIONAL.

THE BOAR'S HEAD

CHORUS

TRADITIONAL.

The boar's head in hand bear I,
Bedeck'd with bays and rosemary;
And I pray you, my masters, be merry;
Quot estis in convivio.

   Caput apri defero,
   Reddens laudes Domino.

The boar's head, as I understand,
Is the rarest dish in all this land;
Which thus bedeck'd with a gay garland,
Let us *servire cantico.*

Our steward hath provided this
In honour of the King of Bliss;
Which on this day to be servèd is,
In Reginensi atrio.

This carol is still sung annually on Christmas Day at Queen's College, Oxford.

THE MISTLETOE BOUGH

SIR H. R. BISHOP (1786–1817): ARR. EDMUND RUBBRA (1939).

The mistletoe hung in the castle hall,
The holly branch shone on the old oak wall,
And the Baron's retainers were blithe and gay,
And keeping their Christmas holiday.
The Baron beheld with a father's pride
His beautiful child, young Lovel's bride,
While she with her bright eyes, seem'd to be
    The star of the goodly company.
        Oh, the mistletoe bough!
        Oh, the mistletoe bough!

'I'm weary of dancing, now,' she cried,
'Here tarry a moment; I'll hide, I'll hide.
And Lovel, be sure thou'rt the first to trace
The clue to my secret lurking place.'
Away she ran, and her friends began
Each tower to search and each nook to scan,
And young Lovel cried: 'Oh, where dost thou hide?
I'm lonesome without thee, my own dear bride.'

They sought her that night and they sought her next
    day,
And they sought her in vain till a week pass'd away.
In the highest, the lowest, the loneliest spot,
Young Lovel sought wildly but found her not.
And years flew by, and their grief at last
Was told as a sorrowful tale long past,
And when Lovel appear'd the children cried,
'See, the old man weeps for his fairy bride!'

At length an oak chest that had long lain hid
Was found in the castle; they rais'd the lid;
And a skeleton form lay mould'ring there
In the bridal wreath of the lady fair.
Oh, sad was her fate! In sportive jest
She hid from her lord in the old oak chest.
It closed with a spring, and her bridal bloom
Lay withering there in a living tomb.

THOMAS HAYNES BAYLY (1797–1839).

OUT OF THE STOCKING

The Twelve Days of Christmas

It was not possible to find room for the music to this charming traditional song. The best setting is that by Frederic Austin, published by Novello.

On the first day of Christmas
My true love sent to me—
A partridge in a pear-tree.
On the second day of Christmas
My true love sent to me—
Two turtle-doves and a partridge in a pear-tree.
On the third day of Christmas
My true love sent to me—
Three French hens, two turtle-doves,
And a partridge in a pear-tree.
On the fourth day of Christmas
My true love sent to me—
Four calling birds,
Three French hens, two turtle-doves,
And a partridge in a pear-tree.
On the fifth day of Christmas
My true love sent to me—
 Five gold rings,
 Four calling birds,
 Three French hens, two turtle-doves,
 And a partridge in a pear-tree.

On the sixth day . . . Six geese a-laying . . .
On the seventh day . . . Seven swans a-swimming . . .
On the eighth day . . . Eight maids a-milking . . .

On the ninth day . . . Nine drummers drumming . . .
On the tenth day . . . Ten pipers piping . . .
On the eleventh day . . . Eleven dames a-dancing . . .
On the twelfth day . . . Twelve lords a-leaping . . .

Love or Spite?

Friday, 28 December 1711.   Mr Spectator, I am a Footman in a great Family, and am in Love with the House-maid. We were all at Hot Cockles last Night in the Hall these Holidays; when I lay down and was blinded, she pulled off her Shoe, and hit me with the Heel such a Rap, as almost broke my Head to Pieces.   Pray, Sir, was this Love or Spite?

RICHARD STEELE, in The Spectator.

Jule-Nissen in Denmark

I do not know how the forty years I have been away have dealt with 'Jule-nissen,' the Christmas elf of my childhood in far-off Denmark. He was pretty old then, grey and bent, and there were signs that his time was nearly over. So it may be that they have laid him away. I shall find out when I go over there next time. When I was a boy we never sat down to our Christmas Eve dinner until a bowl of rice and milk had been taken up to the attic, where he lived with the martin and its young, and kept an eye upon the house—saw that everything ran smoothly. I never met him myself, but I know the house cat must have done so. No doubt they were well acquainted; for when in the morning I went in for the bowl, there it was, quite dry and licked clean, and the cat purring in the corner. So, being there all night, she must have seen and likely talked with him. . . .

JACOB RIIS, The Old Town.

Twelfth-Night Culinary Diversion

In former days, when good housekeeping was in fashion amongst the English nobility, they used to divert their guests with such pretty devices as these following, viz:

A castle made of pasteboard, with gates, drawbridges, battlements, and portcullises, all done over with paste, was set upon a table in a large charger, with salt laid round about it, as if it were the ground, in which were stuck eggshells full of rose or other sweet waters, the meat of the egg having been taken out by a great pin. Upon the battlement of the castle were planted kexes covered over with paste, in the form of cannons, and made to look like brass by covering them with dutch leaf-gold. These cannons being charged with gun-powder, and trains laid so that you might fire as many as you pleased, at one touch; this castle was set at one end of the table.

Then in the middle of the table they would set a stag made of paste, but hollow, and filled with claret wine, and a broad arrow stuck in his side; this was also set in a large charger, with a ground made of salt with eggshells of perfumed waters stuck in it as before.

Then at the other end of the table, they would have a ship made of pasteboard, and covered all over with paste, with masts, flags, sails, and streamers; and guns made of kexes, covered with paste and charged with gunpowder, with a train, as in the castle. This being placed in a large charger was set up-right in as it were a sea of salt, in which were also stuck egg-shells full of perfumed waters. Then betwixt the stag and castle, and the stag and ship, were placed two pies made of coarse paste, filled with bran, and washed over with saffron and the yolks of eggs; when these were baked the bran was taken out, a hole was cut in the bottom of each, and live birds put into one and frogs into the other. Then the holes were closed up with paste, and the lids neatly cut up, so that they might be easily taken off by the funnels, and adorned with gilded laurels.

These being thus prepared, and placed in order on the table, one of the ladies was persuaded to draw the arrow out of the body of the stag, which being done the claret wine issued forth like blood from a wound and caused admiration in the spectators; which being over, after a little pause, all the guns on one side of the castle were by a train discharged against the ship; and afterwards the guns of one side of the ship were discharged against the castle; then, having turned the chargers, the other sides were fired off as in a battle. This causing a great smell of powder, the ladies or gentlemen took up the eggshells of perfumed water and threw them at one another. This pleasant disorder being pretty well laughed over, and the two great pies still remaining untouched, some one or other would have the curiosity to see what was in them; and on lifting up the lid of one pie, out would jump the frogs, which would make the ladies skip and scamper; and on lift/ing up the lid of the other out would fly the birds, which would naturally fly at the light and so put out the candles. And so with the leaping of the frogs below, and the flying of the birds above, would cause a surprising and diverting hurly/burly among the guests, in the dark. After which the candles being lighted, the banquet would be brought in, the music sound, and the particulars of each person's surprise and adventures furnish matter for diverting discourse.

JOHN NOTT (late cook to the Dukes of Somerset and Ormond), *The Cook and Confectioner's Dictionary*, 1726.

The Hodening Horse in Kent

When I was a lad, about forty/five years since, it was always the custom on Christmas Eve, with the male farm/servants from every farm in our parish, to go round in the evening from house to house with the hodening horse, which consisted of the imitation of a horse's head made of wood, life size, fixed on a stick about the length of a broom handle. The lower jaw of the head was made to open with hinges; a hole was made through the roof of the mouth, then another through the forehead coming out by the throat; pulled through this was passed a cord attached at the lower jaw, which, when pulled by the cord at the throat, caused it to close and open; on the lower jaw large-headed hobnails were driven in to form the teeth. The strongest of the lads was selected for the horse; he stooped and made as long a back as he could, supporting himself by the stick carrying the head; then he was covered with a horse-cloth, and one of his companions mounted his back. The horse had a bridle and reins. Then commenced the kicking, rearing, jumping, etc., and the banging together of the teeth.

There was no singing by the accompanying paraders. They simply by ringing or knocking at the houses on their way summoned the inmates to the doors and begged a gratuity. I have seen some of the wooden heads carved out quite hollow in the throat part, and two holes bored through the forehead to form the eyes. The lad who played the horse would hold a lighted candle in the hollow, and you can imagine how horrible it was to any one who opened the door to see such a thing close to his eyes.

A Contributor to the Church Times,
23 Jan. 1891.

Yawns

To the *Spectator*. I hope you will oblige the World with some Reflections upon Yawning, as I have seen it practised on a Twelfth Night among other Christmas Gambols at the House of a very worthy Gentleman, who always entertains his

Tenants at this time of the Year. They yawn for a Cheshire-Cheese, and begin about Midnight, when the whole Company is disposed to be drowsy. He that yawns widest, and at the same Time so naturally as to produce the most Yawns among the Spectators, carries home the Cheese. If you handle this Subject as you ought, I question not but your Paper will set half the Kingdom a yawning, though I dare promise you it will never make any Body fall asleep.

JOSEPH ADDISON, in *The Spectator.*

Old School Holiday Song

Omne bene
Sine poena
Tempus est ludendi
Venit hora
Absque mora
Libros deponendi.

SOS Message

Any man or woman . . . that can give any knowledge, or tell any tidings, of an old, old, very old grey-bearded gentle-man, called Christmas, who was wont to be a verie familiar ghest, and visite all sorts of people both pore and rich, and used to appeare in glittering gold, silk, and silver, in the Court, and in all shapes in the Theater in Whitehall, and had ringing, feasts, and jollitie in all places, both in the citie and countrie, for his comming: . . . whosoever can tel what is become of him, or where he may be found, let them bring him back againe into England.

An Hue and Cry after Christmas, 1645.

INDEX OF AUTHORS

Addison, Joseph, 146, 555
Aubrey, John, 144

Bampfylde, John, 55
Bannatyne MS., 41
Barnes, William, 72
Bayly, T. H., 549
'Beachcomber' (J. B. Morton), 109, 369
Beaumont, Joseph, 38
Bent, J. Theodore, 175
Blake, William, 83
Blanchard, H. H., 248
Bonaventure, St, 130
Bolton, Edmund, 24
Bozman, E. F., 299
Bradford, William, 137
Breton, Nicholas, 80
Bridie, James, 353
Broadcasts, 485-7, 492-7, 499, 500, 503-4
Brodrick, Fr J., 138
Brontë, Emily, 59
Browne, Sir Thomas, 115
Byrom, John, 527

Caliban, 383
Campion, Thomas, x
Canterbury Christmas, 141
Carey, Patrick, 33
Carleton, Sir Dudley, 135
Caswall, E., 525
Chamberlaine, John, 136
Chambers's Journal, contributor to, 489
Chaucer, Geoffrey, 257

Chesterton, G. K., 28, 79
Church Times, 554
Clare, John, 56, 57, 64
Clutton-Brock, A., 163
Coleridge, Hartley, 92
Coleridge, S. T., 36
Commonplace Book of Richard Hill, 74
Congreve, William, 60
Corporation Letter-book, 131
Cotton, Charles, 95
Cowper, William, 55, 57, 58
Crabbe, George, 60
Crashaw, Richard, 28, 36

Dawson, W. F., 118, 129, 505
De la Mare, Walter, 17
Dickens, Charles, 274, 370
Drummond, William, 32
Dugdale, Sir William, 134
Dunbar, William, 51

Eliot, T. S., 36
Elizabeth and her German Garden, x
Evelyn, John, 142, 143

Florence of Worcester, 126
Flying Eagle, The, 142

Garvin, Viola Gerard, 84
Gautier, Théophile, 32
Gay, John, 67
George the Fifth, 164
Gentleman's Magazine, The, 148, 159
Greville, Charles, 160
Grisewood, Frederick H., 311

Hadfield, Miles, 218
Hall, Edward, 133
Hall, Joseph, 14
Harte, Francis Bret, 315
Herbert, George, 53
Herrick, Robert, 21, 42, 54, 69, 97, 100, 101, 247, 506
Hessenstein, Count Alfred, 490
Heywood, Charles, 292
Hilton, James, 275
History of York, 124
Hone, William, 128, 149, 183
Hopkins, J. H., 537
Horace (imitated by Congreve), 60
Hue and Cry after Christmas, An, 556

Irving, Washington, 150

Jonson, Ben, 18, 66

Kinwelmershe, Francis, 13

Le Fanu, J. Sheridan, 337
Lewis, D. B. Wyndham, 378
Luke, St, 113

Macaulay, Rose, 6
MacDonald, George, 108
McMullen, Anna, 90
Madan, Martin, 521
Maitland MSS., 72
Malory, Sir Thomas, 121
Marot, Clément, 25
Martindale, Fr C. C., 103
Matthew, St, 114
Matthews, W. R., Dean of St Paul's, 1
Milton, John, 12, 44
Morley, Henry, 147

Morton, J. B., 109

Nash, Ogden, 89
Neale, J. M., 532
Nott, John, 553

Oakeley, Frederick, 517

Paston, Margery, 132
Patmore, Coventry, 63
Pepys, Samuel, 145
Phillips, Hubert, 258, 460
Pinkney, Myles, 16
Poor Robin's Almanack, 65, 80
Pope, Alexander, 147
Power, Tyrone, 160
Price, Harry, 231
Prynne, William, 140
P. S., 332

Quarles, Francis, 41

Rhys, Ernest, 5
Riis, Jacob, 552
Rossetti, Christina, 15, 19
Round about our Coal Fire, 68
Rowlands, Richard, 34

St Paul's, Dean of, 1
Scott, Captain, 162
Segrave, Edmond, 196
Seneca, 117
Shakespeare, William, 59, 82, 88
Shelley, Percy Bysshe, 99
Sirr, H. C., 504
Southwell, Robert, 27, 38, 82
Spry, Constance, 176
Starkie, Walter, 500
Steele, Richard, 552, 555
Stevenson, Robert Louis, 60
Stow, John, 130
Stubbs, Philip, 134

Sullivan, Frank, 171, 285
Swift, Jonathan, 145

Tate, Nahum, 523
Tennyson, Alfred, Lord, 14, 92, 94
Thackeray, W. M., 78
Tille, Alexander, 120, 125
Times, The, 163, 165
Tusser, Thomas, 67

Vaughan, Henry, 20
Vinogradoff, Igor, 485, 486, 494, 499, 503

Walsh, W. S., 161
Warton, Thomas, 62
Washburne, E. B., 162
Weatherhead, Rev. Leslie D., 166
Weatherhead, Instructor ⁄ Captain R., 404
Webb, Mrs Arthur, 184
Wesley, Charles, 521
Whitefield, George, 521
Wither, George, 74
Wolfe, Humbert, 66
Worby, John, 497
Wordsworth, Dorothy, 149
Wordsworth, William, 63, 83

FIRST LINES OF ANONYMOUS POEMS AND CAROLS

	PAGE
A babe is born all of a may	507
As I passed by a river⁄side	518
Bring us in good ale	70
God rest you merry, gentlemen	509
Here we come a⁄wassailing	545
How happy were those days so old	80
I gave her Cakes and I gave her Ale	77
I saw a faire maiden	26
I saw three ships come sailing in	529
I sing not of Rome or Grecian mad games	70
I sing of a maiden	34
In dulci jubilo	515
In honour of this Christinmas	72
Jerusalem rejoice for joy	41
Joseph was an old man	539
Lestenytz lordyngs both grete and smale	126

	PAGE
Now have good day, now have good day	102
Now thrice welcome Christmas	65
O my deir hert, young Jesus sweit,	170
O you merry, merry souls	68
Omne bene	556
On the first day of Christmas	551
Quho is at my windou, quho?	87
The boar's head in hand bear I	547
The first good joy that Mary had	534
The first nowell the angel did say	512
The Holly and the Ivy	541
The moon shines bright, and the stars give a light	542
The shepherd upon a hill he sat	22
There is no rose of such vertu	40
'Tis late and cold, stir up the fire	87